TER

F

SOUTH BISCAY PILOT

The Gironde Estuary to La Coruña

Robin Brandon

Third Edition

ADLARD COLES LIMITED
GRANADA PUBLISHING
London Toronto Sydney New York

Adlard Coles Ltd
Granada Publishing Ltd
8 Grafton Street, London W1X 3LA

First published in Great Britain by
Adlard Coles Limited 1971
Second Edition 1977
Reprinted 1979
Third edition 1984

British Library Cataloguing in Publication Data
Brandon, Robin
South Biscay pilot.—3rd ed
1. Coastwise navigation—Spain
2. Yachts and yachting—Spain
I. Title
623.89′2946 VK854

ISBN 0 229 11680 9

Photoset by CG Graphic Services, Aylesbury, Bucks
Printed by William Clowes Ltd,
Beccles and London

By the same author

South France Pilot	Imrays
East Spain Pilot	Imrays
South England Pilot	Imrays

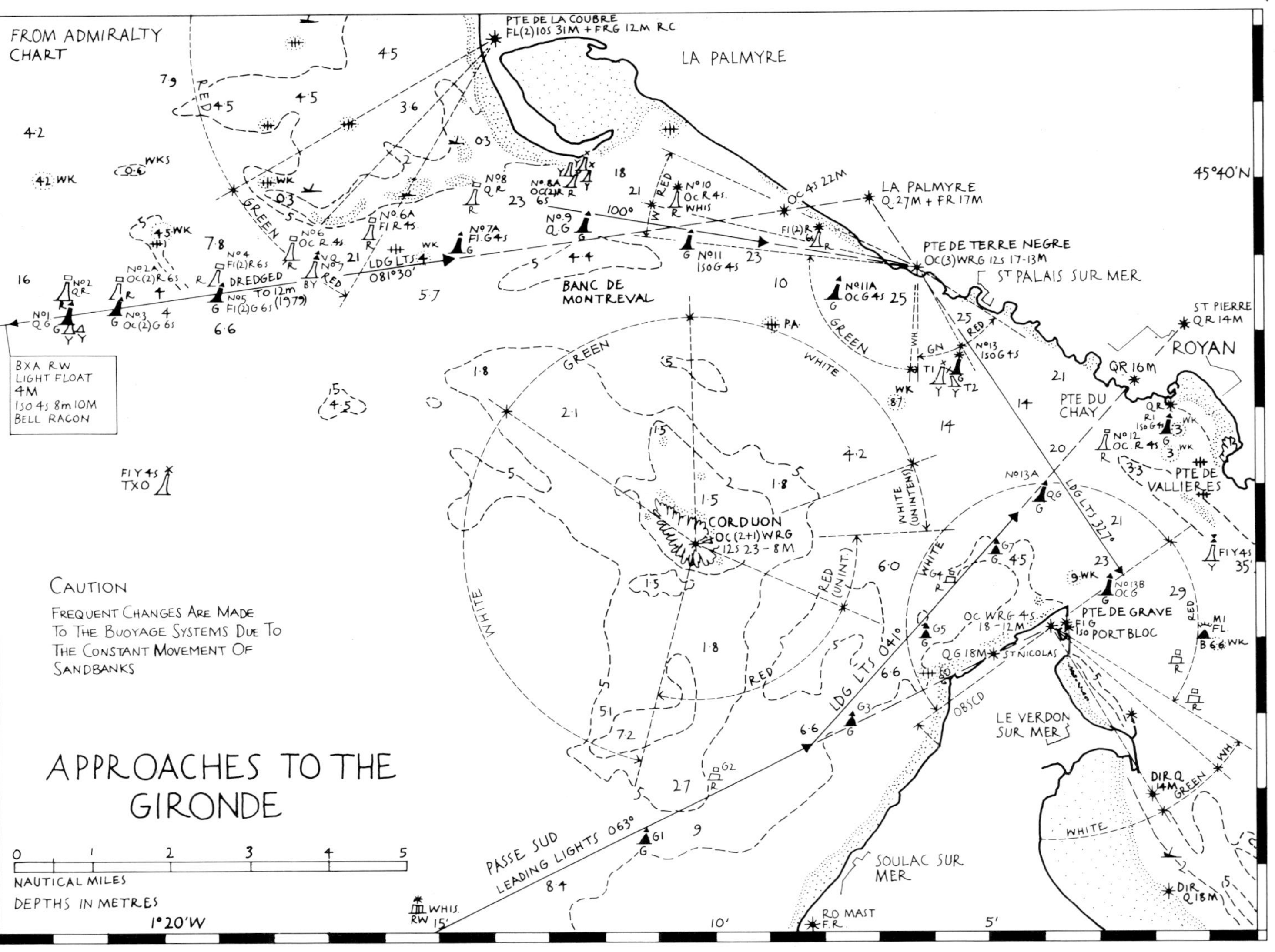

(see Estuaire de la Gironde, p. 43)

Acknowledgments

The chartlets in this book are based on the official British Admiralty, French and Spanish charts as indicated in the text with the sanction of the Hydrographer of the Navy, the authorisation of the *Directeur du Service Hydrographique de la Marine* and the permission of *El Director de Instituto Hidrografico* respectively. Extracts from the Admiralty *Tide Tables*, *List of Lights*, *List of Radio Stations* and *Sailing Directions* were made with the sanction of the Controller of HM Stationery Office.

The encouragement, help and advice from members and officials of the Royal Cruising Club was of great assistance in the preparation of this work.

Without the assistance of John Fletcher who drew the charts, Jim Cooper, Pat and Paddy White, Mrs Hillhouse, M. Rincon, Dr A. Cusham, A. N. Black, J. H. Trafford and many others who helped with typing and checking, etc. this book would never have been published.

The revisions to the charts for this edition have been carried out by Messrs Imray, Laurie, Norie and Wilson, and to them many thanks are due.

Nor can I ever forget the crew members who helped me so nobly, some for many months on end, many times short-handed, getting my yacht from port to port with the maximum efficiency and minimum complaint.

To many who have helped in this project I send my warmest thanks.

Robin Brandon

Last Corrections

This work has been corrected to 9 February 1983 and Admiralty Notices to Mariners No. 45 of 12 November 1983. See page x for further late corrections.

Corrections by Readers

Users of this guide are themselves asked to report any changes, omissions or corrections to the Author or Publishers. A correction reported briefly when noted, on a postcard or by rough sketch, may subsequently prevent another yachtsman getting into difficulty. Your co-operation in this matter is therefore earnestly requested.

Preface to Third Edition

It is over thirteen years since I made the original reconnaissance of this coast and naturally many changes have taken place during this period. What is surprising is that the greatest changes have not been hydrographical, geographical or even navigational, but have been sociological.

Thirteen years ago the north Spanish coast was an area of extreme poverty and in parts it was almost medieval. Under the Franco regime, progress was being made to improve the life style of the inhabitants even though they were still subject to the harsh discipline of a police state. Today all is changed and there are many signs of prosperity to be seen. A materialistic consumer society is rapidly taking over from the traditional society of the past. Large numbers of new houses are to be seen but unfortunately, in some areas, large, ugly tenement blocks have been erected. Shops in small towns and villages have multiplied many times and are well stocked with goods. This improvement has been reflected in the provision of extra facilities at many harbours. The inhabitants are better dressed and look in better health, beggars and cripples are now rarely to be seen. The numbers of Spanish yachts and cars, albeit of small size, have multiplied several times.

However, since the end of the Franco regime there has been a considerable relaxation in the activities of the police and other officials with the result that law and order has suffered. It is no longer safe to leave cars or yachts unattended unless they are locked, nor is it said to be safe for young girls to wander about at night. Another result of this relaxation has been the upsurge of Basque nationalism which is manifest on the eastern end of the north Spanish coast. One obvious sign of this is the official or unofficial changing of the names on road direction signs, with the consequent confusion of the visitor. For instance Gijon is now sign posted with the Basque spelling Xixon.

Mass tourism has been confined to the same eastern section of the coast and there are only a few signs of any increase further to the west. The fishing fleet has increased considerably and many harbours which only had a few small local fishing boats now sport a number of deep sea boats. Extra harbours and facilities have been built for them. The continued prosperity based on the expansion of industry, fishing and the production of user goods seems assured always, provided that the political arena remains calm.

In this, the third edition, I have endeavoured to bring the data and information given for each harbour up to date as the result of personal reconnaissance but I would like to thank those who have taken the trouble to write in with details of changes and corrections. In particular, I would like to thank members of the Royal Cruising Club, and Adlard Coles Limited's editorial team for their help.

Robin Brandon
Port Grimaud

SOUTH BISCAY PILO

LIMITS OF AREAS COVERED

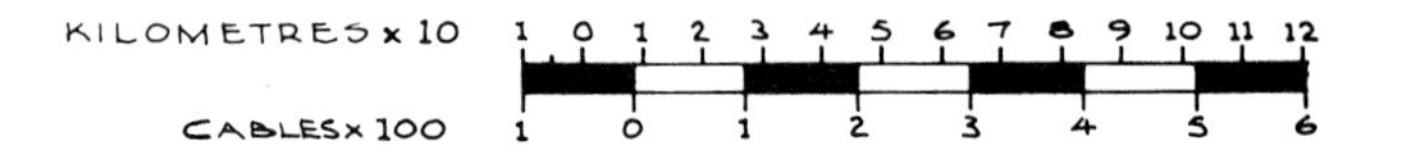

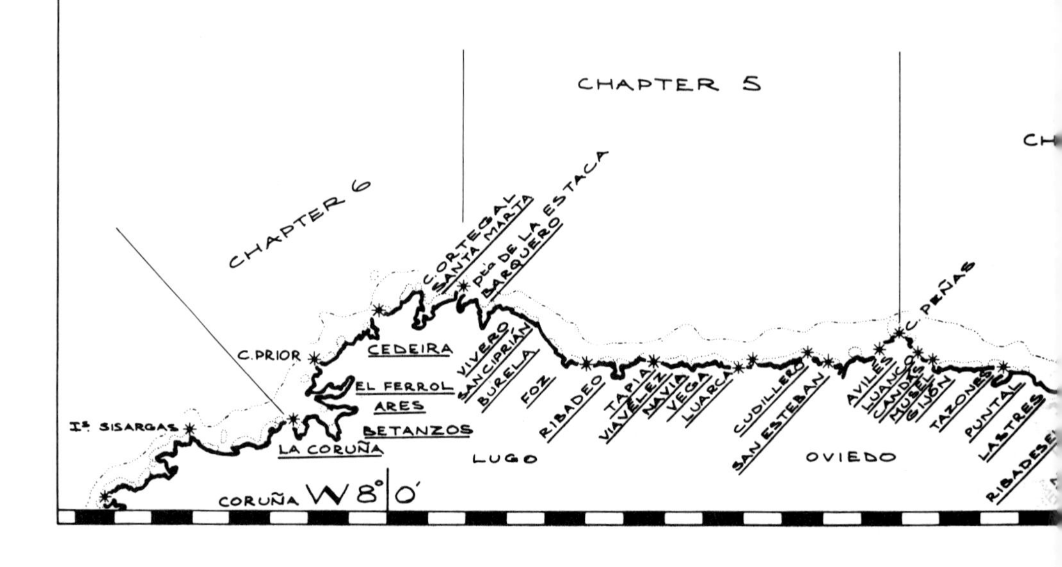

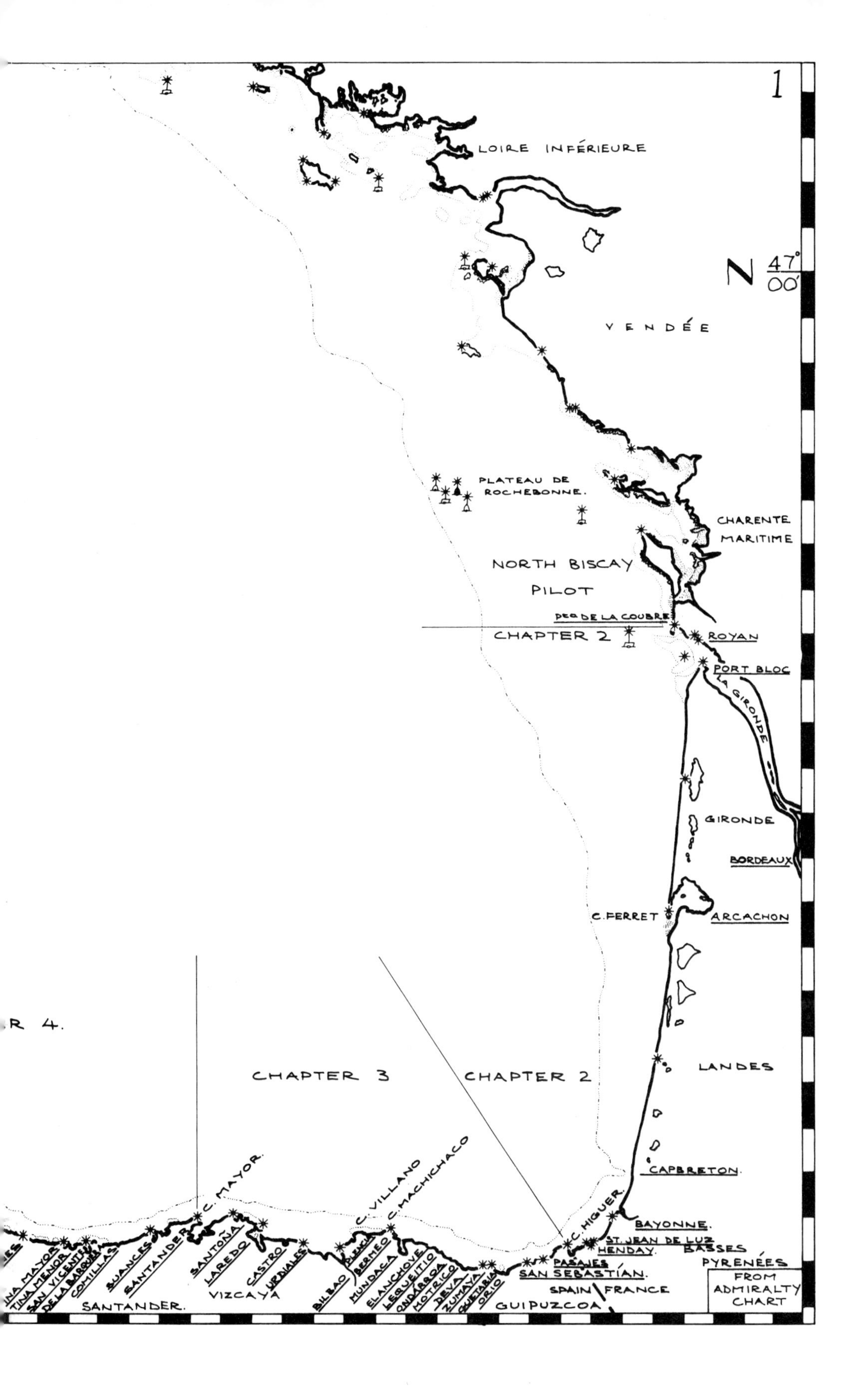

1
LOIRE INFÉRIEURE
N 47° 00′
VENDÉE
PLATEAU DE ROCHEBONNE.
CHARENTE MARITIME
NORTH BISCAY PILOT
PTE DE LA COUBRE
CHAPTER 2
ROYAN
PORT BLOC
LA GIRONDE
GIRONDE
BORDEAUX
C. FERRET
ARCACHON
R 4.
CHAPTER 3
CHAPTER 2
LANDES
CAPBRETON.
C. MAYOR.
C. VILLANO
C. MACHICHACO
C. HIGUER.
BAYONNE.
ST. JEAN DE LUZ
HENDAY.
BASSES PYRENÉES
TINA MAYOR
TINA MENOR
SAN VICENTE DE LA BARQUERA
COMILLAS
SUANCES
SANTANDER
SANTOÑA
LAREDO
CASTRO URDIALES
BILBAO
BERMEO
MUNDACA
ELANCHOVE
LEQUEITIO
ONDÁRROA
MOTRICO
DEVA
ZUMAYA
GUETARIA
ORIO
PASAJES
SAN SEBASTIÁN.
SPAIN FRANCE
SANTANDER.
VIZCAYA
GUIPUZCOA
FROM ADMIRALTY CHART

Late Corrections

P. 37, 45, 46, 47: BXA replaced by safe water pillar light and whistle buoy, radar transponder beacon (BXA Iso. with Racon). (*Ref. A.N. to Ms. No 41/83*)

P. 379, 381: **Muelle del Centariario** (marked by WORKS on chart) FRs on N and E corners, FG on S corner. (*Ref. A.N. to Ms. No 41/83*)

P. 190–193: **Santander**. Light buoys beacons Nos 2,3,4,5,6,8,10,12 and 14 moved slightly. **La Comba** light beacons to be deleted. (*Ref. A.N. to Ms. No 47/83*)

P. iii and 46–48: **La Gironde**. No 23 light buoy moved SE 1000 m; No 22 light buoy moved SE 1200 m; Light 2 FBu at 45°12.1′N, 0°44.7′W and light close SSE to be deleted. (*Ref. A.N. to Ms. No 51/83*)

P. 294–296: **Luarca**. Light Fl (2) R 6 sec 13 m 3 M: amend to VW (2) R 6 sec 13 m 3 M. (*Ref. A.N. to Ms. No 5/84*)

Contents

Chapter 1

Introduction, Information and Data

Introduction

Why is it that so many yachtsmen have such a fear of the Bay of Biscay? I think that this is the result of years of unconscious propaganda. From earliest youth they will have heard their parents speak with awe of the terrible waves and storms in the Bay. They have read books about fine square-rigged ships lost upon this coast. At school they have learnt lines such as Macaulay's 'Their ranks are breaking like thin clouds before a Biscay gale', or sung Andrew Cherry's 'The Bay of Biscay'. Finally, as yachtsmen, when they study *Ocean Passages of the World* they find many warnings to the navigators of sailing ships to stay clear of these waters.

These can be dangerous waters, but in general are *far* less perilous than, say, the North coast of Brittany, and the average weather conditions for these two areas are very similar.

How did all these stories of the horrors of the Bay arise? In two ways perhaps—firstly, if a square-rigged ship met a W or NW gale and became embayed in the Bay of Biscay there was little chance, due to her very poor windward performance, of beating her way out again, especially if a gale blew for several days and set up strong currents towards the SE corner of the Bay.

The advice in *Ocean Passages* still holds good for such square-rigged ships—if any still exist—'stay well clear of this area', but it is not applicable to a modern well-found yacht which can make progress to windward or at least hold her own in storm conditions.

Secondly, steamships bound from England to almost any part of the world except North America pass down the English or Irish Channel in a short choppy sea without much rolling, and it is not until they reach Ushant and the Bay that they encounter the long ocean swells with all the fetch of the Atlantic behind them, which cause these ships to roll abominably; hence the reputation for the terrible Biscay seas.

It is true that we do not experience these long swells on our English coasts, and when first seen they are inclined to be rather intimidating but will be found much more pleasant to sail on than the steep sharp waves of the Channel.

From the point of view of a yachtsman this N Spanish coast has many desirable features and advantages. It is not a difficult coast from the navigational and pilotage angle; the tide range is not great; there are almost no outlying dangers and the water is usually clear.

It is not overrun with other yachts and yachtsmen nor is the greater part of this coast crowded with land-based tourists. The food and drink are remarkably good and cheap. The local inhabitants are very friendly and helpful. The coast itself is for the large part very beautiful and the weather is better than in the British Isles. The air and the sea are much warmer. The author visited at least a dozen ports where, according to the locals, no other yacht had been before. There were also a large number of ports where it was reported that no British yacht had previously visited.

It would seem that the few British yachts that have visited the area over the years have either gone to the NW corner of Spain on their way to more distant parts, or only visited the major ports on the N coast. One wonders if they knew what they missed.

About this Pilot Book

Chartlets

The chartlets in this Pilot have been based, as indicated, on Admiralty, French or Spanish charts and have been brought up to date by inspection of the port by the author. However, due to limited facilities for measurement these chartlets should be used with caution for navigation and pilotage, especially as alterations may have been made after the Author's visit.

Bearings

True bearings may be taken from these chartlets by the use of a Douglas protractor, by virtue of the side edges of the chartlets being orientated N, S, E and W. These bearings should, however, be used with caution. Magnetic variation is included in the relevant text of the section concerned.

As far as possible only details essential to pilotage by yachtsmen have been included and many of the details which are to be found in the original charts are excluded in order to simplify navigation.

Soundings

Soundings and heights are in metres (m) as shown on the French and Spanish charts and the latest issue of Admiralty charts.

An approximation to the 2 metre (1 fathom) and the 5 metre (3 fathom) lines are also shown dotted. Various spot soundings are included where they will be useful to navigators.

Leading lines are drawn in and lettered to connect with the text.

Photographs

The majority of the photographs which accompany the text were taken by the Author, sometimes under conditions of poor light while piloting his yacht into what was usually a strange port. The quality of these photos in some cases is not of a high standard, especially those enlarged from coloured slides. In other cases local coloured picture postcards have been used and these do not always reproduce satisfactorily for technical reasons.

Classification of ports by code

In order to simplify the planning of a cruise on this coast each port has been classified according to the code given below. It must be emphasised that this classification represents the personal views of the Author and every effort has been made to form a fair judgement on these places. In addition, a single visit to a nice port on a day with poor weather conditions may produce a lower grading than if the weather was fine. Also any unfortunate occurrence such as going aground or even an excess of fishing boats in the harbour tends to down-grade a port.

The classification consists of three sets of numbers each with a range of 1 to 5. The first covers the attractiveness of the port and the area around it, the second the ease of entrance and the third the facilities to be found ashore.

Code system used

Attractiveness First number.

1. A most attractive place to visit, *make every effort to go there* if prudent.
2. An attractive port, visit and if necessary *go a little out of your way* to do so.
3. Normal for this part of the coast; *if convenient* visit the port concerned.
4. Visit only if alternatives listed above are unavailable. *Expect to be disappointed* and subject to inconvenience.
5. Only visit *if really necessary* by virtue of bad weather, breakdown or other troubles. Do not expect to find it attractive. You may be inconvenienced by coal dust, etc.

Ease of approach and entrance Second number.

1. This port can be entered under *gale* conditions with winds from *any direction.*
2. Can be entered under *gale* conditions with winds from any direction *except from one quarter.*
3. Can be entered in *strong* winds from all quarters with the exception of one.
4. Can only be entered in *light conditions* of winds and swell.
5. Can only be entered in *calm* and *settled* conditions with *no swell.*

Facilities available Third number.

1. *All possible facilities* available that a yachtsman may require for yacht and crew.
2. *Many facilities* available including all domestic requirements, but no major hull, engine and radio repairs possible and only a limited amount of chandlery available.
3. *All domestic facilities* available but probably only a slip for hauling out and perhaps a yard which could do a limited amount of rough work.
4. Only *simple everyday domestic requirements* can be met, usually only local produce, wine and water.
5. *Virtually nothing* available unless prepared to walk some distance to a village for simple domestic goods.

Background Information

General and personal

Special and extra equipment for yachts

It is virtually impossible to buy any yacht chandlery at ports on the South Biscay coast, with the exception of **San Sebastián**, **Santander**, **Bilbao**, **La Coruña** and the major French ports and marinas, where a very limited amount of expensive imported dinghy and motor yacht equipment may be found. Heavy ship-type chandlery for the use of the local fishing fleets may be found in most ports and the prices are not unreasonable.

It is not recommended to have goods sent out from England. Stores and equipment for yachts may be subject to considerable delay in getting Customs clearance. Duty may have to be paid, although this can be reclaimed with difficulty at the last Spanish port of call. There is a fair certainty that the items may never be received. Small items sent by air under a green label Customs declaration may be received.

It is assumed that any yacht visiting this coast will be properly fitted out and equipped for a medium distance sea crossing and the items listed below should be included if possible.

Ground tackle

A second bower anchor with a 50 m (30 fathom) warp of strength equal to the yacht's anchor chain, in addition to the normal light kedge.
A second anchor trip line and buoy.
A set of legs to enable many smaller ports to be visited. Legs if available should always be carried.
A short length of chain to avoid chafe on rough and rusty mooring buoys.

Berthing tackle

At least four really large fenders 0·25 m (10 in) or more in diameter, in addition to the yacht's usual complement. Many harbour walls have underwater projections.
Two extra long warps, 50 m (30 fathoms), making a total of four. One of these could be the warp referred to under 'ground tackle', above.
A griping spar to reduce wear on fenders and hull, as most berths alongside suffer from the disadvantage of the swell.

Water

Hose pipe to pipe water from quay to yacht: about 50 m (60 yd) or more of ½ in diameter light plastic hose is recommended.
A really large plastic bowl which will take a fouled warp so that it may be cleaned. This will double as a bath.
A good supply of rags, cotton waste, paraffin (or diesel) to clean hull, fenders and warps.
A rope ladder about 3 m (12 ft) in length to scale quaysides.

Domestic

Plastic container 10 litres (2 gal) size to collect wine from *bodegas* (wine shops).
Plastic net shopping bags. Shops and markets expect customers to bring their own carriers.

If paraffin is used for cooking or heating a good supply should be taken, as Spanish paraffin (*petróleo*) is inclined to be smelly.

Flags Small Spanish ensign to fly as a courtesy flag.

Papers The yacht's Certificate of Registration as it is liable for occasional inspection.

Batteries Special type dry batteries, e.g. for Brookes and Gatehouse equipment, are very difficult to obtain so adequate spares should be carried.

Gas Yachts using gas for cooking etc. should either bring adequate supplies of full Calor gas cylinders or obtain an adaptor to fit International Camping Gaz cylinders, the refills of which are obtainable at even the very smallest port and village at a cost much below that in the UK and France for similar containers.

Clothing Normal simple clothing of the type used when sailing in the English Channel in summer is all that is required, but visiting yachtsmen and their crew must remember that there are certain dress conventions which must be observed ashore.

Bathing and sunbathing dress must only be worn on the beach and should never be worn in towns and villages, cafés or shops. The wearing of shorts, especially abbreviated versions, by either men or women is not acceptable ashore except on the beach. When visiting the interior of churches women must have their heads and arms covered. The more formal and social type of yacht club does not approve of visitors in sloppy or dirty yachting clothes. However, there appear to be no objections today to women wearing bikinis on the beaches and trousers almost anywhere.

Documents All crew members should have valid passports; special visas are not necessary. It is advisable to insist that passports are stamped *Entrada* on first arrival in Spain by a Customs or Immigration official, especially if the crew member concerned is returning by other means. This can only be done at major ports. Although this rule still exists it is not enforced at the moment.

Health Although adequate medical facilities exist in all the major ports there are many small places, where doctors and hospitals are only to be found some distance away. Most simple medicines can be brought at the *farmacia* in any fair sized port, but special and 'branded' drugs should be bought in England before leaving.

It is always advisable to take out medical insurance to cover the cost of any medical attention. The premiums are modest.

As hygiene has not reached a high standard in parts of this area, it is advisable to boil all drinking water even when the locals insist that the *agua potable* (drinking water) is pure. Alternatively, water purification tablets can be used. Fruit and vegetables which are eaten raw should be washed first in a solution of disinfectant such as permanganate of potash.

The food eaten ashore is usually cooked in olive oil and possibly served with an oily sauce. This, together with the wine which is so cheap that one is inclined to drink more than usual, often has a laxative effect.

The lower level of hygiene can also produce stomach upsets, therefore effective medicines to cure these complaints should be obtained from one's own doctor before leaving home.

In hot spells heat exhaustion and even heat stroke are possible and an adequate intake of salt is essential to prevent this happening.

Although most yachtsmen are fully conversant with the dangers of sunburn at sea there are others who do not appreciate that, due to reflection of rays of sun off the water and the effects of wind and salt water, a bad case of sunburn can develop after only a few hours of exposure. This effect is naturally heightened in South Biscay as the sun is more powerful and the necessary precautions must be taken.

Up-to-date vaccination against smallpox and inoculation against typhoid and tetanus are advised but not compulsory.

Customs

Some weeks before leaving Britain it is worthwhile to visit the Customs officer at your home port. It may be found possible to ship duty-free bonded stores for consumption on the cruise. He will brief you on the procedure to be adopted and the forms to be completed. The Customs in any case should be notified before your departure. On arrival in France or Spain the local Immigration and Customs officers should be visited with all documents and your arrival reported. If laying up for the winter and not already in possession of a Spanish Customs card (*Permiso aduanero*), this should be obtained, though it is rarely asked for by officials. On leaving France or Spain a similar visit is required by the Customs and Immigration.

Bonded stores may also be obtained from major French ports such as Brest, La Rochelle, Bayonne etc. In Spain it was found impossible to get duty-free stores, but as the local wines and spirits are so cheap it did not matter.

On return to the UK it is essential to clear Customs in the normal way.

Laying up in Spain

In order to have two seasons' cruising in the area some yachtsmen may wish to lay up their yacht in Spain.

While the cost is bound to be much less than in England there are some problems. Firstly, there is only one yard on the coast, at Bilbao, which is capable of undertaking major yacht repairs. There are, of course, many yards which can deal with minor repairs in a rough way. Secondly, yacht-type fittings and spares are almost impossible to obtain and if found are expensive. Thirdly, help by skilled workmen, other than painters, is difficult to obtain.

However, if only a berth either ashore or afloat is required, then this can be found at most major and many minor ports. Check the availability and location of berths with the officers of the nearest yacht club. If hauling out make sure personally that the cradle is adequate for your yacht as experience in dealing with deep-keeled yachts is limited.

Air/sea routes to South Biscay

At the time of writing the following services are available; these can be used to change crews, etc.

Sea Southampton–Bilbao three times a week, 36 hours.
Southampton–Lisbon once a week, 2½ days.
Southampton–La Coruña once or twice a month, 2 days.

Air Direct from UK to Bilbao, Oporto and Lisbon.
Other routes are possible via such centres as Paris, Madrid, Lisbon, Vigo, Oporto etc. using local air, rail or road transport to get to the coast. Your local travel agent will advise.

Security There has been a considerable relaxation in the activities of the police and similar organisations in the post Franco era with the result that there has been an increase in crime and a noticeable decrease in self-discipline. Yachts left unattended should be locked and attractive items stowed below. In the larger ports it is not wise to allow individual crew members, especially women, to wander around alone after dark.

Background Information

Technical

Charts Admiralty, French and Spanish charts for the area of South Biscay are listed below. The information is correct to 1975 only.

Not unnaturally, the French charts are the best for the French parts of the coast and the Spanish for the North Spanish coast. They are more up to date and are usually easier to read than the Admiralty charts of the area.

At the time of writing all three nations' charts for many of the smaller ports are in need of major correction, as commercial development has taken place and training walls have been built which in some cases have altered the position of the channels very considerably.

Neither the French or Spanish charts have compass roses, so the use of protractor, such as a Douglas protractor or similar instrument, is necessary in order to obtain bearings.

French and Spanish charts are obtainable from the following chart agents in England:

Messrs Imray, Laurie, Norie and Wilson Ltd, Wych House, Saint Ives, Cambs.
Messrs H. Browne (Depot) Ltd, P & O Deck, P & O Building, Leadenhall St, London EC3.
Messrs J. D. Potter Ltd, 145 Minories, London EC3.
Messrs Kelvin Hughes Ltd, 31 Mansell St, London E1 8AA.

At least three weeks' notice should be given to enable the chart agents to obtain copies of the charts concerned.

In Spain, the Spanish charts are usually obtainable from the *Commandancia Militar de Marina* at the major ports or from the *Instituto Hydrografico de la Marina*, Cadiz.

In France, the French charts can be obtained from the *Librairie Maritime* at the larger ports, or from the *Service Hydrographique et Océanographique de la Marine*, 29283 Brest Cedex, France.

Admiralty charts

French coast of South Biscay

No.	Title	Scale (1:)
1104	Bay of Biscay	1,000,000
2648	Pointe de la Coubre to les Sables d'Olonne, Port of Les Sables d'Olonne	150,000
2664	Pointe d'Arcachon to Pointe de la Coubre	150,000
2665	Pointe d'Arcachon to Guetaria	149,000
2910	Entrance to La Gironde	75,000
2916	La Gironde—Royan to Bordeaux	75,000
1343	Plans in the Bay of Biscay:	
	L'Adour—entrance to Bayonne, St Jean de Luz	10,000
	Rada de Higuer or Baie de Fontarabie	25,000

Spanish coast of South Biscay

No.	Title	Scale (1:)
73	Puerto de Pasajes	7,500
2925	San Sebastián to Santander	150,000
75	Plans on the north coast of Spain:	
	Puerto de San Sebastián	7,500
	Puerto de Guetaria and Puerto de Bermeo	15,000
	Puerto de Lequeitio and Puerto de Castro Urdiales	10,000
	Ría de Santoña, Ría de Suances	25,000
	Puerto de Ondárroa	10,000
1170	Approaches to Puerto de Bilbao	50,000
74	Abra de Bilbao	10,000
	Continuation of Ría de Bilbao	25,000
76	Puerto de Santander	10,000
2926	Santander to Gijón	150,000
77	Plans on the north coast of Spain:	
	Ría de San Vicente de la Barquera and Puerto de Ribadessella	10,200
	Ría de Tina Mayor and Ría de Tina Menor	25,000
	Ensenada de Luanco	10,000
	Concha de Gijón and Ría de Avilés	12,500
2927	Gijón to Foz	150,000
78	Plans on the north coast of Spain:	
	Puerto de San Estéban and Ría de Pravia	7,500
	Puerto de Luarca	15,000
	Ría de Ribadeo	12,500
	Ensenada de San Ciprían, Rías de Vivero, del Barquero and de Cedeira	25,000
1755	Foz to Camariñas	200,000
	Ría de Corme y Lage, Ría de Camariñas	50,000
79	Rías El Ferrol del Caudillo, La Coruña and Betanzos	41,700
80	Ría de El Ferrol del Caudillo	10,000

Spanish charts

Spanish coast of South Biscay

No.	Title	Scale (1:)
1201	Golfo de Vizcaya, de La Isla D'Ouessant a Cabo Finisterre	863,400
39	De La Isla de Ré a Cabo Mayor	350,000
40	De Cabo Ajo a Cabo Ortegal	350,000
125A	De Cabo Toriñana a La Estaca de bares	156,800
126A	De la Estaca de Bares a Cabo Peñas	156,096
127	De Cabo Peñas a Cabo Ajo	175,000
128	De Cabo Ajo a Cabo Higuer	156,982
136A	De Cabo Machichaco a Río Gironde	325,000
945	De La Desembocadura del Río Adour al Cabo de Santa Catalina	92,600
13B	Puertos de Gijón y El Musel	8,000
18A	Ría del Barquero	15,000
4082	Ría de Vivero	15,000
4084	Puertos de Cariño y Espasante	15,000
61A	Ría de Navia	15,000
550A	Ría de Ribadeo	10,000
721B	Ría y Puerto de San Esteban de Pravia	5,000
731A	Ensenada de San Ciprián	15,000
	Puerto de Luarca	15,000
	Puerto de Viavález	2,200
748A	Puertos du Candás y Luanco	10,000
929	De Punta Frouseira a Las Islas Sisargas, con Las Rías de El Ferrol del Caudillo, Ares, Betanzos, La Coruña	55,000
930	De Cabo Ortegal a Cabo Prior	40,250
	Plano inserto: Ría de Cedeira	20,000
931	De San Ciprián a Cabo Ortegal	40,250
932	De Las Pantorgas a San Ciprián	40,280
933	De Luarca a Las Pantorgas	40,280
934	De San Estéban de Pravia a Luarca	40,280

No.	Title	Scale (1:)
935	De Cabo San Lorenzo a Cabo Vidio	50,000
936	Del Arenal de Moris al Cabo de San Lorenzo	40,331
9290	Rías de El Ferrol del Caudillo, Ares, Betanzos y La Coruña	25,000
4126	Ría y Puerto de La Coruña	5,000
4122	Ría de El Ferrol del Caudillo (Hoja I), Desde La Entrada hasta El Puerto	5,000
4123	Ría de El Ferrol del Caudillo (Hoja II), Desde El Castillo de San Felipe hasta el fondo de La Ría	10,000
	Planos insertos: Ría de El Ferrol del Caudillo, entre La Punta de S. Carlos y El Castillo de La Palma	5,000
	Arsenal de El Ferrol del Caudillo	5,000
9350	Ría de Avilés	5,250
9351	Ría de Avilés (Hoja I), Des La Entrada hasta el fondeadero del Monumento	3,000
9352	Ría de Avilés (Hoja II), Desde el fondeadero del Monumento hasta del fondo de la Ría	3,000
16A	Puerto de Motrico	5,000
19B	Puerto de San Sebastián	5,000
24B	Ría de Santoña	15,000
165A	Puerto de Castro Urdiales	5,000
3912	Rada de Higuer y Ría de Fuenterrabia	12,500
9410	Abra y Ría de Bilbao	10,000
199A	Bahía de San Juan de Luz	5,000
303A	Ría de Orio, Ensenada de Zarauz y Concha de Guetaria	15,100
321A	Fondeadero de Elanchove	15,133
4031	Barra Y Puerto de Ribadesella	10,000
4021	Ría y Puerto de San Vicente de La Barquera	10,000
4041	Puerto del Puntal y Tazones	10,000
4032	Puerto de Lastres	10,000
642A	Puerto de Lequeitio	5,000
659	Ría de San Martin de La Arena o de Suances	10,000
660	Ría de Astillero	10,000
663A	Bahía y Puerto de Santander	10,000
707	Puerto y Barra de Ondárroa	5,000
868A	Barra y Ría de Zumaya	6,400
914	Barra y Río de Deva	5,000
917	Mundaca, Bermeo y Fondeadero de Cabo Machichaco	15,000
937	De La Punta de La Ballota al Arenal de Moris	40,382
938	De Comillas al Puerto de Llanes	40,393
939	De La Virgen del Mar a La Ría de La Rabia	40,382
940	De La Ría de Santoña a La Virgen del Mar	40,415
941	Del Abra de Bilbao a la Ría de Santońa	40,409
942	De Cabo Ogoño al Abra de Bilbao	40,409
943	De Guetaria a Cabo Ogoño	40,470
944	De Río Bidasoa a Guetaria	40,443
9440	Ría y Puerto de Pasajes	4,000
	Plano inserto: Canal de Entrade, de Punta de Las Cruces a Punta de la Torre	2,500

French charts

French coast of South Biscay

No.	Title	Scale (1:)
6335	De L'Ile d'Oléron à Cordouan – Pertuis de Maumusson 1961.	47,000
6572	Golfe de Gascogne (partie centrale) 1967	219,954
6336	De La Pointe de la Coubre à la Pointe de la Négade – Embouchure de La Gironde 1961	48,300
6141	Embouchure de La Gironde. Rades de Royan et du Verdon 1972	15,000
6139	La Gironde, Du Verdon à Pauillac, Port de Pauillac 1973	48,000
6140	La Gironde, La Garonne et La Dordogne jusqu'à Bordeaux et Libourne, Port de Blaye 1970	48,000

No.	Title	Scale (1:)
4610	Cours de La Garonne. De Bec d'Ambès à Bordeaux 1968	15,000
6766	Environs du Bassin d'Arcachon, Port et Mouillage d'Arcachon 1955	125,600
5722	*Etang d'Hourtin et de Carcans 1931	20,000
5723	Anse de Contau 1949	5,000
6571	Golfe de Gascogne (partie sud) 1967	224,791
5875	*Etang de Biscarosse et de Parentis 1938	20,000
6586	Capbreton—Etang d'Hossegor 1973	8,500
6536	Cours de L'Adour. Port de Bayonne 1968	10,000
6558	De Bayonne à Saint Sébastien 1973	50,000
6526	Baie de Saint Jean de Luz 1967	7,500
6556	Baie de Fontarabie 1967	12,500
6557	De Vieux—Baucau à Bayonne 1973	49,630

* Inland lakes

Spanish coast of South Biscay

No.	Title	Scale (1:)
4991	De Cap Ferret à Llanes 1938	296,600
6571	Golfe de Gascogne (partie sud) 1967	224,791
6375	Port de Passajes 1961	7,500
6379	Ports de La Côte Nord d'Espagne: Ría de Orio, Port de Guetaria, Ría de Zumaya, Río Deva, Port de Motrico, Port de Ondárroa, Port de Lequeitio 1964	10,000
6380	D'Elanchove au Cap Machichaco 1963	15,000
6774	Port de Bilbao (entree du Río–Nervion)—Suite du Río–Nervion 1931	different
3542	Port de Santoña, Port de Castro Urdiales 1931	different
3308	Port de Santander 1956	10,000
2042	Barre et Entree de La Riviére de San Martin de la Arena, Mouillage de Comillas, Port de Candás, Port de Luanco 1929	different
5009	De Llanes au Cap Ortegal, Cartouches: Baie de Santa Marta, Mouillages d'Espasante et de Caríño 1929	297,600
6381	Port de Luarca—Rivière Pravia et Port de San Estéban Ports de Musel et de Gijón, Port de Ribadesella, San Vicente-de-la-Barquera 1968	different
6382	Ría de Avilés 1962	10,000
6383	Ports de La Côte Nord d'Espagne: Ría de Ribadeo, Anse de San Ciprían, Ría de Vivero, Ría del Barquero, Ría de Cedeira 1964	25,000
6665	Baies du Ferrol et de La Corogne 1925	41,700
5546	Port du Ferrol 1962	20,000

Streams, currents and tides

Basic current

The prevailing current in the Bay of Biscay is an offshoot of the North Atlantic Current which is itself a continuation of the Gulf Stream. A part of this offshoot carries on to become the Portuguese and, further S, the Canary Current. This current flows into the head of the Bay and sweeps round, emerging again off the NW corner of Spain, creating a W-going current along the N coast of Spain.

Wind currents

This prevailing current is severely modified by surface currents induced by winds. If winds are strong and have been blowing for several days currents of up to 2 knots may be experienced in the open sea and much stronger near the coast. For instance a long lasting W to NW gale can induce an E-going current along the N coast of Spain, which turns N along the French coast with a velocity which can reach 5 knots.

Counter currents When the main current is S-going there is a local counter-current N along the coast of France as far as La Gironde, but this is only found very close inshore, and vice-versa with a N-going main current.

Tidal streams Tidal streams are very weak, especially in the offing. However, in the narrow entrances to some estuaries and around points, headlands and inshore islands these streams can be strong.

Conclusions When crossing the mouth of the Bay of Biscay allowance must be made for an E set due to currents, especially if the winds are from SW through W to NW and are strong.

When coasting checks must be made to ascertain the direction and speed of currents by navigational methods or by observing the flow of water past the buoys of the many lobster and crab pots to be found near the coast.

Prediction of tidal heights and times

Data from the Admiralty *Tide Tables* Vol. I has been used throughout this Pilot as most yachts proceeding to this coast will probably continue further and they will need this volume for use on the coast of the rest of the Iberian peninsula and also for the Mediterranean.

In order to simplify the procedure, Time and Height differences have been extracted and included with the data for each port in this Pilot so that if the Tidal Predictions for the standard port of Pointe de Grave is extracted from Vol. I and pinned up in the chart room no further reference to the Admiralty *Tide Tables* is necessary.

Under normal conditions simple methods of interpolation are quite adequate. If, however, an especially accurate result is required, full instructions are to be found in the first part of the Admiralty *Tide Tables*.

Times in these tables are in local time. France and Spain keep the same time, one hour being added to GMT in winter and two in summer.

Heights used are the heights above Chart Datum of the latest Admiralty charts, and on the Spanish and French coasts this is normally Lowest Astronomical Tide (LAT). Except under unusual conditions about 0·3 m (1 ft) extra depth can be expected at Mean Low Water Springs (MLWS).

Depths are only mentioned in the text when they are less than 3 m (10 ft) unless special reference to them is necessary.

Meteorology

General The climate and weather on the S Biscay coast is considered below, but only for the summer months of June to September. Any yachtsmen who plan to visit this coast in the winter should study the Admiralty *Sailing Directions for the Bay of Biscay* (No. 22) and the *West Coasts of Spain and Portugal* (No. 67) for additional data.

In general it is fair to say that the weather is similar to that experienced in the English Channel, but about 5°C (10°F) warmer. A study of the tables in the Admiralty *Sailing Directions* will show this similarity.

Pressure The weather is variable and is normally effected by the movements of low pressure areas passing near to or crossing the British Isles, and by any secondary depressions formed on cold fronts to the S of the main depression. The Azores high pressure areas and the Central European low form a background pressure gradient from SW or W to E.

Winds Along the N Spanish coast the prevailing winds are from SW to NW, but in midsummer are frequently from NE. Unless a strong secondary depression forms or a rare depression crosses the Bay itself these winds are not of great strength and are generally steady. However any winds from SE through S to SW are squally and gusts may reach gale force as they sweep down from the mountains. When a cold front from a depression to the N passes along the Spanish coast a very sudden increase in wind strength from the NW, locally called a *galerna*, may be experienced.

In calm conditions land and sea breezes will be encountered near the coasts, especially the flat French coast, due to the temperature differences between the land and sea.

In hot and thundery weather line squalls may occur near the coast and precautions should be taken if a long low line of cloud is seen to approach. Sometimes these squalls are accompanied by very powerful gusts and at other times very little increase in wind strength will be encountered as the clouds pass overhead.

There is a close similarity between the S coast of England and the N Spanish coast in the amount of cloud and sunshine that can be expected. The W end of the Spanish coast has a better record for sunshine, but in every case when the sun does shine it is much more powerful than that experienced in S England.

Rainfall Again there is not much difference in rainfull compared with S England. Rain in summer is usually associated with thunderstorms.

Line squall.

Fog and mist In the summer months, the early morning mist on calm days can present a problem to pilotage. The low clouds which sometimes obscure the tops of hills and the lighthouses on them can be dangerous during a night approach to the coast. Fog itself is very rare.

Temperature In general the air and sea temperatures are above the figures which are normal for S England. The air temperature can reach 90°F for days on end in the summer.

Radio

Introduction Although the various radio facilities are not so numerous or comprehensive as in the area around the coast of Britain, they are more than adequate for normal requirements.

Yachtsmen are advised to make a last minute check before leaving Britain to see if there are any amendments to the data given below as some of these stations may change operational times and frequencies with the minimum of warning.

Attention is directed to the very low power of some of the transmissions and their consequent limited range.

Radiobeacons (reference: Admiralty *List of Radio Signals* Vol. II).

Station	Frequency kHz	Range miles power	Call sign	Period	Group Remarks
Belle Isle	303·4	100	BT	6 min.	Grouped
Goulphar lighthouse			(– · · · / –)		
Ile de Sein	303·4	50	SN	6 min.	
NW lighthouse			(· · · / – ·)		
Pointe de la Coubre	303·4	100	LK	6 min.	
lighthouse			(· – · · / – · –)		
Les Baleines	303·4	50	BN	6 min.	
Ile de Ré lighthouse			(– · · · / – ·)		
BXA	291·9	5	BX	10 sec.	
light float			(– · · · / – · · –)		
Pointe de Grave	308	5	VR		
Rear lighthouse			(· · · – / · – ·)		
Cap Ferret	296·5	100	FT	6 min.	Grouped
lighthouse			(· · – · / –)		
Cabo Machichaco	296·5	100	MA	6 min.	
lighthouse			(– – / · –)		
Cabo Mayor	296·5	50	MY	6 min.	
lighthouse			(– – / – · – –)		
Llanes	301·1	50	IA	6 min.	Grouped
lighthouse			(· · / · –)		
Cabo Peñas	301·1	50	PS	6 min.	
lighthouse			(· – – · / · · ·)		
Estaca de Bares			BA		
lighthouse	301·1	100	(– · · · / · –)	6 min.	
Torre de Hércules	305·7	30	L	6 min.	Grouped
lighthouse			(· – · ·)		
Cabo Prioriño	305·7	50	C	6 min.	
lighthouse			(– · – ·)		

Station	Frequency kHz	Range miles power	Call sign	Period	Group Remarks
Cabo Villano lighthouse	310·3	100	VI (· · · – / · ·)	6 min.	Grouped
Cabo Finisterre lighthouse	310·3	100	FI (· · – · / · ·)	6 min.	
Cabo Silleiro lighthouse	310·3	200	RO (· – · / – – –)	6 min.	
Lugo **(Otero del Rey)** 43°14′53″N 7°28′56″W	285	200 1·5 kW	LG (· – · · / – – ·)	1 min.	Continuous

Aero radiobeacons

Station	Frequency kHz	Range miles power	Call sign	Remarks
Biarritz-Bayonne **(Anglet)** 43°28′17″N 1°25′44″W	249·5	35	BZ (– · · · / – – · ·)	Continuous
Bordeaux (Mérignac) 44°55′55″N 0°33′53″W	393	200	BDM (– · · · / – · · / – –)	Continuous
Cazaux 44°31′58″N 1°09′10″W	382	50	CAA (– · – · / · – / · –)	Day only
Dax (Castels) 43°53′55″N 1°07′57′W	341	40	DXN (– · · / – · · – / – ·)	Continuous
Bilbao 43°19′34″N 2°58′30″W	370	70	BLO (– · · · / · – · · / – – –)	Continuous
Asturias (Gijón) 43°33′30″N 6°01′37″W	325	60	AVS (· – / · · · – / · · ·)	Continuous
La Coruña 43°21′56″N 8°19′42″W	401	40	LRA (· – · · / · – · / · –)	Day only
San Sebastian **(Fuenterrabia)** 43°23′15″N 1°47′39″W	328	0·2 kW	HIG (· · · · / · · / – – ·)	Continuous
Santander 43°28′N 3°46′W	338	0·3 kW	SNR (· · · / – · / · – ·)	Day only
Monteferro 42°09′16″N 8°50′43″W	353	0·25 kW	MTF (– – / – / · · – ·)	Day only

Radio weather messages

(reference: Admiralty *List of Radio Signals* Vol. III)

The following table gives details of radio weather messages which include the area covered by this Pilot. Again, a last minute check on times and frequencies is advised before leaving the UK.

Some of these stations are so low powered that they may only be heard near the transmitter concerned.

The forecasts from three national sources, British, French and Spanish, often differ materially from each other and are frequently different from the weather actually experienced on the coast.

Additional weather forecasts are transmitted in Morse (A1 and A2) by all three nations. Details are contained in the Admiralty *List of Radio Signals* Vol. III.

The French and Spanish television weather transmissions are worth seeing and, being mainly diagrammatic, are easy to understand without knowledge of the language.

Radio weather messages—South Biscay

Station	Frequency kHz Channel	Type of transmission	Power/range	Timings GMT Storm	Timings GMT Forecast	Remarks
BBC Radio 4	200	Speech AM	50 – 400	At programme junctions & after news	0015*, 0625*, 1355*, 1750*	**English** – Biscay, Finisterre, Trafalgar
Soulac C.R.O.S.S.A.	Channel 06, 09, 10, 12	Speech FM			On request	**French** – Rochebonne to Spanish Frontier
	Channel 13	Speech FM		0800*, 1430	0800*, 1430	
Bordeaux – Arcachon (FEC)	421	Morse	1.0	On receipt, at end of next two silent periods.		**French** – Sables d'Olonne to Spanish Frontier
	1820	Speech SSB		At 18 mins past every other even hour	On request and at 0730, 1730	
	1862	Speech SSB		7 min past every even hour		
	Channel 82	Speech FM	0.05		0633*, 1133*	
Royan	Channel 23	Speech FM	0.05	On receipt & at end of next two silent periods	0633*, 1133*	**French** – Sables d'Olonne to Spanish Frontier
Radio France Allouis	164	Speech AM	2000		0825, 1950	**French** – Sables d'Olonne to Spanish Frontier
Bordeaux	1205	Speech AM	100		0615, 1105	
	89.7 MHz	Speech FM	5		0615, 1105	
Bayonne	1492	Speech AM	40		0615, 1105	
	89.0 MHz	Speech FM	4		0615, 1105	
Bayonne	Channel 24	Speech FM	0.05	On receipt & at end of next two silent periods	0633*, 1133*	**French** – Sables d'Olonne to Spanish Frontier
Machichaco	1704	Speech SSB		1103, 1733	1103, 1733	**Spanish** – Areas 1 & 2
Cabo de Peñas (EAS)	441	Morse			1118, 1818 1103, 1733	**Spanish** – Areas 2 & 3
	1730	Speech SSB			1118, 1818 1103, 1733	
La Coruña	1748	Speech SSB		1103, 1733	1103, 1733	**Spanish** – Areas 4 & 6

Note: * 1 hour earlier during Summer.

Coast radio stations (reference: Admiralty *List of Radio Signals* Vol. I). The following coast radio stations give fair coverage over S Biscay during normal conditions.

Station	Frequency kHz Channel	Type of Transmission	Power/ Range	Timings GMT	Traffic lists – GMT	Remarks
Royan	(Numbers in bold type indicate prime frequency) Channel 16, 23, 25 (02, 83)	Speech FM	0·05	24 hours		French
Bordeaux	Channel 16, 27 (63)	Speech FM	0·05	24 hours		French
Bordeaux/ Arcachon (FFC)	**410**, 421, 500*, 512*	Morse	1·0	24 hours	50 min past even hours on 421 kHz	French
	1862, 2182* 2775, 3722	Speech SSB	1·0	24 hours	07 min past even hours on 1862 kHz	French
	1820	Speech SSB	0·1	24 hours		
	Channel 16, 28, 82	Speech FM	0·05	24 hours		
Bayonne	Channel 16, 24 (03)	Speech FM	0·05	24 hours		French
Choritoquieta (San Sebastián)	Channel 16, 20, **25**, 26, **27**	Speech FM		24 hours	0233, 0633, 0833, 1033, 1233, 1633, 1833, 2233 on Channel 27	Spanish
Machichaco	**1704**, 2083, 2182, 2191, 2586, 3283	Speech SSB	1·0	24 hours	33 min past every odd hour on 1704 kHz	Spanish
	Channel **04**, 16, 24, 26, 27	Speech FM		24 hours	0233, 0633, 0833, 1033, 1203, 1633, 1833, 2233 on Channel 24	
Algorta (Bilbao)	Channel **20**, 25, **26**, 27	Speech FM	0·05	24 hours	0233, 0633, 0833, 1033, 1233, 1633, 1833, 2233 on Channel 26	Spanish
Praves	Channel 16, **23**, 26, 27, **28**	Speech FM	0·05	24 hours	0233, 0633, 0833, 1033, 1233, 1633, 1833, 2233 on Channel 23	Spanish
Cabo de Penas (EAS)	**441**, 500, 512, 425*, 468*, 480*, 500*, 512*	Morse	5·0	24 hours	3 min past each even hour	Spanish
	1730, 2013*, 2182*, 2191*, 2649, 3231	Speech SSB	1·0	24 hours	33 min past each odd hour on 1730 kHz	
	Channel 16 **24**, 25, **26**, 27	Speech FM		24 hours	0303, 0703, 0903, 1103, 1303, 1703, 1903, 2303 on Channel 26	Spanish
Boal (Gijon)	Channel 16, 24, **25**, 26, **27**	Speech FM		24 hours	0303, 0703, 0903, 1103, 1303, 1703, 1903, 2303 on Channel 27	Spanish
La Coruña	**1748**, 2122*, 2182*, 2191*, 2596, 3290*	Speech SSB	1·0	24 hours	33 min past every odd hour on 1748 kHz	Spanish
	Channel 16, **20**, 25, **26**, 27	Speech FM	0·05	24 hours	0303, 0703, 0903, 1103, 1303, 1703, 1903, 2303 on Channel 26	

Port Radio Stations, Pilots and Tugs. (reference Admiralty List of Radio Signals Vol VI)
The following Port Operations, Pilot Services, Tugs and Traffic Surveillance radio stations operate and can be communicated with in the event of difficulty in the area of the port concerned.

Station	Time	Frequency kHz Channel No.	Type	Telephone	Remarks
La Gironde		2182	Speech SSB	29.11.97	**French** Send ETA 12 hrs in advance
Pilots	24 hrs	06, 12, 16	Speech FM		
Le Verdon	24 hrs	12, 16	Speech FM	59.63.91	
Radar	24 hrs	14, 16	Speech FM		Guidance and traffic information in French
Pauillac	24 hrs	09, 12, 16	Speech FM	59.01.60 59.12.16	
Bordeaux	24 hrs	12, 16	Speech FM		
Cap Breton	X	09	Speech FM		**French**
L'Adour	X	12, 16	Speech FM	63.16.18	**French** Send ETA 12 hrs in advance
Pilots	X	12, 16	Speech FM		0800 – 1200 and 1400 – 1800 local time
Bayonne	24 hrs	12, 16	Speech FM	25.00.02	Tug 'Barclan' Ch 12
Pasajes	24 hrs	11, 12, 13, 14, 16	Speech FM		**Spanish**
Guetaria	X	2182 2700	Speech SSB Speech SSB		**Spanish**
Lequitio	X X	2182 2700	Speech SSB Speech SSB		**Spanish**
Bermeo	X X	2182	Speech SSB Speech SSB		**Spanish**
Bilbao	24 hrs	12, 13, 16, 20	Speech FM		**Spanish**
Tugs	24 hrs	08	Speech FM		
Pilots	24 hrs	12, 16	Speech FM		
Sig Stn	X	12, 13, 16	Speech FM		
Refinery	24 hrs	11, 14, 16	Speech FM		
Santoña	X	2182 1840	Speech SSB		**Spanish**
Santander					
Pilot Vessel	24 hrs	06, 12, 14, 16	Speech FM		**Spanish** Send ETA 24 hrs in advance
Pilots	24 hrs	09, 12, 14, 16	Speech FM		**Spanish**
Gijon	24 hrs	1, 12, 14, 16	Speech		**Spanish**
Aviles				560313	
Pilot Vessel	24 hrs	06, 09, 12, 14, 16	Speech FM	566856	**Spanish**
Pilots	24 hrs	11, 12, 14, 16	Speech FM		
Burela	X	2182 1810	Speech SSB Speech SSB		**Spanish**

San Cripián	X	12, 14, 16	Speech FM	**Spanish**
Cillero	X	2182	Speech SSB	**Spanish**
	X	1691·5	Speech SSB	
Cedeira	X	2182	Speech SSB	**Spanish**
	X	1800	Speech SSB	
El Ferrol	24 hrs	10, 11, 12, 13, 14, 16	Speech FM	**Spanish**
Sada	X	2182	Speech SSB	**Spanish**
	X	1707	Speech SSB	
La Coruña Pilots and Port	X	12, 16, 26	Speech FM	**Spanish**

Note: 'X' means no specific hours but usually when harbour is open to traffic

Buoyage System

General The IALA Maritime Buoyage System has now been fully established on this section of coast. Both the Lateral and Cardinal Marks are used.

Lateral marks

	Port hand marks	**Starboard hand marks**
Colour:	Red	Green
Shape (Buoys):	Cylindrical (can), pillar or spar	Conical, pillar or spar
Topmark (if any):	Single red cylinder (can)	Single green cone, point upward
Light (when fitted):	Red, any other than composite group flashing (2 + 1)	Green, any other than composite group flashing (2 + 1)

At the point where a channel divides, when proceeding in the conventional direction of buoyage, a preferred channel may be indicated by modifying Port or Starboard lateral marks as follows.

	Preferred channel to Starboard	**Preferred channel to Port**
Colour:	Red with one broad green horizontal band	Green with one broad red horizontal band
Shape (Buoys):	Cylindrical (can), pillar or spar	Conical, pillar or spar
Topmark (if any):	Single red cylinder (can)	Single green cone, point upward
Light (when fitted):	Red, composite group flashing (2 + 1)	Green, composite group flashing (2 + 1)

Cardinal Marks The four quadrants (North, East, South and West) taken from the point of interest. A cardinal mark is named after the quadrant in which it is placed. The name of a cardinal mark indicates that it should be passed to the named side of the mark.

	North Cardinal Mark:	**East Cardinal Mark:**
Topmark:	2 black cones, one above the other, points upward	2 black cones, one above the other, base to base
Colour:	Black above yellow	Black with a single broad horizontal yellow band
Shape:	Pillar or spar	Pillar or spar
Light (when fitted):	White, VQ or Q	White, VQ (3) every 5 s or Q (3) every 10 s

	South Cardinal Mark:	**West Cardinal Mark:**
Topmark:	2 black cones, one above the other, points downward	2 black cones, one above the other, point to point
Colour:	Yellow above black	Yellow with a single broad horizontal black band
Shape:	Pillar or spar	Pillar or spar
Light (when fitted):	White, VQ (6) + long flash every 10 s or Q (6) + long flash every 15 s	White, VQ (9) every 10 s or Q (9) every 15 s

Isolated danger mark

This is a mark over an isolated danger which has navigable water all round it

Topmark:	2 black spheres, one above the other
Colour:	Black with one or more broad horizontal red bands
Shape:	Pillar or spar
Light (when fitted):	White, Fl. (2)

Safe water marks

Indicate that there is navigable water all round the mark; these include centre line marks and mid-channel marks. Such a mark may also be used as an alternative to a cardinal or a lateral mark to indicate a landfall.

Colour:	Red and white vertical stripes
Shape:	Spherical, pillar with spherical topmark or spar
Topmark (if any):	Single red sphere
Light (when fitted):	White, Isophase, occulting, one long flash every 10 s or Morse A

Special Marks

Marks not primarily intended to assist navigation but which indicate a special area or feature, e.g: Ocean Data Acquisition Systems (ODAS) marks: Traffic Separation marks where use of conventional channel marking may cause confusion; Spoil Ground marks; Military Exercise Zone Marks; Cable or pipe line marks; Recreation Zone marks.

Colour:	Yellow
Shape:	Optional but not conflicting with navigational marks (e.g. yellow can buoy will not be used in a 'starboard' situation)
Topmark (if any):	Single yellow 'X' shape
Light (when fitted):	Yellow

Storm and harbour signals

The following signals may be flown or displayed from prominent sites near the entrance to harbours on the Spanish coast. Some harbours have non-standard signals, details of which are given in the section dealing with the port concerned.

	By day	By night	Meaning
Storm signals	Cone point up	Two red lights vertically	NW gale probable
	Two cones points up vertically	Red over white light	NE gale probable
	Cone point down	Two white lights vertically	SW gale probable
	Two cones points down vertically	White over red light	SE gale probable
	Ball	White over green light	Bad weather probable
Additional storm signals (used in conjunction with above)	Two balls vertically	Two red lights horizontally	Storm or strong gale probable
	Black flag or cylinder	—	Wind probably veer
	Two black flags or cylinders vertically	—	Wind probably back
Traffic signals	Three balls vertically	Three red lights vertically	Emergency: entry prohibited
	Cone point up between two balls vertically	White light between two red vertically	Entry prohibited
	Two cones points together above another cone point down all vertically	White light between two green all vertically	Departure prohibited
	Ball between two cones points together vertically	Green above red above white lights vertically	Entry and departure prohibited
Additional traffic signals	Square shape	Red light between two white vertically	Local gale, boat traffic suspended
	Two cones points together	White over two red lights vertically	Moderate gale port closed to small craft
	Two cones bases together	Three red lights vertically	Severe gale port closed
	Red pendant over blue pendant at yardarm	Two red over one white light vertically	Bar cannot be crossed
	Blue pendant over red pendant at yardarm	Two green over one white light vertically	Ships at anchor should put to sea
	Blue pendant at mast head red at yardarm	Three green lights vertically	Ships may enter or depart if signal is visible to them
	Red pendant at one yardarm blue at other	Green over white over red light vertically	Departure prohibited

Note: There is an additional series of signals for the use of pilots directing ships into harbour. These are detailed in the *Bay of Biscay Pilot*, Admiralty *Sailing Directions* No. 22.

Note: Red pendant has a white circle on it and the Blue pendant has two yellow stripes.

Lights

A very complete reference to lights has been made in this Pilot to ease one of the navigator's most difficult problems, the night approach and entrance to an unknown harbour.

A list of the major coast lights will be found at the beginning of each of the parts dealing with a section of the coast. Another list of the lights near each port is given for each port, which also includes the smaller lights in the area. In addition, where referred to in the text under the headings 'Approach' and 'Entrance', the characteristics of the lights are also given.

Heights of the lights are expressed in metres and feet from Mean High Water Spring (MHWS) to the focal plane of the light.

The range is given in nautical miles and where there are two figures the lesser figure represents the normal range of the light. If under clear conditions it may be seen at greater distances, then the greater figure gives this range. The 'loom' may be seen still further under exceptional conditions.

In the approach to the coast when clouds are low no reliance should be placed upon seeing the lights on the higher cliffs and mountains as they may be obscured by mist and cloud. Minor lights sometimes do not work or show inaccurate characteristics.

Bearings

Throughout the bearings are true bearings in the 0°–360° notation; magnetic variation based on the latest data is given for each port in this Pilot. It should be noted that French and Spanish charts do not have compass roses as on the Admiralty charts. Bearings of leading lights and marks are landward, i.e. the course to be sailed, and bearings of normal coast lights are seaward, i.e. from the light outwards, as is usual.

Swell

Yachtsmen who have sailed only in the English Channel or North Sea will not have encountered the Atlantic swell which is a feature of the Bay of Biscay. It is quite alarming to see it for the first time and to find full size ships vanishing from sight in the troughs. It is in fact nothing like so dangerous as it appears, and is usually more pleasant to sail upon than the short chop of the Channel. It is, however, dangerous in shallow water when it breaks and in severe conditions may do so over banks as deep as 11 m (6 fathoms) or more. Under these conditions all banks should be carefully avoided. Only ports with wide deep-water entrances should be used when there is a heavy swell. Skippers and navigators should remember that swell reduces the depth of water by half the height of the swell, and that the height of the swell increases as the water shallows.

Sand bars

Many ports on the coast of South Biscay have sand bars at their entrances and some of these bars virtually dry out at low water.

Entrance should not be attempted in conditions of heavy swell but under calm or normal conditions they can be entered during the last two or three hours of the flood tide. In general they should never be attempted on the ebb tide when the ebbing tidal stream added to the river current can cause the seas to break heavily.

In most harbours it is possible to approach quite close to the bar in deep water and to heave to for a short time to observe whether the bar is breaking or not. In this case do not be put off by the seas breaking either side of the entrance, which in some cases is quite narrow.

Care should be taken to carry out these observations over at least ten minutes to allow for any extra large rogue waves.

Breakwaters

The ends of breakwaters should not be approached too closely as there are often underwater obstructions or rocks in the vicinity.

Coastal Anchorages

A number of anchorages have been listed in the first part of each chapter, and others which are near a port in the section dealing with the nearby port. Many other coastal anchorages are possible but in all cases anchorages on this coast should be used with caution owing to the swell, depth of water, steeply shelving sea bed and, in most places, large areas of rocky bottom with poor holding ground.

Glossary of Spanish words applicable to this pilot

Below are listed a limited number of Spanish words with their English equivalents. Further information can be found in the Admiralty *Sailing Directions No. 22, The Bay of Biscay Pilot*, and from that most useful book, *Ready About* by Barbara Webb (Adlard Coles, £1.05), which also includes French and Spanish terms beyond the scope of this pilot.

Abra	Cove, creek, haven opening
Ancho	(adj) Wide, broad
Arena	Sand
Arenal	Extensive area of sand
Arrecife	Reef
Astillero	Shipyard
Atalaya	Watchtower
Bahia	Bay
Bajio	Shoal
Bajo	(n) Shoal (adj) Low (adv) Below, under
Baliza	Beacon
Banco (de Arena)	Bank, sandbank
Bancha	Bank
Barra	Bar (of a river etc.)
Blanco, a	(n) Target (adj) White
Boca	Mouth
Cabo	Cape
Cala	Narrow cove or creek with steep sides
Canal	Channel
Canto	Bluff
Casa	House
Castillo	Castle
Castro	Headland, hillock surmounted by ruins
Catedral	Cathedral
Chico, a	Small
Ciudad	City
Co	Rocky shoal, rock
Concha	Bay or cove
Contramuelle	Breakwater
Convento	Convent
Cordillera	Mountain range
Cruz	Cross
Cueva	Cave
Dársena	Basin, dock, backwater
Desembarcadero	Landing place
Dique	Mole, dock, embankment, levee
El	Definite article (masc)
Ensenada	Bay
Entrada	Entrance
Ermita	Hermitage
Escollera	Rubble breakwater
Espigón	Station
Estación	Arm of mole, pier
Este	East
Faro	Lighthouse
Fondeadero	Anchorage
Frontón	Wall-like cliff face
Golfo	Gulf
Gran, Grande	Large, great, big
Iglesia	Church
Isla	Island

Islote	Barren islet	*Playa*	Beach
La, las	Definite article (fem)	*Poniente*	Western
Lago	Lake	*Provincia*	Province
Laguna	Lagoon, pond	*Pueblo*	Town
Levante	Eastern	*Puente*	Bridge
Los	Definite article (masc)	*Puerto*	Port, harbour
Lugar	Village, place	*Punta*	Point
Malecón	Quay, mole	*Puntal*	Narrow point
Mar	Sea	*Redondo, a*	Round
Meridional	Southern	*Restinga*	Reef
Monasterio	Monastery	*Ría*	Sunken valley forming a narrow inlet or estuary
Montaña	Mountains	*Río*	River
Monte	Mount	*Roca*	Rocky
Morro	Headland, bluff, head of breakwater	*Rojo*	Red
Muelle	Pier, jetty, mole	*Rompeolas*	Breakwater
Negro	Black	*Rompientes*	Breakers
Norte	North	*San, Santo, a*	Saint
Nuevo	New	*Septentrional*	Northern
Occidental	Western	*Sierra*	Mountain range
Oeste	West	*Silla*	Saddle
Oriental	Eastern	*Sud, Sur*	South
Palacio	Palace	*Surgidero*	Anchorage
Paseo	Promenade, avenue	*Tenedero*	Holding ground, anchorage
Pasaje	Passage	*Tierra*	Land
Paso	Pass	*Torre*	Tower
Peninsula	Peninsula	*Vega*	(n) plain
Peña	Rock	*Verde*	Green
Petón	Pinnacle	*Vigia*	Lookout
Pico	Peak	*Villa*	Town, villa
Piedra	Stone, rock		
Placer	Shoal		

Conversion tables

Metres–Feet			Centimetres–Inches		
m	ft or m	ft	cm	in or cm	in
0·31	1	3·28	2·54	1	0·39
0·61	2	6·56	5·08	2	0·79
0·91	3	9·84	7·62	3	1·18
1·22	4	13·12	10·16	4	1·57
1·52	5	16·40	12·70	5	1·97
1·83	6	19·69	15·24	6	2·36
2·13	7	22·97	17·78	7	2·76
2·44	8	26·25	20·32	8	3·15
2·74	9	29·53	22·86	9	3·54
3·05	10	32·81	25·40	10	3·94
6·10	20	65·62	50·80	20	7·87
9·14	30	98·42	76·20	30	11·81
12·19	40	131·23	101·60	40	15·75
15·24	50	164·04	127·00	50	19·69
30·48	100	328·09	254·00	100	39·37

Kilogrammes–Pounds

kg	lbs or kg	lbs
0·45	1	2·20
0·91	2	4·41
1·36	3	6·61
1·81	4	8·82
2·27	5	11·02
2·72	6	13·23
3·18	7	15·43
3·63	8	17·64
4·08	9	19·84
4·54	10	22·05
9·07	20	44·09
13·61	30	66·14
18·14	40	88·19
22·68	50	110·23
45·36	100	220·46

Litres–Imperial Gallons

L	L or gals	gals
4·55	1	0·22
9·09	2	0·44
13·64	3	0·66
18·18	4	0·88
22·73	5	1·10
27·28	6	1·32
31·82	7	1·54
36·37	8	1·76
40·91	9	1·98
45·46	10	2·20
90·92	20	4·40
136·38	30	6·60
181·84	40	8·80
227·30	50	11·10
340·95	75	16·50
454·60	100	22·00
909·18	200	44·00
2272·98	500	110·00
4545·96	1000	220·00

Kilometres–Statute Miles

km		M
1·61	1	0·62
8·05	5	3·11
12·87	8	4·97

Kilometres–Statute Miles Cont'd

km		M
16·00	10	6·00
32·00	20	12·00
48·00	30	19·00
64·00	40	25·00
80·00	50	31·00
121·00	75	47·00
161·00	100	62·00
402·00	250	155·00
805·00	500	311·00

Metres–Fathoms

m	fathoms	ft
0·91	½	3
1·83	1	6
3·66	2	12
5·49	3	18
7·32	4	24
9·14	5	30
18·29	10	60
36·58	20	120
54·86	30	180

lb/in^2–kg/cm^2

lbs/in^2	kg/cm^2	lbs/in^2	kg/cm^2
10	0·703	32	2·250
12	0·844	34	2·390
14	0·984	36	2·531
16	1·125	40	2·812
18	1·266	45	3·164
20	1·406	50	3·515
22	1·547	60	4·218
24	1·687	70	4·921
26	1·828	80	5·625
28	1·969	90	6·328
30	2·109	100	7·031

Cubic Capacity

1 cu in	16·387 cc
1 cu ft (1728 cu in)	0·028 m^3
1 cu yard (27 cu ft)	0·765 m^3
1 cu centimetre	0·061 cu in
1 cu decimetre	61·023 cu in
1 cu metre (1000 cdm)	35·315 cu ft
1 cu metre	1·31 cu yd

Background Information

Spain

General Spain, perhaps more than most countries, is a land of contrasts. Almost everywhere you look you will see side by side the extremes of riches and poverty, beauty and ugliness, cleanliness and filth, efficiency and inefficiency, modern and ancient. The juxtaposition of these contrasting features makes it a fascinating country to visit.

The N coast of Spain was never settled by the Moors who invaded the country in the eighth century and the local inhabitants not unnaturally consider themselves as a superior race compared to the rest of the country.

A Spaniard is a man of dignity. No matter how poor he is, how menial his job or how rough his dress, he is a proud man and should be treated as a *caballero* (gentleman). If treated with courtesy he will be a sound and helpful friend who will go out of his way to assist you.

As with any nationality Spaniards have their peculiarities. They will often reply to a question with the answer which they think will please you most but which may not be entirely correct. Their measure of time can be elastic. *Mañana* (tomorrow) may be several days ahead!

Yacht clubs Many of the larger ports on this coast have yacht clubs of various types and there is a very considerable difference to be found between them. In some of the larger ports there are yacht clubs concerned with yachting in name only which are in fact purely social clubs in no way connected with yachting. There are some clubs which perform a dual function of encouraging yachting and at the same time have a large non-yachting social membership. At the other end of the scale there are some smaller clubs which are concerned primarily with yachting. In addition there are some clubs whose main concern is fishing and yachting is of less importance. Finally there are some clubs which are only interested in fishing.

In the larger commercial fishing ports there are co-operative clubs for the local fishermen who fish for a living.

It will be realised that the behaviour and dress requirements of these many types of clubs, to say nothing of the cost and quality of drinks, food etc., vary very considerably and one can only advise that the standard is much higher than that which is currently normal in a similar club in England.

Information offices Most ports have information bureaus which are worth visiting on first arrival as they often supply, free of charge, maps and details of local places and events which are of interest to visitors.

Before leaving England a lot of useful local information can be gleaned from the brochures about the area which can be obtained from the Spanish and French Tourist Offices. These offices can be found as follows:
Spanish National Tourist Office, 70 Jermyn St, London SW1, 01-930-8578 French Government Tourist Office, Official Information Centre, 178 Piccadilly, London W1, 01-493-3171.

Officials and formalities

Spanish officials of all grades and services are courteous and helpful to visiting yachtsmen despite any stories circulating to the contrary. They react to a friendly and polite approach by assisting in any way within their power.

On first reaching a Spanish port a yacht should be issued with a Customs Card. But as this card is almost never asked for, visiting yachtsmen should not be too worried if they do not have it.

On arrival at a Spanish port a yacht may be visited by officials from any of the following services: Guardia Civil, Guardia Costa, local police, Customs, Captain de Puerto, Militar Marine, Obras del Puerto. Normally the official who visits the yacht will pass any information obtained on to the others, but occasionally a visit will be made by more than one official. In some ports the official will come out in his own launch, in others in an old fishing boat. Have plenty of fenders ready as they are inclined to come alongside rather fast. In other ports the official will be seen waiting on the quayside. In this case take all personal documents and ship's documents ashore to him. Sometimes it will be necessary to visit the official in his office.

The preparation of a form given below will simplify proceedings and speed up matters in most ports. In others the officials may have their own special form which will have to be completed.

Occasionally passports and ship's papers are examined to see if they agree with the form. Never forget that despite these officials' usual friendliness they are generally armed and have powers of instant arrest if they consider that the bounds of normal modest behaviour have been exceeded. In recent years there has been a considerable relaxation in the application of existing rules and procedures; these rules still exist and are used to get rid of undesirable visitors.

Suggested form

Información des yates

NOMBRE DEL YATE .... *Name of yacht*
MATRICULA .... *Country of Registration*
PUERTO ASIENTO .... *Port of Registration*
NUMERO ASIENTO .... *Registration number*
TONELADA ASIENTO PESO NETO .... *Net Registered tons weight*
ESLORA .... *Length (metres)*
MANGA .... *Beam (metres)*
CALADO .... *Draft (metres)*

PROPRIETARIO .... *Owner of yacht*
NOMBRE DEL CAPTAIN DEL YATE .... NUMERO PASSPORTS ....
(*Name of captain of yacht*) (*Passport number*)
NOMBRE DEL TRIPOLANTES .... NUMERO PASSPORTS ....
(*Names of crew*) .... ,, ...
.... ,, ...
PUERTO ULTIMO—PROCEDENTE .... *Last port of call*
PUERTO PROXIMO—DESTINO .... *New port of call*
ARRIBO PON .... HORAS .... *Time/Date of arrival in port*
TURISTA .... *Reason for visit*
(*Tourist*)

Post, telephone and telegraph

In most Spanish ports the Post, Telephone and Telegraph offices are to be found in different buildings, often on the outskirts of town; only in major cities will they be found together near the centre of the city.

The Post Office (*Correos*) has a good system of 'poste restant' (*lista*) and in addition they will forward (*redirecta*) letters from one post office to another.

However, when collecting mail care should be taken as letters may be filed under 'M' for Mr or 'E' for Esquire, or other combinations. The Spanish postal clerks are not accustomed to English surnames and methods of address.

Fishing boats

The thousands of brightly painted fishing boats of all sizes are a feature of this coast. They range in size from small one-man dinghies to huge ocean-going ships. The powerful and graceful lines of these wooden craft make them most attractive to the eye. Even some of the newer and larger craft which are made of steel still follow the traditional designs.

The fishermen themselves are delightful people, always ready to help and quick to share their food and wine with foreign yachtsmen. The skill with which they operate their craft is a pleasure to watch. There are, however, a few problems connected with them which are worth knowing. As they have no experience with yachts their advice and help should be treated with caution; their boats are so strong and powerful that they can do a lot of damage coming alongside a lightly built yacht in any seaway.

The larger boats when fishing for *atun* and *bonito* (tunny fish) will have built-in tanks full of live sardines for use as bait. These sardines are kept alive by pumping salt water through the tanks and the overflow gushes from the side of the boat at a rate which would sink a dinghy or fill the cockpit of a yacht in a few moments.

These pumps are operated by powerful diesel engines which are very noisy and at night in harbour they can be very disturbing.

Naturally enough, they have to unload their catches and if they find a yacht alongside 'their' piece of quay they will move the yacht, but not being used to yachts may not resecure them in the approved way.

Spaniards as a nation like to do most things with a flourish and the fisherman is no exception. He will enter and leave port at full speed creating a tremendous wash and will often pass quite close to a visiting yacht out of interest, with dire consequences. This deplorable habit is unfortunately copied by most Spaniards in motor yachts and a good lookout for heavy washes should be kept when using a dinghy in any of the harbours.

At sea the larger boats fishing for tunny will have a series of troll lines astern and some out on long bamboo poles each side. They usually are steaming fast on a straight course. The boats catching sardines usually steam in circles herding the sardines into a catching area. In due course they will put a trawl net over the side and will then proceed to haul it in. In both these cases it is advisable to keep well clear of the area concerned.

At night these boats operate with a mass of working lights in addition to their normal navigation lights and are quite unmistakable; the larger boats may be found far out to sea. A single very bright light may be seen closer inshore: this is usually a small boat using this light to attract fish to the surface for ease in catching and may, in a heavy swell, look like a flashing navigational light. Small one- or two-man fishing boats may be found close inshore at night with no navigation lights.

Fishermen returning to port may often be very useful in showing where the deepest part of the channel lies, especially in ports with sandbars and banks which are inclined to move. They will often lead a visiting yacht in if they think that it will help. Fishermen will often offer help in the event of difficulties such as grounding and a reward such as some English cigarettes or whisky is usually very welcome.

During the summer months most of the larger fishing boats are away catching *bonito* (tunny fish) off the coast of Africa. They return to their home ports towards the end of August, and a harbour which one day has been quite empty will suddenly be full up.

Food and drink

Meals in restaurants are very much cheaper than an equivalent meal in England. However, to eat and drink at this low cost one has to observe certain rules: buy foodstuffs from the market soon after it opens or from shops near the market. As far as possible buy locally grown or caught food; never buy imported goods, which are heavily taxed. Never hesitate to go around the market checking prices from various stalls and choose the goods yourself from the stall.

When eating ashore visit the various restaurants which by law have to have a priced menu in the window, and choose one to suit your purse and requirements. The times of meals are usually about one to two hours later than is normal in England.

The following foods are impossible or difficult to buy, if found are very expensive compared to English prices, and may be of poor quality. An adequate supply should be brought from the UK of marmalade, sausages, bacon, coffee (instant and normal), fruit juice (concentrated), meat, except for pork and occasionally lamb.

Conversely, the following are much better than usually found in Britain: all fish and shellfish, tomatoes, lettuce, many types of vegetables and fruit, cold sausage meats. Some items are particularly cheap compared to English prices; the best buys are: Spanish wine, Spanish brandy, bread, fish, fruit, olive oil for cooking.

When buying wine it is best to take a large container to a wine shop—*bodega*—and buy the wine straight from the cask. The tasting of the various types of wine available before making a choice is a pleasant and educational procedure. *Vino tinto* (red wine) is usually better than *rosado* (rosé) or *blanco* (white) and a *Riojas* (from Castile) better than *vino corriente* (local wine). Wine is generally cheap.

The following are some of the specialities worth buying or choosing as a course in a restaurant.

Basque
- *Bacalao a la Vizcaina*—a cod dish — Drink *chacoli*
- *Besugo a la guipuzcoana*—sea bream
- *Angulas*—eel fry
- *Chipirones*—baby squid

Asturias
- *Fabada*—a dish of beans, ham, pork, trotters, black pudding, sausage and tomato sauce. — Drink *cider*
- *Callos*—tripe

Galicia

Caldeirada—a fish stew.
Lácon con grelos—ham and turnip tops
Pote Gallego—a hot pot
Merluza a la Gallega—hake

Drink *Monterrey* and *Ribeiro de Avia*

General

Fish

Marisco—sea food dish of shell and small fish
Merluza—hake } no relation in taste to the UK version
Bacalao—cod }
Bonito—small tunny fish
Atun—tunny fish
Gambas—large prawns

Sweets

Turron jijona—a nougat type sweet
Carne de membrillo—quince jelly

All are excellent.

If you get the chance try *sardinas fritas*, large sardines grilled over charcoal and eaten with bare fingers with chunks of bread and local wine.

A visit to a cider bar in Asturias to watch how the cider is poured out to aerate it and to taste it yourself is a well worth while entertainment. Between six and eight in the evening make a tour of the many bars and sample the varied dainty *tapas* (snacks) with your drinks while watching the evening promenade.

Shopping Shops are normally open from 0900 to 1300 and from 1530 to 2000 or later. With the exception of a few food shops which may be open late in the morning, shops are all closed on Sundays, days of fiestas and on special religious and civil holidays.

Ice Ice is usually obtainable at the larger ports and any of the fishing ports where a small ice factory will be found alongside the harbour wall. It is not advisable to use this ice in drinks etc. as it may come from impure sources of water.

Fuel *General* In Spain *Campsa*, a government monopoly, supplies all fuel at a price similar to that which has to be paid in the UK.

Diesel The diesel oil available in Spain is called *gas oil* and can be obtained from a red pump on the quayside in almost every harbour. It is usually situated in a convenient place for the local fishing craft to come alongside and fill up. Difficulty may be encountered in obtaining supplies in the very small ports which yachts only occasionally visit. At some of the larger ports a diesel bunkering service is available and this is noted in the appropriate text. Credit cards may be used for this purpose; details of this service can be obtained from the major fuel suppliers in the UK. Keep a reserve can aboard in case pump diameter is too large.

Petrol Petrol, called *gasolina*, is usually to be obtained from a single red pump of antique design on the outskirts of the village or town usually beside the main road. In large cities two or even three grades of petrol may be available.

Oil Engine oils (*aceite*) are often of well known international brands but it may be difficult to locate the exact type of oil required, without much waste of time and effort, although normal SAE classification is used. It is advised to bring supplies from the UK.

Paraffin Paraffin (*petróleo*) is more volatile and smelly than the English equivalent. It is advised to bring out adequate supplies.

Methylated Spirit Meths (*alcohol para quemar*) is difficult to obtain so bring supplies with you.

Gas Gas for cooking is cheap, good and easily obtained. *Camping Gaz* is universally available no matter how small the port or village. There are other brands in very large cylinders for household cooking available but your cooker valve connection may not have the same screw thread.

Fiestas Fiestas are a feature of the Spanish way of life and any yachtsman visiting this coast is likely to be in some port at some time when there is a fiesta. These fiestas are usually of a religious nature and start with a church service followed by a procession often headed by a sacred image, which may be continued by a procession of boats. In the evening a band often plays for public dancing in the main *plaza* and this may carry on until the small hours of the morning.

Fiestas are announced by a series of explosions of fireworks sometimes starting early in the day culminating in a fusillade of firecrackers near the time of commencement.

Public holidays There are a number of official public holidays in Spain; these are listed below. In addition each port has a number of local holidays. Details of some of these are given in the section dealing with the port concerned.

1 Jan.	New Year's day	18 July	National Labour day
6 Jan.	Epiphany	25 July	St James day
19 Mar.	St Joseph's day	15 Aug.	Feast of the Assumption
	Holy Thursday	12 Oct.	Columbus day
4 April	Good Friday (movable)	1 Nov.	All Saints day
1 May	Independence day	8 Dec.	Immaculate Conception
17 June	Corpus Christi (movable)	25 Dec.	Christmas day
29 June	Sts Peter and Paul		

Harbour dues Harbour dues are normally only charged in major commercial ports and for prolonged stays in marinas. These dues are not very high for yachts of normal size.

Field sports The N of Spain is famous for its fishing, both fresh and saltwater, and for shooting and hunting. Full details can be obtained from the Spanish National Tourist Office (page 28).

Bibliography

Navigational—Admiralty Published by the Hydrographer of the Navy.

Admiralty Sailing Directions No. 22 Bay of Biscay Pilot (1970), Pointe de Penmarch to Cabo Ortegal and Supplement No. 8.

No. 67 West Coasts of Spain and Portugal Pilot. Punta de La Estaca to Gibraltar (1972) and Supplement No. 6

Admiralty List of Lights, Vol. D Eastern Shores of the North and South Atlantic Oceans, from Goulet de Brest southward (1981).

Admiralty List of Radio Signals, Vol. I Coast Radio Stations, etc. Part 1 (1981).

II Radio Navigational Aids (1981).

III Radio Weather Services (1981).

V Radio Time Signals, Radio Navigational Warnings, Ice Reports and Position Fixing Systems (1982).

VI Port Operations, Pilot Services and Information Services, Part 1 (1981).

Admiralty Tide Tables Vol. I European Waters (including Mediterranean), published annually.

Navigational—general

Guide Renault Marine des Ports de France (*Blondel La Rougery* and Iliffe-NTT International Ltd, London). Details of French ports, particularly the facilities ashore.

Petits Ports d'a Côté, Jean Merrien (*Denoël, Paris*) now out of print. Includes Capbreton to La Coruña.

Foreign Port Information Folio: South Biscay. The Royal Cruising Club, available only to members of the Royal Cruising Club and Cruising Club of America. The Cruising Association also holds a copy.

France

Guides Michelin (Pneu Michelin, Paris)

Spain

Blue Guide: Northern Spain (Ernest Benn, London). A detailed guide to the country.

Spain's Magic Coast, Nina Epton (Weidenfeld and Nicolson, London). A pleasant, readable description of the coast from the Miño to the Bidassoa.

Spain: Collins Holiday Guide, R. A. N. Dixon (Collins, London). A simple guide to the country and its customs.

Spain 1969: Holiday Fact Book, J. and M. Hawkes (Dickens Press, London). A simple pocket-sized book useful for shopping.

Collins Spanish Phrasebook, D. S. Gifford (Collins, London).

General

Yachtsman's 8-Language Dictionary, Barbara Webb (Adlard Coles, London). A very handy technical dictionary for yachtsmen.

Foreign Cruising, R. L. Hewitt (Pelham). A simple guide for foreign cruising.

Many useful publications and leaflets can be obtained from the respective national tourist bureaus in London and overseas, mostly free of charge.

Chapter 2

The coast between Pointe de la Coubre and Cabo Higuer

The coast between Pointe de la Coubre and Cabo Higuer

2 General description

La Côte des Landes and La Côte d'Argent

SW Aquitaine, Gironde, Landes, Basses Pyrénées

General

The French coastline in South Biscay is completely unlike the rugged and mountainous Spanish coast further S. From the estuary of **La Gironde** as far as the **Río Bidasoa** which forms the boundary between France and Spain, the coast is low-lying and sandy, backed by pinewood forests and sand dunes, with a few low hills and a short stretch of low cliffs at the extreme S end. The number of recognisable and conspicuous objects are few and far between. With the exception of shoal waters off **La Gironde, Bassin d'Arcachon, Saint-Jean de Luz** and **Hendaye** there are no outlying dangers. In heavy storms from S through W to N this coast offers no safe shelter, with the possible exception of the **Baie de Saint-Jean de Luz** and **Río Bidasoa.**

Warnings

An air force, naval and artillery range is situated off the coast between **La Gironde** and **Capbreton** (see page 42).

Data

Charts

Admiralty Nos. 2664, 2665
Spanish Nos. 945, 1201, 39
French Nos. 6338, 172, 174

Buoy marking firing range danger area. Now yellow.

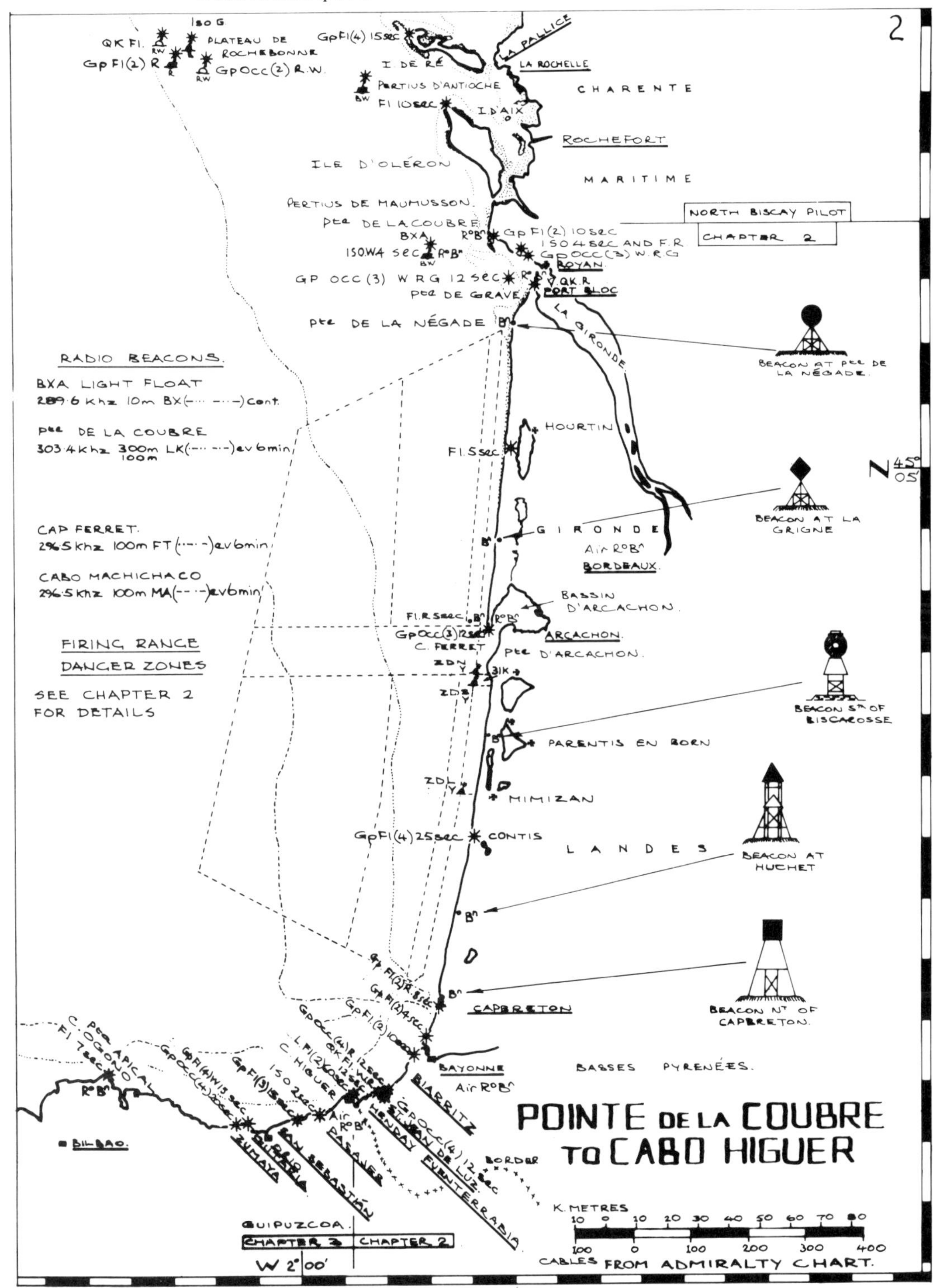
POINTE DE LA COUBRE TO CABO HIGUER
RADIO BEACONS.
BXA LIGHT FLOAT
289·6 khz 10m BX(-··· -··-) cont.
Pte DE LA COUBRE
303·4khz 300m 100m LK(-··· -·-)ev 6min
CAP FERRET.
296·5khz 100m FT(··-· -)ev6min
CABO MACHICHACO
296·5khz 100m MA(-- ·-)ev6min
FIRING RANGE DANGER ZONES
SEE CHAPTER 2 FOR DETAILS
NORTH BISCAY PILOT
CHAPTER 2
CHARENTE
MARITIME
LA ROCHELLE
ROCHEFORT
I. DE RÉ
ILE D'OLÉRON
ROYAN
PORT BLOC
LA GIRONDE
GIRONDE
BORDEAUX
BASSIN D'ARCACHON
ARCACHON
HOURTIN
PARENTIS EN BORN
MIMIZAN
CONTIS
LANDES
CAPBRETON
BAYONNE
BASSES PYRENÉES
BIARRITZ
BEACON AT Pte DE LA NÉGADE
BEACON AT LA GRIGNE
BEACON Sth OF BISCAROSSE
BEACON AT HUCHET
BEACON Nth OF CAPBRETON
BILBAO
GUIPUZCOA
CHAPTER 3
CHAPTER 2
W 2°00'
K. METRES
CABLES FROM ADMIRALTY CHART.

Tidal information

Currents Normally in summer there is a half knot N-going current 5 to 6 miles offshore and a similar counter-current going S 1 mile offshore. W gales if long continued may increase the N-going current to 5·5 knots. N winds tend to check or reverse these currents and counter-currents.

Major lights

La Coubre (La Gironde). Group Flashing (2) White, 10 seconds, 64 m (210 ft), 31 miles. White round tower, red top, white dwelling. *Also* Fixed RG, 42 m (138 ft), 11 miles. Visible R 030°–043°, G 043°–060°, R 060°–110°. Ro Bn and Signal Station.

Cordouan (La Gironde). Group Occulting (2+1) White, Red, Green sectors, 12 seconds, 60 m (197 ft), White 23, Red 19, Green 19 miles. White conical tower, dark grey band and top. White 014°–126°, Green 126°–178·5°, White 178·5°–250°, White 250°–267°, Red 267°–014°. Obscured in Gironde estuary when more than 285°.

Pointe de Grave (La Gironde). Occulting White, Red, Green sectors, 4 seconds, 26 m (85 ft), White 18, Red 12, Green 11 miles. White square tower, black corners and top. Red 233·5°–303°, White 303°–312°, Green 213°–330°, White 330°–233·5°. Obscured when less than 053°. Unwatched.

Hourtin. Flashing White, 5 seconds, 55 m (180 ft), 23 miles. Red square brick tower.

Cap Ferret (Arcachon). Flashing Red, 5 seconds, 53 m (175 ft), 26 miles. White round tower, red top. Radiobeacon *also* Group Occulting (3) White, 12 seconds, 46 m (151 ft), 14 miles. Visible 045°–135°.

Contis. Group flashing (4) White, 25 seconds, 50 m (164 ft), 23 miles. White round tower, black diagonal stripes. Fixed Red on radio mast 16·5 miles NNE.

Capbreton (Estacade Nord). Group Flashing (2) Red, 6 seconds, 13 m (43 ft), 10 miles. White tower, red top. Fog signal Reed, 30 seconds. Unwatched.

L'Adour (Digue du Large head). Isophase Red 4 seconds, 11 m (36 ft), 5 miles. Square white tower, red top.

Pointe Saint-Martin. Group Flashing (2) White, 10 seconds, 73 m (240 ft), 31 miles. White tower, black top.

Cabo Higuer—lighthouse from the east.

Sainte-Barbe (Saint-Jean de Luz). Group Occulting (1+3) Red, 12 seconds, 30 m (98 ft), 16 miles. White masonry hut. Intensified 95°–107°.
Le Socoa (Saint-Jean de Luz). Quick Flashing White, Red 36 m (118 ft), White 12, Red 8 miles. White square tower, black vertical stripe. Red 264°–282°, White 282°–264°. Signal Station.
Cabo Higuer. Group Long Flash (2) White, 60 seconds, 63 m (207 ft), 16 miles. White stone tower and lantern. Aeromarine light, visible 072°–340°.

Life saving Lifeboats are stationed at **Port Bloc**, **Cap Ferret**, and **Saint-Jean de Luz**. Life saving apparatus at **L'Adour**.

Radio *Radiobeacons* The radiobeacons in this area are listed below; for other beacons outside this area see page 16.

Station	Frequency kHz	Range miles	Call sign	Period	Group Remarks
BXA light float	291·9	5	BX (– · · · / – · · –)	10 sec.	
Pointe de la Coubre lighthouse	303·4	100	LK (· – · · / – · –)	6 min.	Three others in group
Cap Ferret lighthouse	296·5	100	FT (· · – · / –)	6 min	**Cabo Machichaco** MA (– – / · –) **Cabo Mayor** MY (– – / – · – –)
Biarritz-Bayonne Anglet air beacon 43°28′17″N 1°25′44″W	249·5	35	BZ (– · · · / – – · ·)		Continuous
Bordeaux Mérignac air beacon 44°55′55″N 0°33′53″W	393	200	BDM (– · · · / – · · / – –)		Continuous
Cazaux air beacon 44°31′58″N 1°09′10″W	382	80	CAA (– · – · / · – / · –)		Day only
Dax-Castets air beacon 43°53′45″N 1°07′57″W	341	40	DXN (– · · / – · · – / – ·)		Continuous

Signal stations Coast, port and pilot radio stations, weather and navigational messages, see pages 19–21.
Signal stations are established at **Pointe de la Coubre**, **St Jean de Luz**, **Cap Ferret** and **L'Adour.** Ship-to-shore messages may be passed by International Code of Flag Signals.

Ports, harbours, anchorages and landing places

Pointe de la Coubre
3 ESTUAIRE DE LA GIRONDE
East bank – La Gironde
Bonne Anse. Anchorage in settled weather. Drying harbour.
St Palais-sur-Mer. Anchorage in settled weather.
4 PORT DE ROYAN (3-2-3) see page 51.
St Georges-de-Didonne. Anchorage and quay. Breakwater.
Meschers-sur-Gironde. Anchorage and quay.
Mortagne-sur-Gironde (la Rive). Basin, dock and anchorage.
Port Maubert. Anchorage.
Blaye (Sainte-Luce). Anchorage, moorings, berths.
Roque-de-Thau. Anchorage.
Bec d'Ambès. Berths.
La Dordogne
Bourg. Anchorage.
Libourne. Anchorage.
La Garonne
Lambert. Anchorage.
Le Marquis. Anchorage.
Lamarque – port. Anchorage.
West bank – La Gironde
5 BORDEAUX (2-2-1) see page 55.
Médoc – port. Anchorage.
Beychevelle. Anchorage.
Pauillac. Yacht harbour.
Trompeloup. Anchorage.
Le Maréchal. Anchorage.
Saint-Christoly-de-Médoc. Anchorage.
Le Verdon-sur-Mer. Anchorage.

50 miles
50 miles

6 PORT BLOC (3-2-4) see page 60.
Pointe de Grave
Pointe de la Négade
Cap Ferret
7 BASSIN D'ARCACHON (3-3-2) see page 64.
Pointe d'Arcachon
Mimizan. Mouth of stream, jetty drying. Small harbour for fishing launches. Low bridge.
Contis. Very small stream and jetty, both drying.
Huchet. As above.
Vieux Boucau. As above.
8 CAPBRETON (2-3-3) see page 70.
9 L'ADOUR – BAYONNE (3-3-2) see page 76.
Pointe Saint-Martin
Biarritz. Small drying harbour with a wet dock entrance 0·8 m (2·5 ft) depth. Masts must be lowered.
Rade de Biarritz. Anchor in up to 12·8 m (7 fathoms) off **Pointe Saint-Martin** in fair weather only.
Guéthary. Very small harbour, slip.
Pointe Sainte-Barbe
10 CIBOURE, SOCOA, SAINT-JEAN DE LUZ (2-2-2) see page 83.
Pointe Sainte-Anne
11 HENDAYE (3-3-3) see page 90.
11 FUENTERRABIA see page 92.
11 GURUTZEAUNDI see page 93.
Cabo Higuer

70 miles
60 miles
9 miles
10 miles
5 miles
1 mile
2 miles

Port de Biarritz – looking W.

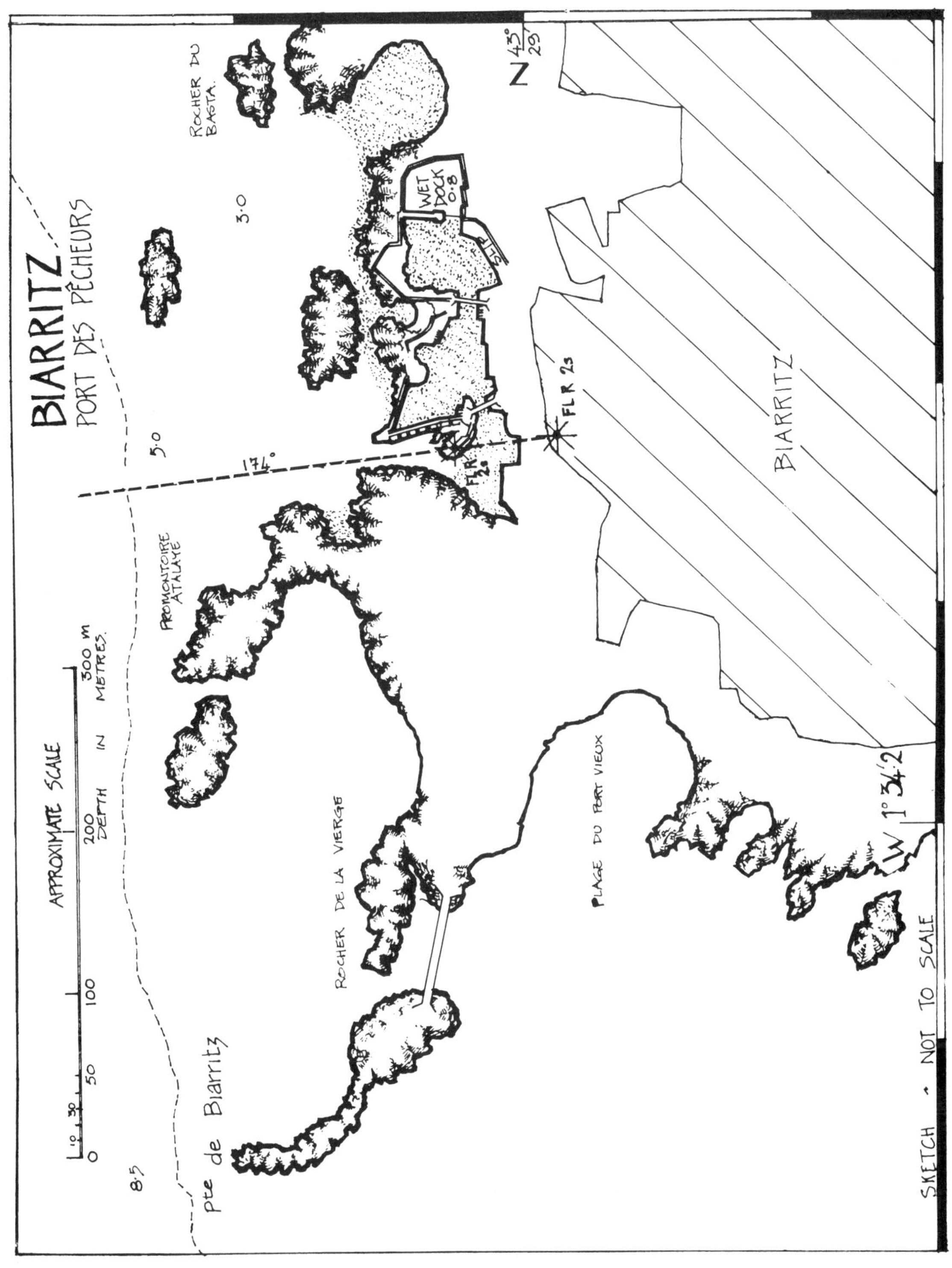
BIARRITZ
PORT DES PÊCHEURS
ROCHER DU BASTA
WET DOCK 0·8
3·0
5·0
174°
FL R 2s
FL R 2s
N 43° 29'
BIARRITZ
PROMONTOIRE ATALAYE
APPROXIMATE SCALE
0 10 30 50 100 200 300 M
DEPTH IN METRES
ROCHER DE LA VIERGE
PLAGE DU PORT VIEUX
pte de Biarritz
8·5
W 1° 34'2
SKETCH - NOT TO SCALE

Cabo Higuer—lighthouse from the north west.

Firing range danger area

An air to sea, ground to sea, and sea to sea firing range exists off the coast from **Pointe de la Négade**, by the **Estuaire de La Gironde**, to **Capbreton**. It is divided into a number of areas identified by prefix 31 and a code (see chartlet below). The ground to sea firing takes place from the area **Pointe d'Arcachon** to **Mimizan**. This area is marked by three blue and white conical light buoys 3 miles off the coast as shown.

Zones 31K, 31S 12–27 and 31N 12–27 are usually prohibited weekdays 0800–1800 and Saturdays 0800–1200; other areas which are dangerous and which it is forbidden to enter are announced after the weather bulletins from Radio **Bordeaux/Arcachon** (see pages 18–19).

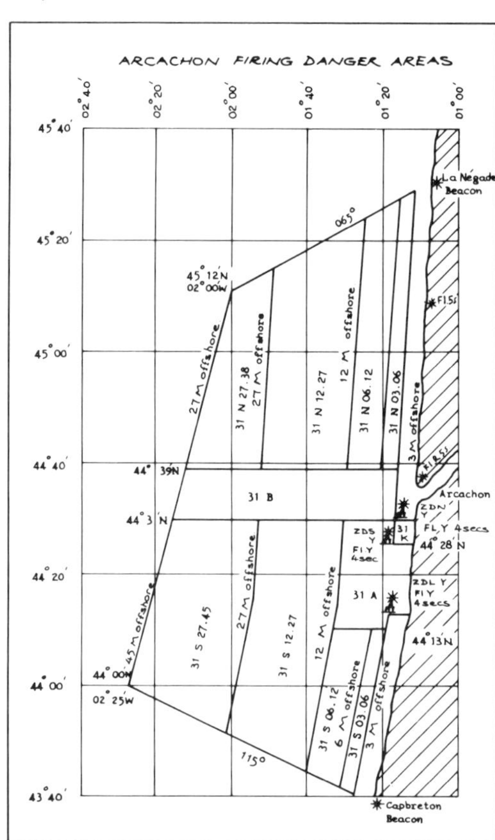

3 Estuaire de La Gironde (see chart at beginning of book)

General

This wide and long estuary leads to the city of **Bordeaux** and to the large rivers of **La Garonne** and **La Dordogne**. The **Canal Lateral à La Garonne** and the **Canal du Midi** can be entered from **La Garonne** above **Bordeaux** and may be used by craft smaller than 30 m (98·5 ft) long, 5·25 m (17 ft) wide, 1·6 m (5 ft 3 in) deep, 3 m (10 ft) high. Details and documents from *Ministère de l'Equipement, Service des Voies Navigables, 2ᵉ Bureau, 244 Blvd. Saint-Germain, Paris 7ᵉ.*

There are two good yacht harbours just inside the entrance to the estuary: **Royan** on the N bank (page 51) and **Port Bloc** on the S (page 60). There are various minor harbours further up the estuary and also a marina, quays and basins at **Bordeaux** (page 55).

The estuary is dangerous to enter in heavy weather or swell from the SW through W to NE, or in conditions of poor visibility. Approach to the estuary by night is normally easier than an approach by day.

Though **Bordeaux**, one of the largest cities in France, is a pleasant place to visit, the estuary is not particularly attractive. Unless wishing to enter the canal system it is not really worth the effort necessary to ascend some 55 miles of tidal river just to visit it. It is possible with a yacht capable of maintaining 3 to 3½ knots and starting at LW to carry a single tide up to **Bordeaux**; also by leaving **Bordeaux** well before HW to carry the ebb down to the mouth of the estuary.

Warnings

The tidal and river currents are very strong and do not always follow the expected direction, especially at the mouth of the estuary (overfalls); constant checks are necessary to avoid being set outside the channels. Care is necessary near No. 4A entrance buoy as a similar buoy, No. 4, to the N could, if mistaken, cause a yacht to go onto one of the sandbanks which infest the mouth of this estuary. It is advisable to follow the line of the starboard hand buoys which leads well clear to **Banc de la Mauvaise** when using the **Grande Passe de l'Ouest.**

As some of the sandbanks change their position during winter storms, an up-to-date chart and information must be obtained before proceeding to the estuary. The latest amendments to the *Admiralty Sailing Directions No. 22, Bay of Biscay Pilot*, should be studied in advance as buoys and lights are altered and moved to suit the new conditions. *Notices to Mariners* should also be consulted. Due to these constant variations no chartlet is provided in this Pilot.

Groups of white buoys marked TX should be avoided as they mark areas where work is in progress. Fishing nets sometimes across river near **Bec d'Ambes.**

Data

Charts

Admiralty	Nos. 2910, 2916, 2664
Spanish	No. 40
French	Nos. 6336, 6335, 6141, 6139, 6140, 4610

Magnetic variation 5° 30′W (1984) decreasing about 5′ a year.

Tidal information

	HW		LW		MHWS	MHWN	MLWS	MLWN
Pointe de Grave	0600 1800	0000 1200	1000 2200	0400 1600	5·4 m 17·6 ft	4·2 m 13·8 ft	0·9 m 3·0 ft	2·0 m 6·8 ft
LA GIRONDE								
Royan	−0·10	0	−0·05	−0·05	−0·2 m −0·6 ft	−0·2 m −0·7 ft	−0·0 m −0·1 ft	−0·2 m −0·5 ft
Lamena	−0·05	+0·20	+1·30	+0·55	+0·2 m +0·9 ft	+0·3 m +0·8 ft	−0·2 m −0·6 ft	−0·3 m −0·8 ft
Pauillac	+1·15	+0·40	+2·20	+1·30	+0·3 m +1·0 ft	+0·2 m +0·6 ft	−0·4 m −1·5 ft	−0·6 m −1·8 ft
Blaye	+1·30	+1·05	+2·55	+2·25	+0·1 m +0·4 ft	+0·0 m +0·1 ft	−0·5 m −1·6 ft	−1·1 m −3·4 ft
LA GARONNE								
Bordeaux	+2·50	+1·55	+4·40	+4·00	−0·1 m −0·3 ft	−0·1 m −0·2 ft	−1·0 m −3·4 ft	−1·8 m −5·7 ft
LA DORDOGNE								
Bourg	+2·05	+1·20	+4·00	+2·55	−0·1 m −0·3 ft	−0·2 m −0·7 ft	−0·1 m −0·3 ft	−1·4 m −4·4 ft
Asques	+2·55	+1·50	+4·45	+4·00	−0·1 m −0·3 ft	−0·2 m −0·7 ft	+0·1 m +0·3 ft	−1·3 m −4·2 ft
Libourne	+3·30	+2·45	+6·05	+5·40	−0·7 m −2·2 ft	−0·9 m −3·1 ft	−0·4 m −1·5 ft	−1·7 m −5·4 ft

Wind effect Winds between S and NNW raise the water level up to 1 m (3 ft) and advance the time of HW by up to 15 minutes. Winds from N through E to S decrease the level by up to 0·3 m (1 ft) and retard the time of HW by up to 15 minutes.

Tidal streams The tidal streams near the mouth of **La Gironde** are complex and use should be made of the tidal data on Admiralty chart No. 2910. The following table is a simplification based on HW **Pointe de Grave**.

Position	Flood begins	Spring rate knots	Ebb begins	Spring rate knots
Rade de Royan	−0445	3·8	+0045	3·8
Mouth of estuary	−0430	2·6	+0100	3·3
Rade de Verdon	−0445	2·8	+0115	3·8
Off Richard old lighthouse	−0515	2·8	+0145	3·8
Off La Maréchale	−0400	2·8	+0200	3·8
Off Pauillac	−0315	2·8	+0215	3·8
Off Béchevelle	−0315	2·8	+0315	3·8
Off Bordeaux (La Garonne)	−0115	2·8	+0315	3·8
Off Libourne (La Dordogne)	+0045	3·8	+0410	4·7

Lights **BXA light float.** Isophase White, 4 seconds, 9 m (30 ft), 10 miles. Red ball on red and white hull and light tower. Bell, Radiobeacon. Racon.

La Coubre. Group Flashing (2) White, 10 seconds, 64 m (210 ft), 31 miles. Red round tower, lower part and dwellings white. *Also* Fixed RG, 42 m (138 ft), 12 miles. Visible R 030°–043°, G 043°–060°, R 060°–110°. Ro Bn. Signal station **La Palmyre leading lights** 090°.

Front. Occulting White, 4 seconds, 22 m (72 ft), 21 miles. White round mast on dolphin. Intensified 080·5°–082·5°.

Rear. Quick flashing white, 57m (186 ft), 27 miles. White radar tower. Intensified 080·5°–082·5° *Also* Fixed Red, 57 m (186 ft), 17 miles. Intensified 325°–329°.

Terre-Nègre leading lights 327°. Group Occulting (3) White, Red, Green sectors, 12 seconds, 39 m (121 ft). White 16, Red 13, Green 13 miles. White tower with red top on W side. Red 304°–319°, White 319°–327°, Green 327°–000°, White 000°–004°, Green 004°–097°, White 097°–104°, Red 104°–116°.

Cordouan. Group Occulting (2+1) White, Red, Green sectors, 12 seconds, 60 m (197 ft), White 23, Red 19, Green 19 miles. White conical tower, dark grey band and top. White 014°–126°, Green 126°–178·5°, White 178·5°–250°, Red 294·5°–014°, obscured in estuary when bearing more than 285°. Danger Signals.

St Nicholas leading lights 063°.

Front. Quick Flashing Green, 22 m (71 ft), 18 miles. White square tower. Intensified 060°–066°.

Rear (**Pointe de Grave**). Occulting White, Red, Green sectors, 4 seconds, 26 m (85 ft), White 18, Red 12, Green 11 miles. White square tower, black corners and top. Red 233·5°–303°, White 303°–312°, Green 312°–330°, White 330°–233·5°. Obscured when bearing less than 053°.

Le Chay leading lights 041°.

Front. Quick Flashing Red, 33 m (108 ft), 16 miles. White tower, red top. Intensified 039·5–042·5°. Obscured 325°–335°.

Rear (**Saint-Pierre**). Quick Flashing Red, 61 m (200 ft) 14 miles. Light grey water tower, red support. Intensified 039°–043°.

Note 1 Lights for **Royan**, **Port Bloc** and **Bordeaux**, pages 51, 60, 55, respectively.

Note 2 There are a large number of lights and lighted buoys marking the fairway up the estuary of **La Gironde** and the river **La Garonne** which are best seen on Admiralty charts 2910 and 2916.

Radio Large yachts equipped with radio and transmitter should contact **Bordeaux/ Arcachon** and inform the Commandant of the Port of their E.T.A., size, draft and speed (see page 20). Radar guidance is available.

Radiobeacons In the area are as follows:

BXA light float. 291·9 kHz, 5 miles, BX (– · · · / – · · –) continuous.

Pointe de la Coubre lighthouse. 303·4 kHz, 100 miles, LK (· – · · / – · –) every 6 minutes.

Pointe de Grave rear lighthouse. 308 kHz, 5 miles, VR (· · · – / · – ·) every 10 seconds. Day only.

Life saving A lifeboat is maintained at **Port Bloc.**

Signal stations A port signal station and lookout is situated close within the point of **Pointe de Grave** and another at **Pointe de la Coubre**.

Consul A British Consular Officer is stationed at **Bordeaux**.

Grande Passe de l'Ouest

Approach

Day *From N* The low-lying sand-edged **Isle d'Oléron** and the sand dunes which line the coast immediately N of the entrance have no conspicuous features other than the white church tower at **Saint-Pierre d'Oléron**, which looks like a lighthouse, and the following lighthouses:
Chassiron. White round tower black bands. 50 m (163 ft).
La Cotinière leading lights. White column, and two white metal frame towers, red bands. 13 m (43 ft), 6 m (20 ft) and 14 m (46 ft).
La Coubre. Red round tower, lower part white and dwelling 64 m (210 ft). It is essential to be at least 5 miles off the coast in the closer approach to the entrance to avoid the dangerous shoal waters of **Banc de la Mauvaise**. The corner should not be cut and landfall on the BXA light float is advised. This float has a radio beacon bell, racon and radar reflector.

From S Again, the low, straight, sandy coast backed by dunes and fir woods has few conspicuous features. A large, waisted, water tower at **Montlivet les Bains**, the black ball beacon at **Pointe de la Négade**, the **Pointe de Grave** lighthouse with its white square tower with black corners and edges, and the **Cordouan** lighthouse, a white conical tower with dark grey band and top on a low rocky island, should be easy to recognise. Care should be taken to navigate far enough offshore to clear the dangerous shoal **Banc des Olives**. Landfall on the BXA light float is advised. TXO yellow pillar light buoy (Fl. Y 4 sec.) may assist.

Night *From N* the lights are:
Chassiron (Fl.W. 10 sec. 28 M.), **La Cotinière leading lights** (Dir. Oc. W.R.G. 3 sec, Oc. (2) W 6 sec), **La Coubre** (Fl. (2) W. 10 sec. 31 M.), **BXA light float** (Iso. W 4 sec, 9 M.), which enable a night approach to be made.
In the close approach the lighted channel buoys should be seen as well as the lights detailed under *entrance*, *night* below.
From S only the lighthouses **Hourtin** (Fl. W. 5 sec. 23 M.) and **Cordouan** (Oc. (1+2) W.R.G. 12 sec. 24/19 M.) and **BXA light float** (Iso W 4 sec 9 M.) assist in the night approach. In good visibility the lights detailed under *entrance*, *night* may be seen. TXO yellow pillar light buoy (Fl. Y 4 sec.) may assist.

Entrance

Day Having located the BXA light float (red ball, white and red hull and light-tower) proceed on 081° for 4 miles and identify the first pair of channel marking buoys. Green odd-numbered buoys are to starboard; red even-numbered buoys are to port. Enter between and follow close to the line of the starboard hand buoys in a general direction just N of E until No. 9 buoy is reached, when course should be altered to 100° to pass near to No. 10A buoy. If proceeding to **Royan** a course of 125° should be set towards **Pointe de Chay** and No. R1 buoy, green wreck buoy (Iso G 4 sec). If proceeding to **Port Bloc** or up-river, set a course of 140° to Nos. 13A and 13B buoys.

Night From the BXA light float (Iso W.4 sec, 9 M) bring the **La Palmyre** lights into line on 081° (*Front*: Oc. W 4 sec 21 M. *Rear*: Q. Fl. W 27 M. Both intensified 080°–082°) and enter the channel between a series of buoys detailed below as far as No. 7A buoy.

Port hand buoys	*Starboard hand buoys*
No. 2 (Q.Fl.R)	No. 1 (Fl.Y 2 sec), (Q.Fl.G) and (Fl. (5) Y 20 sec)
No. 2A (Oc. (2) R 6 sec)	No. 3 (Oc. (2) G 6 sec)
No. 4 (Fl. (2) R 6 sec)	No. 5 (Fl. (2) G 6 sec)
No. 6 (Oc. R 4 sec)	No. 7 (V.Q.Fl. W)
No. 8 (Q.Fl. R)	No. 7A (Fl. G 4 sec)

Then alter course to 60° to pass in a shallow curve S of No. 8A buoy (Oc. (2) R 6 sec) and N of No. 9 (Q.Fl. G).
Now bring the sectored lights of **Terre Nègre** into the white sector on 100° (Oc. (3) W.R.G., 12 sec 16 M.—R 104°+, G 097°) until just S of No. 10A buoy (Fl. (2) R 6 sec). Then on a 125° course parallel with the shore. If proceeding to **Royan** see page 51. If proceeding to **Port Bloc** bring the sectored lights of **Terre Nègre** onto 327° astern in the white sector with a red sector 331° plus and a green sector 326° minus. Next pass N of No. 13 (Iso. G 4 sec), No. 13A (Q.Fl. G) and No. 13B (Oc.G) and S of No. 12 (Oc.R 4 sec), then alter course at No. 13B buoy (page 62). If proceeding up river keep the white sector of **Pointe de Grave** (Oc. W.R.G. 4 sec 16/15 M.) astern on 307·5° with a red sector at 303° minus and a green sector at 213° plus, passing N of **La Verdon sur Mer** mole (Fl. (3) W.G. 12 sec 8/4 M.) and N of No. 15 buoy (F.G.) and No. 19 (F.G.), and S of No. 16 (F.R.). Follow the line of port and starboard hand buoys up the estuary. An up to date Admiralty chart No. 2910 is essential.

Passe Sud (or Passe de Grave)

Approaches

Day and night *From N* There is no advantage to be gained or reason to use this pass from a N direction, so no details are given.

From S see page 46 under **Grande Passe de l'Ouest**, *approaches, day and night.*

Entrance *Warning* This pass should not be used in conditions of bad visibility or heavy swell. The minimum depth is 4·3 m (14 ft) in this channel, but it varies.

Day Close No. G red and white whistle buoy with the X topmark and set course on 063° towards No. G1 green conical buoy with tall up-pointing triangular topmark. Locate the leading marks on **Pointe de Grave** and bring these into line on 063°, *Front:* white square tower 22 m (71 ft) high, *Rear:* white square tower black corners, edges and top, 26 m (85 ft) high. When 2 miles from land diverge from this line and leave No. G2 red can buoy to port and No. G3 green conical buoy to starboard. Change course onto 041° to bring the **Royan** leading marks into line, *Front:* **Le Chay**, white tower with red top 33 m (108 ft) high, *Rear:* **Saint-Pierre**, light grey water tower, red support and top 61 m (200 ft) high. Both difficult to see.

Leave No. G5 green conical buoy and No. G4 red can buoy to starboard; proceed to a position 1 cable due S of No. G7 green can buoy when turn to starboard on 100° towards No. 13B green conical light buoy, then proceed as described from the **Grande Passe de l'Ouest** (*entrance*, *day*, page 47) above. Green starboard hand buoys have up pointed triangular top marks and red port hand buoys have red can top marks.

Night *Warning* Entrance at night is only safe in conditions of little swell and good visibility, and also near HW as the line of leading lights crosses shoal water.

Approach the area of the red and white whistle buoy in the white sector of **Cordouan** (Oc. (2+1) 12 sec. 23/19 M.) and bring the leading lights on **Pointe de Grave** in line on 063° (*Front:* Q.Fl.G. 18 M. intensified 061°–065°, *Rear:* Occ. W.R.G. 4 sec. 18/11 M.) until **Le Chay/Royan** leading lights are nearly closed on 041°, when set course towards them and slowly bring them in line (*Front:* **Pointe du Chay** Q.Fl. R. 16 M. intensified 039·5°–042·5°, *Rear:* **Saint-Pierre** (Q.Fl. R. 14 M. intensified 039°–043°). Keep to this line until the **Pointe de Grave** light (Occ. W.R.G. 4 sec.) bears 125°, then alter course to 100° towards No. 13B buoy (Oc.G.) and proceed as detailed under **Grande Passe de l'Ouest**, *entrance*, *night*, page 47 above.

Anchorages in the approach

Other than the harbours of **Royan** and **Port Bloc** (pages 51, 60) the following anchorages are available to await the tide.

Rade de Royan in up to 5·5 m (3 fathoms) sand and mud, but only to be used in good weather and absence of swell from SW or W. Close to the entrance to the harbour.

La Gironde Estuary—Passe Sud—front leading light—Saint Nicolas.

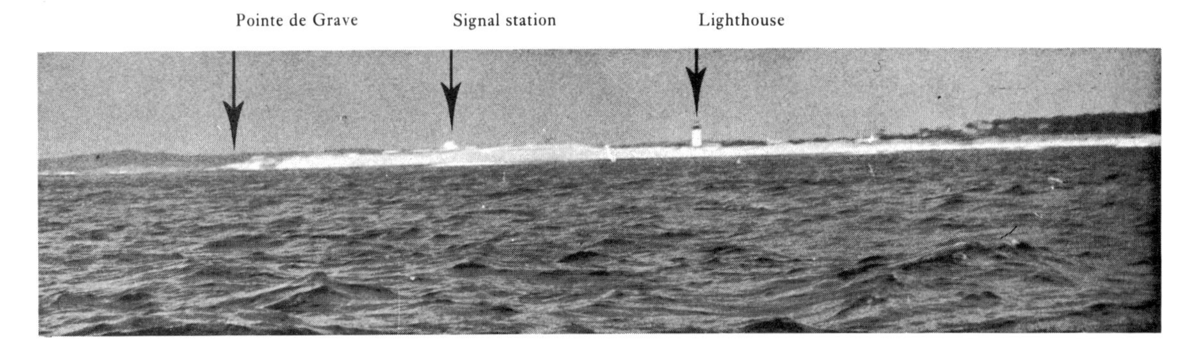

La Gironde Estuary—Passe Sud—rear leading light – Pointe de Grave.

Verdon sur Mer, off **Mole d'Escale** and **Pointe de la Chambrette**, as close inshore as draft permits. Yachts drawing 2 m (1 fathom) or less can anchor in mud due S of the point and about ½ cable away from it.
Bonne Anse ½ mile NE of the point and as far inshore as draft permits, but it is open to swell from SW and W. Small drying harbour 1m in entrance.

Anchorages in the estuary

Yachts should have no difficulty in anchoring out of the main channel in soft mud almost anywhere in the estuary above **Pointe de Grave** that draft permits. However, consideration should be given to the strength and direction of flow of the current, especially the ebb, when choosing any anchorage because mud is very soft. The following locations are the recognised places for anchoring.

E bank (right bank)
Saint-Palais-sur-Mer. Anchorage in settled weather. **Club la Voile de St Palais.**
Saint-Georges-de-Didonne. Anchorage in up to 3 m (1·5 fathoms) and drying quay. It has little protection from swell from W and NW. **Club Société des Régates de St Georges-de-Didonne.** Short breakwater, lighthouse, moorings.
Meschers-sur-Gironde. Small canalised river. Anchorage in 2·6 m (1·3 fathoms) and drying quay, water available. **Club Nautique de Merchers.**
Mortagne-sur-Gironde (La Rive). Anchorage—see also *berths*.
Port Maubert. Anchorage, narrow river, quays and pontoons.
Blaye (Sainte-Luce). Anchorage—see also *moorings* and *berths*.
Rogue-de-Thau. Anchorage.
Bourg (Dordogne). Anchorage. Pontoons. **Club Centre Nautique Bourguais.**
Libourne (Dordogne). Anchorage.
Lambent (Garonne). Anchorage.
Le Marquis (Garonne). Anchorage.
Lamarque-Port S (Garonne). Anchorage.

W bank (left bank)
Médoc – port. Anchorage.
Beychevelle. Anchorage.
Trompeloup. Anchorage.

Le Maréchal. Anchorage.
Saint-Christoly-de-Médoc. Anchorage.
Le Verdon-sur-Mer. Anchorage. A marina is planned for this area. VHF Ch. 12·16.

Moorings

Moorings are sometimes available for yachts as follows:
Blaye. A few buoys are available near the town near the ferry landing jetty. There is also a small club, **Blaye Nautique**, and provisions can be obtained from the town.

Berths

Other than at **Bordeaux**, the only berths available are as follows and they are normally used for commercial vessels:
Pauillac. A yacht harbour with entrance on SE side and all normal facilities. There is also the yacht club **Croiseurs d'Aquitaine**. Normal provisions can be obtained from the town. VHF Ch. 16·9. Tel (56) 59-12-16.
Blaye. berths in 7·5 m (4 fathoms) alongside wharf, crane 3 tons, drying tidal basin.
Furt. Small port. Berths in 4·0 m (2 fathoms).
Bec d'Ambés. Berths in 7·5 m (4 fathoms) alongside oil wharf. VHF Ch. 12·16.
Mortagne-sur-Gironde (La Rive). Basin and wet dock 3·5 m (1·8 fathoms) deep, 200 m (656 ft) long, 75 m (246 ft) wide. Water from the quay, supplies from the town. Pontoons for yachts. 6 ton crane, Chandlery, mechanics. Wet dock open HW–1 to HW.

Small harbours are being developed at
E bank (right bank)
Saint-Georges de Didonne
Meschers sur Gironde
Talmont sur Gironde
Callonges
Porte Neuve
Freneau
Plassac
W bank (left bank)
Saint-Estèphe
Goulée

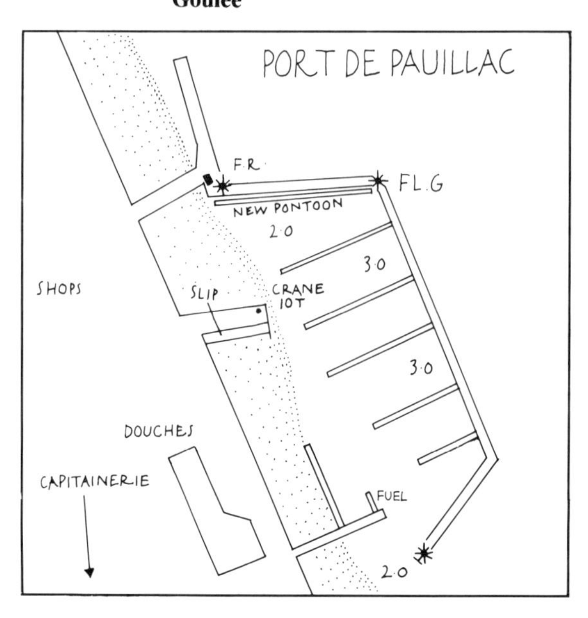

4 Port de Royan

Population 11,000 to 100,000 (summer) Rating 3-2-3 Position 45°37·2′N 1°01·9′W

General

This small port and attractive modern town has a marina which offers a good staging point for yachts which have missed their tide on the way to **Bordeaux**.

Provided weather and sea conditions permit the entry to **La Gironde** estuary then this harbour can also be entered without danger. Approach and entrance are simple. The entrance is dredged to 1·5 m (5 ft) and yachts drawing up to 2·25 m (8 ft) can lie afloat inside. Good shops and facilities exist for visiting yachtsmen. The local yacht club welcomes visitors. The area is a well known holiday resort with good train services to **Paris** and a ferry service to **Port Bloc**. A good place to step or unstep masts. Very crowded in the season.

Warnings

Due to powerful currents in the approach to this harbour particular care is necessary to avoid being set away from a desired course. Silts, but dredged.

Data

Charts Admiralty Nos. 2910, 2916
French Nos. 6141, 6139, 6336

Magnetic variation 5°32′W (1984) decreasing by 05′ each year.

Tidal information see page 44.

Tidal currents Off the entrance of the harbour there is an eddy which runs continuously S at 1 knot on a rising tide and 3 knots on a falling tide.

Lights **Jetée Sud head.** Very quick flashing Red 11 m (34 ft), 12 miles. White tower with red base. Visible 199°–116°. Obscured by **Pointe du Chay**. Foghorn (2) 20 sec. HW±2½ hours.
Nouvelle Jetée head. Group Occulting (2) Red 6 seconds, 8 m (26 ft), 6 miles. White metal pylon, red top.
Jetée Est head. Flashing Green, 2 seconds, 2 m (6 ft), 6 miles. White post green top.
Wreck buoy R1, Isophase Green, 4 seconds. Green pillar buoy up pointed cone.

Approach

Day *From NW* No. 13 buoy (page 47) is left to starboard and course set for No. R1 green wreck buoy which is S of **Pointe due Chay**. When the white tower with a red base on the **Jetée Sud** head bears 020° alter course towards a point about 50 m (150 ft) E of Môle Nord head spur which has a white metal pylon.

From SE Proceed across the neck of **Banc de St Georges**, which is S of **St Georges-de-Didonne**, and along the channel N of this *banc* towards the white tower

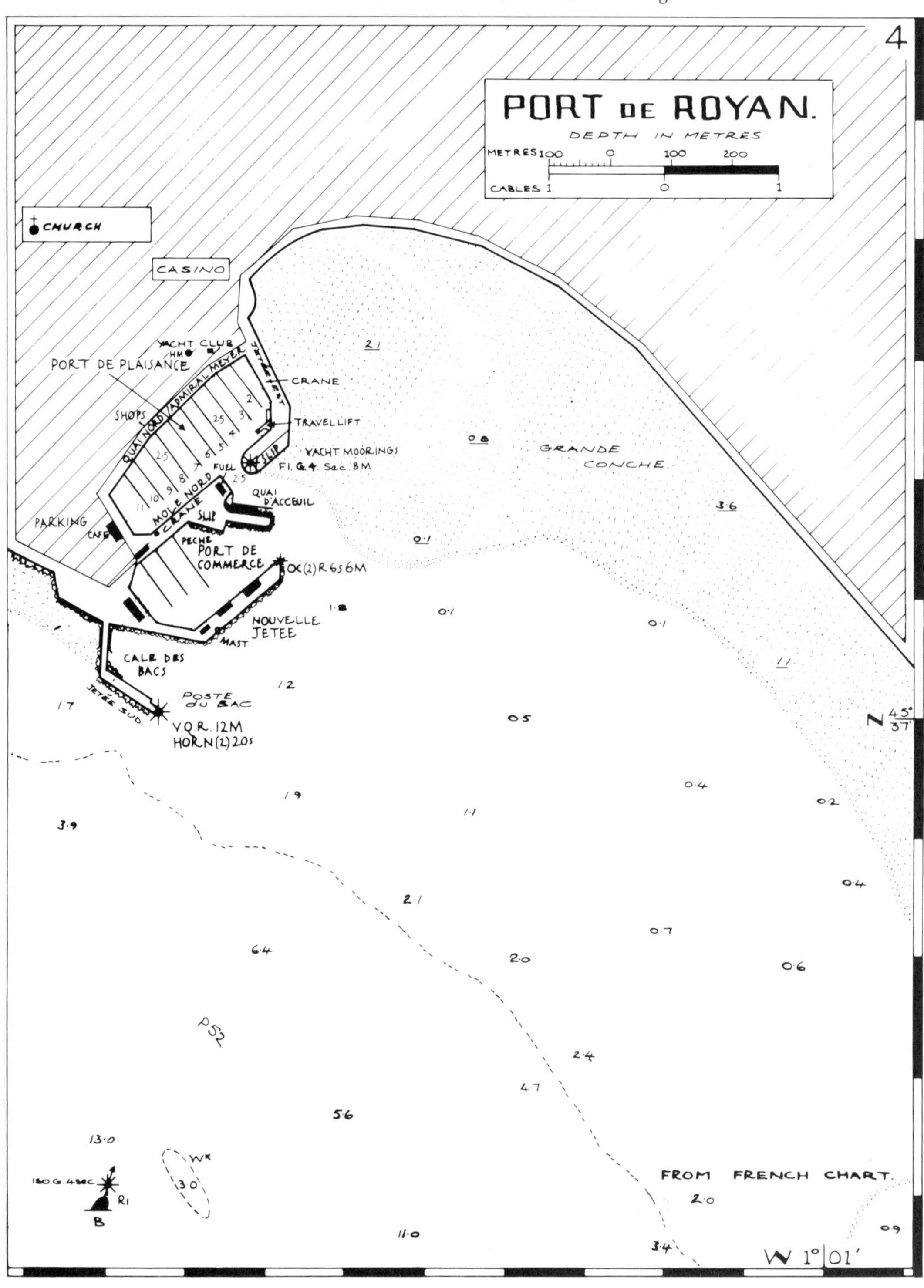

4
PORT DE ROYAN.
DEPTH IN METRES
METRES 100 0 100 200
CABLES 1 0 1
CHURCH
CASINO
YACHT CLUB
HM
PORT DE PLAISANCE
QUAI NORD
ADMIRAL MEYER
SHOPS
CRANE
TRAVEL LIFT
YACHT MOORINGS
FI. G. 4. Sec. 8M
SLIP
FUEL
QUAI D'ACCEUIL
MOLE NORD
CRANE
SLIP
PARKING
CAFE
PECHE
PORT DE COMMERCE
OC(2)R 6s 6M
NOUVELLE JETEE
MAST
CALE DES BACS
POSTE du BAC
JETEE SUD
VQR. 12M
HORN(2)20s
GRANDE CONCHE
N 45° 37'
WK
R1
B
FROM FRENCH CHART.
W 1° 01'

Port de Royan—approach looking N.

with a red base on the **Jetée Sud** head. When 2 cables S of the **Nouvelle Jetée** head alter course towards it to leave it to port.

Night *From NW* Approach from No. 10A buoy (Fl. (2) R 6 sec) on 125° (page 46) leaving buoys Nos. 11A (Oc. G 4 sec) and 13 (Iso. G 4 sec) to stbd. When the light of **Jetée Sud** at **Royan** harbour (V.Q.Fl. R., 11 m, 12 M.) is on 020° follow this direction until 1 cable from **Jetée Sud** head, then give this a 50 m (150 ft) berth and proceed on 020° towards **Nouvelle Jetée** head (Oc. (2) R. 6 sec. 8 m 6 M.) leaving it 50 m (150 ft) to port round into the entrance. Leave **Jetée Est** to starboard.

From SE Using **Pointe de Grave** light (Oc. W.R.G. 4 sec. W. 16/15 M., R. 12 M., G. 11 M.) enter the channel N of **Banc de St Georges**. When clear of **Pointe de Vallières** bring **Jetée Sud** head (V.Q.Fl. R. 11 m, 12 M.) onto 330° and approach this until 1 cable off when proceed as in *approach*, *night*, *NW* above.

Entrance

Day Enter the yacht harbour between spur of **Nouvelle Jetée** and head of **Jetée Est** in mid-channel leaving the entrance to the **Port de Commerce** to port.

Night Enter harbour between **Nouvelle Jetée** head (Oc. (2) R. 6 sec. 8 m, 6 M.) and **Jetée Est** head (Fl.G. 2 sec. 6 M.).

Anchorage

Anchorage is possible off the harbour entrance in up to 12 m (6 fathoms) sand and mud. Anchor as far N as draft permits to reduce the amount of swell.

Berths

Berths are usually available to visiting yachts on pontoons equipped with 'fingers'. On arrival secure to the Quai d'Accueil.

Moorings

There are a few but unlikely to be available.

Formalities

It is necessary on arrival to visit the Bureau du Port, on the NW side of the harbour, and to fill in a form. Should Customs clearance be necessary the staff will advise. The *Douane's* office is on the W corner of the harbour.

Port de Royan – looking NE.

Facilities

Water	From taps on pontoons.
Diesel and petrol	From fuel pumps at port side of entrance.
Shops	Large number of modern shops close to harbour also launderette.
Chandlery	Several chandlery shops near harbour and a sailmaker.
Hard	NE outer wall of harbour has a large hard and there is a small one in the **Port de Commerce**.
Crane	Crane at end of **Jetée Est**—6 tons, and an elevator 26 tons.
Yacht club	**Société des Régates de Royan** (05-28-38) welcomes yachtsmen and can provide showers, toilets, etc. but not food or drink which is available at the Casino restaurant and bar nearby.
Showers	Also available on NW side of the harbour.
Hotels	A large number of hotels of all types are available.
Information	*Syndicat d'Initiative, Rond Point de la Poste.*
Visits	A very modern church, Notre Dame de Royan, is of an interesting design.
Beaches	A good sandy beach alongside the harbour.

5 Port de Bordeaux

Population 285,000 Rating 2-2-1 Position 44°52·5′N 0°32·4′W

General

A very pleasant city and port in the centre of the famous wine producing area. The approach up the long estuary of **La Gironde** and the river **La Garonne** is simple but should only be undertaken with the rising tide. Berths in up to 3 m (1·5 fathoms) at a yacht harbour or in a commercial wet dock outside the city are available. Also it is possible to moor alongside the wharfs on the W bank in the city but the current here is very strong.

All requirements a yachtsman may need are available.

Warnings

The current of this river, especially on the ebb, is very strong and at springs with the river in spate may reach 5 knots. In addition a considerable amount of flotsam including whole trees may be encountered. Doubled ground or mooring gear is advised.

Large merchant vessels which cannot keep to the starboard hand side of the channel display a black ball on the forestay by day and a red light at the foremast by night and must be given right of way.

Data

Charts Admiralty No. 2916
French Nos. 5508, 6141, 6140, 6139, 3508

Magnetic variation 5°30′W (1984) decreasing by about 05′ each year.

Tidal information See page 44.

Lights There are a very considerable number of lights and lighted buoys marking the deep-water channel from **Pointe de Grave** to **Bordeaux.**

La Gironde—Bec d'Ambès junction.

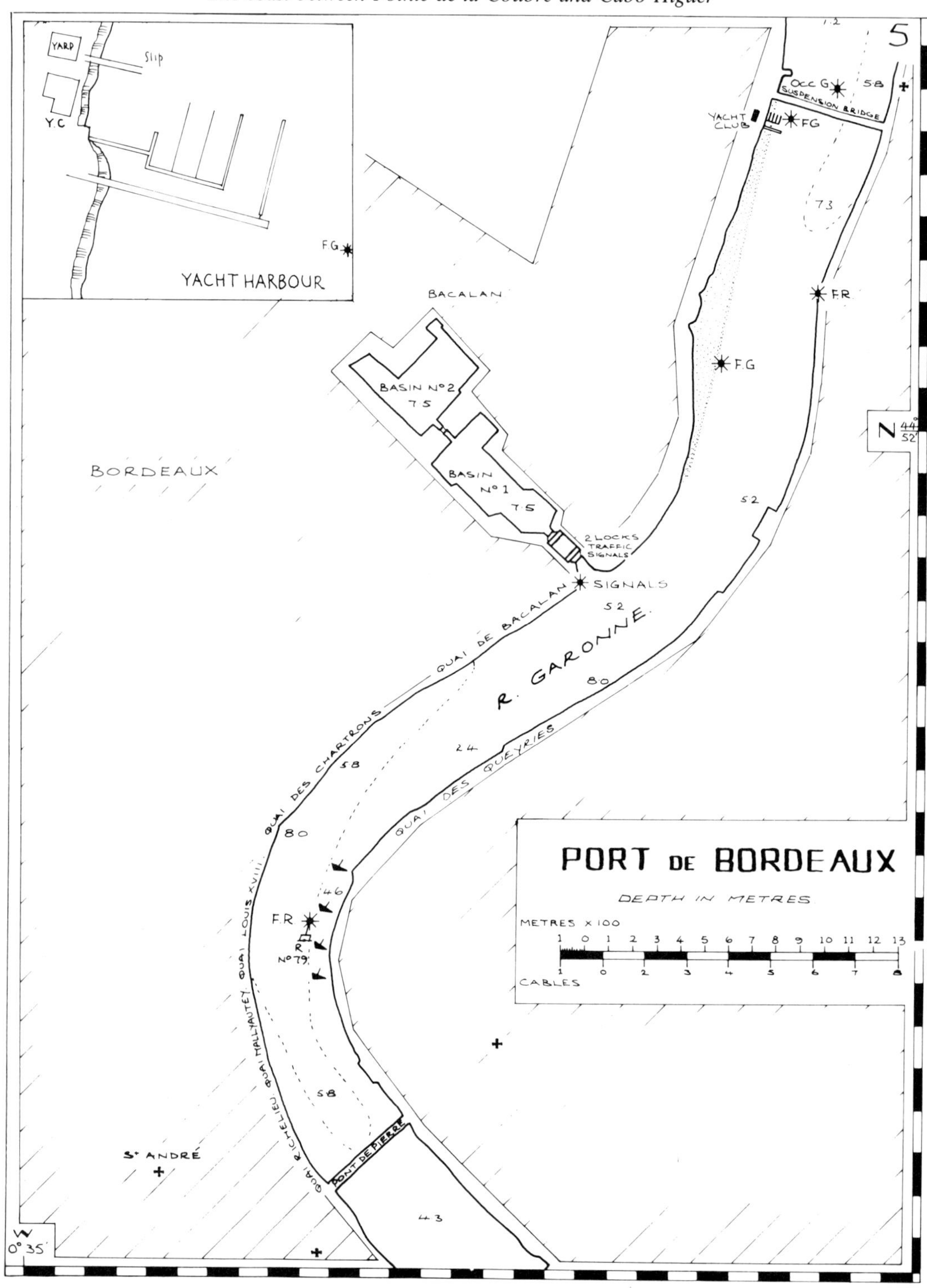

5
YARD
Slip
Y.C
F.G.
YACHT HARBOUR
Occ G
58
SUSPENSION BRIDGE
YACHT CLUB
FG
73
F.R
BACALAN
F.G
BASIN No 2
7.5
BASIN No 1
7.5
N 44° 52'
BORDEAUX
52
2 LOCKS TRAFFIC SIGNALS
SIGNALS
52
QUAI DE BACALAN
R. GARONNE
80
24
QUAI DES CHARTRONS
58
QUAI DES QUEYRIES
80
46
F.R
R No 79
QUAI LOUIS XVIII
QUAI MAL LYAUTEY
QUAI RICHELIEU
PORT DE BORDEAUX
DEPTH IN METRES
METRES x 100
CABLES
58
PONT DE PIERRE
St ANDRÉ
43
W 0° 35'

The use of Admiralty chart No. 2916 or French charts Nos. 3508 and 6139 is essential. In general white lights are leading marks, green are starboard hand and red port hand buoys or marks.

Radio See page 20 for port radio details.

Signals Signals from the entrance to *Basin No.* 1 are by lights showing from the centre of lock and also from the top of the pylon beside the river.

Lights showing from centre of lock		Lights showing from top of pylon	Meaning
Pointing towards basin	Pointing towards river		
Red	Red	Green	No movement
Red	Orange	Green	Prepare to enter
Red	Green	Green	Enter
Red	Red	Green	Ship in lock
Orange	Red	Orange	Prepare to leave
Green	Red	Orange	Leave
Red	Red	Orange	Ship in lock

Approach

Day From **Pointe de Grave** follow the line of buoys in a general direction of 145° leaving even-numbered red can buoys to port and odd-numbered black conical buoys to starboard.

After No. 28 buoy close to starboard bank and hold the curves of this bank at ½ mile leaving the **Iles de Trompeloup**, **St Louis**, **Vasand** and **Pâté** to port until buoy No. 57, when cross over to mid-river and leave **Ile Verte** to starboard. Then head straight for the oil refinery on **Bec d' Ambès** at the junction of **La Dordogne** and **La Garonne** rivers.

At buoy No. BAO close the bank of **Ile Cazeau** to 2 cables until level with the oil refinery when cross over to the port hand bank, which course hold at 2 cables distance until buoy No. 66. Now cross over to the starboard bank at 1 cable until No. 67 buoy when keep in mid-channel as far as the suspension bridge, then cross to the starboard bank which can be held at 1 cable until the stone bridge in the centre of the city bars further up-river progress by yachts with masts, etc. not lowered for transit of the canal system.

Anchorage

Anchoring in the river near **Bordeaux** is not advised owing to soft mud and strong currents, but it is possible below **Bec d'Ambès**.

Mooring

Mooring buoys for yachts may be available just upstream of the suspension bridge near the W bank.

Berths

Marina The yacht club **Société Nautique de La Gironde** has established a small marina about 2 miles downstream from the city centre on the W bank, just upstream from the new suspension bridge. Berth alongside the outer pontoon in

Bordeaux—yacht club and marina. An extra pontoon now located outside others.

3 m (1·5 fathoms) using the special berthing arms to hold the yacht away from the pontoon as there is considerable wash from passing vessels. A charge is made for the use of this marina. A crane is available to step masts at slack water.

Basin No. 1 About 1½ miles downstream from the city centre on the W bank is a lock leading to a pair of wet docks. These can be entered only during the two hours before local HW. Tie up on the starboard hand side just inside the first basin in 7·5 m (4 fathoms). Sometimes water is covered with oil. A crane is available but is expensive.

City wharfs Wharfs extend from *Basin No.* 1 to the *Pont Pierre*, the lower of the two stone bridges, and there is usually any amount of vacant space to make fast alongside in up to 6 m (3 fathoms) near the centre of the city. Unfortunately the current here is very strong and adequate fenders and doubled warps are essential. Special care is necessary at low and high water when the direction of the stream changes.

Formalities

Nil. Customs office on **Quai de la Douane.**

Facilities

Water From wharfs, docks and marina pontoons by pipe.

Diesel, petrol From garage near marina.

Electricity 220v a.c. points on the pontoons.

Shops Normal supplies available from shops near marina. **Bordeaux** has shops to cover all requirements.

Cranes	A crane is available at the marina for unstepping masts up to 12 m long, also at wet docks and wharfs.
Slip	A 10 ton slip near the yacht club house.
Yacht clubs	**Société Nautique de La Gironde** (29-45-01) is near the marina; bar, lounge, showers. In **Bordeaux** is the **Yacht-Motor Club d'Aquitaine** (48-37-75), and the **Cercle de la Voile de Bordeaux**.
Hotels and restaurants	Many and varied, covering all tastes.
Information	The *Syndicat d'Initiative* at the end of *Alle de Tourney*, 1 *Cours de 30 Juillet* will supply maps and information about the city and area.
Visits	Many old and interesting buildings, churches, ruins and museums, some dating from Roman times.
British Consulate	15 Cours de Verdun, 33081 Bordeaux. Cédex. (Tel: 52-28-35, 52-89-51, 52-48-86.)

6 Port Bloc

Population 100 Rating 3-2-4 Position 45°34·1′N 1°03·6′W

General

A small ferry harbour and yacht marina with easy entrance provided the conditions are suitable for the approach to the mouth of **La Gironde** estuary. Moorings and berths in up to 3 m (1·5 fathoms) are possible but space is limited. Facilities ashore consists of two cafés, a yacht club, a fish shop and kiosk. It is a useful port while waiting for a tide to **Bordeaux**. There is also a train service to **Verdon-sur-Mer** and **Bordeaux**.

Warnings

There are very strong tidal streams and currents which cause eddies between **Pointe de Grave** and the harbour entrance of up to 4 knots at springs.

Ferry boats run a regular service to **Royan** and entry or exit should not be attempted when they are leaving, entering or manoeuvring.

Data

Charts Admiralty No. 2910
French Nos. 6336, 6141, 6139

Magnetic variation 5°32′W (1984) decreasing by 5′ each year.

Tidal information See page 44.

Lights **Pointe de Grave**. Occulting White, Red, Green sectors, 4 seconds, 26 m (85 ft), White 18, Red 12, Green 12 miles. White square tower black corners and top. Red 233·5°–303°, White 303°–312°, Green 312°–330°, White 330–233·5°. Obscured when less than 053°. Radiobeacon.

Port Bloc—entrance as seen from Pointe de Grave—high water.

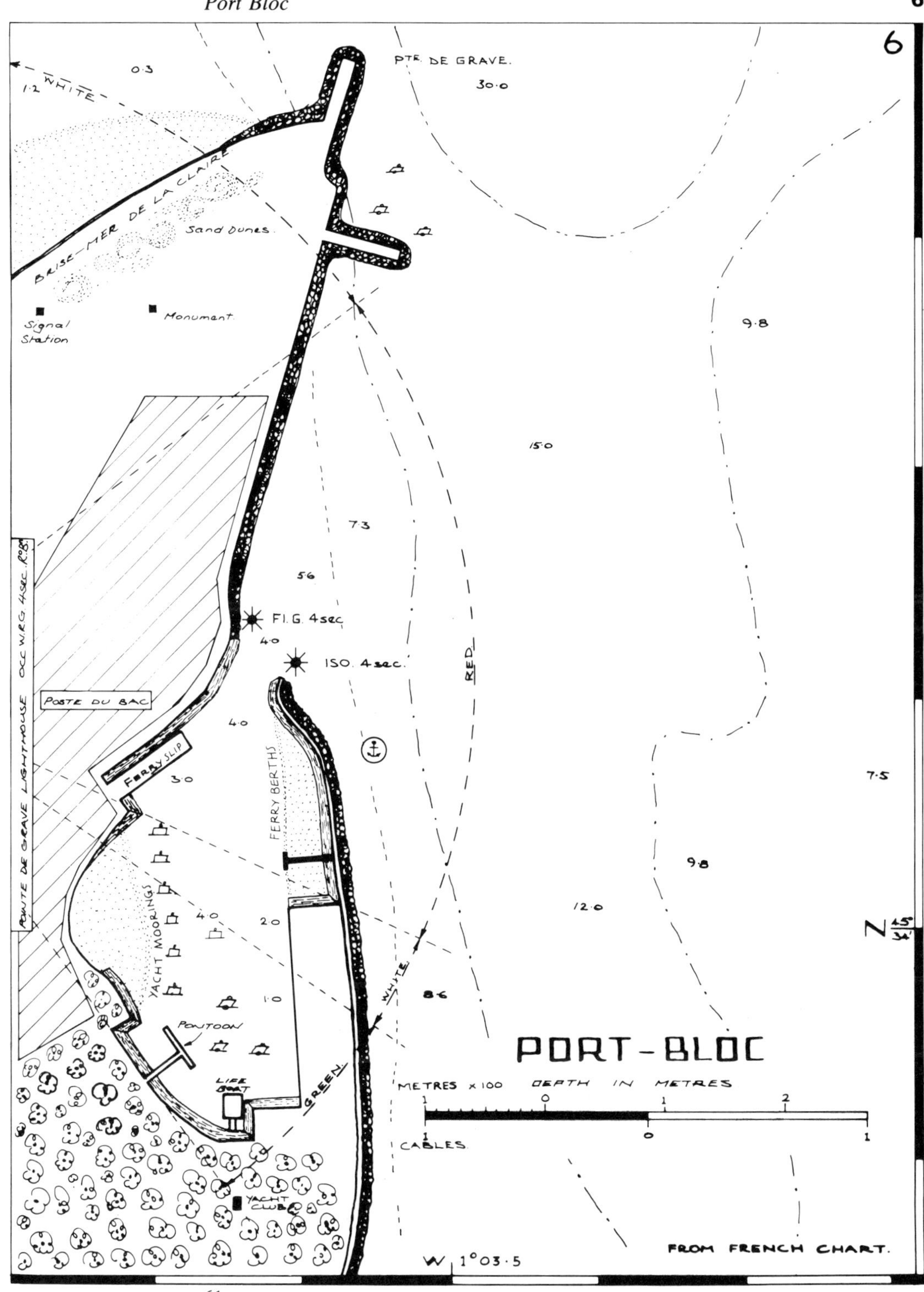
6
PTE. DE GRAVE.
30·0
WHITE
BRISE-MER DE LA CLAIRE
Sand Dunes
Signal Station
Monument
POINTE DE GRAVE LIGHTHOUSE OCC.W.R.G. 4sec.
POSTE DU BAC
FERRY SLIP
Fl. G. 4sec
ISO. 4sec.
FERRY BERTHS
YACHT MOORINGS
PONTOON
LIFE BOAT
YACHT CLUB
GREEN
WHITE
RED
PORT-BLOC
METRES x 100
DEPTH IN METRES
CABLES
FROM FRENCH CHART.
W 1°03·5
N 45° 34'

Estacade Nord. Flashing Green, 4 seconds, 8 m (26 ft), 5 miles. White tower, green top.
Estacade Sud. Isophase Red, 4 seconds, 8 m (26 ft), 6 miles. White tower, red top.

Approaches

Day

From NW Leave No. 13A and 13B buoys to starboard. See page 47.

From SW Having left buoy No. 10A to port (page 48) leave Nos. 13 and 13B, green conical buoys with up-pointing cone and topmarks, to starboard, also the mole at the tip of **Pointe de Grave** to starboard. Keep careful and constant check on the direction of set due to the tidal streams and currents. The harbour entrance, which is difficult to see, then opens up some 4 cables along the E coast of **Pointe de Grave**. The harbour entrance is marked by two small white towers, to port with a red top and to starboard with a green top.

From SE Follow the main channel leaving No. 15 buoy and the **Le Verdon** jetty complex to port at a distance of about 4 cables. Then set course for the tip of **Pointe de Grave** until the harbour entrance is seen. This is located some 4 cables S of the point.

Night

From NW Follow the line of the leading lights of **Pointe de Terre Nègre** on a stern bearing of 327° (*Front:* Oc. (3) W. sector, 12 sec. 17 M. *Rear:* F.R. 17 M.) until the red sector of **Pointe de Grave** light (Oc.W.R.G. 4 sec. 12 M.) is entered near No. 13B buoy (Oc.G.) when turn towards **Pointe de Grave** light and enter between the two harbour entrance lights **Estacade Nord** (Fl.G. 4 sec. 5 M.) to starboard, **Estacade Sud** (Iso.R. 4 sec. 8 M.) to port.

From SE Leave No. 15 buoy (F.G.) to port and keep in the white sector of **Pointe de Grave** light (Oc.W.R.G. 4 sec. 18 M.) on 100° until the two harbour entrance lights **Estacade Nord** (Fl.G. 4 sec. 5 M.) to starboard, **Estacade Sud** (Iso.W. 4 sec. 6 M.) to port are seen, then enter between.

Port Bloc—entrance—showing projecting deep-water channel marks, which have now been removed.

Port Bloc—looking northwards—low water.

Entrance

Day and night The entrance is narrow, about 30 m (98 ft) wide, and has walls which slope out under water.

Moorings

A line of yacht moorings in about 2 to 2·5 m (1 to 1·4 fathoms) parallel to the W side of the harbour can usually be used by visiting yachts.

Berths

A floating pontoon is established in about 3 m (1·5 fathoms) water in the SW corner of the harbour and, if lucky, a space may be found here.

Anchorages

Anchoring inside the harbour is not advised owing to constant movement of ferries, buoy maintenance vessels and the lifeboat, which operate in the E and N halves of the harbour. Anchoring is now permitted outside the harbour, S of the entrance, but very strong currents will be encountered.

Formalities

Capitaine du Port at **Verdon** (05-43-82), Douane at **Verdon** (56-60-23 and 59-61-97).

Facilities

Water From pipe on pontoon.

Diesel, petrol Both some distance away on road to **Verdon-sur-Mer.**

Shops Only at **Le Verdon**. A train service is available from **Port Bloc**.

Yacht club The **Moto Yachting Club de la Pointe de Grave** is established in a huge catamaran on land to the S of the harbour. (59-61-58).

Crane 10 tons

Visits A short walk over the sand dunes to the monument and signal station gives a good view of the estuary mouth.

Beaches Sandy beaches below signal station, but watch out for the current.

Future development
A 1500 berth yacht harbour at **Verdon.**

7 Bassin d'Arcachon

Population 16,000 to 150,000 (summer) Rating 3-3-2 Position 44°39·5′ N 1°08·6′ W

General

A large inland tidal lake connected to the sea by a long winding channel between sandy shoal waters upon which the seas break spectacularly in any wind or swell. Entry is not possible at night or in heavy weather from SW through W to N. A considerable area of the lake is navigable even at LW via various channels. A large modern marina offers berths to visitors where all normal facilities are provided. The shops, though some distance away, cater for all normal requirements. Yacht and engine repairs can be undertaken. A casino, good bathing beaches, the largest sand dune in Europe, cheap oysters (the culture of which is the main industry) and Roman ruins are some of the local attractions. Good safe bathing beaches, ideal for a young family.

Warning

The entrance channel is remarked each year as it is changed by the winter storms. However, it can change again after remarking so care should be exercised. Do not enter during the period 1 hour after HW until 3 hours after LW. Good visibility is important.

A sea to sea, air to sea and land to sea practice range is in constant use just S of the entrance to the harbour (page 42). The mud is soft in places and holding is poor. Good visibility is important because the entrance buoys are far apart.

Data

Charts Admiralty No. 2664
French No. 6766
If exploring the basin a pair of charts can be purchased from the local book shop covering the area on a very large scale. These are produced by *Feret et Fils* from drawings by Jean-Marie Bouchet.

Magnetic variation 5°32′W (1984) decreasing by about 5′ each year.

Tidal information

	HW		LW		LHWS	MHNW	MLWS	MLWN
Pointe de Grave	0600 1800	0000 1200	1000 2200	0400 1600	5·4 m 17·6 ft	4·2 m 13·8 ft	0·9 m 3·0 ft	2·1 m 6·8 ft
Bassin d'Arcachon (Cap Ferret)	0·00	no data	+0·55	no data	−1·6 m −5·0 ft	no data	−0·6 m −2·1 ft	no data

At the entrance to the channel the flood stream commences at HW **Pointe de Grave** −0520, and the ebb at HW **Pointe de Grave** −0045. The flood stream runs E up to 2 knots and the ebb NW up to 3·5 knots.

Off **Arcachon** the flood stream begins at HW **Pointe de Grave** −0525 springs, 3

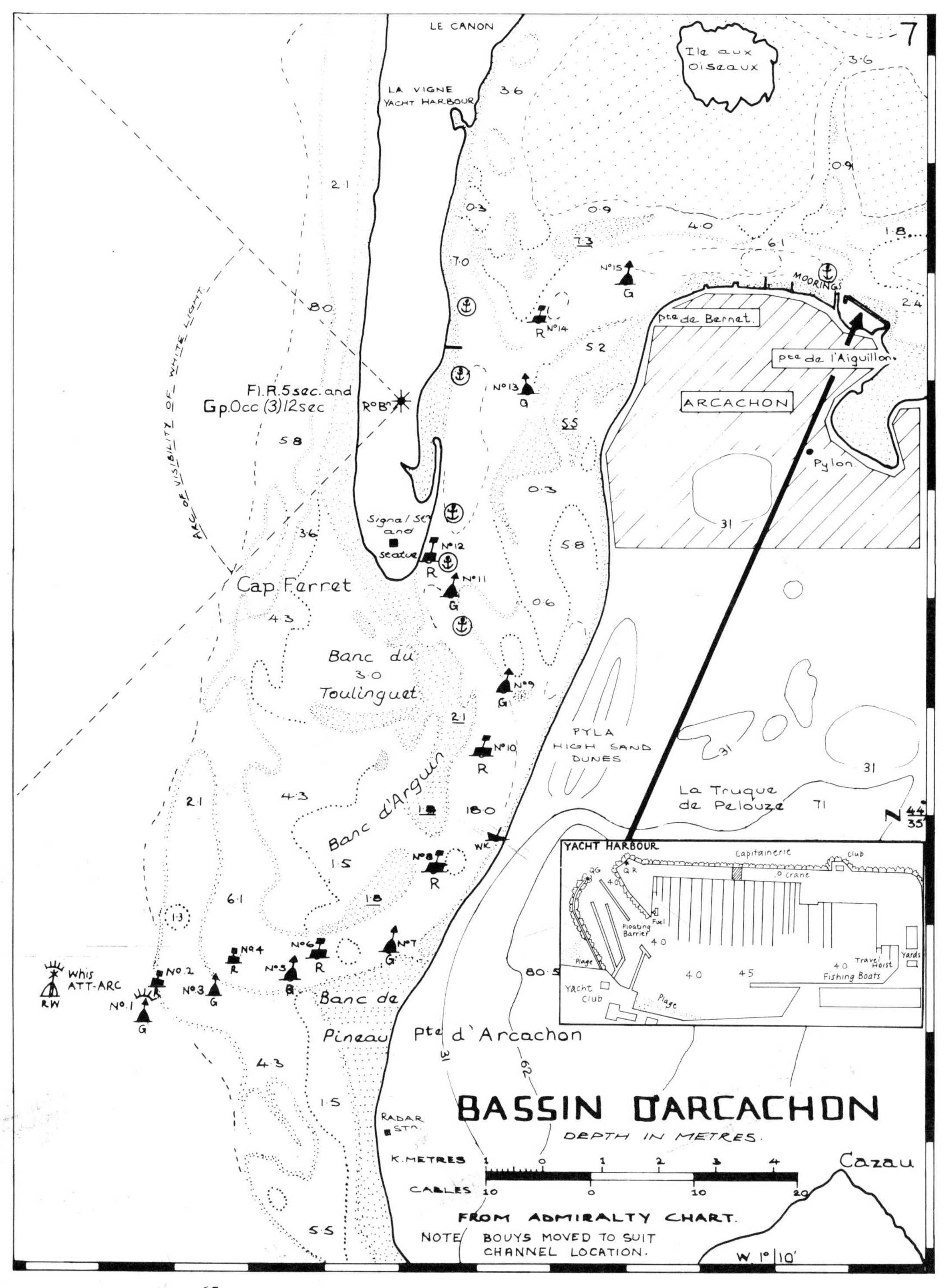
7
LE CANON
LA VIGNE
YACHT HARBOUR
Ile aux Oiseaux
Pte de Bernet.
Pte de l'Aiguillon.
MOORINGS
ARCACHON
Pylon.
Fl.R.5sec. and
Gp.Occ (3) 12sec
ARC OF VISIBILITY OF WHITE LIGHT
Signal Stn and seature
Cap Ferret
Banc du Toulinguet
Banc d'Arguin
PYLA
HIGH SAND DUNES
La Truque de Pelouze
Banc de Pineau
Pte d'Arcachon
Whis ATT-ARC
RW
RADAR STN.
YACHT HARBOUR
Capitainerie
Club
Floating Barrier
Fuel
Travel Hoist
Yards
Fishing Boats
Plage
Yacht Club
BASSIN D'ARCACHON
DEPTH IN METRES.
K.METRES
CABLES
FROM ADMIRALTY CHART.
NOTE BOUYS MOVED TO SUIT CHANNEL LOCATION.
Cazau
W. 1° 10'
N 44° 35'

knots; −0455 neaps at 1·9 knots. The ebb stream begins HW **Pointe de Grave** springs +0040 at 3·5 knots, neaps +0035 at 2–3 knots.

Five to 6 miles off the coast the current is usually N at 0·5 knots with a similar counter-current within 1 mile of the coast. The N-going current can reach 5 knots after prolonged W gales. Strong N gales result in a S-going current.

Lights **Contis.** Group Flashing (4) White, 25 seconds, 50 m (164 ft), 23 miles. White round tower, black diagonal stripes. Radio mast (F.R.) 16·5 M. NNE.

Cap Ferret. Flashing Red, 5 seconds, 53 m (175 ft), 26 miles. White tower, red top. *Also* Group Occulting (3) White, 12 seconds, 46 m (151 ft), 14 miles. Visible 045°–135°. Radiobeacon.

Hourtin. Flashing White, 5 seconds, 55 m (180 ft), 23 miles. Red square brick tower.

La Salie wharfhead, Q.Fl. (9) W 15 sec 19 m (62 ft), 10 miles; yellow structure, black band.

Buoys Conical Yellow ZDN, Flashing Yellow, 4 seconds, 8 miles.

Conical Yellow ZDS, Flashing Yellow, 4 seconds. 3·75 miles.

Pillar whistle buoy, red and white vertical stripes, radar reflector 5·5 m to SW of **Cap Ferret.**

No. 1 light buoy, Green Isophase green. 5·5 miles WSW of **Pointe d'Arcachon**.

Can buoy, Red over White, Group Flashing 2 White, 6 seconds. Can buoy, Red and White Q.Fl. Red 3·25 miles SW **Pointe d'Arcachon**.

Can buoy Red over White, Fl. (2) W. 6 sec. 5 miles SSW **Pointe d'Arcachon**.

Lifesaving A lifeboat is maintained at **Cap Ferret**.

Radio A radiobeacon operates from **Cap Ferret** lighthouse as follows:

296·5 kHz, 100 miles, FT (· · – · / –) 6 minutes.

For **Bordeaux/Arcachon** coast radio see page 19.

Approaches

Day *From S* From **Capbreton** there are miles of almost unbroken sand dunes bordered by pine forests which are virtually featureless. The **Contis** lighthouse, a white round tower with black diagonal stripes, the **Bicarosse** beacon, a black pyramidal framework with a black ball with a hole through it on top, and the firing range buildings, towers and instrument houses painted white to the N of it, are the main conspicuous objects. There are several villages but they are very similar to each other. If coasting N close in a careful watch on soundings should be kept to avoid the shoals off the **Pointe d'Arcachon**. In any swell it is advisable to commence to enter the channel from W of No. 1 pillar buoy, or from near the whistle buoy which is painted with red and white vertical stripes, with an X topmark and ATT-ARC marked on it. It is not advised to cut the corner.

From N A similar type of coast extends from the estuary of **La Gironde**, the only conspicuous and identifiable objects being the beacon with a black ball on top at **Pointe de la Négade**, **Hourtin** lighthouse, a red square brick tower showing over the fir trees with a disused and similar lighthouse and a cable further S, the beacon at **La Grigne** with diamond topmark, **Cap Ferret** lighthouse, a white tower with

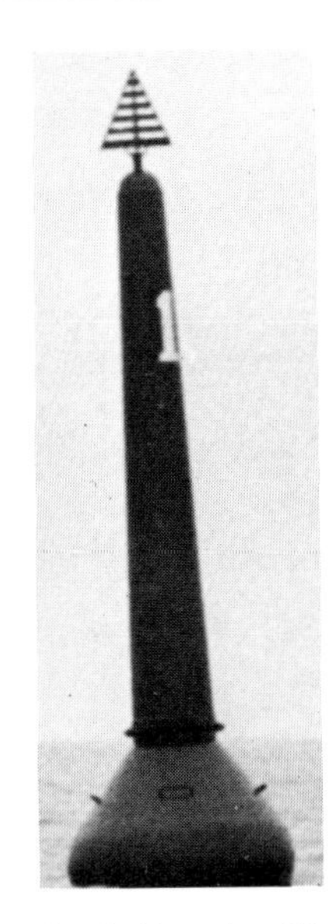

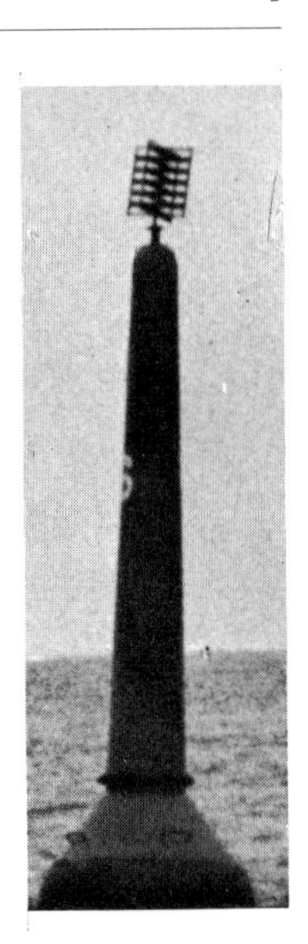

Bassin d'Arcachon—landfall whistle conical buoy red and white stripes 'X' top mark and ARC-ATT.
Bassin d'Arcachon—entrance channel buoy No. 1 green starboard hand (now has radar reflector).
Bassin d'Arcachon—entrance channel buoy No. 6 red port hand.

red top, and the **Cap Ferret** signal station, a white house with white tower and mast. Again, care should be taken, if coasting close in, to stand out to sea to clear the sand banks near the channel entrance.

Night *From S* Only the **Hourtin** lighthouse (Fl.W. 5 sec. 20 M.) and the various light buoys off **Pointe d'Arcachon** together with **Cap Ferret** lighthouse (Fl.R. 5 sec. 19 M.) give some help.

From N There is in addition **Contis** lighthouse (Fl. (4) W. 25 sec. 23 M.).

Entrance

Day It is advisable to enter from a position near the whistle buoy with red and white vertical stripes during the last half to quarter of the flood, and to follow the channel indicated by a series of pillar buoys, green and odd numbers to starboard and red and even to port. The channel proceeds E and then curves round N close inshore behind a large sand bank. It then crosses towards **Cap Ferret**. During all these 5 miles vessels are subject to confused seas due to waves, swell, current and shallow water. Once under the lee of **Cap Ferret** it is a simple matter to follow the channel round for a final 5 miles past the town of **Arcachon** and its piers to the entrance of the yacht harbour which is marked by a large stone anchor on the port hand side of the entrance. Due to length of this channel, timing is important.

Night Entrance at night is not recommended.

Anchorages

Anchorages are possible in most parts of the *Bassin* but the following is

Bassin d'Arcachon—entrance to marina.

recommended: off the E side of **Cap Ferret** peninsula in up to 11·8 m (6·5 fathoms) sand for the first three miles N of the point and also W of No. 14 buoy and off the marina.

Berths

Berths in 4·5 m (2·5 fathoms) in the marina in the **Port de Plaisance** are available on the W side of the first pontoon from the entrance.

Formalities

Visitors must report to the *Bureau de Port de Plaisance* (83-22-44) and to the *Douane* (Customs) (83-08-27/83-05-89) in the building on the N side of the marina on arrival, with ship's papers and passports.

Facilities

Water — From pipe on pontoon.

Diesel and petrol — From special floating pontoon near entrance of harbour.

Bassin d'Arcachon—inside harbour looking E. Fuel berth in foreground.

Shops	The shops are some distance by foot as one has to walk all round the harbour wall. The use of a dinghy to the yacht club, a short distance away, reduces this walk by half a mile.
Repairs	A number of yacht building and repairing yards exist near the harbour.
Chandlery	A number of chandlery shops are to be found around the town.
Yacht clubs	The **Cercle de la Voile d'Arcachon** (83-05-92) together with **Le Yacht Motors Club de la Côte d'Argent** (83-22-11) are situated at the SW corner of the port and provide bars, showers and club rooms. Visitors are welcome.
Hotels and Pensions	A large number from 3-star downwards are available.
Restaurants and bars	A considerable assortment to suit all tastes.
Information	*Syndicat d'Initiative, Place Roosevelt*, near the station, will supply maps etc.

Other Harbours There are a large number of small harbours around the **Bassin d'Arcachon** suitable for small shallow draft yachts. Many are used by local fishermen and those involved in oyster culture.

South Coast

La Teste A largish drying harbour for oyster boats, fuel, slip, provisions from town.
La Hume Small drying harbour for yachts and oyster boats, slip, quay.
Gujan–Mestras Several harbours for oyster boats, shops in town.
Biganos 3 kms from mouth of river Eyre is a small yacht harbour.

East Coast

Audenge Small drying harbour for yachts and oyster boats.
Cassy Harbour for oyster boats and yachts. Pontoons, quays, slip, crane, water, yacht club, shops.
Taussat Oyster boat and yacht harbour that dries out, sailing school.
Fontain Vielle A private marina for 200 yachts, pontoons, slip, fuel, yacht club, restaurant.
Betey Small yacht harbour open to SW, fuel, slip, yacht club.
Andernos A harbour for oyster boats, also a long pier, slip, chandlery, mechanic, shops in town nearby.
Lége Small harbour for oyster boats, quays, water.
Arés Mooring area dug out of sand, yacht club.

West Coast

Claouey Mooring in channel, yacht club, shops in village.
Le Grand Piquey Moorings in channel, slip, shops in village.
Pirallan Three small harbours for oyster boats, dries.
La Vigne A private marina for 300 yachts with all facilities including navigation lights 1 m at LWS.
Belisaire Landing jetty, moorings in channel.

8 Capbreton

Population 4,450 Rating 2-3-3 Position 43°39·3′N 1°26·4′W

General

This is a small port almost entirely devoted to yachting and the better class holiday visitors. It has a narrow canalised entrance which is dangerous in strong winds and swell from N and W and a yacht harbour with pontoons for boats drawing up to 2 m (1 fathom). Entrance is only possible 2 hours before HW until about 1 hour afterwards.

However, considerable dredging is due to be completed before 1988 when entrance should be possible at all states of the tide. The whole harbour will then have 1·5 to 2·5 m (0·4 to 1·5 fathoms) minimum depth. Marina-type pontoons are provided for 700 yachts, to be increased to 1500.

There is an excellent yacht club with showers, bar and restaurant. Adequate shops are available about two miles away. Good bathing beaches nearby.

Warnings

Due to development the chart may not be accurate or up to date, so care should be exercised.

Le Fosse (or **Le Gouf**) **de Capbreton**, a 100-fathom deep submarine valley which runs at right angles to the coast and ends only 2 miles away, prevents seas breaking in heavy weather, whereas in the shallower waters on either side they may be breaking.

Data

Charts Admiralty No. 2665
French Nos. 174, 175, 6586

Magnetic variation 5°31′W (1984) decreasing by about 5′ each year.

Tidal information

	HW		LW		MHWS	MHWN	MLWS	MLWN
Pointe de Grave	0600 1800	0000 1200	1000 2200	0400 1600	5·4 m 17·6 ft	4·2 m 13·8 ft	0·9 m 3·0 ft	2·0 m 6·8 ft
Capbreton	0·20	−0·30	−0·0	−0·10	−1·4 m −4· ft	−0·8 m −2·7 ft	−0·5 m −1·3 ft	−0·7 m −2·5 ft

The current about 5 to 6 miles offshore is N ½ knot. A counter-current may sometimes be encountered close to the shore. Strong W winds may increase this offshore current to 4 to 5 knots. Strong N winds may reverse the flow.

Lights **Capbreton Estacade Sud.** Iso.G. 4 sec. 7 m (23 ft), 9 miles. Grey tower, Green top. **Jetée Nord.** Fl. (2) R. 6 sec. 13 m (43 ft) 11 M Grey White tower, Red top. Fog signal Horn, 30 sec.

Port Radio See page 20.

Approaches

Day *From S* Between the entrance to **L'Adour Rivière (Bayonne)** and **Capbreton** the

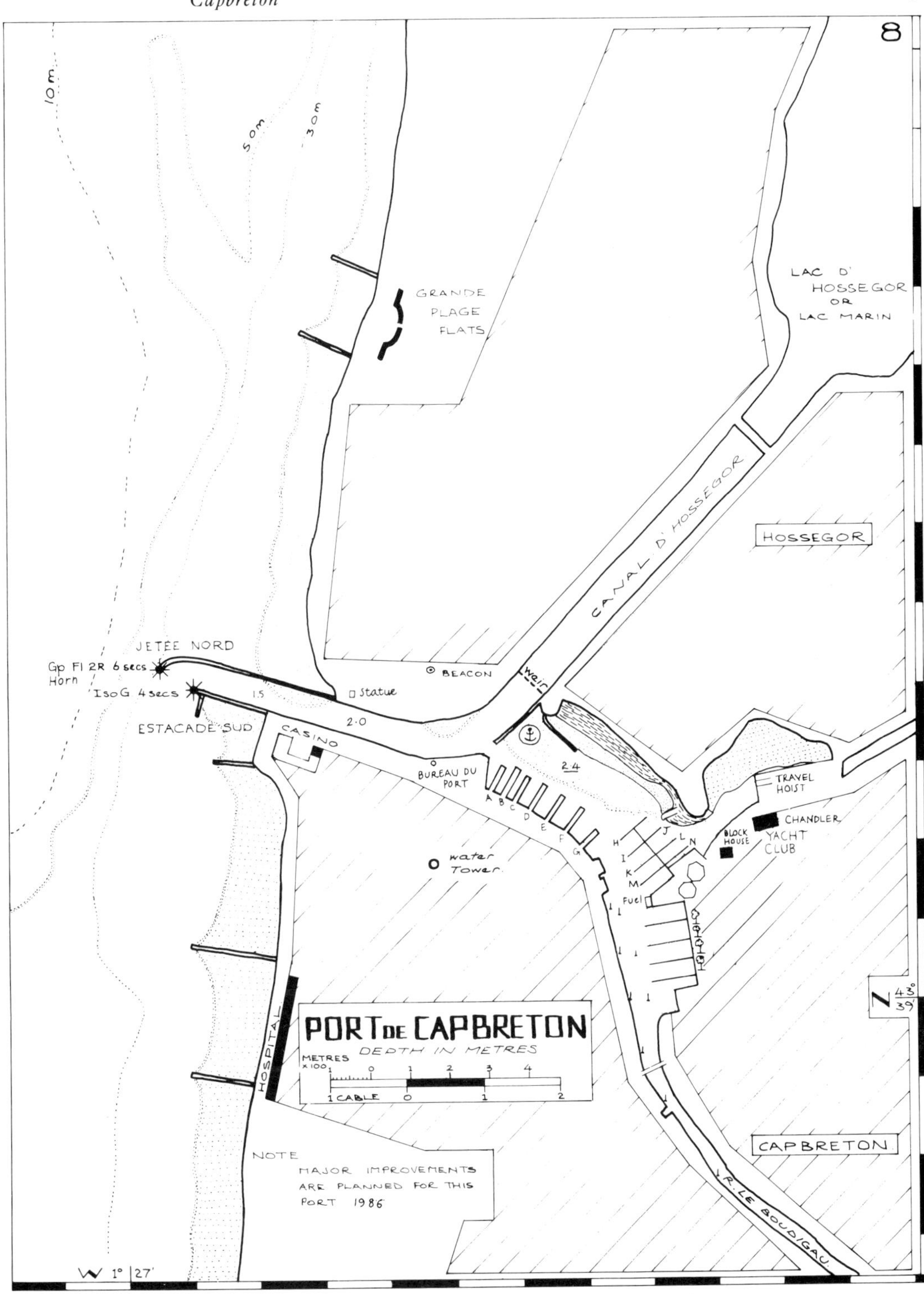
8
10 m
50 m
30 m
GRANDE PLAGE FLATS
LAC D' HOSSEGOR OR LAC MARIN
CANAL D' HOSSEGOR
HOSSEGOR
JETEE NORD
Gp Fl 2R 6 secs Horn
Iso G 4 secs
ESTACADE SUD
1.5
2.0
2.4
Statue
BEACON
Weir
CASINO
BUREAU DU PORT
A B C D E F G
H I J K L M N
Fuel
TRAVEL HOIST
CHANDLER
BLOCK HOUSE
YACHT CLUB
Water Tower
HOSPITAL
PORT DE CAPBRETON
DEPTH IN METRES
METRES x100
1 CABLE
CAPBRETON
R. LE BOUDIGAU
NOTE
MAJOR IMPROVEMENTS ARE PLANNED FOR THIS PORT 1986
W 1° 27'
N 43° 39'

Capbreton—looking south east.

coast consists of low, featureless sand dunes bordered by fir woods and no very conspicuous points, the possible exception being the coastguard building at **Ondres**. **Capbreton** itself is easily identifiable by the large, long, red-roofed hospital and the line of buildings to the N of it, culminating in the *Casino* and the entrance jetty which has a small grey lighthouse on its seaward end.

From N A similar featureless straight coastline exists, of which the **Contis** lighthouse appearing over the treetops, the beacon at **Huchet** consisting of two triangles one above the other and the beacon at **Capbreton**, a black square on a white pyramidal framework, are the only conspicuous points. There are also visible several seaside villages but these are not easy to identify. The houses of **Capbreton** and its jetty are easily identified when approaching the port.

Night *From S* **L'Adour (Le Boucau)** (Q.Fl.W. 14 M.) **Capbreton Estacade Sud** (Iso.G. 4 sec. 9M.) and **Jetée Nord** (Fl. (2) R. 6 sec. 22 M).

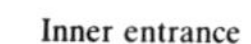

Capbreton – entrance from head of **Estacade Sud** – half tide.

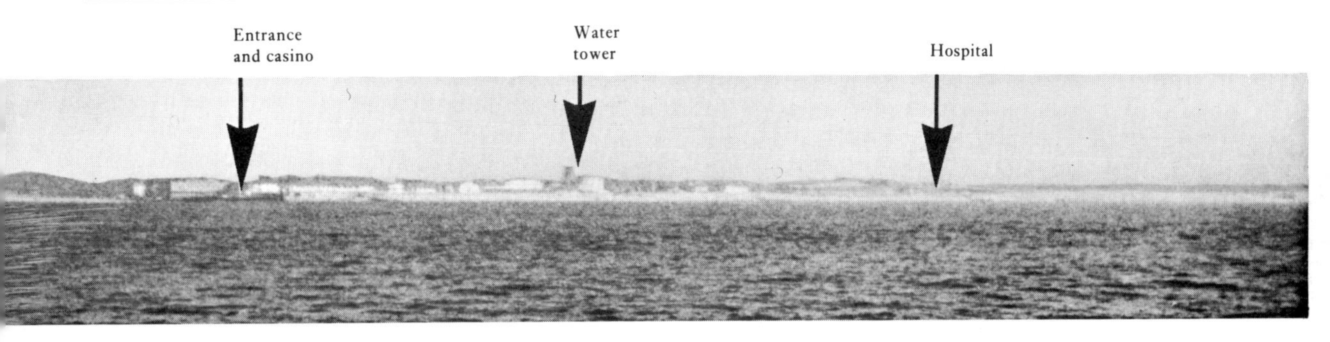

From N **Contis** lighthouse (Fl. (4) W. 25 sec. 23 M.) and **Capbreton Estacade Sud** and **Jetée Nord** are the only lights for night approach.

Entrance
Day

Until dredging is completed entrance should only be attempted under good or fair conditions during the last two hours of the flood and the first hour of the ebb. Do not enter if waves are breaking in the middle of the channel. They do, however, break on each side under most conditions.

Enter leaving the **Estacade Sud**, a wooden pier with a small grey tower at its seaward end, to starboard, and the **Jetée Nord** 15 metres to port. Keep one third of the width of the channel from the **Jetée Nord** until you are level with the Casino, after which you should keep one third from the S quay. Beware of the cross current from the **Canal d'Hossegor** when entering the Port de Plaisance between the two stone jetty heads.

Capbreton – approach to inner entrance – half tide.

Capbreton – Panorama from top of block of flats looking N.

Night Entrance at night is not recommended without a previous visit by day plus knowledge of the conditions at the entrance.

Anchorages

Deep-water anchorages are not currently available but are included in future plans.

Moorings

Deep-water moorings in 2 m (1 fathom) may be available for a limited number of yachts.

Berths

One hundred pontoon berths are available for visitors and more are planned.
Note: It is advisable to contact the club on arrival regarding moorings, berths and anchorages available, owing to changes planned in the near future.

Formalities

It is normally only necessary to report arrival to the Bureau du Port, quai Pompidou (72-21-23) VHF Ch. 9 0600–2200 in season. A visit to Customs, if from a foreign port, should be made with ship's papers, green card and passports to obtain clearance.

Facilities

Water, diesel, petrol	From quay at high water. Also water points on pontoons.
Shops	A good selection of shops at **Hossegor** and **Capbreton** villages.
Repairs	A small yacht yard with its own club—**Club Nautic C.H.S.** (72-05-43)—can undertake limited repairs.
Cranes	30 ton travel hoist.
Yacht club	**Le Yacht Club Landais** had a new clubhouse, bar, restaurant, showers but it was burnt down. A new building is expected.
Showers	At Bureau du Port.
Information	*Syndicat d'Initiative*, **La Plage** and **Pont-Lajos**.
Visits	A dinghy trip at HW up the **Canal d'Hossegor** to **Lac Marin** is rewarding.

9 L'Adour Rivière et Port de Bayonne

Population 41,000 Rating 3-3-2 Position 43°27·5′N 1°28·5′W

General

Four miles of river estuary lead to the city of **Bayonne** where berths alongside in up to 5·5 m (3 fathoms) are available and most of the facilities of a small city can be found. The town is pleasant and attractive and the river, considering the factories lining its bank, is surprisingly clean. There is a modern marina.

The entrance is simple and can be undertaken under all conditions except heavy swell or storm from the SW through W to NW.

The minimum depth on the bar is normally 7 m (4 fathoms). A yacht marina has been built just inside the river mouth.

Warnings

The entrance and channel are narrow for the large commercial craft which use this harbour and they must be given an adequate berth. It may be necessary to stand off the entrance when large craft are entering or leaving.

If there is any sea running, entrance should only be attempted from 4 hours before HW until 1 hour after.

Data

Charts Admiralty No. 1343
French Nos. 175, 6536, 174

Magnetic variation 5°30′W (1984) decreasing by about 5′ a year.

Tidal information French tide tables are available for this port.

	HW		LW		MHWS	MHWN	MLWS	MLWN
Pointe de Grave	0600 1800	000 1200	1000 2200	0400 1600	5·4 m 17·6 ft	4·2 m 13·8 ft	0·9 m 3·0 ft	2·0 m 6·8 ft
Le Boucau (half way to **Bayonne**)	−0·30	−0·40	−0·30	−0·15	−1·1 m −3·4 ft	−0·8 m −2·8 ft	−0·1 m −0·3 ft	−0·5 m −1·6 ft

Currents and streams The current is normally 1 knot N-going off the entrance but can be stronger in winter or after W gales.

The tidal streams at the mouth on the flood run E up to 3–4 knots and the ebb W up to 5 knots, which can be increased to 6–7 knots when the rivers are in spate. At **Bayonne** the flood stream begins at −0050 HW **Pointe de Grave** and the ebb at +0010 HW **Pointe de Grave**.

There is a tide gauge showing height of water above chart datum at the Signal Station. Other gauges up-river show chart datum plus 0·3 m (1 ft).

Lights **Digue du Large head**. Isophase Red 4 seconds, 11 m (36 ft), 5 miles. White square tower, red top.

Le Boucau leading lights. 090° Line Ⓐ.
Front Quick Flashing White 9 m (30 ft), 14 miles. Red day mark on white pylon,

red top. Intensified 086·5°–093·5°.
Rear Quick Flashing White 15 m (49 ft), 14 miles. Red day mark on white pylon, red top. Intesified 086·5°–093·5°.
Jetée Nord head. Group Occulting (2) Red, 12·8 m (42 ft), 9 miles. Red and white mast.
Jetée Sud head. Isophase Green 4 seconds, 9 m (30 ft), 7 miles. White tower, green top. Shows Fixed Red in bad weather.
Entrance leading lights 111·5° Line Ⓑ.
Front Fixed Green 6 m (20 ft), 12 miles. Hut, visible 108°–114°. Movable. Lit only when entrance possible.
Rear Fixed Green, 16 m (52 ft), 12 miles. White tower, black bands. Visible 110°–116°.
Port d'Anglet. Fixed White 4 m (13 ft) 2M.

A series of red and green lights on shore and on buoys mark the river channel. Three pairs of leading lights show the river bend at **Le Boucau** (see chart).

Signal station A 13·4 m (44 ft) white tower with a vertical black stripe, on the S side of the river mouth, displays the following light signals on up and down stream sides.

Lights facing sea and inland	Meaning
Red White Red	Entrance prohibited. Exit permitted.
Green White Red	Entrance and departure prohibited.
Green White Green	Departure prohibited. Entry permitted.
No lights	Entrance and departure permitted.
White light level with lowest light	Yachts may enter or leave irrespective of other signals.

L'Adour Rivière—entrance—signal tower.

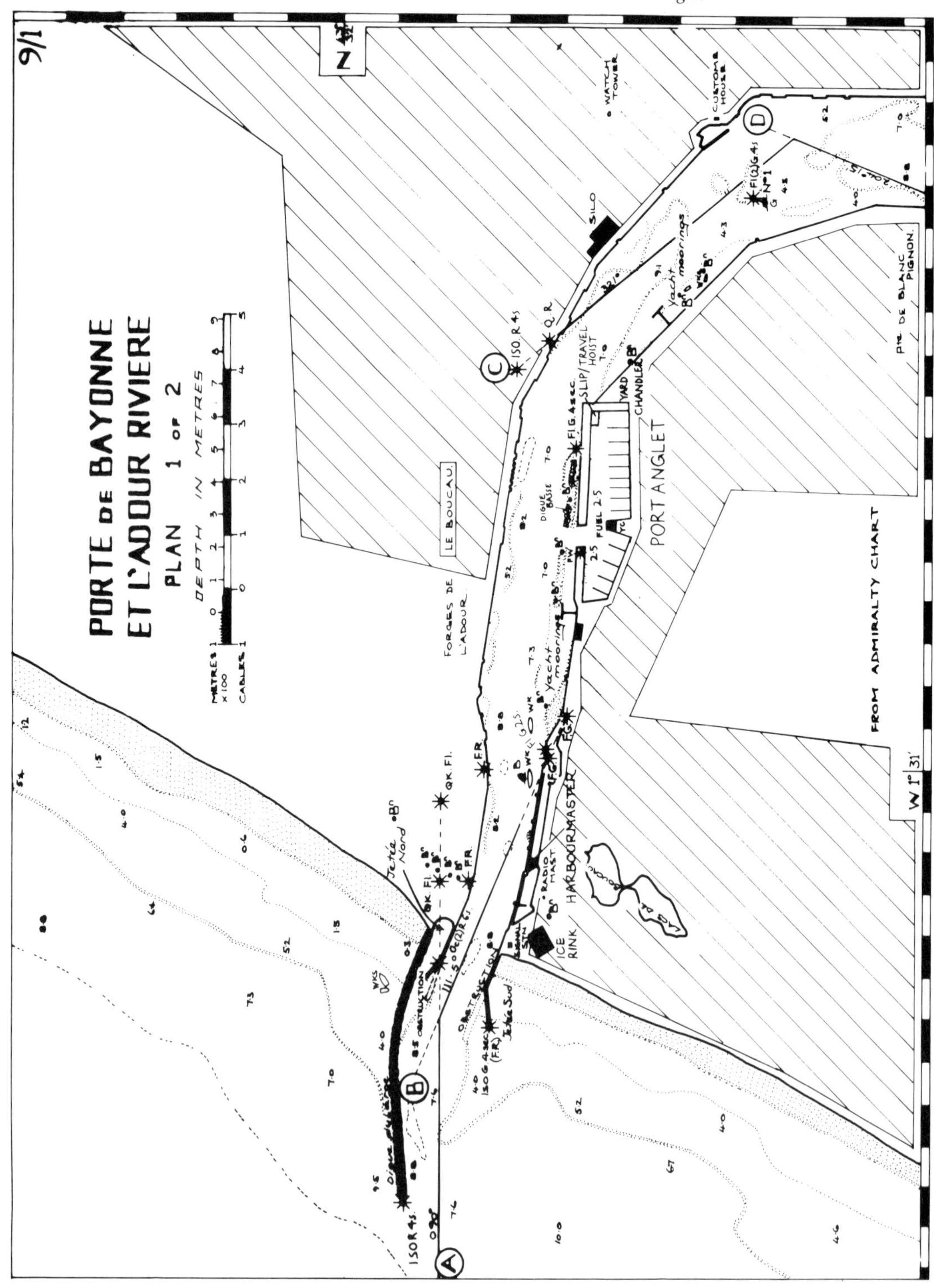
9/1
PORTE DE BAYONNE
ET L'ADOUR RIVIERE
PLAN 1 OF 2
DEPTH IN METRES
METRES x100
CABLES
LE BOUCAU
FORGES DE L'ADOUR
PORT ANGLET
HARBOURMASTER
ICE RINK
RADIO MAST
SILO
WATCH TOWER
CUSTOMS HOUSE
SLIP/TRAVEL HOIST
YARD
CHANDLER
FUEL 2.5
DIGUE BASSE
Yacht moorings
Jetée Nord
Jetée Sud
OBSTRUCTION
PTE DE BLANC PIGNON
FROM ADMIRALTY CHART
W 1° 31'
ISO.R.4s
ISO G 4sec (F.R)
QK.FI.
F.R
Q.R
ISO.R 4s
F.G.
F.I.G. 4sec
Fl(2)G.4s G No1

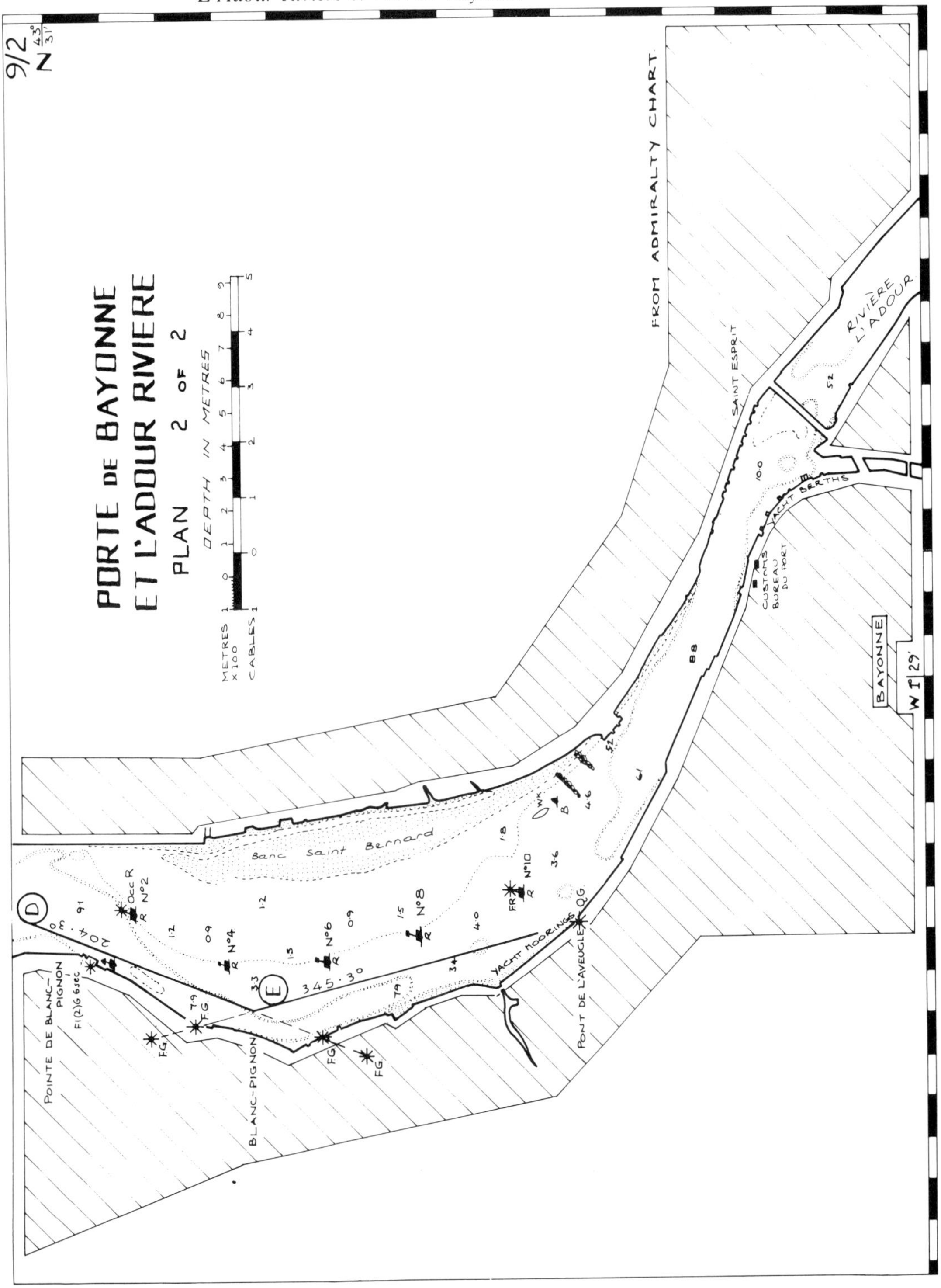

9/2
N 43° 31'
PORTE DE BAYONNE
ET L'ADOUR RIVIERE
PLAN 2 OF 2
DEPTH IN METRES
METRES x 100
CABLES
FROM ADMIRALTY CHART
SAINT ESPRIT
RIVIERE L'ADOUR
YACHT BERTHS
CUSTAMS
BUREAU DU PORT
BAYONNE
W 1° 29'
Banc Saint Bernard
Occ R
Nº2
Nº4
Nº6
Nº8
Nº10
FR
Wk
YACHT MOORINGS
Q.G
PONT DE L'AVEUGLE
345·30
204·0
Pointe de Blanc-Pignon
Fl(2)G 6 sec
BLANC-PIGNON
FG

L'Adour Rivière—opposite signal station—looking upstream.

Radio See page 20 for details of port radio.

Approach

Day *From S* The low coastline is broken by the rocky outcrop of **Pointe Sainte-Martin** with its conspicuous lighthouse. The several skyscrapers of **Biarritz** with the sandy beaches below are also conspicuous. On closer approach to the river entrance the breakwater, signal station tower and some large white sheds are conspicuous, as is the silo at **Le Boucau**.

From N Only the **Ondres** coast guard station, church tower, jetty and the rifle butts one mile N of the entrance break the line of sand dunes from **Capbreton** until **L'Adour** breakwater; the large white sheds and the signal tower at the entrance of the harbour are easily seen from this direction. The silo at **Le Boucau** may also be seen above the trees.

L'Adour Rivière—just below the marina looking up river.

Night *From S* The lighthouse on **Pointe Saint-Martin** (Fl. (2) W. 10 sec. 31 M) with the Aero light at **Biarritz** (Mo L (· – · ·) W. 7·5 sec. 80 m).

From N The light of **Capbreton** (Iso. G. 4 sec. 12 M.) enables an approach to be made to the entrance where a landfall buoy (Fl. (2) W. 6 sec.) will be seen.

Entrance

Day From the vicinity of the landfall buoy, a pillar light buoy marked BA with Red and White vertical stripes, enter the harbour 80 m (90 yards) S of the **Digue du Large** head and follow the curve of the breakwater for half of its length, then proceed to enter the river mouth halfway between **Jetée Nord** and **Sud**. After this follow the centre of the river as marked by series of port and starboard buoys and marks. From **Pointe de Blanc Pignon** onwards keep to the starboard hand bank until the town of **Bayonne** is reached or the marina is entered.

L'Adour Rivière-Bayonne—landfall buoy.

Night

From near the landfall buoy (Fl. W 10 sec) proceed towards the head of the **Digue du Large** (Iso.R. 4 sec. 5 M.) and leave it 80 m (90 yards) to port. Bring the first set of leading lights, Line Ⓐ, into line on 090° (*Front:* Q.Fl. W. 14 M. *Rear:* Q.Fl. W. 14 M. Both intensified on leading line). Follow this line until the light on **Jetée Sud** head (Iso.G. 4 sec. 7 M.) is almost abeam when turn to the second set of leading lights, Line Ⓑ, on 111·5° (*Front:* F.G. 12 M. *Rear:* F.G. 12 M.) and bring them into line. Follow this until abeam of the signal tower when keep to the centre of the river leaving various port and starboard marks and buoys on their correct side. Around the **Le Boucau** curve three sets of front and rear leading lights assist. The first is a rear mark (Iso. R 4 sec and QR) Line Ⓒ, the second a front mark (F.G.) Line Ⓓ, the third a rear mark (F.G.) Line Ⓔ; after this keep the bank close to starboard until the town is reached.

Anchorage

It is possible to anchor out of the main fairway in 2 to 4 m (1 to 2 fathoms) in mud and sand in many places in this estuary, but beware of the very strong currents. Up-river of the yacht club or just down-river of the town on the S bank are best. It is dangerous to anchor near the head of the **Digue du Large**.

Moorings

Moorings are established in the same vicinity as the recommended anchorages (see above) and can be used if not required by their owners. Contact the secretary of the yacht club first.

Berths

Berths in yacht harbour on S bank ½ M. inside entrance, or alongside Nos. 2, 3 or 4 wooden jetties beside the town. Other jetties may be used only with prior permission of the port authorities. These jetties are very narrow and care is needed in berthing due to the strong currents in the area.

Formalities

When secure it is necessary to report to the Marina Office (63-05-45) or *Bureau du Port* (25-00-02), located near the Pilot Station at the entrance. The latest weather reports and the state of the sea on the bar is posted outside the *Bureau du Port* and at the Marina. The *Douane* office is at **Bayonne**.

Facilities

Water Available from water points on the quay at **Bayonne**. Contact the Chamber of Commerce for man with key and pipes. At the yacht harbour it is available from taps on the pontoons.

Electricity 220 V a.c. points on the pontoons

Bayonne—looking up river—half tide.

Diesel, petrol	From garage near bridge at **Bayonne**, and from Total bulk supply pier on S side of **Le Boucau** bend. Bunkering facilities are available at this port and from the yacht marina pontoon.
Shops	There is a very good assortment of shops in the city.
Yacht Club	A yacht club, **Club Nautique de Bayonne**, is located about ½ mile up-river from the entrance on the S bank. Bar, restaurant and showers are available. A hard for hauling out is also there and a pontoon landing with fuel pumps.
Repairs	A number of small yards can handle yacht and engine repairs. Cranes are also available up to 30 tons and a travel hoist of 13 tons.
Visits	A thirteenth century cathedral and chateau are worth a visit, also the Basque museum. Bus service to **Bayonne** from the Marina.

Information Syndicat d'Initiative, 29 Quai du Pont-Mayou.

British Consulate Société Basque Automobile, Allée Paulny, 64100 Bayonne. (Tel: 55-84-12).

10 Saint-Jean de Luz, Ciboure and Socoa

General

A beautiful bay which contains three harbours, **Saint-Jean de Luz**, **Ciboure** and **Socoa**. The latter dries out at LW. There is also a considerable area in the bay where anchorage is possible in 4 m (2 fathoms) or more.

The bay can be entered under all conditions except NW storm. However, the anchorage is very uncomfortable if there is any swell from N or NW.

The town of **Saint-Jean de Luz** is a lively gay place with good facilities to cater for all the requirements of the tourists, of which there are many in August. There is a first class yacht club at **Socoa**.

Warnings

There are a number of outlying banks which must be avoided in heavy weather as they break. In heavy W or NW winds only the pass between **Illarguita** and **Belhara Perdun** shoals should be attempted.

There is a dangerous submerged obstruction in the SE corner of the bay of **Saint-Jean de Luz** (see chart).

Data

Charts Admiralty Nos. 2665, 1343
French Nos. 6526, 177, 174

Magnetic variation 5°30′W (1984) decreasing by 5′ each year.

Tidal information French tide tables are available for this port.

	HW		LW		MHWS	MHWN	MLWS	MLWN
Pointe de Grave	0600 1800	0000 1200	1000 2200	0400 1600	5·4 m 17·6 ft	4·2 m 13·8 ft	0·9 m 3·0 ft	2·0 m 6·8 ft
Socoa	−0·30	−0·40	−0·35	−0·10	−1·2 m −3·7 ft	−1·0 m −3·3 ft	−0·5 m −1·7 ft	−0·7 m −2·3 ft

Currents and streams A tide gauge stands at the head of the E breakwater of **Socoa** harbour. The flood stream enters the E entrance to the bay and follows the bay edge to the **Rivière Nivelle**. The ebb stream runs from this river out of the W entrance. In the **Rade de Socoa** the flood stream is ½ knot N-going and the ebb 1 knot N-going. The ebb stream in the river is very strong when the river is in spate. The flood stream begins at HW −0600 **Pointe de Grave** and the ebb at HW **Pointe de Grave**.

Lights **Pointe Sainte-Barbe leading lights** 101° Line Ⓑ.
Front Group Occulting (3+1) Red, 12 seconds, 29 m (95 ft), 16 miles. White masonry hut. Intensified 095°–107°.

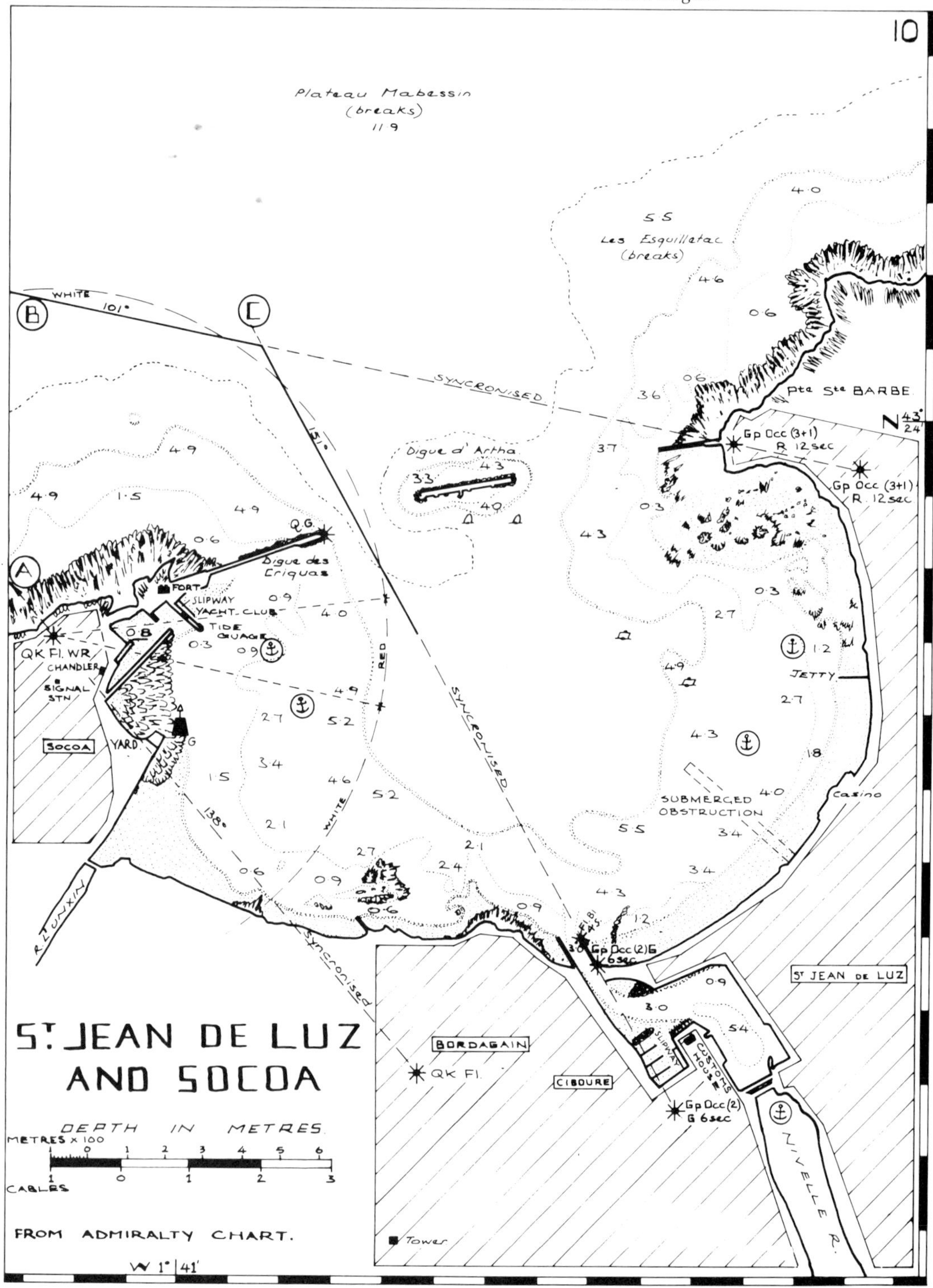
10
Plateau Mabessin
(breaks)
11.9
Les Esquillatac
(breaks)
WHITE
101°
SYNCRONISED
Pte Ste BARBE
Digue d'Artha
Gp Occ (3+1)
R 12sec
Q.G.
Digue des Criquas
FORT
SLIPWAY
YACHT CLUB
TIDE GUAGE
QK Fl. WR
CHANDLER
SIGNAL STN
SOCOA
YARD
JETTY
SUBMERGED OBSTRUCTION
Casino
R. UNXIN
WHITE
RED
Gp Occ (2) G
6sec
ST JEAN DE LUZ
BORDAGAIN
QK Fl
CIBOURE
SLIPWAY
CUSTOMS HOUSE
Gp Occ (2)
G 6sec
NIVELLE R.
Tower
ST. JEAN DE LUZ
AND SOCOA
DEPTH IN METRES
METRES x 100
CABLES
FROM ADMIRALTY CHART.
W 1° 41'
N 43° 24'

Rear Red synchronised with above 47 m (154 ft), 16 miles. White square tower, black top. Intensified 095°–107°.
Saint-Jean de Luz. Inner harbour leading lights 151° Line Ⓒ.
Front Group Occulting 2 Green, 6 seconds, 18 m (59 ft), 14 miles. White square tower with red vertical stripe. Intensified 148·5°–153·5°.
Rear Green synchronsied with above, 27 m (88 ft), 14 miles. White square tower, green vertical stripe. Intensified 148·5°–153·5°.
Le Socoa/Bordagain leading lights 138° Line Ⓐ.
Front **Le Socoa** Quick Flashing White, Red sectors, 36 m (118 ft) White 12, Red 8 miles. White square tower, black vertical stripe. Red 264°–282°. White 282°–264°. Signal station.
Rear White synchronised with above, 67 m (220 ft), 20 miles. Black and white square on metal framework tower. Intensified 135·5°–140·5°.
Digue des Criquas head. Quick Flashing Green 11 m (30 ft), 9 miles. Grey Square tower, Unwatched.
Finger Mole Head. Fl.Bl. 4 sec. 3 m (10 ft) 5 M. white pillar.

Signal station There is a signal station near **Le Socoa** lighthouse to which messages can be sent by International Code of Flag Signals.

Approaches

From S The coast consists of the wide **Rade de Higuer** with sandy beaches backed by the buildings of the towns of **Hendaye Plage** and **Fuenterrabia**. **Pointe Sainte-Anne** is conspicuous as is the **Chateau d'Abbadie** on it. The cliffs between this point and **Saint-Jean de Luz** are low and of whitish hue.

From N The coast consists of low hills and cliffs from **Pointe Saint-Martin**, which is a conspicuous rocky headland with the **Biarritz** lighthouse on it, to **Pointe Sainte-Barbe**. To the N of this part of the coast the shore is lined with low sand dunes. Behind **Saint-Jean de Luz** is a high conical mountain, **La Rhune**, which has a radio tower and buildings on its summit. In clear weather it is very conspicuous.

Day *From NE* In good conditions only, follow the coast at about 1 mile distance, inside the shoal patches and just outside the 20 m (10 fathoms) contour, until the

Saint-Jean de Luz—Le Socoa—Bordagain leading lights—line Ⓐ.

Saint-Jean de Luz—Pointe Sainte-Barbe—leading lights—line Ⓑ.

Tour de Bordagain (a tall stone tower on top of a hill with green trees around it) bears 193°. Follow this course of 193° and enter by the E entrance. Do not cut this corner owing to **Les Esquilletac** shoal.

From NW Approach in all weathers between **Illarguita** and **Belhara Perdun** shoals keeping **Tour de Bordagain** (see above) just S of the **Le Socoa** lighthouse (a white square tower with a black vertical stripe) on 138° until the rear mark (a latticework tower with a black and white square on it) can be seen. Now bring this into line with **Le Socoa** lighthouse, Line Ⓐ, and follow this course until the leading marks on **Pointe Sainte-Barbe**, Line Ⓑ, are in line, and then proceed as detailed in *approach*, *W* below.

From W Approach in normal weather only between **Belhara Perdun** shoal and **Les Briquets** rocks. Bring the leading marks on **Pointe Sainte-Barbe** into line on 101°, Line Ⓑ (*Front:* White square building with a white triangle on top; *Rear:* a similar square white building with a black triangular top). Stay on this course until

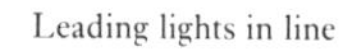

Saint-Jean de Luz—inner harbour leading lights—line Ⓒ.

the leading marks alongside the entrance to **Saint-Jean de Luz** inner harbour, Line Ⓒ, are in line on 151° (*Front:* a tall white tower with a red vertical stripe; *Rear:* a similar taller tower with a green vertical stripe). Follow this line through the W entrance.

Night In the distance approach **Cabo Higuer** (L.Fl. (2) W. 60 sec. 16 M.) and **Pointe Sainte-Martin** (Fl. (2) W. 10 sec. 31 M.) will assist.

From NW Bring the leading lights **Le Socoa/Bordagain** into line on 138°, Line Ⓐ (*Front:* Q.W.R., W. 282°–264°, R. 264°–282°, 12/8 M. synchronised with *Rear:* Q. W. 20 M. Intensified 135°–140·5°). Keep in the white intensified sector until the leading lights of **Pointe Sainte-Barbe** are in line, Line Ⓑ, then proceed as below.

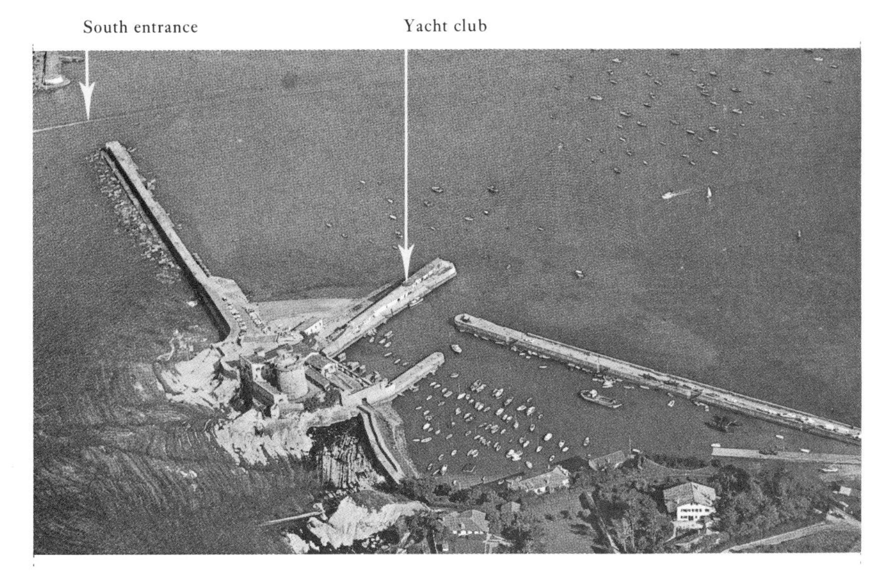

Saint-Jean de Luz—Socoa harbour and anchorage. *Photo: L. Chatagneau*

From W Bring the leading lights on **Pointe Sainte-Barbe** into line on 101°, Line Ⓑ (*Front:* Oc. (3+1) R. 12 sec. 16 M. Intensified 095°–107°; *Rear:* Synchronised with front, Oc. (3+1) R. 16 M. Intensified 095°–107°). Keep in intensified sector until the **Saint-Jean de Luz** inner harbour lights are in line on 151°, Line Ⓒ, (*Front:* Oc. (2) G. 6 sec. 14 M. Intensified 148·5°–153·5°. *Rear:* Synchronised with front, Oc. (2) G. 6 sec. 14 M. Intensified 148·5°–153·5°). Follow these lights into the W entrance leaving the head of **Digue des Criquas** (Q.Fl.G. 9 M.) to port.

Entrance

Day The anchorage and harbour at **Socoa** are visible to starboard on entering the bay; if there is sufficient water proceed straight towards the entrance, otherwise go towards the anchorage. The entrance to **Saint-Jean de Luz** and **Ciboure** is between two rocky training walls just SW of the leading marks, Line Ⓒ. Enter in mid-channel, which has been dredged recently to 3 m (1·5 fathoms). **Ciboure** yacht harbour lies ahead. If there is a heavy swell in the bay enter only at HW as the bar at the mouth of the harbour breaks.

Night Follow the **Saint-Jean de Luz** inner harbour lights, Line ©, until in the red sector of **Le Socoa** light when turn towards it and approach **Socoa** anchorage and harbour.
Or: **Saint-Jean de Luz** and **Ciboure** inner harbours, continue on the original line passing 20 m (22 yards) SW of Fl.Bl. 4 sec. and the front light tower at the entrance.

Anchorage The normal yacht anchorage is off **Socoa** between the harbour entrance and a point about 2 cables SSE, according to draft of the craft, in sand over rock. Care must be taken to avoid a patch of rock due S of the harbour entrance. In heavy weather a pair of anchors is advised as the holding is not too firm. Landing can be made just inside **Socoa** harbour near the fuel pumps on the starboard side.

An alternative anchorage is in the SE corner of the bay. There is a landing jetty on the E side of the bay. Yachts with lowering masts may proceed under two bridges up *La Nivelle* river to anchor.

Moorings Some private yacht buoys are laid and might be available. Contact the yacht club.

Berths

Drying berths are possible in the harbour at **Socoa**. Contact the yacht club officials first. **Ciboure** yacht harbour has pontoons. 3 places for visitors (2·5 m).

Berths alongside the fishing craft in the **Saint-Jean de Luz** inner harbour may be possible in up to 4 m (2 fathoms). It all depends on the fisherman chosen but it is well worth trying if the swell is bad in the bay. As with most fishing ports it is smelly and the quay walls are covered with oil.

Formalities

Normal requirements by Customs Bureau at Port de Ciboure (26-34-04) who will want to see the yacht's documents and the crew's passports.

Facilities

Socoa

Water, diesel, petrol and outboard fuel from the yacht club on inner side of NE breakwater just inside harbour. Attendant available about 2 hours either side of HW. Also water from pontoons.

Shops Adequate shops in village for food, etc., also chandlery shops with yacht fittings.

Repair Good yacht repair facilities, a crane and a slipway inside habour.

Yacht club The **Yacht Club Basque** is a lively concern which welcomes visitors. Showers, restaurant and bar are available and every assistance is offered to foreign yachtsmen (26-18-31).

	Visits	Bus every hour into **Saint-Jean de Luz**. The view from the top of the **Tour de Bordagain** is worth the climb.
	Beach	An excellent sandy beach nearby.
Saint-Jean de Luz and Ciboure	*Water*	From quay near Customs house and pontoons.
	Electricity	220V a.c. on pontoons.
	Petrol	From N corner of harbour.
	Shops	Many and varied to NE of port.
	Chandlery	On quay beside harbour.
	Beaches	Superb sandy beaches all round the bay.
	Hard	A good hard in S corner of the harbour.
	Casino	On sea front.
	Hotels, restaurants, cafés	Many of all classes.
	Information	*Syndicat d'Initiative, Place Maréchal-Foche.*

11 Rada de Higuer or Baie de Fontarabie

Population 8,600 Rating 3-3/3-3 Position 43°22′N 1°46·9′W

General

This interesting bay, estuary, harbour and river lies between France and Spain and consequently a large part of its waters are international, the boundaries of which are very complex.

There is one very small attractive fishing harbour of **Gurutzeaundi**, with easy approach and entrance, and there are a number of protected and secure anchorages in up to 2·2 m (1·25 fathoms) near the towns of **Fuenterrabia** in Spain and **Hendaye** in France. These towns lie on the **Río Bidasoa**, which can be entered in normal weather during the top half of the tide. Under conditions of heavy swell or storm entry of this river should not be attempted. Normal facilities only are available at these two towns.

Warnings

Due to the new training walls and considerable dredging which is still taking place, the channel may be different to that shown on the charts.

Les Briquets, off **Pointe Sainte-Anne**, are dangerous and care should be taken to give them a wide berth.

Data

Charts

Admiralty Nos. 2665, 1343
Spanish No. 3912
French Nos. 6556, 177, 174

Magnetic variation 5°30′W (1984) decreasing by about 5′ a year.

Tidal information

	HW		LW		MHWS	MHWN	MLWS	MLWN
Pointe de Grave	0600 1800	0000 1200	1000 2200	0400 1600	5·4 m 17·6 ft	4·2 m 13·8 ft	0·9 m 3·0 ft	2·0 m 6·8 ft
Rade de Higuer	−0·30	−0·35	−0·28	0·00	−1·1 m −3·7 ft	−1·1 m −3·6 ft	−0·5 m −1·8 ft	−0·6 m −2·0 ft

Streams and currents in the **Río Bidasoa** are strong, especially on the ebb at spring tides near the mouth of the river.

Lights

Cabo Higuer. Group Long Flashing (2) White, 60 seconds, 63 m (207 ft), 16 miles. White stone tower and lantern. Visible 072°–340°. Aeromarine light.

Puerto Gurutzeaundi

Dique Norte head. Fixed Green, 8·2 m (27 ft), 4 miles. Mast.

Dique Norte Extension. Flashing Green 2 seconds 10 m (33 ft), 4 miles, Masonry structure.

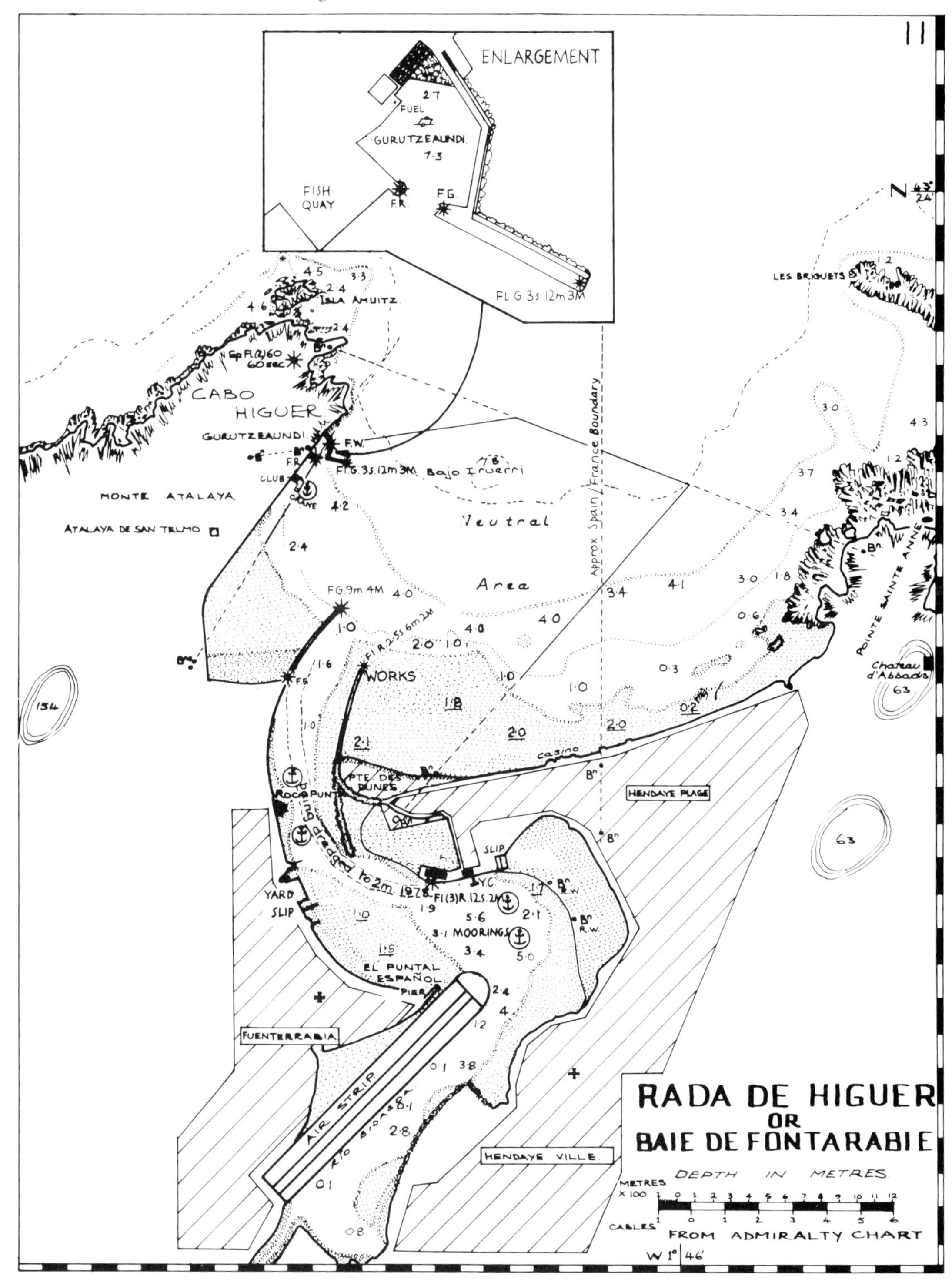
11
ENLARGEMENT
FUEL
GURUTZEAUNDI
FISH QUAY
F.R.
F.G.
FL G 3s 12m 3M
ISLA AMUITZ
CABO HIGUER
GURUTZEAUNDI
F.W.
CLUB
F.G. 3s. 12m 3M
Bajo Iruerri
MONTE ATALAYA
ATALAYA DE SAN TELMO
Neutral Area
Approx Spain / France Boundary
LES BRIQUETS
POINTE SAINTE ANNE
Chateau d'Abbadia
F.G. 9m 4M
Fl.R. 2.5s 6m 2M
WORKS
casino
PTE DES DUNES
HENDAYE PLAGE
ROCA PUNTA
dredged to 2m. 1978
SLIP
YC
Fl (3) R. 12s. 2M
YARD
SLIP
MOORINGS
EL PUNTAL ESPAÑOL PIER
FUENTERRABIA
AIR STRIP
RIO BIDASOA
HENDAYE VILLE
RADA DE HIGUER
OR
BAIE DE FONTARABIE
DEPTH IN METRES
METRES x 100
CABLES
FROM ADMIRALTY CHART
N 43° 24'
W 1° 46'

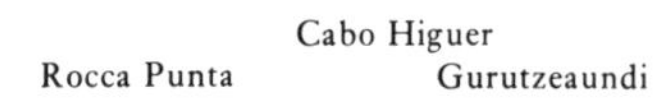

Funeterrabia and **Río Bidasoa**. *Photo: Alarde*

Dique Sur Head. Fixed Red, 8 m (26 ft), 4 miles. Mast.
Fuenterrabia
Head of training wall from Roca Punta. Fixed Green, 9·5 m (31 ft). 4 miles. Mast. Fixed Green on Training Wall.
Hendaye
Training wall head. Flashing Red 2·5 sec, 6 m (20 ft), 2 miles. Red support.
La Floride Head. Group Flashing (3) Red 12 sec 4 m (13 ft) 2 miles. Red support.

Approaches

Day *From W* The high sloping cliffs gradually reduce in height towards **Cabo Higuer**

Río Bidasoa—entrance—looking south west—high water.

Río Bidasoa—from Roca Punta looking south east—high water.

and are broken in several places. **Cabo Higuer** is high inland and slopes gently to the sea. The lighthouse on it is conspicuous as is the large building nearby.

From E The French coast is low and is backed by a high pyramid-shaped mountain **La Rhune** with radio tower and buildings on the top. **Pointe Sainte-Anne** is conspicuous as is the chateau on it. The houses of **Higuer** stand out clearly above a wide sandy beach and the town of **Fuenterrabia** on its hill shows up well in the background.

Night The lights of **Cabo La Plata (Pasajes)** (Iso.W. 2 sec. 15 M.), **Cabo Higuer** (Fl. (2) W. 60 sec. 16 M) and **Sainte-Barbe (Saint-Jean de Luz)** (Oc. (3+1) R. 12 sec. 16 M.) enable night approach to the bay to be made.

Entrance

Day **Puerto Gurutzeaundi** can be approached from 040° to 220° but in any swell **Bajo Iruarri** should be avoided. Keep at least 22 m (25 yards) away from the SE corner of the entrance owing to underwater obstructions.

Río Bidasoa should be approached from NE avoiding **Bajo Iruarri** in any heavy weather. Enter about 22 m (25 yards) off the W rocky training wall head and

Río Bidasoa—from buoy—looking east—high water.

Panorama of **Río Bidasoa** taken from Héndaye Plage.

keep this distance until abreast the end of this wall, when move out to 45 m (49 yards). When level with a large wall with a series of bas relief sculpture on it near **Roca Punta**, alter course to port towards some large fishing boat moorings with their dinghies or the actual fishing boats on them. Pass near these and about 45 m (49 yards) S of a large concrete conical beacon which leans to one side. Then pass near a small black buoy and towards the anchored yachts, off **Hendaye Plage**.

Night The entrance to **Puerto Gurutzeaundi** is possible at night using the **Dique Norte head** (F.G. 4 M.) extension (Fl.G 3 sec 3 M) and **Dique Sur Head** (F.R.)
The entrance to **Río Bidasoa** is not recommended at night without a prior daylight visit.

Anchorages

It is possible to anchor in the following places.
1–2 cables S of **Puerto Gurutzeaundi** in 2·5 m (1·5 fathoms).
In the river N and SW of **Roca Punta** near large fishing craft in 2·5 m (1·5 fathoms) mud and sand.
In the yacht anchorage 1 cable SW of landing point at **Hendaye Plage** in 3·6 m (2 fathoms) sand.
Inside **Puerto Gurutzeaundi** near middle of harbour.

Gurutzeaundi—harbour entrance—looking north west.

Moorings

There are moorings for fishing craft in **Puerto Gurutzeaundi** which can be used if available.

Formalities

As this area is the boundary between Spain and France the Customs officials are very active and several visits may be paid. At **Hendaye Plage** it is advisable to report to the *Douane* (20-00-35) in his office next to the yacht club on arrival.

Facilities

Puerto Gurutzeaundi	*Water*	From spring on N side of harbour.
	Diesel	From pump on W side of harbour.
	Shops, etc.	Nil.
Fuenterrabia	*Water*	From fish auction market or ice factory near landing jetty.

Gurutzeaundi—harbour—looking south.

	Shops	Adequate shops on road parallel to sea front.
	Cafés, hotels, etc.	Some rather poor hotels and restaurants in town, but a Parador hotel in the old castle on top of the hill is good.
	Visits	Eleventh century church on top of hill. Ancient towers and medieval stronghold walls still in existence, also **Hostal del Jaizquibel** and **San Telmo Castle** a few miles away.
	Beaches	Fine sandy beach.
Hendaye Plage	*Water*	From quay.
	Diesel	From quay.
	Petrol	Near yacht club.
	Shops	Good shops, cafés, restaurants in centre of town about 1–2 km away. Chandlers on quay.
	Yacht club	**Club Maritime d'Hendaye** (20-03-02) welcomes visiting yachtsmen and offers its full co-operation and help. The club house, which has showers, is at the head of the landing stage.
	Visits	A visit to **Hendaye Ville**, the old town, is worth while.
	Information	*Syndicat d'Initiative, Rue des Aubépines.*
	Future developments	A yacht harbour with pontoons is being developed at **Hendaye** and another in the NE corner of the **Baie de Chingoudy**.

Chapter 3

The coast between Cabo Higuer and Cabo Mayor

The coast between Cabo Higuer and Cabo Mayor

12 General description

Costa de la Plata, Cornisa Cantabrica and the Country of the Basques

Guipuzcoa, Vizcaya, Santander

General

This part of the coast is remarkable for the considerable number of both small and large mountains close to the seaboard increasing in elevation inland to a series of mountain ranges, the peaks of which are snow covered for most of the year and can be seen far out to sea.

The coastline in general is rocky and barren and has steep cliffs falling straight into deep water. There are virtually no outlying dangers. Ports and harbours are to be found in shallow breaks in the coast or at the mouths of the various rivers.

The only ports of refuge in stormy weather from the N are **Pasajes**, **Bilbao** and **Santander**. There are many other small harbours which can be entered in normal conditions.

Warnings

In strong winds from the SW, W and NW powerful currents up to 5 knots set towards the French coast, for which allowance should be made. Most of the villages and ports tip their rubbish over the cliffs and set it alight, the smoke from which is noticeable by day and the fires by night. The coast road runs along the sea and cliff edge and at night the lights of cars may be seen. These two sources of light could be confused with the lights of lighthouses. By day the flat slate surfaces on some of the cliffs reflect the sun when wet.

The coast between **Cabo Machichaco** and **Cabo Villano**, 8·5 miles further W, can have very steep and broken seas off it, due to an uneven bottom. It is advisable to keep 2 to 3 miles off the coast.

Isla San Antón—the Guetaria "mouse"—from the west.

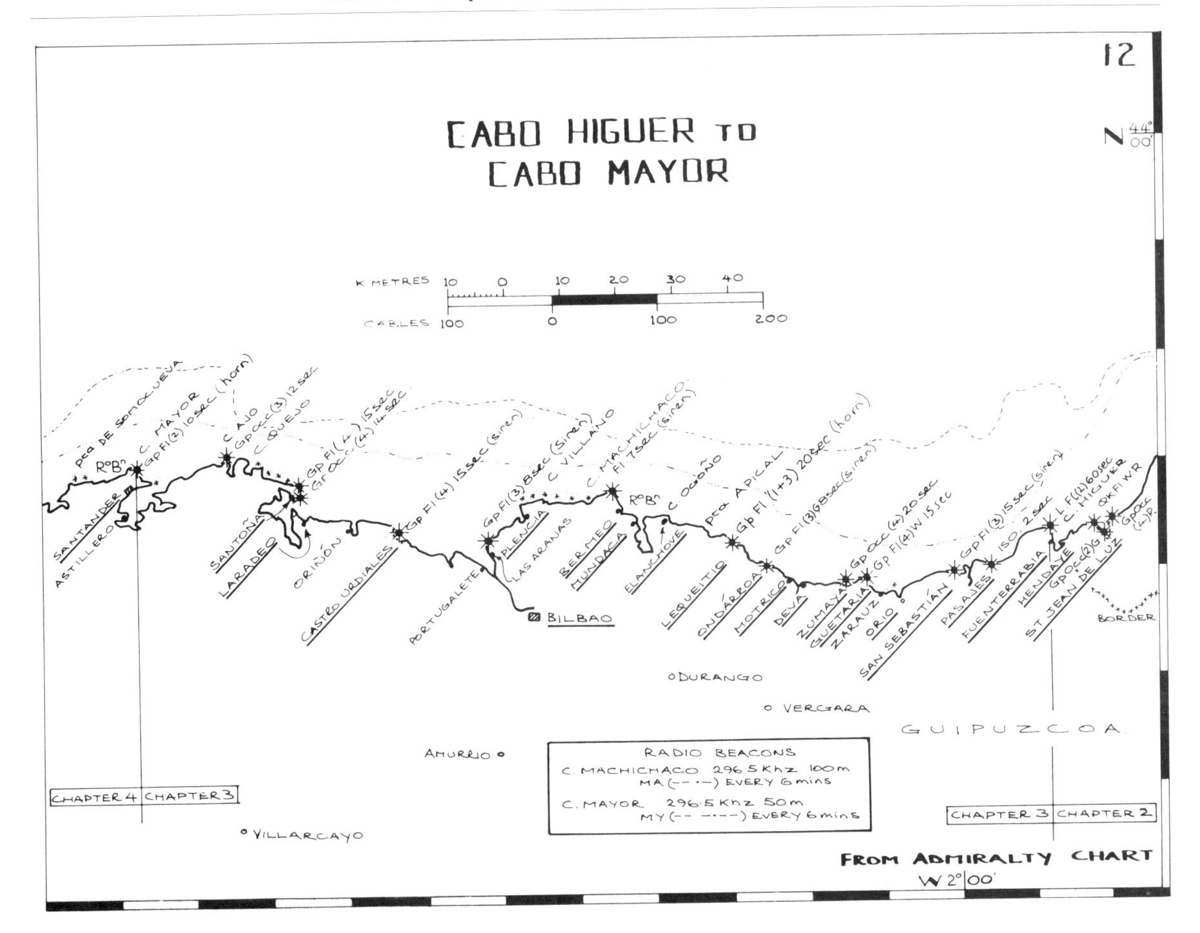

Data

Charts

Admiralty	Nos.	2665, 2925
Spanish	Nos.	127, 128, 940, 941, 942, 943, 944, 39
French	Nos.	4991, 177, 174

Currents and streams Winds from the W quarter set up strong West going currents, which flow N on meeting the French coast. Winds from the E set up weak currents towards the W. These currents are usually stronger away from the coast. Tidal streams are only noticeable in narrow waters near the coast and around points.

Major lights **Cabo Higuer (Fuenterrabia)**. Group Long Flashing (2) White, 60 seconds, 63 m (207 ft), 16 miles. White stone tower and lantern visible 072°–340°. Aero marine light.

Cabo La Plata (Pasajes). Iso.W. 2 sec. 151 m (496 ft), 16 miles visible 285°–250°. White castellated building. 6 Fixed Red lights on radio mast 1 mile WSW.

Igueldo Sebastián) Group Flashing (2+1) White, 15 seconds, 132 m (430 ft), 26 miles. White round tower on N face of building.

Isla San Antón—looking south.

Isla de San Antón (Guetaria). Group Flashing (4) White, 15 seconds, 91 m (295 ft), 21 miles. White 8-sided tower on W face of house. Visible 061°–331°.
Zumaya. Group Occulting (1+3) White, 20 seconds, 39 m (128 ft), 12 miles. Grey 8-sided tower, white cupola and dwelling. Port signals.
NE breakwater (Ondárroa). Group Flashing (3) White, 8 seconds, 13 m (43 ft), 12 miles. Grey conical brick tower. Fog Siren 3, 20 seconds, 368 m (1210 ft) to NW of lighthouse.

Punta de Santa Catalina and lighthouse. Note stacks of wood on cliff top.

Ría de Ea.

Punta de Santa Cataline (Lequeitio). Group Flashing (1+3) W. 20 seconds, 44 m (144 ft), 17 miles. Grey conical tower on 8-sided base. Fog Horn Morse L (· – · ·), 20 seconds.
Cabo Machichaco (**Bermeo**). Flashing White, 7 seconds, 120 m (395 ft), 24 miles. Stone tower on NW corner of grey building, aluminium lantern. Fog Siren 2, 60 seconds. Radiobeacon.
Punta Galea (**Bilbao**). Group Flashing (3) White, 8 seconds, 82 m (269 ft), 19 miles. Stone tower with dwelling, red and white cupola. Visible 011°–227°. Fog Siren 3, 40 seconds, 194 m (640 ft) NNW of lighthouse.
Castillo de Santa Ana (**Castro Urdiales**). Group Flashing (4) White, 15 seconds, 47 m (152 ft), 17 miles. White conical tower on old fortress. Fog Siren Morse C (– · – ·) 60 seconds. *Note:* do not confuse with **Punta Pescador** below.
Punta Pescador (**Santoña**). Group Flashing (3+1) White, 15 seconds, 37 m (122 ft), 17 miles. Conical grey stone tower. *Note:* do not confuse with **Castillo de Santa Ana** above.
Punta del Caballo. Group Occulting (4) White, 14 seconds, 24 m (79 ft), 12 miles. Grey-blue conical stone tower.
Cabo Ajo. Group Occulting (3) White, 12 seconds, 69 m (227 ft), 13 miles. Grey round tower, aluminium cupola, in front of grey dwelling with red roof.
Cabo Mayor (**Santander**). Group Flashing (2) White, 10 seconds, 89 m (291 ft), 21 miles. White tower, first story 8-sided, remainder round. Fog Horn (2), 40 seconds. Radiobeacon.

Life saving The following ports maintain lifeboats and/or line throwing apparatus: **San Sebastián**, **Ondárroa**, **Santurce**, **Bilbao** and **Portugalete**, **Castro Urdiales**, **Santander**, **Lequeitio.**

Cabo Ogono looking south west.

Radio

Radiobeacons The radiobeacons in this area are listed below; for other beacon outside this area see page 16.

Station	Frequency kHz	Range miles	Call sign	Period minutes	Group remarks
Cap Ferret lighthouse	296·5	100	FT (· · – · / –)	6	Grouped
Cabo Machichaco lighthouse	296·5	100	MA (– – / · –)	6	Grouped
Cabo Mayor lighthouse	296·5	50	MY (– – / – · – –)	6	Grouped
Bilbao air beacon 43°19′34″N 2°58′30″W	370	20	BLO (– · · · / · – · · / – – –)	Continuous	
San Sebastian (Fuenterrabia) 43°23′15″N 1°47′39″W	328	0·2 kW	HIG (· · · · / · · / – – ·)		Continuous
Santander 43°28′N 03°46′W	338	0·3 kW	SNR (· · · / – · / · – ·)		Day only

Coast, port and pilot radio stations, weather and navigational messages, see page 18–20.

Cabo Machichaco looking south west.

Signal stations **Bilbao** and **Santander** have signal stations. Messages by International Code of Flag Signals may be used.

Consul British Consul offices at **Bilbao**.

Ensenada de Isla.

Cabo Quejo—looking east—note TV tower.

Puerto de Arminza—looking west.

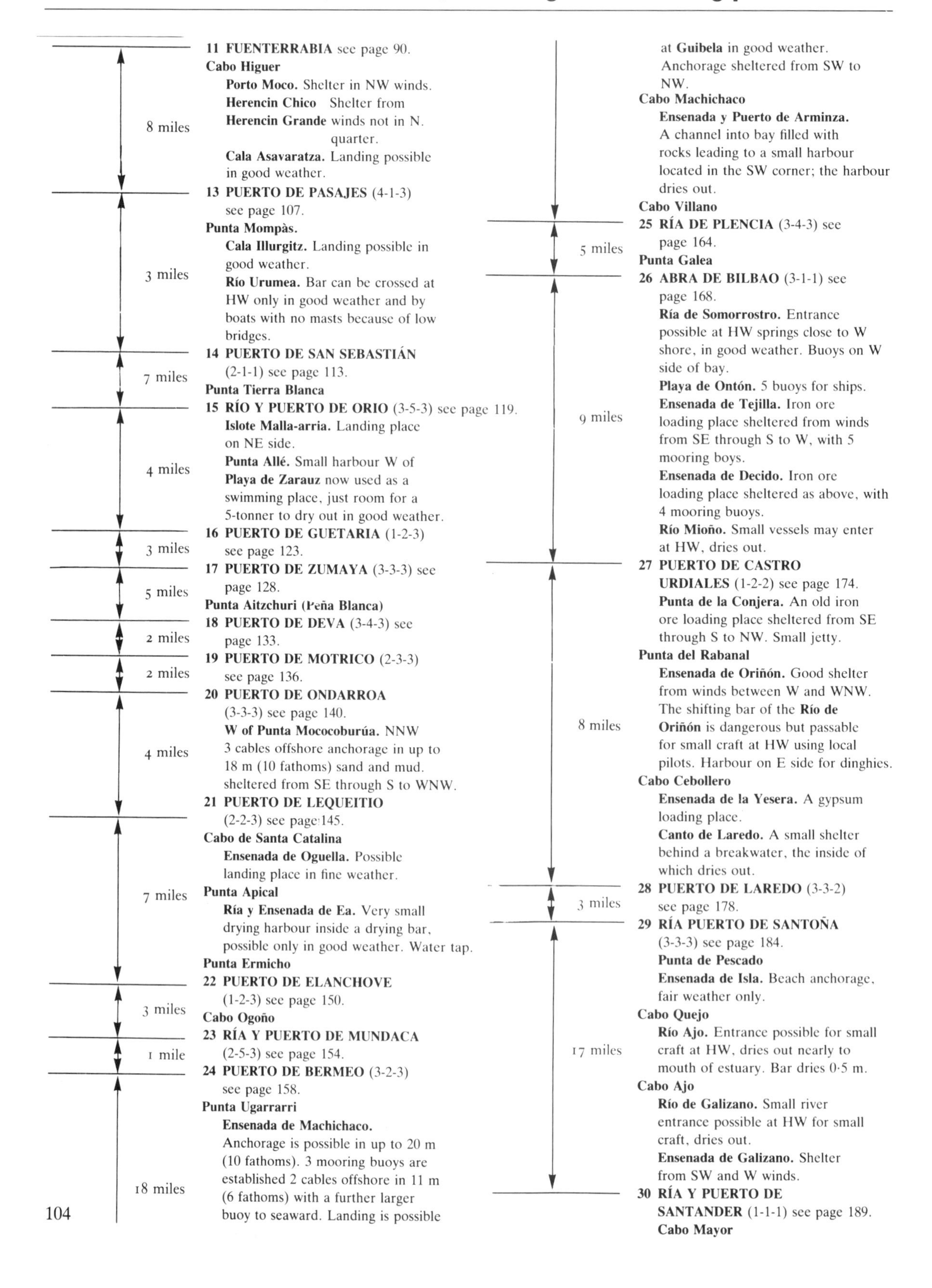

8 miles

11 FUENTERRABIA see page 90.

Cabo Higuer

Porto Moco. Shelter in NW winds.

Herencin Chico Shelter from
Herencin Grande winds not in N. quarter.

Cala Asavaratza. Landing possible in good weather.

3 miles

13 PUERTO DE PASAJES (4-1-3) see page 107.

Punta Mompàs.

Cala Illurgitz. Landing possible in good weather.

Río Urumea. Bar can be crossed at HW only in good weather and by boats with no masts because of low bridges.

7 miles

14 PUERTO DE SAN SEBASTIÁN (2-1-1) see page 113.

Punta Tierra Blanca

4 miles

15 RÍO Y PUERTO DE ORIO (3-5-3) see page 119.

Islote Malla-arria. Landing place on NE side.

Punta Allé. Small harbour W of **Playa de Zarauz** now used as a swimming place, just room for a 5-tonner to dry out in good weather.

3 miles

16 PUERTO DE GUETARIA (1-2-3) see page 123.

5 miles

17 PUERTO DE ZUMAYA (3-3-3) see page 128.

Punta Aitzchuri (Peña Blanca)

2 miles

18 PUERTO DE DEVA (3-4-3) see page 133.

2 miles

19 PUERTO DE MOTRICO (2-3-3) see page 136.

4 miles

20 PUERTO DE ONDARROA (3-3-3) see page 140.

W of Punta Mococoburúa. NNW 3 cables offshore anchorage in up to 18 m (10 fathoms) sand and mud. sheltered from SE through S to WNW.

7 miles

21 PUERTO DE LEQUEITIO (2-2-3) see page 145.

Cabo de Santa Catalina

Ensenada de Oguella. Possible landing place in fine weather.

Punta Apical

Ría y Ensenada de Ea. Very small drying harbour inside a drying bar, possible only in good weather. Water tap.

Punta Ermicho

3 miles

22 PUERTO DE ELANCHOVE (1-2-3) see page 150.

Cabo Ogoño

1 mile

23 RÍA Y PUERTO DE MUNDACA (2-5-3) see page 154.

18 miles

24 PUERTO DE BERMEO (3-2-3) see page 158.

Punta Ugarrarri

Ensenada de Machichaco. Anchorage is possible in up to 20 m (10 fathoms). 3 mooring buoys are established 2 cables offshore in 11 m (6 fathoms) with a further larger buoy to seaward. Landing is possible at **Guibela** in good weather. Anchorage sheltered from SW to NW.

Cabo Machichaco

Ensenada y Puerto de Arminza. A channel into bay filled with rocks leading to a small harbour located in the SW corner; the harbour dries out.

Cabo Villano

5 miles

25 RÍA DE PLENCIA (3-4-3) see page 164.

Punta Galea

9 miles

26 ABRA DE BILBAO (3-1-1) see page 168.

Ría de Somorrostro. Entrance possible at HW springs close to W shore, in good weather. Buoys on W side of bay.

Playa de Ontón. 5 buoys for ships.

Ensenada de Tejilla. Iron ore loading place sheltered from winds from SE through S to W, with 5 mooring boys.

Ensenada de Decido. Iron ore loading place sheltered as above, with 4 mooring buoys.

Río Mioño. Small vessels may enter at HW, dries out.

8 miles

27 PUERTO DE CASTRO URDIALES (1-2-2) see page 174.

Punta de la Conjera. An old iron ore loading place sheltered from SE through S to NW. Small jetty.

Punta del Rabanal

Ensenada de Oriñón. Good shelter from winds between W and WNW. The shifting bar of the **Río de Oriñón** is dangerous but passable for small craft at HW using local pilots. Harbour on E side for dinghies.

Cabo Cebollero

Ensenada de la Yesera. A gypsum loading place.

Canto de Laredo. A small shelter behind a breakwater, the inside of which dries out.

3 miles

28 PUERTO DE LAREDO (3-3-2) see page 178.

17 miles

29 RÍA PUERTO DE SANTOÑA (3-3-3) see page 184.

Punta de Pescado

Ensenada de Isla. Beach anchorage, fair weather only.

Cabo Quejo

Río Ajo. Entrance possible for small craft at HW, dries out nearly to mouth of estuary. Bar dries 0·5 m.

Cabo Ajo

Río de Galizano. Small river entrance possible at HW for small craft, dries out.

Ensenada de Galizano. Shelter from SW and W winds.

30 RÍA Y PUERTO DE SANTANDER (1-1-1) see page 189.

Cabo Mayor

III
28
23
19
23
17
11
3·3
0·9
12
12
Pta Monte
Grande de
Arminza
1·9
Ensa. de
Arminza
5·8
1·0
2·2
N 43° 26'
PUERTO DE ARMINZA
DEPTH IN METRES
METRES. 0
500
1000
CABLES. 0
5
W 2° 54'
FROM SPANISH CHART.

Cabo Ajo and lighthouse looking south—note flat sloping rocks to east.

Ensenada de Oriñón—small harbour.

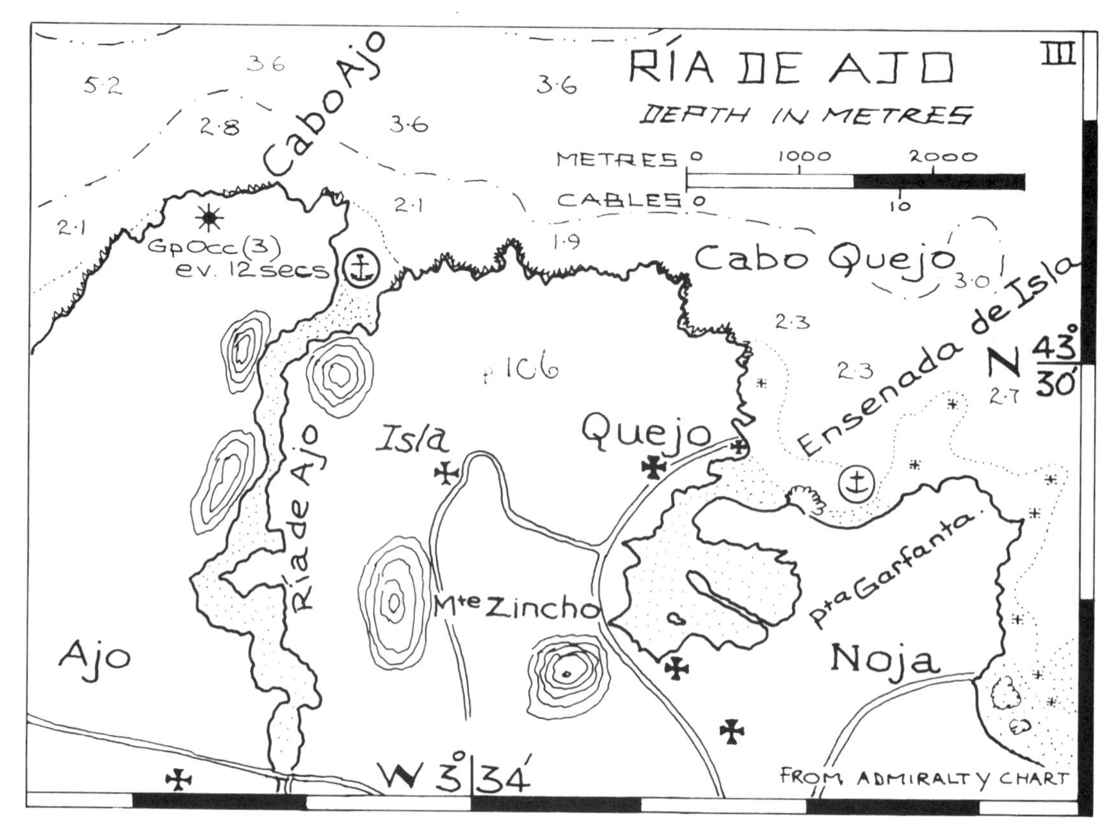

13 Puerto de Pasajes

Population 19,000 Rating 4-1-3 Position 43°20·3′N 1°55·1′W

General

This is one of the most impressive entrances to any harbour on this coast and can be used under all conditions. It leads to two charming unspoilt Basque villages, **Pasajes de San Pedro** and **Pasajes de San Juan**, both of which are ruined by the huge commercial port of **Pasajes Ancho** beyond them. Anchorages and moorings in over 4 m (2 fathoms) are available almost anywhere. All facilities are available. The oil and rubbish in the harbour and the constant movement of large boats spoil what could be a delightful harbour.

Warnings

In heavy swell enter during the last quarter of the flood tide to minimise the effect of the waves. Keep well clear of **Bancha del Este** and **Bancha del Oeste** shoals.

Dredging is taking place continually in the harbour.

Data

Charts

Admiralty Nos. 2665, 73, 2925
Spanish Nos. 9440, 944
French Nos. 177, 4991, 6375

Magnetic variation 5°08′W (1984) decreasing by about 5′ a year.

Tidal information Spanish tide tables are available for this port.

	HW		LW		MHWS	MHWN	MLWS	MLWN
Pointe de Grave	0600 1800	1100 2300	0000 1200	0500 1700	5·4 m 17·6 ft	4·2 m 13·8 ft	0·9 m 3·0 ft	2·1 m 6·8 ft
Pasajes	−0·30	−0·30	−0·20	+0·10	1·2 m −3·7 ft	1·2 m −3·9 ft	0·5 m −1·8 ft	0·6 m −1·8 ft

The outgoing tidal streams can reach 2 knots and when the river is in spate this can be exceeded.

Lights

Cabo La Plata (Frontón). Isophase White 2 seconds, 150 m (496 ft), 15 miles. White castellated building. Visible 285°–250°. 6 Fixed Red lights on radio mast 1 mile WSW.

Arando Grande. Group Flashing (2) Red, 6 seconds, 10m (33 ft), 8 miles, Masonry tower.

Leading lights 156° Line Ⓐ , on **Punta de las Cruces.**

Front Directional Group Occulting (2) White, Red, Green sectors, 15 seconds, 50 m (163 ft), White 8, Red 4, Green 3 miles. White tower and building. Green 129·5°–154·5°, White 154·5°–157°, Red 157°–190°. Dark bands between colours.

Centre Quick Flashing White, 67 m (244 ft), 18 miles. Masonry tower.

Rear Occulting White, 3 seconds, 87 m (284 ft), 18 miles. Masonry tower.

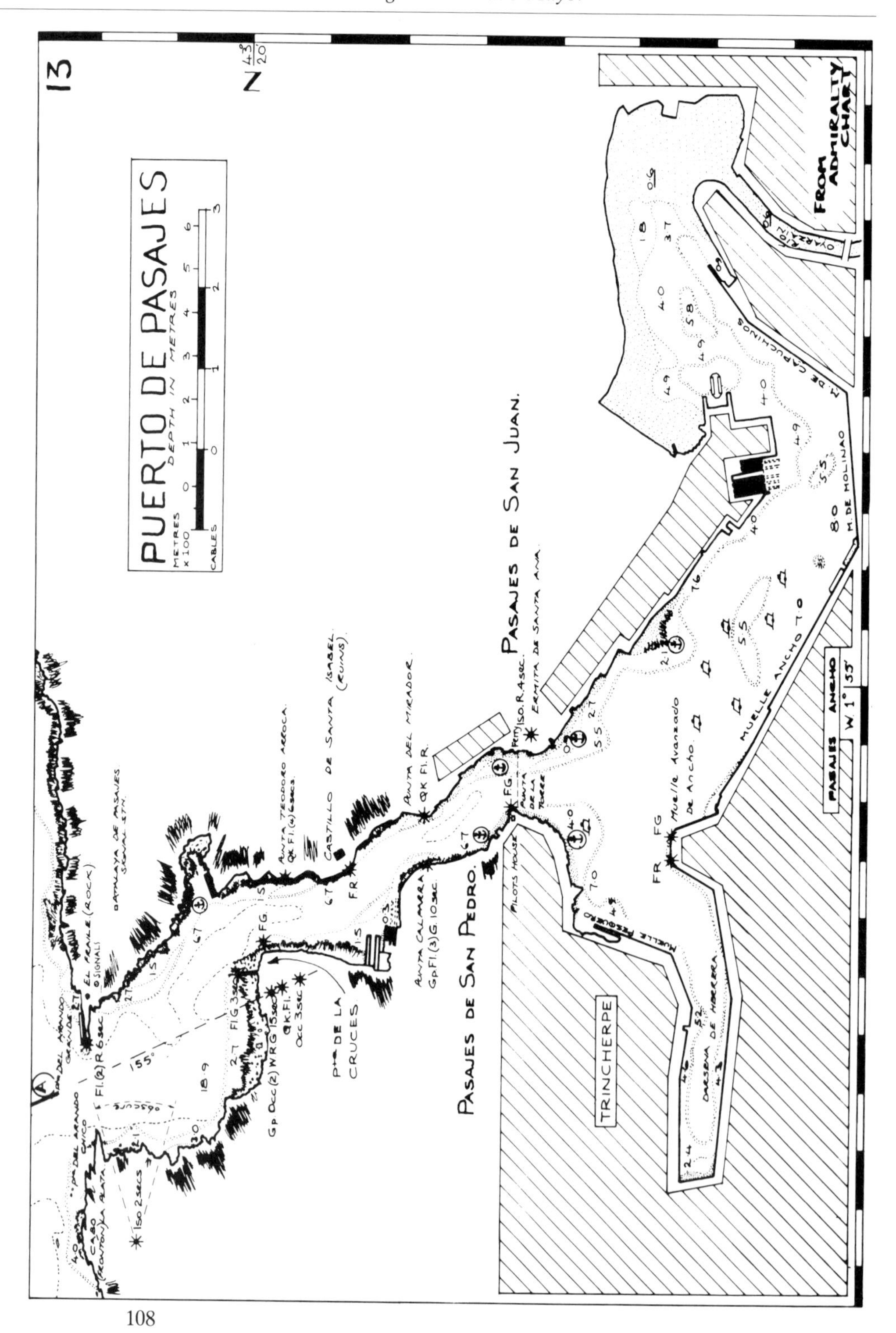
13
PUERTO DE PASAJES
DEPTH IN METRES
METRES x 100
CABLES
Pasajes de San Juan.
Pasajes de San Pedro.
TRINCHERPE
Muelle Ancho
M. de Capuchinos
M. de Molinao
Ermita de Santa Ana
Castillo de Santa Isabel (Ruins)
Punta del Mirador
Pilots House
Punta de la Torre
Muelle Avanzado de Ancho
Darsena de Herrera
Muelle Pesquero
Pta de la Cruces
Atalaya de Pasajes Signal Stn
El Fraile (Rock)
Rio Oyarzun
Cabo (Fronton) La Plata
Pasajes Ancho
W 1° 55'
N 43° 20'
FROM ADMIRALTY CHART

Castillo de Santo Isabel. Fixed Red, 11 m (35 ft), 8 miles. Masonry tower.
Punta del Mirador. Quick Flashing Red, 11 m (36 ft) 7 miles. Stone tower and arch.
Ermita de Santa Ana. Isophase Red, 4 seconds, 32 m (107 ft), 7 miles. Bracket on masonry tower.
Dique de Senocozulúa head on **Punta de Las Cruces**. Flashing Green, 3 seconds, 12 m (42 ft), 5 miles. White column on masonry hut.
Punta de Las Cruces. Fixed Green, 9 m (30 ft), 11 miles. White column.
Punta Teodora Arroca. Group Quick Flashing (4) white, 6 seconds, 20 m (66 ft), 10 miles. White column.
Punta Calparra. Group Flashing (3) Green, 10 seconds, 9 m (30ft), 8 miles. White column.
Punta de la Torre de San Pedro. Fixed Green, 10 m (33 ft), 8 miles. White column.
Muelle Avanzado de Ancho, NE corner. Fixed Green. **NW corner** Fixed Red, 6 m (21 ft), 5 miles. Concrete posts.

Port Radio See page 20.

Signal station A signal station is established on the East side of the entrance. Day and night signals are displayed as follows:

Light Signal	Meaning
Green White Green	Entry permitted Departure forbidden.
Red White Red	Departure permitted Entry forbidden.
Green White Red	Entry and Departure forbidden.

These signals are normally only used for commercial craft but may be used for larger yachts.

Approach

Day

From W The cliffs from **San Sebastián** are steep, high and rugged until they drop suddenly at **Cabo La Plata** into the estuary of **Passajes**, which appears as a 'V' in the line of cliffs. Navigate to a position due N of the harbour entrance about 1 mile off.

From E **Cabo Higuer**, a sloping rugged bare point with a conspicuous lighthouse and large buildings nearby. The coast between **Cabo Higuer** and **Pasajes** is high and sloping with a few indentations and diagonal breaks along the cliff face. The actual entrance to the estuary is difficult to see until N of it as it is so narrow and steep-sided. The lighthouse on **Cabo La Plata** and the old signal station on the hill opposite are quite conspicuous, also **El Fraile**, a rock shaped like a monk's head. Navigate to a position due N of the harbour entrance about 1 mile off.

Puerto de Pasajes – entrance seen from 5 miles to the north.

Night *From W* The lights of **Igueldo (San Sebastián)** (Fl. (2+1) W. 15 sec. 26 M.), **Isla de Santa Clara** (Fl.W. 4 sec. 9 M.) and **Cabo La Plata** (Iso. W. 2 sec. 15 M.) make approach from this direction easy. Navigate to a position due N of the harbour entrance about 1 mile off.

From E Other than the light at **Cabo La Plata** the only light is at **Cabo Higuer** (L.Fl. (2) W. 60 sec. 16 M.), which can be used for approach from the E. Navigate to a position due N of the harbour about 1 mile off.

Entrance

Day Enter between the headlands on Line Ⓐ with the lighthouse and two concrete beacons on **Punta de Las Cruces** in line on 156° until the light tower on **Punta del Arando Grande** is abeam. Change to 144°, keeping the E side of the estuary and the square building on the hill **Ermita de Santa Ana** in line.

Night From a position about 1 mile N of the entrance bring the three leading lights on **Punta de Las Cruces** into line on 155°, Line Ⓐ , (*Front:* Oc. (2) W.R.G. 15 sec.,

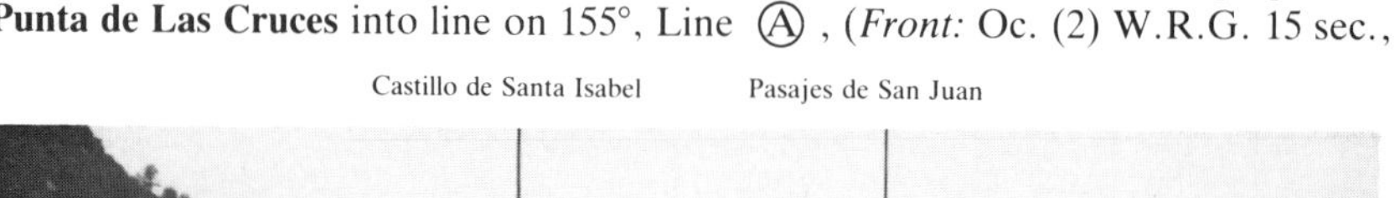

in the white sector; *Centre:* Q.Fl. W.; *Rear:* Oc.W. 3 sec.) and approach the entrance.
When the light on **Punta del Arando Grande** (Fl. (2) R. 6 sec.) is abeam set course for **Punta Teodoro Arroca** (Q.Fl. (4) W 6 sec.) leaving it to port and follow the centre of the estuary leaving **Punta de Las Cruces** (F.G.) to starboard, then **Punta del Mirador** (Q.Fl.R) to port and **Punta Calparra** (Fl. (3) G. 10 sec.) and **Punta de la Torre** (F.G.) to starboard.

Mooring
Light on Punta del Miradore
Light on Ermita de Santa Ana

Puerto de Pasajes—entrance from south.

Anchorages

As most of the harbour has been dredged there are many anchorages over 4 m (2 fathoms) available. The following are suggested.
Off **Pasajes de San Juan** NW and SW of **Ermita de Santa Ana** outside existing moorings in 4 m (2 fathoms) mud, handy for the best shops and restaurants.
Off **Pasajes de San Pedro** NW and SW of pilot house in 4 m (2 fathoms) mud, outside existing moorings.
Off rocks SE of **Pasajes de San Juan** in 4 m (2 fathoms) mud. This is the least noisy berth and not subject to wash from passing boats.
In cove opposite **Punta de Las Cruces** in fine weather only. This is the cleanest anchorage.

Moorings

It is possible to pick up moorings at **Pasajes de San Juan**, but the rightful owner may turn up – usually a large fishing boat. Do not use the vacant moorings near the ferry: they are used by the ferry boats at night.

Berths

It is not recommended to use berths alongside as the quay walls are thick with oil and are used by commercial craft.

Formalities

Nil.

Facilities

Water	From point on quay at **San Juan or Pasajes Ancho.**
Diesel	A supply point in **Pasajes Ancho** is available for bunkering.
Petrol	On road out of **Pasajes de San Pedro** or in **Pasajes Ancho.**
Repairs	Major repairs can be carried out here.
Shops	Adequate food shops and chandlery in **San Juan** and **San Pedro.**
Restaurants, cafés	First class fish restaurants in **San Juan.**
Yacht club	Small **Club Maritimo de San Juan**, mostly for local fishermen.
Visits	Bus leaves **San Pedro** for **San Sebastián** every 30 minutes and takes about 20 minutes for the trip. Fourteenth century Basque church in **San Juan** is worth a visit, as it is the museum in the town hall (*Ayuntamiento*).
Fiestas	28 June–2 July, regatta for power boats.

Puerto de Pasajes—Anchorages off **San Juan** and **San Pedro.**

14 Puerto de San Sebastián

Population 135,000 Rating 2-1-1 Position 43°19·3′N 1°59·3′W

General

Together with its commercial port of **Pasajes** (page 107), **San Sebastián** is the major city on the E end of the N coast of Spain.

This elegant and cosmopolitan city is the summer seat of the government. It is situated around a beautiful bay behind two hills and an island, and provides every conceivable facility from the point of view of a yachtsman. The entrance is easy and can be undertaken in all except storm conditions. Once inside there are two possible anchorages and a small enclosed yacht harbour. There is an excellent yacht club and good bathing beaches. Unfortunately this is a major tourist resort and is very crowded in the summer months.

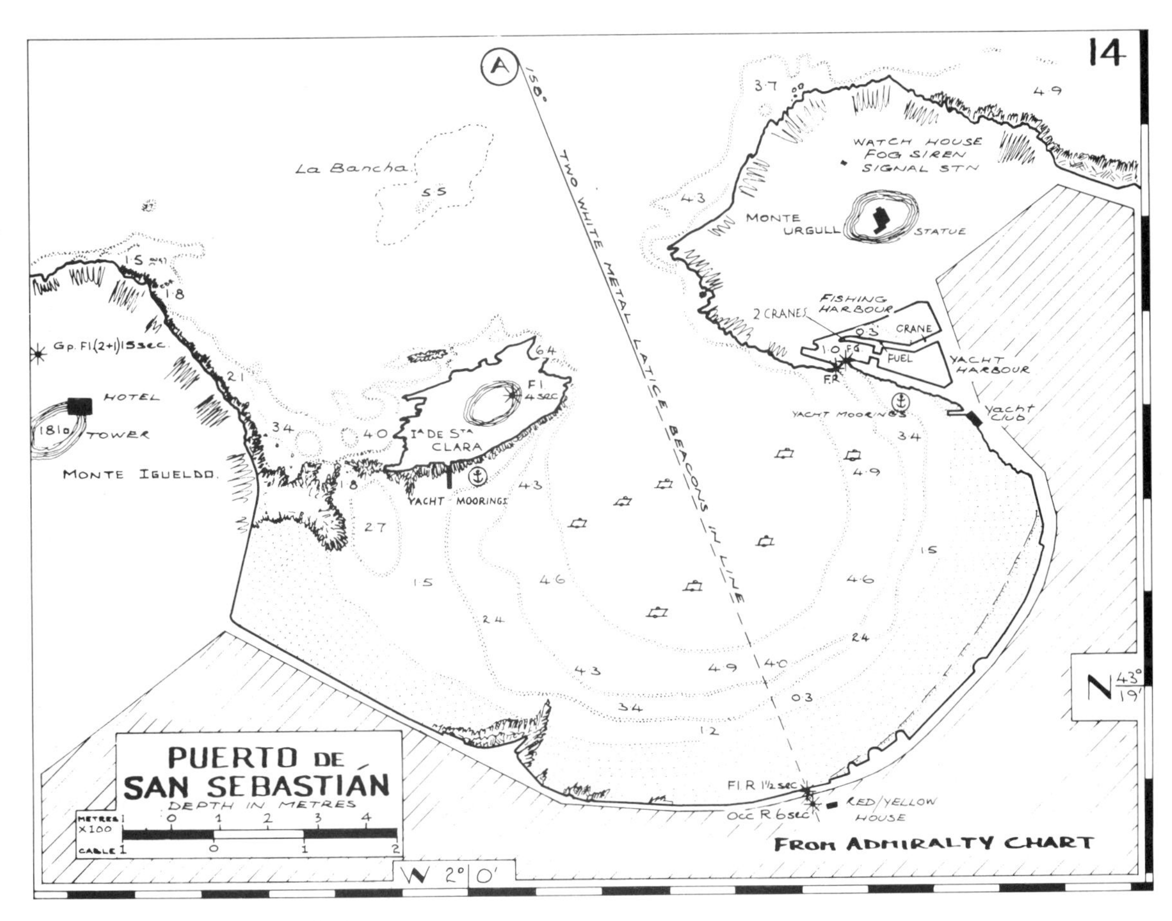

Warnings

Keep clear of **La Bancha** shoal in conditions of heavy swell.

Do not mistake **Monte Urgull** for **Isla de Santa Clara** in bad visibility and enter **Río Urumea** by mistake. This error has led to many wrecks.

Data

Charts

Admiralty Nos. 2665, 75
Spanish Nos. 19B, 944
French Nos. 177, 3581, 4991

Magnetic variation 5°06′W (1984) decreasing by about 5′ a year.

Tidal information

	HW		LW		MHWS	MHWN	MLWS	MLWN
Pointe de Grave	0600 1800	1100 2300	0000 1200	0500 1700	5·4 m 17·6 ft	4·2 m 13·8 ft	0·9 m 3·0 ft	2·2 m 6·8 ft
San Sebastián	−0·20	−0·20	−0·10	+0·15	−1·2 m −3·9 ft	−1·2 m −4·0 ft	−0·5 m −1·7 ft	−0·6 m −1·8 ft

Strong winds between SW and NW raise the level of the water by up to 0·5 m (1·5 ft). Winds from NE and SE lower it by the same amount. Tidal streams inside the bay are very slight.

Lights

Monte Urgull. Fog Siren Morse U (· · –), 60 seconds. Watch house.
Isla de Santa Clara. Flashing White 4 seconds, 51 m (166 ft), 9 miles. White round tower on N face of house.
Monte Igueldo. Group Flashing (2+1) White, 15 seconds, 131 m (430 ft), 26 miles. White round tower on N face of house.
La Concha leading lights 158° Line Ⓐ .
Front Flashing Red 1·5 seconds, 10 m (33 ft) 8 miles. White latticework tower, orange band. Visible 143°–173°. Itensified on leading line.

San Sebastián—entrance from north west.

Rear Isophase Red 6 seconds, 17 m (56 ft), 8 miles. White laticework tower, orange band. Visible 154°–162°. Intensified on leading line.
Darsena de la Concha E breakwater head. Fixed Green 11 m (36 ft) 2 miles. Column. **W. breakwater head**. Fixed Red 10 m (33 ft) 2 miles. Column.

Signal station Situated on **Monte Urgull**, a square white tower with red horizontal stripes.

Life saving A motor lifeboat and line throwing apparatus are maintained.

Approaches

Day *From W* The coast consists of a cliff of smooth rock sloping back at 45° similar to but higher than those to W of **Zumaya**. These cliffs stop short at **Monte Igueldo**, which has a conspicuous lighthouse and is topped by a large watch tower and modern hotel.

From E The higher rocky cliffs around the entrance to **Pasajes** suddenly drop away to **Playa de Gros**, and rise again to **Monte Urgull**, which has a large statue on top of it. This appears from seaward as a large island, and the smaller **Isla de Santa Clara** just shows beyond it.

Night The lights of **Isla San Antón (Guetaria)** (Oc. (3) W. 10 sec. 21 M.), **Igueldo** (Fl. (2+1) W. 15 sec. 26 M.) and **Cabo La Plata** (Iso.W. 2 sec. 15 M.) make night approach possible from E and W.

Entrance

Day Navigate to a position when the centre of the passage between **Monte Urgull**, identified by a huge statue on its peak, and **Isla de Santa Clara** becomes 158° at ½ mile. Locate a large conspicuous house with red and yellow vertical colouring on the edge of the road running round the bay. The leading marks, two white latticework towers with orange band, are about 23 m (25 yards) W of this house and are very difficult to see. Enter with these marks in line on 158°, Line Ⓐ, until the top of **Isla de Santa Clara** is due W.

San Sebastián—leading lights.

Night Bring the leading lights into line on 158°, Line Ⓐ, (*Front:* Fl.R. 1·5 sec. 8 M.; *Rear:* Iso.R. 6 sec. 10 M.) and enter the bay. Do not confuse with street lights. *Note:* the lights are intensified on the leading line. In summer there are a large number of extra street and beach lights and **Isla de Santa Clara** and **Monte Urgull** are floodlit, as are a number of buildings. If bound for the harbour enter between the two lighted breakwater heads (F.R. and F.G.). Note that these are reversed in the approach and a 'U' turn is necessary to enter; also that there are a number of moored yachts near the entrance.

Anchorage

S of **Isla de Santa Clara** in sand up to 4 m (2 fathoms). The closer in to the islands the less the effect of any swell. A regular ferry service from the small jetty on the

San Sebastián—close up of leading lights with red and yellow house.

island to the yacht harbour runs during daylight. The water is clean for bathing. Mooring buoys are available but it is preferable to anchor as they are very large.

Another location is W of the yacht club in up to 4 m (2 fathoms) sand, as far N as possible to reduce the effect of the swell. This is rather crowded with permanent moorings. It is advisable to buoy anchors for this reason. Keep clear of the harbour entrance.

Moorings

Moor inside the crowded yacht harbour at E end with bow facing W. It is usually necessary to make fast alongside other yachts owing to restricted space. If anchoring buoy anchor as bottom is foul with chains and moorings. Watch out for ferry, pleasure and fishing craft entering and leaving at speed.

Formalities

Normal form to be completed for local officials when in harbour.

San Sebastián—yacht harbour—low water.

Facilities

Water	By hose from quayside. Contact blue uniformed officials with the initials CAT embroidered on their pockets, organising rowing boats. Water is also available from yacht club dinghy park just inside entrance where there are floating pontoons.
Diesel	From quay in fishing port. Contact CAT officials.
Petrol	From garage across bridge over **Río Urumea**, some distance away.
Shops	Every variety to S and E of yacht harbour.
Slips	Two small slips in harbour.

Hotels 3 de luxe, 8 first class, A, 4 first class B, 8 second class and 10 third class.

Yacht club **Réal Club Nautico de San Sebastián** welcomes visiting yachtsmen but first see the secretary and fill in a form. Hot showers, drinks, restaurant etc. available (412820).

Visits A tour of the old city is worth while, also a visit to the top of **Monte Igueldo** or **Monte Urgull** for a rewarding view. Many churches in old town to the E.

Puerto y Concha de San Sebastián—looking east. *Photo: Fournier*

Beaches **Playa de La Concha** and **Onderetta** beaches are famous.

Fiestas 20 January for **San Sebastián.**
15 August is *Semana Grande* of general festivities including bull fights.
Also many other entertaining events during the summer months.

15 Rio y Puerto de Orio

Population 2,500 Rating 3-5-3 Position 43°16·5′N 2°7·9′W

General

A large river the entrance to which is canalised, leading through an attractive valley to a country town which is on the main E–W coast road. Anchorage, moorings or berths are available at **Orio** in up to 3 m (1·5 fathoms). However, there is a bar which breaks in any heavy swell from the NW through N to NE. Entry is only possible in the last two hours of the flood. The area is famous for its oarsmen who take part in whaler races and regattas.

Warnings

A new low bridge across the river (1978) below the town considerably restricts access for sailing craft. Clearance is 18 m (60 ft) approx. Approach the river entrance with caution: the sands there shift.

Data

Charts Admiralty Nos. 2925, 2665
Spanish Nos. 303A, 944
French Nos. 6379, 4991

Magnetic variation 5°06′W (1984) decreasing by about 5′ a year.

Tidal information

	HW		LW		MHWS	MHWN	MLWS	MLWN
Pointe de Grave	0600 1800	1100 2300	0000 1200	0500 1700	5·4 m 17·6 ft	4·2 m 13·8 ft	0·9 m 3·0 ft	2·6 m 6·8 ft
Río de Orio	−0·20	−0·17	−0·10	+0·17	−1·2 m −3·9 ft	−1·2 m −4·0 ft	−0·5 m −1·7 ft	−0·5 m −1·8 ft

Freshets in the river cause strong currents on the ebb.

Lights **Río de Orio, W side entrance**. 5 Fixed White lights 38 m (125 ft) located 25 m (82 ft) apart with reflectors.
W bank 6 Small Fixed White lights line the W bank of the river.
Orio Quay. Quick Flashing Green. 3 miles.

Approaches

Day *From W* The **Playa de Zarauz** is a very conspicuous yellow beach with modern blocks of flats behind it. The small **Isla Malla-arriá** with landing steps on its NE side is easily identified.

From E The cliff face from **Puerto de San Sebastián** to **Río de Orio** is of flat sloping slate similar to the coast between **Zumaya** and **Deva** but might higher. There is a small sandy beach just E of the river entrance.

Night The lights of **Isla San Antón** (Fl. (4) W. 15 sec. 21 M.) and **Igueldo (San Sebastián)** (Fl. (2+1) W. 15 sec. 26 M.), together with the 5 F.W. lights and reflectors at the entrance, make a night approach possible but dangerous.

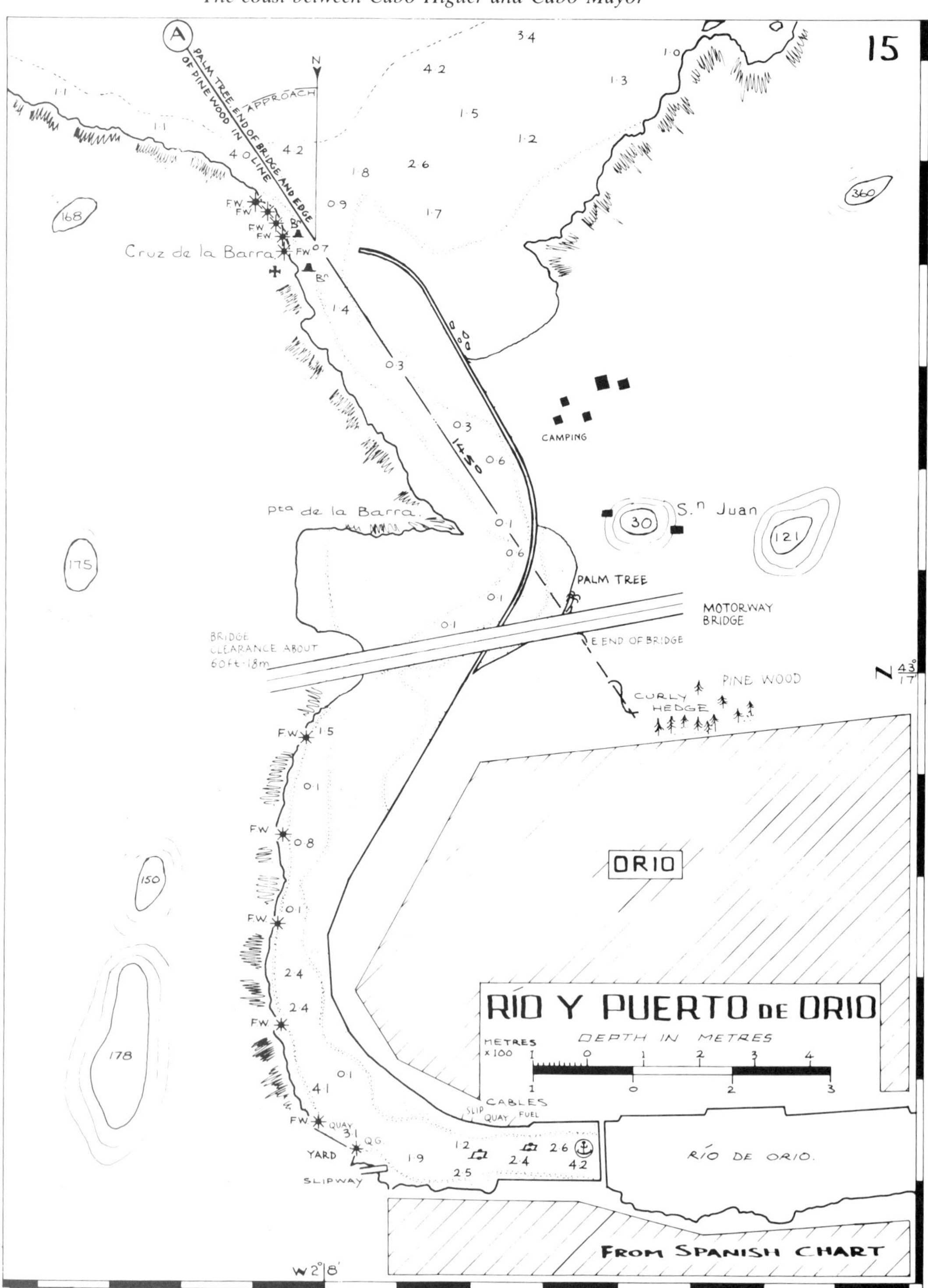
15
A
PALM TREE, END OF BRIDGE AND EDGE OF PINEWOOD IN LINE
APPROACH
N
Cruz de la Barra
Pta de la Barra
CAMPING
S.n Juan
PALM TREE
MOTORWAY BRIDGE
BRIDGE CLEARANCE ABOUT 60ft-18m
E END OF BRIDGE
CURLY HEDGE
PINE WOOD
ORIO
RÍO Y PUERTO DE ORIO
DEPTH IN METRES
METRES x100
CABLES
SLIP
QUAY
FUEL
YARD
SLIPWAY
RÍO DE ORIO
FROM SPANISH CHART
W 2°8'
N 43° 17'

Río y Puerto de Orio—entrance from head of training wall.

Entrance

Day From a position due N of the entrance, which is to be seen between a training wall to the E and a cliff with a large white cross on it to the W, approach the river entering close to the W side about 20 m (66 ft) off the cliff edge, leave two small concrete beacons with broken topmarks to starboard and follow the cliff face at this distance for a quarter of a mile. A lone palm tree in line with the left (E) end of the road bridge and the right (W) edge of a pine wood on a bearing of 145°, may help. When the cliff face drops back at **Punta de la Barre** follow the E bank, and then cross back again to the W bank under the centre span of the bridge where the river runs in a big curve along a steep cliff face. This part of the river is marked with a series of white lights on short posts about 180 m (200 yards) apart. Hold this curve at about 20 m (66 ft) off the cliff face until a large fishing boat slip is reached, then follow a course in mid river.

Río y Puerto de Orio looking north. The new road bridge is not shown. The shallows to the east of the training wall (top right) have now been filled in to make a camping site.

Puerto de Orio—moorings and berths—high water.

Night Night entrance without previous daytime experience is not recommended as there are no leading lights.

Anchorage

Anchorage in up to 3 m (1·5 fathoms) mud is possible opposite the town and below the bridge.

Moorings

Two mooring buoys in 3 m (1·5 fathoms) are established in mid-stream and if free may be used in conjunction with an anchor if considered necessary.

Berths

A berth is possible in 2 m (1 fathom) on the E bank by the town where the quay is a solid wall. The best place to berth is just downstream of the pier-type quay.

Formalities

Normal.

Facilities

Water From nearby cafés.

Diesel Pump on quay.

Petrol Pump on main road.

Shops A fair selection suitable for normal requirements.

Cafés Some good cafés of a simple type.

Visits A 10-mile trip in a motorised dinghy is possible up **Río de Orio** through attractive hilly country. The local sixteenth century church is of curious design.

Beaches Small beach near entrance to harbour.

16 Puerto de Guetaria

Population 2,500 Rating 1-2-3 Position 43°18·3′N 2°12·1′W

General

A charming, picturesque, unspoilt fishing port with easy approach and entrance. Berths or anchorages are available inside the harbour in up to 4 m (2 fathoms), or behind the **Dique Exterior**, protected from all but an E or NE storm.

There are very good cafés, bars etc., nearby sandy beaches, a famous old church and a friendly yacht club. The harbour is clean except when the fishing fleet is in, which also fills it right up.

This is the birthplace of Juan Sebastián de Elcano, the first man to complete a circumnavigation of the world. His ship, the *Victoria*, was the sole survivor of Magellan's fleet of five (1519–22).

Warnings

Buoy anchor as there are ground moorings all over the harbour bottom. Though the harbour and anchorage is well protected from NW storms, these winds can blow over **Isla San Antón** down onto the harbour with great violence.

Data

Charts

Admiralty Nos. 2925, 2665, 75
Spanish Nos. 303A, 944, 943
French Nos. 4991, 6379

Magnetic variation 5°07′W (1984) decreasing by about 5′ each year.

Tidal information

	HW		LW		MHWS	MHWN	MLWS	MLWN
Pointe de Grave	0600 1800	1100 2300	0000 1200	0500 1700	5·4 m 17·6 ft	4·2 m 13·8 ft	0·9 m 3·0 ft	2·1 m 6·8 ft
Guetaria	−0·20	−0·15	−0·10	+0·20	−1·2 m −3·9 ft	−1·2 m −4·0 ft	−0·5 m −1·7 ft	−0·6 m −1·8 ft

Lights **Isla de San Antón**. Group Flashing (4) White, 15 seconds, 89 m (291 ft), 21 miles. White 8-sided tower on W face of house. Visible 061°–331°.
Malecón de Levante head. Fixed Green, 9·7 m (32 ft), 2 miles. Wood mast.
Malecón de Poniente head. Fixed Red, 8 m (26 ft), 2 miles. Wood mast.
New quay Head. Fixed Red.
Dique Exterior head. Flashing Green, 3 sec, 2 M.

Port Radio See page 20.

Signal station A signal station is sited on top of **Isla San Antón**, now used as a lookout.

Approaches

Day *From W* Between the conspicuous lighthouse on its steep-sided headland

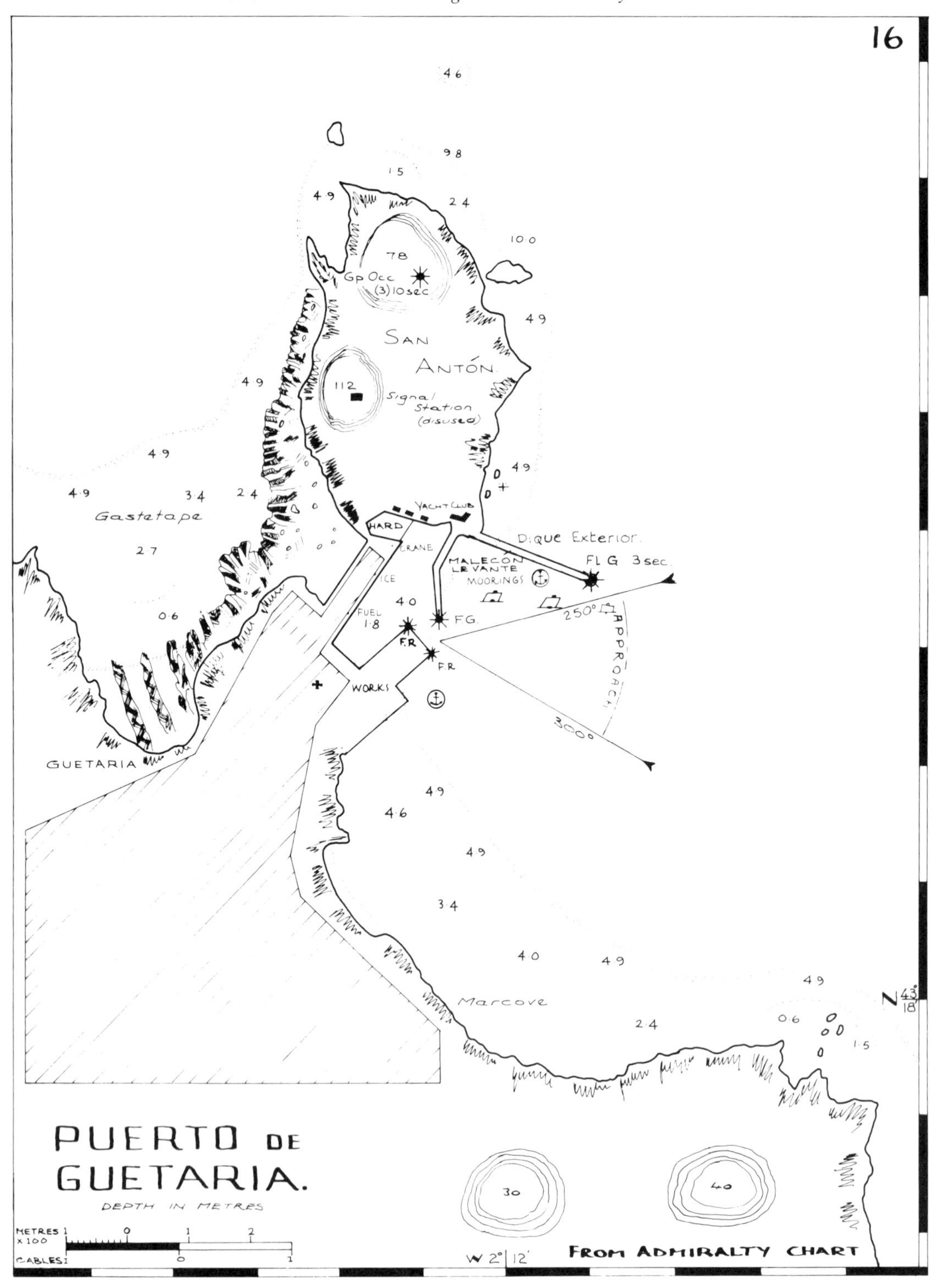
16
San Antón
Gp Occ (3) 10sec
Signal Station (disused)
Yacht Club
Hard
Crane
Ice
Fuel
Dique Exterior
Malecón Levante
Moorings
Fl G 3sec
FG.
F.R
F.R
250°
Approach
300°
Works
Gastetape
Guetaria
Marcove
PUERTO DE GUETARIA.
DEPTH IN METRES
METRES x 100
CABLES
W 2° 12'
N 43° 18'
FROM ADMIRALTY CHART

at **Zumaya** and the even more conspicuous toy mouse-shaped **Isla San Antón** is the coastal road running along the bottom of the cliffs. This has a very obvious white concrete rail alongside it which can be seen from some distance away.

From E The large sandy **Playa de Zarauz** and **Isla San Antón** are very conspicuous. The coast road between these two places is carried on a series of concrete arches.

Night The lights of **Zumaya** (Oc. (1+3) W. 20 sec. 12 M.), **Isla San Antón** (Oc. (4) W. 15 sec. 21 M.) and **San Sebastián** (Fl. (2+1) W. 15 sec. 26 M.) enable a night approach to be made.

Anchorage/Moorings in approach

Anchorage is possible behind the Dique Exterior in up to 8 m (4 fathoms) sand. Mooring buoys are also available in this area.

Entrance

Day Approach the entrance between 250° and 300° and enter between the breakwater heads leaving Dique Exterior to starboard. Check fishing boats leaving at speed by observing their masts over the top of the breakwater wall.

Night Approach the entrance marked by two F.R. and one F.G. lights (2 M.) between 250° and 300° leaving Fl.G. 3 sec. to starboard and enter between. If approaching from N or NE keep a lookout for large white mooring buoys in the line of approach.

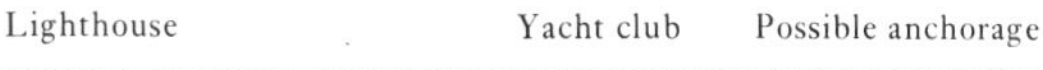

Guetaria looking north. *Photo: Alarde* Note: New Dique Exterior not shown.

Anchorage

It is advised to anchor behind the **Dique Exterior** but sometimes one can anchor using buoyed anchor with stern line to **Malecón Levante** (NE harbour wall) just inside harbour to starboard. Occasionally up to 30 large fishing craft spend the night in harbour, which restricts space considerably.

Berths

A temporary berth is possible in the absence of fishing boats alongside the NW quay or the **Malecón Poniente** (SW harbour wall).

Guetaria—half tide looking south.

Formalities

Normal.

Facilities

Water From water points by hose on NW quay, also from tap in NE corner of harbour from ice factory, or near the Diesel pump. Expensive.

Diesel From pump in SW corner of harbour but only by a large hose.

Petrol Not available.

Shops Up two streets either side of the church.

Hotels One third class.

Repairs Wood and metal workshops for fishing boats, also good concrete hard, but no slipways.

Slipway For small craft.

Clubs **Club Nautico y Pesca de Guetaria** is a club where yachting clothes may be worn and the officers welcome visiting yachtsmen. Cold showers, bar and restaurant are available (841560).

Visits Fourteenth century Gothic church preserved as a national monument should be visited. A climb to the top of **Isla San Antón** gives a rewarding view of the coast.

Beaches To either side of the harbour are **Gastetape** and **Marcove** beaches.

Fiesta Festivities on 6 August to commemorate the safe return of Juan Sebastián de Elcano.

Puerto de Guetaria—Anchorage from root of new breakwater.

Puerto de Guetaria—Construction of a new Fish Quay

17 Puerto de Zumaya

Population 6,000 Rating 3-3-3 Position 43°17·9′N 2°15·4′W

General

A canalised river leading to a series of quays and a small old country town of Roman origin. Entry is possible during the last two hours of the flood tide under all but gale conditions from the N and NE. Berths in 3 m (1·5 fathoms) are available near the town. There is 2 m (6 ft) on the bar at the entrance.

Warnings

The E breakwater head is submerged at HW.

Data

Charts

Admiralty No. 2925
Spanish Nos. 868A, 943, 128
French Nos. 4991, 6379

Magnetic variation 5°07′W (1984) decreasing by about 5′ a year.

Tidal information

	HW		LW		MHWS	MHWN	MLWS	MLWN
Pointe de Grave	0600 1800	1100 2300	0000 1200	0500 1700	5·4 m 17·6 ft	4·2 m 13·8 ft	0·9 m 3·0 ft	2·1 m 6·8 ft
Puerto de Zumaya	−0·25	−0·20	−0·15	+0·15	−1·2 m −3·9 ft	−1·2 m −4·0 ft	−0·5 m −1·7 ft	−0·6 m −1·8 ft

Times of HW may be retarded or advanced by up to 1 hour depending on the amount of water flowing in the two rivers, **Río Larrondo** and **Río Urola**. The flood stream is weak but the ebb stream may reach 2 knots and runs E from the harbour mouth.

Lights

Zumaya. Group Occulting (1+3) White, 20 seconds, 39 m (128 ft), 12 miles. Grey 8-sided tower, white cupola and dwelling. Port signals mast nearby.
W breakwater head. Flashing Green 5 seconds, 11 m (33 ft), 4 miles. Concrete post.
E breakwater head. Group Flashing (2) Red 10 seconds, 6 m (20 ft), 4 miles. Concrete post.

Signals

Port signals are displayed on a mast by **Zumaya** lighthouse and are normally only used for commercial vessels, but if flying must be observed. These signals may be changed soon.

Day signal	Night signal	Meaning
White flag at masthead	White light	Vessel may enter
White flag at the dip	2 white lights vertically	Vessels may leave.
Red flag at masthead	Red light	Entrance prohibited.
Blue flag with white P	Green light	Vessel off bar requests pilot.

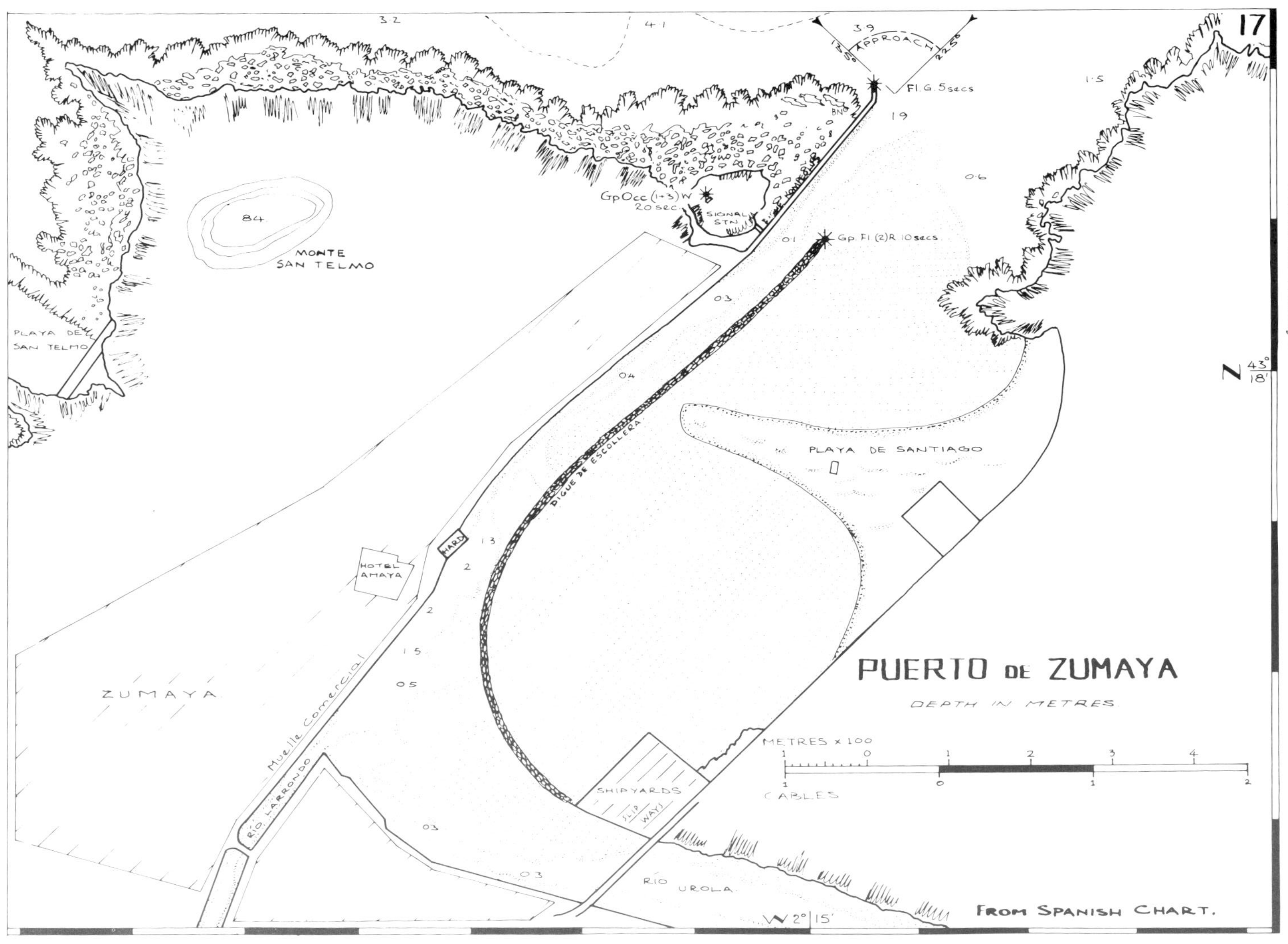
17
PUERTO DE ZUMAYA
DEPTH IN METRES
METRES x 100
CABLES
FROM SPANISH CHART.
APPROACH
135°
225°
Fl. G. 5 secs
Gp. Fl (2) R. 10 secs
Gp Occ (1+3) W 20 sec
SIGNAL STN
MONTE SAN TELMO
84
PLAYA DE SAN TELMO
PLAYA DE SANTIAGO
DIQUE DE ESCOLLERA
HARD
HOTEL AMAYA
ZUMAYA
Muelle Comercial
RÍO LARRONDO
SHIPYARDS
SLIP WAYS
RÍO UROLA
N 43° 18'
W 2° 15'

Approach

Day *From W* The coast has a repetitive series of flat cliff faces which slope back with diagonal stripes. The **Puerto de Deva** at the other end of this line of cliffs is conspicuous. **Zumaya** lighthouse standing on an island with steep sides is easily identified.

From E **Isla San Antón** and **Guetaria** are conspicuous. The cliffs between **Isla San Antón** and **Zumaya** have a road with white railings running along the bottom.

Night The lights of the NE breakwater, **Ondárroa** (Fl. (3) W. 8 sec. 12 M.), **Zumaya** (Oc. (1+3) W. 20 sec. 12 M.) and **Guetaria** (Oc. (3) W. 10 sec. 21 M.) enable a night approach to be made.

Entrance

Day Identify the lighthouse on its island and the W breakwater below it. Approach the head of this breakwater on a course between 135° and 225°. Round the head not closer than 14 m (15 yards) owing to rocks on the N side and close the W breakwater wall to 6 m (7 yards). Follow the wall until 1 cable short of a hard—when alter course nearer mid-stream.

Night Approach the W breakwater head light (Fl. G. 5 sec.) on a course between 135° and 225° round the head of the mole at least 14 m (16 yards) and close the W wall to 6 m (7 yards). Follow this in leaving the E breakwater head light (Fl. (2) R. 10 sec.) to port. Alter course to mid-stream when town is approached.

Berths

Berth alongside in 3 m (1·5 fathoms) just past the hard and the *Hotel Amaya*. There are adequate bollards and a set of steps.

Formalities

Local officials call but are not very interested.

Puerto de Zumaya—looking south up river—low water.

Puerto de Zumaya—entrance—half tide—looking south east.

Facilities

Water Available from tap at a fountain on edge of town or from points on *Muelle Comercial* by pipe.

Diesel By pipe from *Muelle Comercial.*

Petro From pump near bridge.

Shops A small market and an assortment of shops near the church.

Repairs Shipbuilding yards and slips near bridge over **Río Urola**, also metal workshops in the town.

Beaches **Playa de San Telmo** and also **Playa de Santiago** E of harbour entrance.

Visits *Museo Zuloaga* on the E side of the river has El Greco and Goya paintings, also visit the fine XIV Century church.

Puerto de Zumaya—half tide—looking south.

Puerto de Zumaya—looking north—half tide. *Photo: Alarde*

Fiestas 29 June in honour of St Peter.

18 Río de Deva

Population 4,500 Rating 3-4-3 Position 43°17·7′N 2°21·4′W

General

A canalised river with a bar which breaks in heavy N or NE swell and which can only be entered just before or at HW.

Anchorage in up to 3 m (1·5 fathoms) is available in a very limited area. The town has good shops, cafés and hotels etc., but the town and its very nice sandy beach are crowded with tourists in summer. Night entrance is not possible as there are no navigational lights.

Warnings

The river is reputed to change its course and the bar shifts.

The **Dique Rompeolas** head has been washed away and its underwater end is now unmarked.

Data

Charts

Admiralty No. 2925
Spanish Nos. 914, 128, 943
French Nos. 4991, 6379

Magnetic variation 5°05′W (1984) decreasing by about 5′ each year.

Tidal Data

	HW		LW		MHWS	MHWN	MLWS	MLWN
Pointe de Grave	0600 1800	1100 2300	0000 1200	0500 1700	5·4 m 17·6 ft	4·2 m 13·8 ft	0·9 m 3·0 ft	2·1 m 6·8 ft
Río de Deva	−0·25	−0·20	−0·15	+0·15	−1·2 m −3·9 ft	−1·2 m −4·0 ft	−0·5 m −1·7 ft	−0·6 m −1·8 ft

During freshets in **Río Deva** the ebb stream reaches 8 knots.

Lights Nil.

Approaches

Day

From W **Puerto de Motrico** with its houses on the hillside, and the flat grey cliffs sloping back at 45° between **Motrico** and **Deva** are conspicuous.

From E The cliffs form a repetitive pattern with flat sloping cliff faces with diagonal lines. The lighthouse at **Zumaya** is conspicuous.

Night The lights of NE breakwater, **Ondárroa** (Fl. (3) G. 8 sec. 12 M.) and **Zumaya** (Oc. (1+3) W. 20 sec. 12 M.) make approach possible, though they do not give a very good 'cut' close in.

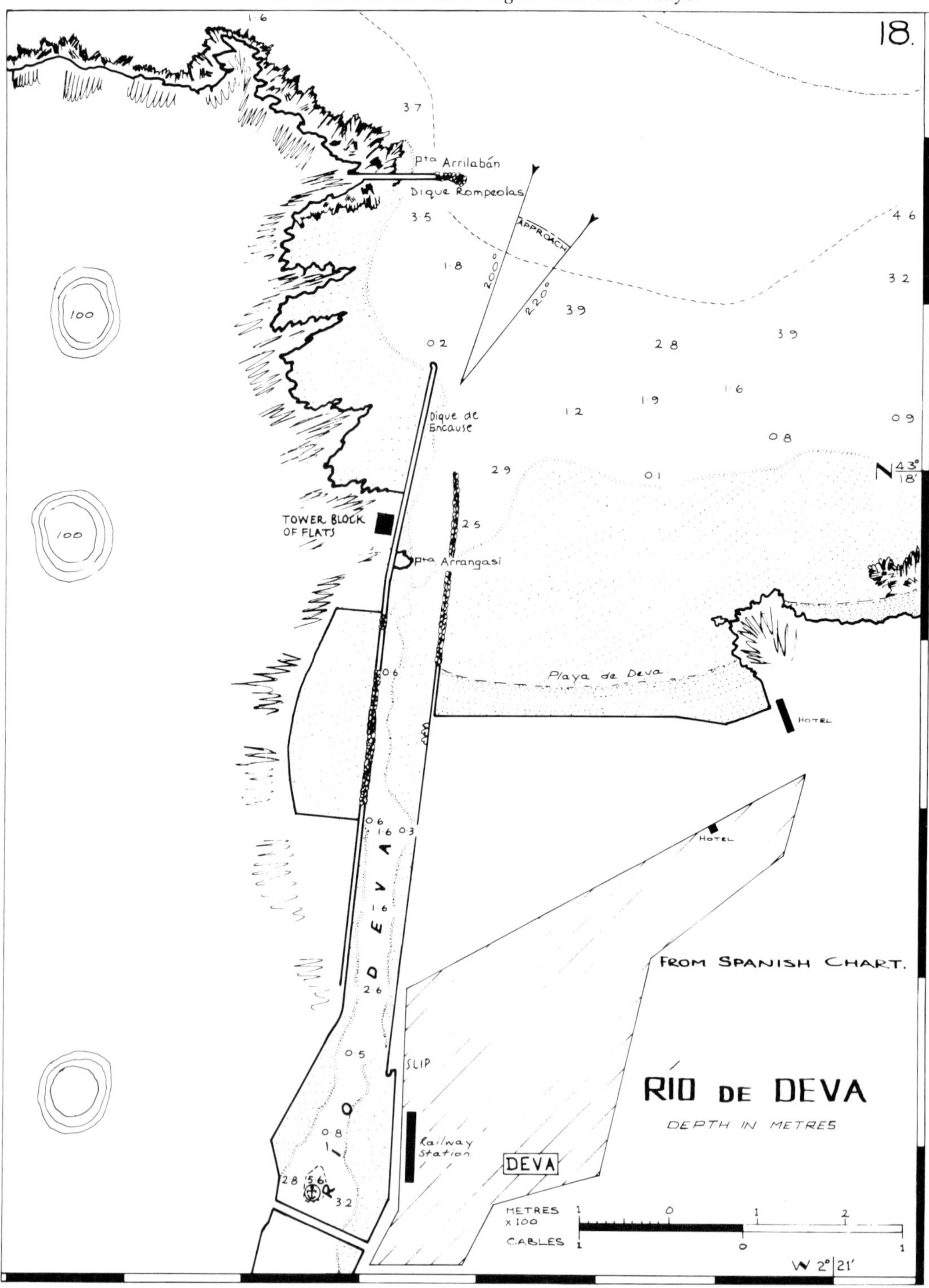
18.
Pta Arrilabán
Dique Rompeolas
APPROACH
200°
220°
Dique de Encause
TOWER BLOCK OF FLATS
Pta Arrangasi
Playa de Deva
HOTEL
HOTEL
RIO DEVA
FROM SPANISH CHART.
SLIP
Railway Station
DEVA
RÍO DE DEVA
DEPTH IN METRES
METRES x 100
CABLES
W 2° 21′
N 43° 18′

Entrance

Day Approach the training walls on a course between 200° and 220° and enter between them one-third away from the E wall. On no account pass near **Dique Rompeolas**, the head of which has collapsed and is not marked. When level with the edge of the beach to the E change course to mid-stream and follow this to the bridge.

Night As there are no navigational lights night entrance is not normally possible. However, after a day visit it would be possible to enter at night owing to the number of street and house lights which illuminate the river.

Formalities

Nil.

Anchorage

The only possible place to anchor is in 3 m (1·5 fathoms), mud and pebbles about 24 m (25 yards) N of the bridge and opposite the second arch from the W. A reconnaissance with echo sounder or lead and line will establish the extent of this hole, which may vary with river conditions.

Facilities

Water From café nearby.

Diesel and petrol From pumps behind railway station.

Shops A good assortment in the town

Visits An attractive church, especially the thirteenth century entrance. A motorised dinghy trip up the river at high water is rewarding.

Beaches **Playa de Deva** is a fine beach but spoilt by the number of tourists on it.

Fiestas 14–24 August, festivities of St Roch.

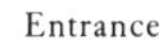

Río de Deva—entrance—looking south south east—high water.

19 Puerto de Motrico

Population, 4,790 Rating 2-3-3 Position 43°18·5′N 2°23′W

General

A charming small Basque fishing port with some beautiful houses (*palacios*). The approach is easy and entrance is simple but narrow. Mooring or anchoring is possible in up to 4 m (2 fathoms) inside the harbour, well protected except for a NE swell. Entrance is not possible during storms from the N or NE.

Warnings

There are rocky shoals either side of the approach, so keep carefully to the leading marks. Harbour dredged to 4·0 m (1976) but tends to silt up.

Data

Charts

Admiralty No. 2925
Spanish Nos. 128, 943, 16A
French Nos. 4991, 6379

Magnetic variation 5°11′W (1984) decreasing by about 5′ each year.

Tidal information

	HW		LW		MHWS	MHWN	MLWS	MLWN
Pointe de Grave	0600 1800	1100 2300	0000 1200	0500 1700	5·4 m 17·6 ft	4·2 m 13·8 ft	0·9 m 3·0 ft	2·1 m 6·8 ft
Puerto de Motrico	−0·25	−0·20	−0·15	+0·15	−1·2 m −3·9 ft	−1·2 m −4·0 ft	−0·5 m −1·7 ft	−0·6 m −1·8 ft

Lights

Malecón de Poniente head. Fixed Green, 10·1 m (33 ft), 2 miles. Concrete mast.
Dique Norte. Fixed Green.
Leading marks 236° Line Ⓐ .
Front **Malecón de Levante head**. Fixed Red, 10·1 m (33 ft), 2 miles. Concrete mast.
Rear **Clock tower, Ermita de San Miguel.** Fixed Red, 63·1 m (207 ft), 2 miles.

Approach

Day

From W **Puerto de Ondárroa** and its blocks of flats are easily identified, also the cliff face of smooth grey rock with dark green trees above it between the two ports. A large red-roofed bungalow on top of the cliff just W of **Motrico** is very conspicuous.

From E The sandy bay of **Playa de Deva** and the smooth grey cliff sloping back at 45° are easily identified. The houses of **Motrico** are also visible from this direction.

Puerto de Motrico—entrance—high water.

Night Lights of **Punta de Santa Catalina** (Fl. (1+3) W. 20 sec. 17 M.), **Ondárroa** NE breakwater head (Fl. (3) W. 8 sec. 12 M.) and **Guetaria** (Fl. (4) W. 15 sec. 21 M.) enable a night approach to be made.

Entrance

Day Bring the harbour entrance onto a bearing of 236° while at least 1 mile off and approach the harbour bringing the leading marks into line on 236°, Line Ⓐ (*Front:* the concrete post at head of E breakwater; *Rear:* the small clock tower near the top of the town on the W side of a large, square, red-roofed building to the right of which and a little above appears a long, low, modern factory.) Follow this line and enter between the two breakwater heads.

Puerto de Motrico looking eastwards.

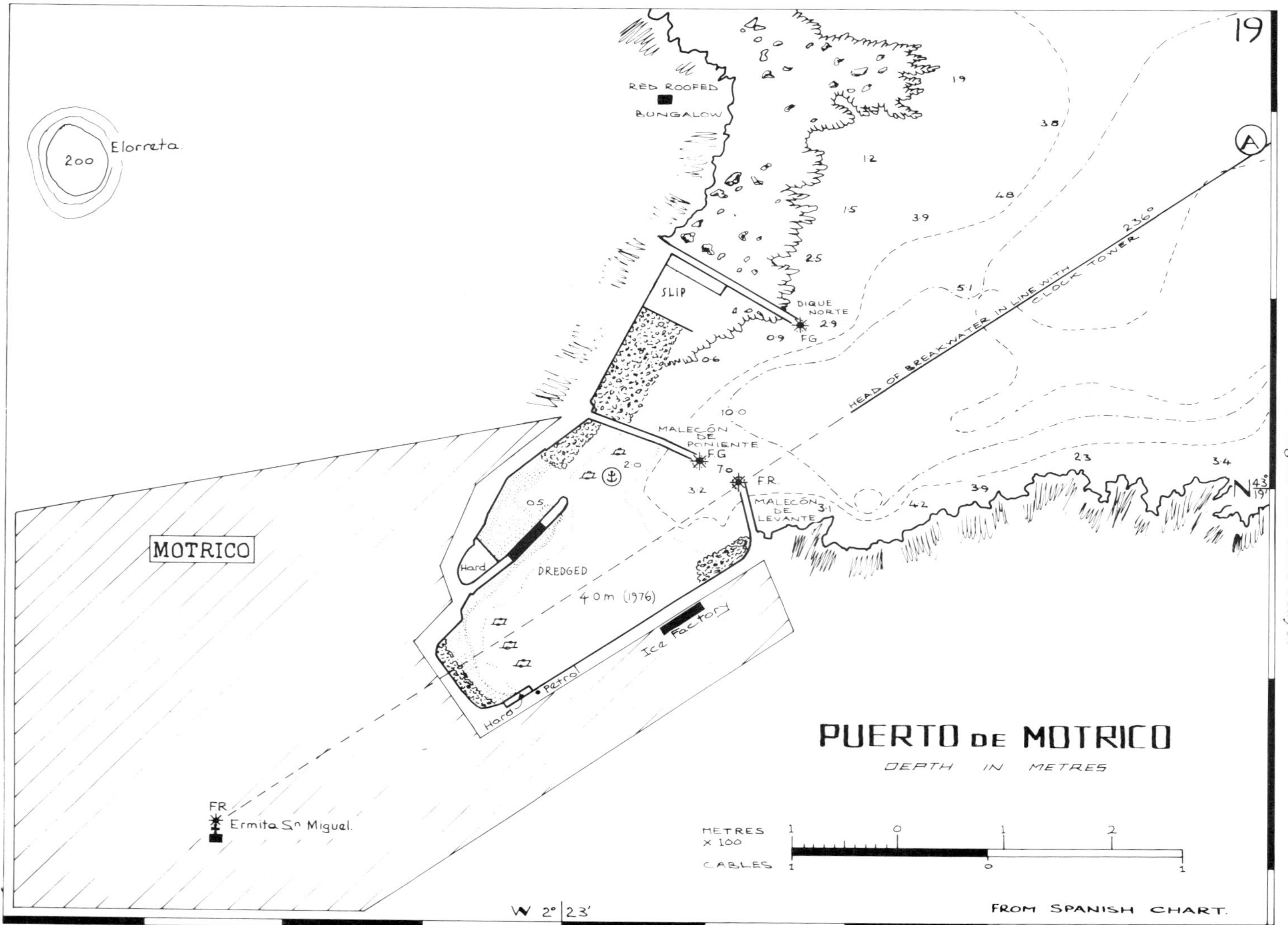
19
PUERTO DE MOTRICO
DEPTH IN METRES
FROM SPANISH CHART.
METRES
X 100
CABLES
HEAD OF BREAKWATER IN LINE WITH CLOCK TOWER 236°
DIQUE NORTE
MALECÓN DE PONIENTE
MALECÓN DE LEVANTE
SLIP
DREDGED
4.0 m (1976)
Ice Factory
Petro
Hard
RED ROOFED
BUNGALOW
MOTRICO
Ermita Sn Miguel.
Elorreta.
200
W 2° 23'
N 43° 19'

Night From a distance off of at least 1 mile bring the two leading lights onto line on 236°, Line Ⓐ. *Front* and *Rear* are F.R. 2 M., the *Rear* being high up in the town. Approach the harbour and enter between F.R. and F.G. on breakwater heads.

Anchorage

Anchor in 4 m (2 fathoms) sand and rock, just inside and W of the entrance, keeping entrance and centre of harbour clear for local fishing boats.

Moorings

Mooring buoys are established inside the entrance to the W in 4 m (2 fathoms) and also at the S end of the harbour in 3 m (1·5 fathoms). Anchor and moor is a possible alternative to restrict swinging.

Berths

Berths may be available alongside the E quay if not used by fishing boats.

Formalities

Nil.

Facilities

Water From ice factory or a tap near bottom of town.

Diesel Near ice factory.

Petrol Pump on E quay.

Shops Distributed up roads to top of town: several supermarkets and some shops of surprisingly good quality.

Visits Visit the old houses in the town, also the church.

Fiestas 22–25 July, festivities in honour of St Mary Magdalene.

20 Puerto de Ondárroa

Population 8,000 Rating 3-3-3 Position 43°19·5′N 2°25·3′W

General

This must have been a most attractive and picturesque port but is now spoilt by commercial fishing development. Parts of the old town up the river and hill are still undeveloped, but the area around the inner harbour, which is oily and dirty and full of fishing craft, has all been modernised.

The entrance is easy and now both inner and outer harbours have been dredged. Mooring and anchorage are available in up to 4 m (2 fathoms). In heavy weather from NE entrance should not be attempted. In heavy weather from N and NW enter only at HW.

Warnings

Dredging is still proceeding, so a greater area for mooring can be expected. The depth at the entrance is now 6 m (3 fathoms).

Data

Charts

Admiralty Nos. 2925, 75
Spanish Nos. 128, 945, 943, 707
French Nos. 4991, 6379

Magnetic variation 5°11′W (1984) decreasing by about 5′ a year.

Tidal inforamtion

	HW		LW		MHWS	MHWN	MLWS	MLWN
Pointe de Grave	0600 1800	1100 2300	0000 1200	0500 1700	5·4 m 17·6 ft	4·2 m 13·8 ft	0·9 m 3·0 ft	2·1 m 6·8 ft
Puerto de Ondárroa	−0·25	−0·20	−0·15	+0·15	−1·2 m −3·9 ft	−1·2 m −4·0 ft	−0·5 m −1·7 ft	−0·6 m −1·8 ft

Lights **NE breakwater.** Group Flashing (3) Green, 8 seconds, 13 m (43 ft), 12 miles. Grey conical brick tower. Fog Siren 3, 20 seconds, 369 m (1210 ft), NW from light.
Mole, E end. Group Flashing (2) Red, 6 seconds, 7 m (23 ft), 6 miles. Grey conical brick tower.
Inner harbour.
N mole. Fixed Green, 7 m (23 ft), 5 miles. White mast.
S mole. Fixed Red, 7 m (23 ft), 5 miles. White mast.

Life saving A line throwing apparatus is maintained.

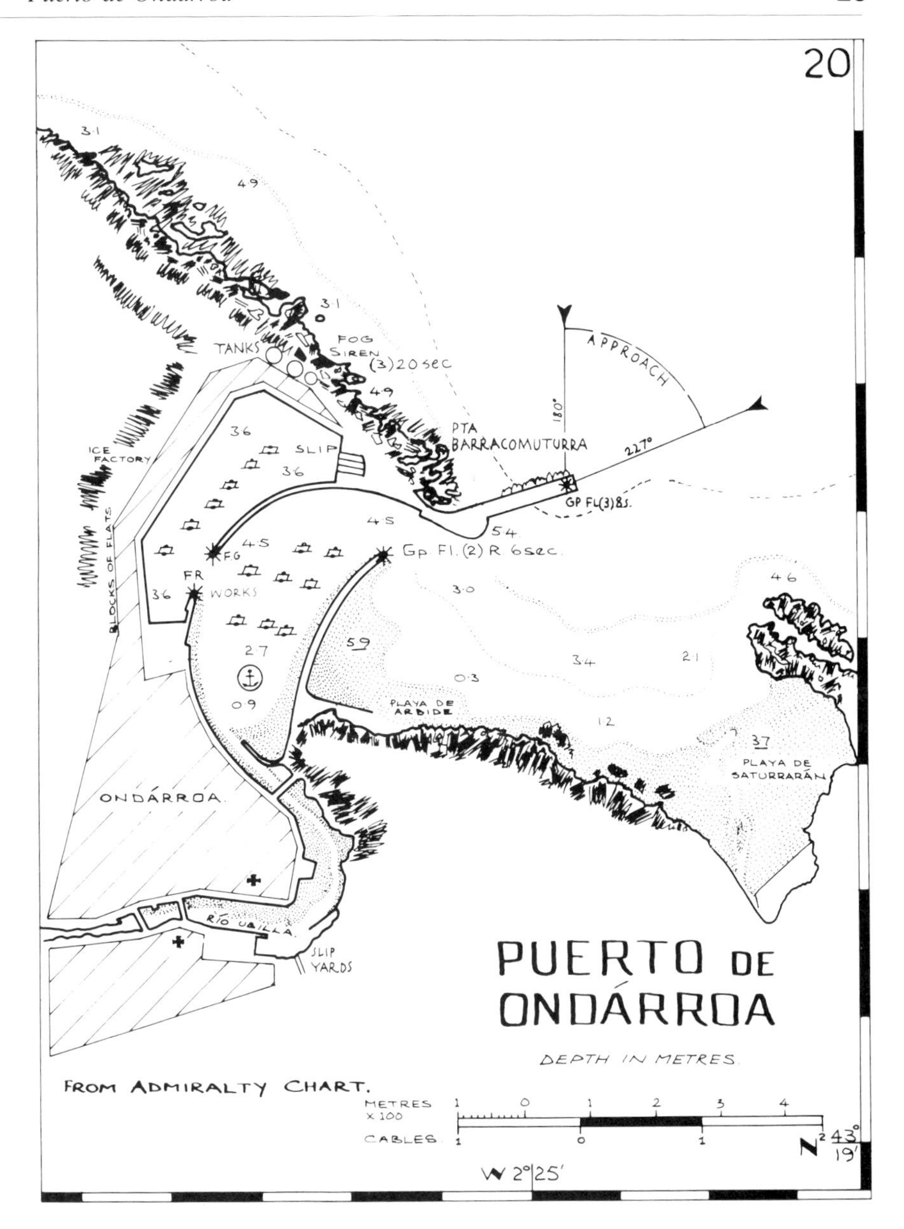

Approaches

Day *From W* There is a rather ordinary, unremarkable, hilly, tree-covered coast starting at **Lequeitio**, which is itself easily identified until **Punta Barracomoturra**, where the valley of the **Río Ubilla** breaks through the hills. The harbour wall of **Ondárroa**, its houses, blocks of flats and the sandy beach to the E are conspicuous.

Puerto de Ondárroa—entrance—looking south west.

From E The coast from **Puerto de Motrico**, the houses of which are easily seen, is rocky with smooth-faced cliffs of slate type rock, the higher hills being covered with dark green trees. **Puerto de Ondárroa** is easily recognised by the large blocks of flats which cover the hillside above the port and by the sandy beach E of the port.

Night Lights of **Cabo (Punta) de Santa Catalina** (Fl. (1+3) W. 20 sec. 17 M.), **Ondárroa** NE breakwater (Fl. (3) G. 8 sec. 12 M.) and **Zumaya** (Oc. (1+3) W. 20 sec. 12 M.) enable an approach to be made.

Puerto de Ondárroa—looking east.

Entrance

Day Approach the entrance between 180° and 227° and round the end of the NE breakwater at 9 m (10 yards). Follow the curve of the starboard hand wall at 14 m (15 yards) until well inside the outer harbour.

Night Approach the light on the head of the NE breakwater. (Fl. (3) G. 8 sec. 12 M.) on a course between 180° and 227° and round the end of the breakwater at 9 m (10 yards). Then follow the starboard hand wall at 14 m (15 yards) until well inside the harbour.

Anchorage

It is possible to anchor in 4 m (2 fathoms) in the outer harbour clear of the mooring buoys. It is recommended to anchor S of these buoys in 2 m (1 fathom) sand, owing to swell in the N part of the outer harbour.

Moorings

No less than eight mooring buoys are established in each of these harbours. It is better to use the outer harbour if the swell permits as it is much cleaner than the inner harbour.

Berths

Though it is possible to berth along the W and NW walls of the inner harbour, it is not recommended owing to oil on the walls and the constant coming and going of large fishing vessels.

Formalities

Local officials do not seem to be interested in yachts.

Facilities

Water By hose from a series of water points on quayside of inner harbour; also from tap at SW corner of outer harbour.

Diesel From bulk supply point at N side of inner harbour.

Petrol On road out of town.

Shops Not very good, but normal requirements can be met.

Repairs Several wooden fishing vessel building yards up river.

Slips Four power-operated slips in NE corner of inner harbour. There is also a concrete hard at S side of inner harbour.

Hotel There is one hotel.

Visits Fourteenth century church is unique in its construction upon arches.

Beaches **Playa de Saturráran** is a pleasant sandy beach.

Fiestas 15–17 August. Festivities of the Assumption and St Roch.

21 Puerto de Lequeitio

Population 6,500 Rating 2-2-3 Position 43°21·9′N 2°30·1′W

General

A very picturesque fishing port and town with fairly easy entrance, good moorings in 3 m (1·5 fathoms) and a fair number of shops, cafés, bars and restaurants of all types, two hotels and a wonderful beach nearby. The harbour is generally clean. Unfortunately, during August there are a lot of tourists of all nationalities in the town and it is very noisy at night with the fishing vessels coming and going and the visitors 'celebrating'.

Warnings

The original leading marks for entrance cannot now be identified because the *Palacio* de *Uribarren* has been pulled down, but a new block of flats built in place of the *Palacio* may be used instead.

Dredging of the S side of the harbour is in hand and there is a project for a yacht harbour for a later date.

Data

Charts

Admiralty Nos. 2925, 75
Spanish Nos. 642A, 943
French Nos. 4991, 6379

Magnetic variation 5°12′W (1984) decreasing by about 5′ a year.

Tidal information

	HW		LW		MHWS	MHWN	MLWS	MLWN
Pointe de Grave	0600 1800	1100 2300	0000 1200	0500 1700	5·4 m 17·6 ft	4·2 m 13·8 ft	0·9 m 3·0 ft	2·1 m 6·8 ft
Lequeitio	−0·30	−0·25	−0·20	+0·10	−1·2 m −3·9 ft	−1·2 m −4·0 ft	−0·5 m −1·7 ft	−0·6 m −1·8 ft

The flood stream is very weak but the ebb, especially W of **Isla de San Nicolas**, is stronger.

Lights

Punta de Santa Catalina. Group Flashing (1+3) W. 20 sec. 44 m (144 ft), 17 miles. Grey conical tower on 8-sided base. Fog Horn Morse L (· – · ·), 20 seconds.

Rompeolas de Amandarri (breakwater) head. Flashing Green, 4 seconds, 17 m (33 ft), 6 miles. Dark grey truncated conical brick tower.

Dique Aislado head. Group Flashing (2) Red, 8 seconds, 5·5 m (18 ft), 4 miles. Masonry tower.

Muelle del Tinglado head. Fixed Green, 5 m (16 ft), 2 miles. White column.

Muelle Sur head. Fixed Red, 4·6 m (15 ft), 2 miles. White column.

Port Radio See page 20.

Lifeboat Lifeboat station here.

Approaches

Day

From W **Cabo (Punta) de Santa Catalina**, a steep-sided promontory with a lighthouse halfway down the cliff, is conspicuous. The top of this promontory is covered with stacks of seasoning timber. The **Isla de San Nicolás** is only obvious on closer approach.

From E The coast is hilly with tree covered slopes. The first conspicuous objects are **Isla de San Nicolás**, which is silhouetted against the red-roofed houses of the town, and the **Playa del El Carraspio** with its yellow sand and modern blocks of flats behind.

Night Lights of **Cabo (Punta) de Santa Catalina** (Fl. (1+3) W. 20 sec. 17 M.) and the weaker lights of **Elanchove** (F.W.R. sectors 8/5 M.) enable an approach to be made from the W. The lighthouse on the **Ondárroa** NE breakwater head (Fl. (3) G. 8 sec. 12 M.) will assist on approach from the E.

Entrance

Day From a position 2 cables N of **Isla de San Nicolás**, steer towards the E end of the breakwater **Rompeolas de Amandarri** on a course of 212°, Line Ⓐ. Identify the head of the N mole, **Muelle del Tinglado**, which has a thin white metal pole with a green lamp, 5 m (16 ft) high. Bring this pole into line with a tall block of flats which has a poplar tree to its E and two smaller blocks of flats alongside to the W. Approach the harbour passing about 3 m (10 ft) from the head of the breakwater and round the head of the mole at a similar distance into the harbour.

Night Approach the harbour with the light on the breakwater (Fl. G. 8 sec. 6 M.) and the light on the head of the N mole (F.G. 2 M.) in line. When **Isla de San Nicolàs** is abeam, open the line of lights towards the E so as to pass 3 m (10 ft) off the breakwater head. Round the N mole head at 3 m (10 ft) and enter the harbour between it and the head of the S mole (F.R. 2 M.).

Anchorages

There is little room to anchor in the inner harbour as the N half is in constant use by large fishing vessels, but the use of an anchor and a line to a mooring buoy is a practical solution. Anchorage is possible in the outer harbour S and clear of the entrance to the inner harbour, but it is open to swell from the N. Anchors should be buoyed as there are many mooring chains on the bottom.

Lequeitio—half tide—entrance looking south.

147

Moorings

Up to six white mooring buoys in the inner harbour are available for yachts. There are two in the outer harbour which can be used as temporary mooring.

Berths

The inside of the **Muelle Sur** and SW quay are possible but not recommended, owing to the number of noisy spectators at all times of the day and night.

Formalities

Local officials not very interested in yachts but sometimes examine passports.

Facilities

Water From hose on N side of harbour (attendant lives in building near NW corner of the harbour).

Diesel As for water. Also from garage behind the Church.

Petrol Pump on W quay operated by the staff of a nearby chandlery shop.

Shops Many small shops distributed around the harbour area.

Puerto de Lequeitio—panorama looking north—high water.

Chandlers Several on the quayside.

Repairs Three wooden fishing boat building yards up the river.

Clubs **Club de Pescador de Atun** has been burnt down (1982).

Visits There are some prehistoric caves near **Artega** and also at **Castillo**, both worth a visit. The eighteenth century church in **Lequeitio** should be visited and a walk past the cemetery behind the church to the top of **Monte Calvario**, with several calvaries on it, gives a good view of the port and coast.

Beaches **Playa del El Carraspio**, though a little crowded, is a wonderful sandy beach.

Fiestas 29 June, festivities by fishermen in honour of St Peter, and 1–8 September, festivities in honour of St Antolin.

22 Puerto de Elanchove

Population 1,448 Rating 1-2-3 Position 43°24·2′N 2°38·3′W

General

A delightful little port and fishing village pinned to an almost vertical cliff face, quite unspoilt and undeveloped. The harbour has easy approach but narrow entrance, with good mooring facilities in up to 4 m (2 fathoms). A few shops provide basic requirements. In a strong NE gale it would be an uncomfortable berth and probably dangerous to enter. The harbour is clean and does not smell.

Warnings

Strong gusts of wind come down on the harbour when the wind is in the W or SW. The inner wall of **Dique Sur** has a projecting ledge.

Data

Charts Admiralty No. 2925.
Spanish Nos. 128, 942, 943, 321A
French Nos. 4991, 6380

Magnetic variation 5°12′W (1984) decreasing by about 5′ each year.

Tidal information

	HW		LW		MHWS	MHWN	MLWS	MLWN
Pointe de Grave	0600 1800	1100 2300	0000 1200	0500 1700	5·4 m 17·6 ft	4·2 m 13·8 ft	0·9 m 3·0 ft	2·1 m 6·8 ft
Puerto de Elanchove	−0·15	−0·10	−0·5	+0·25	−0·9 m −2·9 ft	−0·9 m −3·0 ft	−0·5 m −1·7 ft	−0·6 m −1·8 ft

Lights **Dique Norte head.** Flashing Green 3 sec, 8 m (26 ft), 4 M. Aluminium tower.
Dique Sur head. Fixed Red and White sectors, 7·3 m (24 ft), White 10, Red 6 miles. Green metal column. White 000°–315°, Red 315°–000°.

Approach

Day *From W* The sandy estuary of **Río de Mundaca**, the **Isla Izaro** and the high, vertical sided, rocky **Cabo Ogoño** are readily recognisable.

From E The coast has low rocky cliffs and **Punta Apical** is not especially conspicuous. However, the narrow **Río de Ea** to the W can be identified.

Night The lights of **Cabo Machichaco** (Fl.W. 7 sec. 24 M.), **Punta Lamiaren (Bermeo)** (Occ. (2) W.R. 6 sec. 8 M.) and **Punta de Santa Catalina** (Fl. (1+3) W. 20 sec. 17 M.) enable an approach to be made at night.

Entrance

Day Approach the port on a course between 200° and 270°. The harbour wall and houses on the hillside will be readily visible, but the entrance, to the SE of the

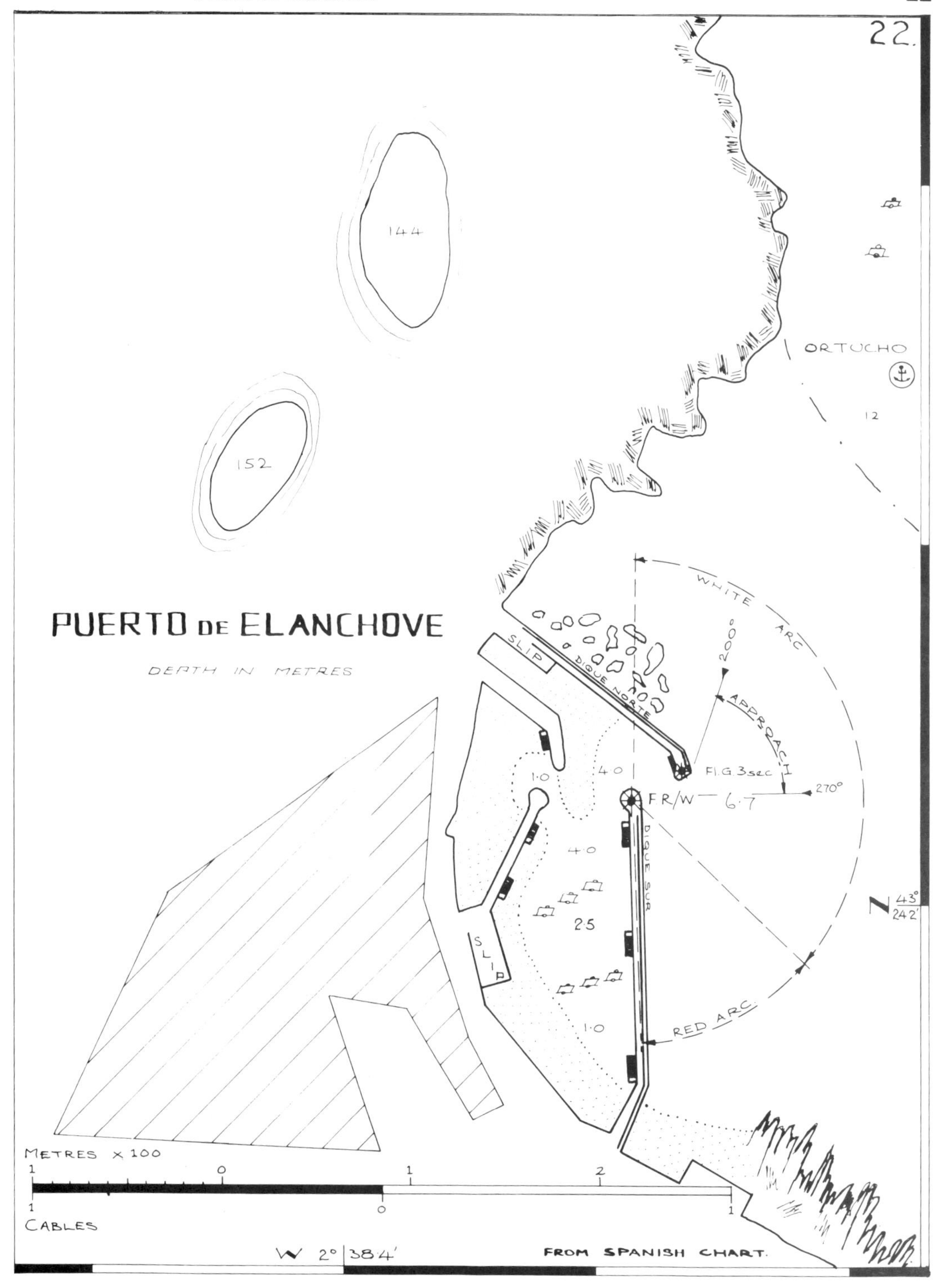
22.
144
152
ORTUCHO
12
PUERTO DE ELANCHOVE
DEPTH IN METRES
WHITE ARC
200°
APPROACH
SLIP
DIQUE NORTE
Fl.G.3sec
270°
1·0
4·0
F.R/W
6·7
DIQUE SUR
4·0
2·5
SLIP
1·0
RED ARC
43°
24.2'
METRES x 100
CABLES
W 2° 38.4'
FROM SPANISH CHART

Puerto de Elanchove—looking west.

higher part of this wall, will not be seen until quite close in. Enter between the breakwater heads slowly, as fishing boats may be leaving and a sharp turn to port will be necessary to enter the inner harbour.

Night Night entrance is not recommended without a previous visit as there are only a few rather weak lights inside the harbour. It is advisable to pick up a mooring buoy 3 cables NNE of the harbour entrance or anchor near it until dawn.

Puerto de Elanchove—looking north west.

Moorings

Large white mooring buoys are established in the harbour and may be used if not already occupied by fishing boats. Alternatively use an anchor and one buoy.

Berths

It is possible to lie alongside the inside of the **Dique Sur**, but care is needed as a ledge sticks out which uncovers at LW springs and a holding off line will be necessary. Yachts drawing over 2·0 m may dry out at springs. Otherwise dry out on the inside of the inner S mole.

Formalities

Local officials are not interested in yachts.

Facilities

Water From water point near root of inner S mole.

Shops Distributed up cobbled street, which goes up hill. A semi-self-service shop is at the top of the hill.

Slip There is a small slip with a power winch near the root of the inner S mole.

Visits A walk to the top of the hill gives a rewarding view of the coast and a taxi trip to **Castillo Arteaga** and the nearby **Basondo** caves is worth while.

23 Ría y Puerto de Mundaca

Population 1,918 Rating 2-5-3 Position 43°24·5′N 2°41·9′W

General

A delightful unspoilt little port and town which can be visited in settled conditions only. The approach requires care. Anchorage in 2 m (1 fathom) sand is available just inside the harbour; alternatively dry out further inside.

Warnings

The use of a pilot from **Bermeo** is advised for the first visit. Or alternatively, a reconnaissance by land at LW before visiting by sea will show how the channel lies.

Data

Charts
Admiralty No. 2925
Spanish Nos. 128, 942, 917
French Nos. 4991, 6380

Magnetic variation 5°16′W (1984) decreasing by about 5′ each year.

Tidal information

	HW		LW		MHWS	MHWN	MLWS	MLWN
Pointe de Grave	0600 1800	1100 2300	0000 1200	0500 1700	5·4 m 17·6 ft	4·2 m 13·8 ft	0·9 m 3·0 ft	2·1 m 6·8 ft
Puerto de Mundaca	−0·10	−0·05	0·00	+0·30	−0·8 m −2·6 ft	−0·8 m −2·7 ft	−0·5 m −1·7 ft	−0·6 m −1·8 ft

The ebb stream can exceed 3 knots when **Río Mundaca** is in spate.

Lights
Rosape, Punta Lamiaren. Group Occulting (2) White, Red, 6 seconds, 35 m (117 ft), White 9, Red 8 miles. White building with red roof and aluminium lantern. Red 100°–199·4°, White 199·4°–232°. Red sector covers the **Bermeo** breakwater.
Punta de la Barra. Fixed White, Occasional.
S breakwater. Fixed Red, Occasional. **N breakwater.** Fixed Green, Occasional.

Approaches

Day
From W The large sloping promontory of **Cabo Machichaco** and its conspicuous lighthouse and **Puerto Bermeo** are easily identified.

From E **Cabo Ogoño** with its high vertical rocky sides and **Isla de Izaro** are conspicuous.
Follow the coast W of the *ría* at 1 cable and pass **Punta de la Barra**, above which a conspicuous hermitage is situated at 50 m (52 yards). Then turn onto 210° (Line

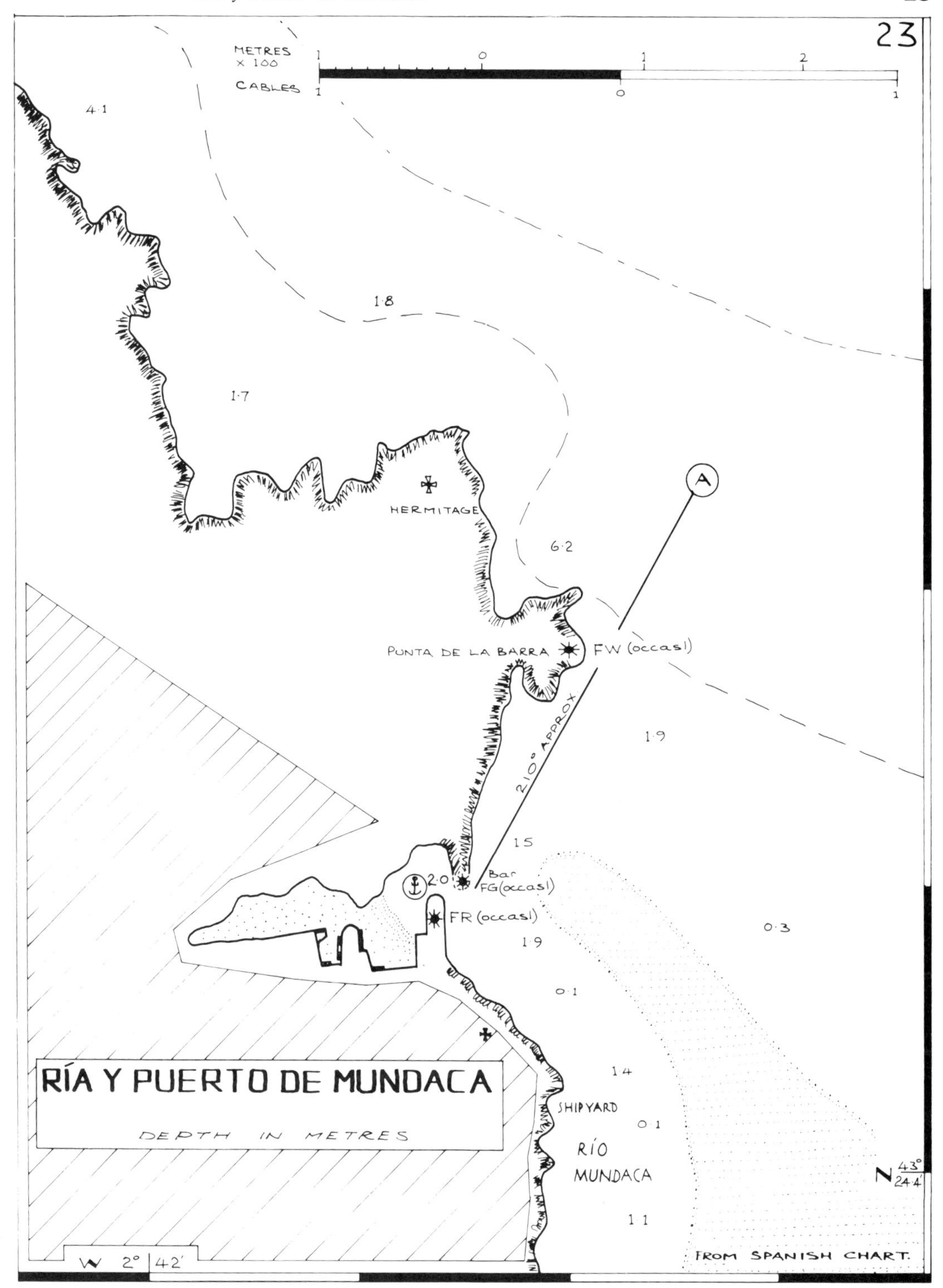
23
METRES x 100
CABLES
1
0
1
2
1
0
1
4·1
1·8
1·7
HERMITAGE
6·2
A
PUNTA DE LA BARRA
FW (occasl)
210° APPROX
1·9
1·5
2·0
Bar
FG(occasl)
FR (occasl)
1·9
0·3
0·1
1·4
SHIPYARD
0·1
RÍO MUNDACA
1·1
RÍA Y PUERTO DE MUNDACA
DEPTH IN METRES
N 43° 24·4′
W 2° 42′
FROM SPANISH CHART.

Ⓐ) rounding a small point with a post on it just N of the harbour at 10 m (11 yards); then direct course for the harbour entrance. Caution is necessary as the sand banks and bar change.

Night Night approach without previous experience is not recommended.

Entrance and Anchorage

Enter between breakwater heads and anchor directly inside. Take kedge out towards head of inner quay, or alternatively dry out along inner side of S breakwater.

Formalities

Officials not interested in visiting yachts.

Facilities

Water From cafés or a tap near the jetties.

Diesel, petrol May be obtained in cans.

Shops Adequate shops around the town.

Sports Popular area for surfing.

Puerto de Mundaca—looking east—low water.

Ría de Mundaca—looking south.

24 Puerto de Bermeo

Population 16,515 Rating 3-2-3 Position 43°25·1′N 2°43·2′W

General

The most important fishing port on this part of the coast, with a good harbour of recent construction. It has an easy entrance which is possible in all conditions except a NE storm. Moorings and berths are available in up to 4 m (2 fathoms), fully protected. The town is very picturesque; undeveloped and unspoilt.

At times other than mid-July to mid-August this port may be crowded with large fishing vessels. Unfortunately, the water in the harbour smells very badly of fish and drains, especially in hot, calm weather. Oil everywhere.

Warnings

The Dique Rompeolas is being still further extended. The harbour is frequently dredged.

Data

Charts Admiralty Nos. 2925, 75
Spanish Nos. 128, 942, 917
French Nos. 4991, 6380

Magnetic variation 5°16′W (1984) decreasing by about 5′ each year.

Tidal information

	HW		LW		MHWS	MHWN	MLWS	MLWN
Pointe de Grave	0600 1800	1100 2300	0000 1200	0500 1700	5·4 m 17·6 ft	4·2 m 13·8 ft	0·9 m 3·0 ft	2·1 m 6·8 ft
Bermeo	−0·10	−0·05	0·00	+0·30	−0·8 m −2·6 ft	−0·8 m −2·7 ft	−0·5 m −1·7 ft	−0·6 m −1·8 ft

Flood stream runs SW and ebb NE, off the harbour entrance.

Lights **Cabo Machichaco.** Flashing White, 7 seconds, 120 m (395 ft), 24 miles. Stone tower on NW corner of grey building, aluminium lantern. Radiobeacon (2 towers). Fog Siren 2, 60 seconds.

Rosape, Punta Lamiaren. Group Occulting 2, White, Red sectors, 6 seconds, 36 m (117 ft), White 9, Red 8 miles. White building with red roof and aluminium lantern. Red 100°–199·4°, White 199·4–232°. Red sector covers new workings.

Espignón Norte head. Fixed Green, 4·8 m (16 ft), 3 miles. Metal tripod.

Espignón Sur head. Fixed Red, 4·6 m (15 ft), 5 miles. Metal tripod.

Dique Rompeolas head. Flashing Green, 4·5 seconds, 8·8 m (29 ft), 5 miles. Metal tripod.

Dique Rompeolas spur. Fixed Green, 4·6 m (15 ft), 2 miles. Metal pole.

Contra Dique head. Flashing Red, 3 seconds, 6 m (20 ft), 3 miles. Red metal tripod.

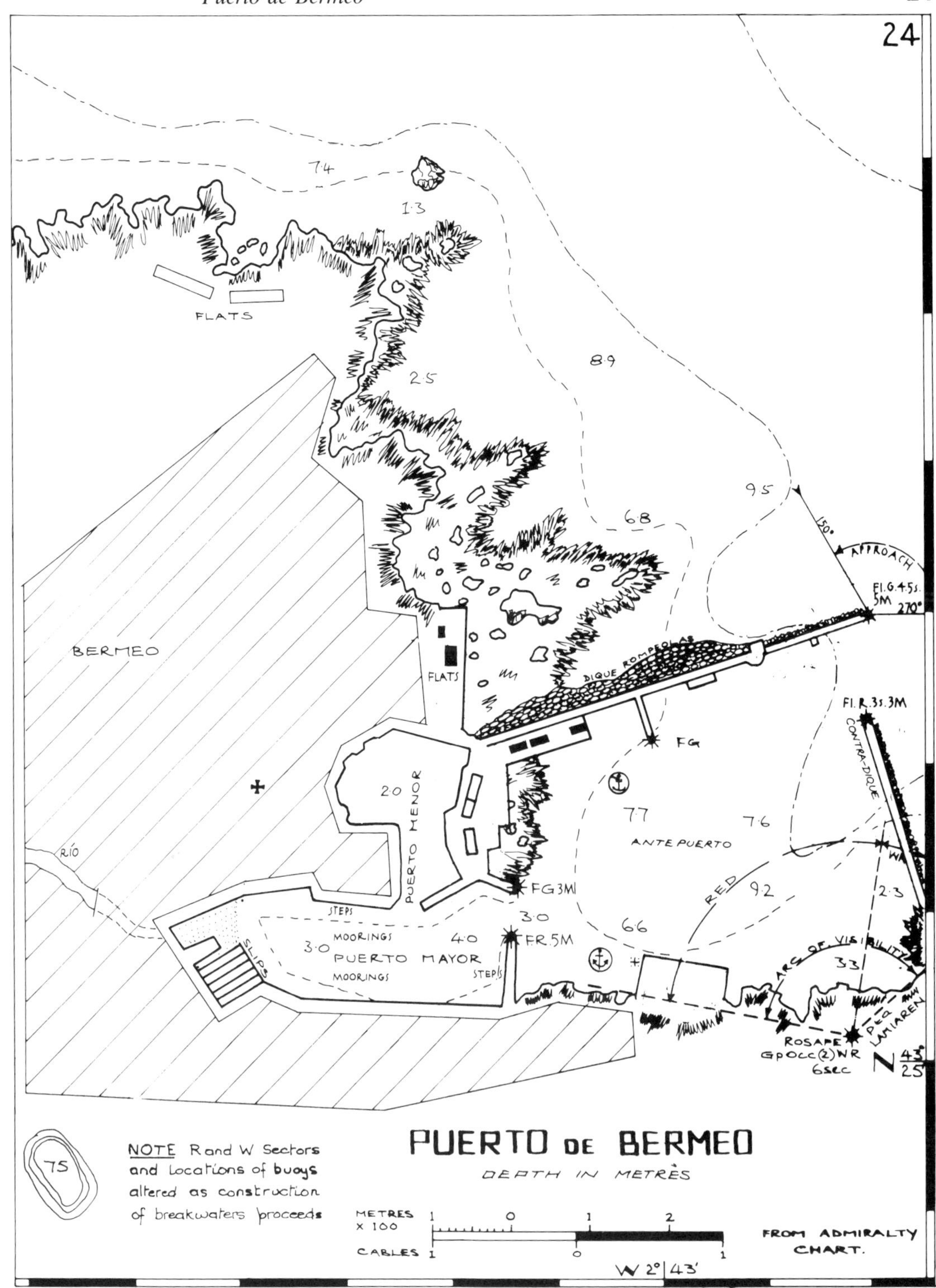
24
FLATS
BERMEO
FLATS
DIQUE ROMPEOLAS
APPROACH
150°
Fl.G.4.5s. 5M 270°
Fl.R.3s.3M
CONTRA-DIQUE
FG
PUERTO MENOR
FG3M
ANTE PUERTO
RED
RÍO
STEPS
SLIPS
MOORINGS
PUERTO MAYOR
MOORINGS
STEPS
F.R.5M
ARC OF VISIBILITY
ROSAPE
GpOcc(2)WR
6sec
Pta LAMIAREN
N 43° 25'
NOTE R and W Sectors and Locations of buoys altered as construction of breakwaters proceeds
PUERTO DE BERMEO
DEPTH IN METRES
METRES x 100
CABLES
FROM ADMIRALTY CHART.
W 2° 43'

Radio A marine beacon operates from **Cabo Machichaco** lighthouse on 296·5 kHz, 100 miles, MA (– – / · –) period 6 minutes.

Port Radio See page 20.

Approaches

Day *From W* The high prominent **Cabo Machichaco** which slopes down towards the sea and has a very large lighthouse and dwelling on it, and also an old lighthouse tower and two radio masts, cannot be mistaken. The new blocks of flats above and N of the town of **Bermeo** are conspicuous as is the new breakwater.

From E The high rocky, vertical sided **Cabo Ogoño** and the sands of **Ría de Mundaca** together with **Isla de Izaro** form an unmistakeable group. Approach between 150° and 270°.

Night **Cabo Machichaco** (Fl.W. 7 sec. 24 M.), **Punta Lamiaren** (Occ. (2) W.R. 6 sec. 9 M.) and **Cabo de Santa Catalina** (Fl. (1+3) W. 20 sec. 17 M.) make approach possible. In approach from E **Elanchove** (F.W.R.) may also assist.

Entrance

Day Round the end of the new breakwater and outside a small green conical buoy marking extension. The entrance to the **Puerto Mayor** is then visible to starboard.

Night The red sector of **Rosape** light covers the breakwater as far as the head where work is taking place.

Puerto de Bermeo—approach looking south.

Puerto de Bermeo—entrance from head of **Dique de Rompeolas.**

Approach in the white sector of the light on **Rosape Punta Lamiaren** (Oc. (2) W.R. 6 sec.) towards the light on the breakwater (Fl. G. 4·5 sec.) and leave it 50 m to starboard. Enter between FR and FG.

Anchorages

It is possible to anchor in 4 to 6 m (2 to 3 fathoms) sand in the N or S side of the Antepuerto.

Moorings

Mooring buoys are established in **Puerto Mayor** but are usually occupied by fishing vessels.

Berths

It is advised to lie alongside in 3 to 4 m (1·5 to 2 fathoms) just inside the entrance to **Puerto Mayor** to port or starboard. It is possible to lie alongside the whole of the S wall to the harbour but it is usually occupied by fishing vessels. The inner harbour (**Puerto Menor**) is usually crowded and not recommended.

Formalities

Officials do not seem to be interested in yachts.

Facilities

Water Water points are established at regular intervals along the S and E quays. Contact man in charge of water.

Diesel Several diesel supply points on E quay, also W side of **Puerto Mayor.**

Puerto de Bermeo—looking north—half tide.

Petrol Near W end of harbour.

Shops Distributed around the town and include several chandlers and ships radio shops.

Slips A set of slips for all medium and small sized vessels at W end of the harbour.

Repairs Two wood-working fishing vessel repair and construction yards.

Visits A trip by an amusing 'Emett'-type train to **Guernica**, famous for its destruction by bombs during the civil war, its *Casa de Juntas* and 'Tree of Privileges'; also a visit to a twelfth century church at **San Petago** near **Cabo Machichaco** are worth while. The ancient fortress of **Arcilla** in **Bermeo**, now a museum, is worth a visit.

Fiestas 22 July, festivities of St Mary Magdalene; 8–16 September, festivities of St Maria Albonica and St Eutemia.

25 Ría de Plencia

Population 2,200 Rating 3-4-3 Position 43°24·8′N 2°57′W

General

A small pleasant little river and harbour which can be entered only in good weather. The river and harbour almost dry out but anchorage is possible on the other side of the bay in 2 m (1 fathom) sand, behind a small jetty. The village has limited facilities. There is a wonderful beach for bathing.

Warnings

Not an anchorage to be used in any swell from NW or N as the bay is wide open in this direction. The river silts up at times.

Data

Charts Admiralty No. 2925
Spanish Nos. 128, 942
French No. 4991

Magnetic variation 5°35′W (1984) decreasing by about 5′ each year.

Tidal information

	HW		LW		MHWS	MHWN	MLWS	MLWN
Pointe de Grave	0600 1800	1100 2300	0000 1200	0500 1700	5·4 m 17·6 ft	4·2 m 13·8 ft	0·9 m 3·0 ft	2·1 m 6·8 ft
Ría de Plencia	−0·40	−0·20	−0·30	−0·25	1·3 m −4·1 ft	1·2 m −3·9 ft	0·5 m −1·8 ft	0·7 m −2·3 ft

Lights **Molehead**. Fixed White, 3 m (17 ft) 2 miles. Small post.

Approaches

Day *From W* The white cliffs around **Punta Galea** cease a short distance before a small sandy bay which gives way to the **Ría de Plencia**.

From E The high rugged **Cabo Villano**, with a small island with a very jagged outline off it, is conspicuous.

Night Night approach and entrance is not recommended.

Entrance

Day Enter the bay midway between the headlands and direct course towards the breakwater head, keeping it in line with a large white building, on approximately 127°, Line Ⓐ.

Round the head of the breakwater to starboard at 14 m (15 yards) and follow it, passing a concrete beacon close to starboard and rounding a black can buoy at 14 m (15 yards) to port. Proceed up the river about a third nearer to the W side. Keep midstream after the first bend to starboard.

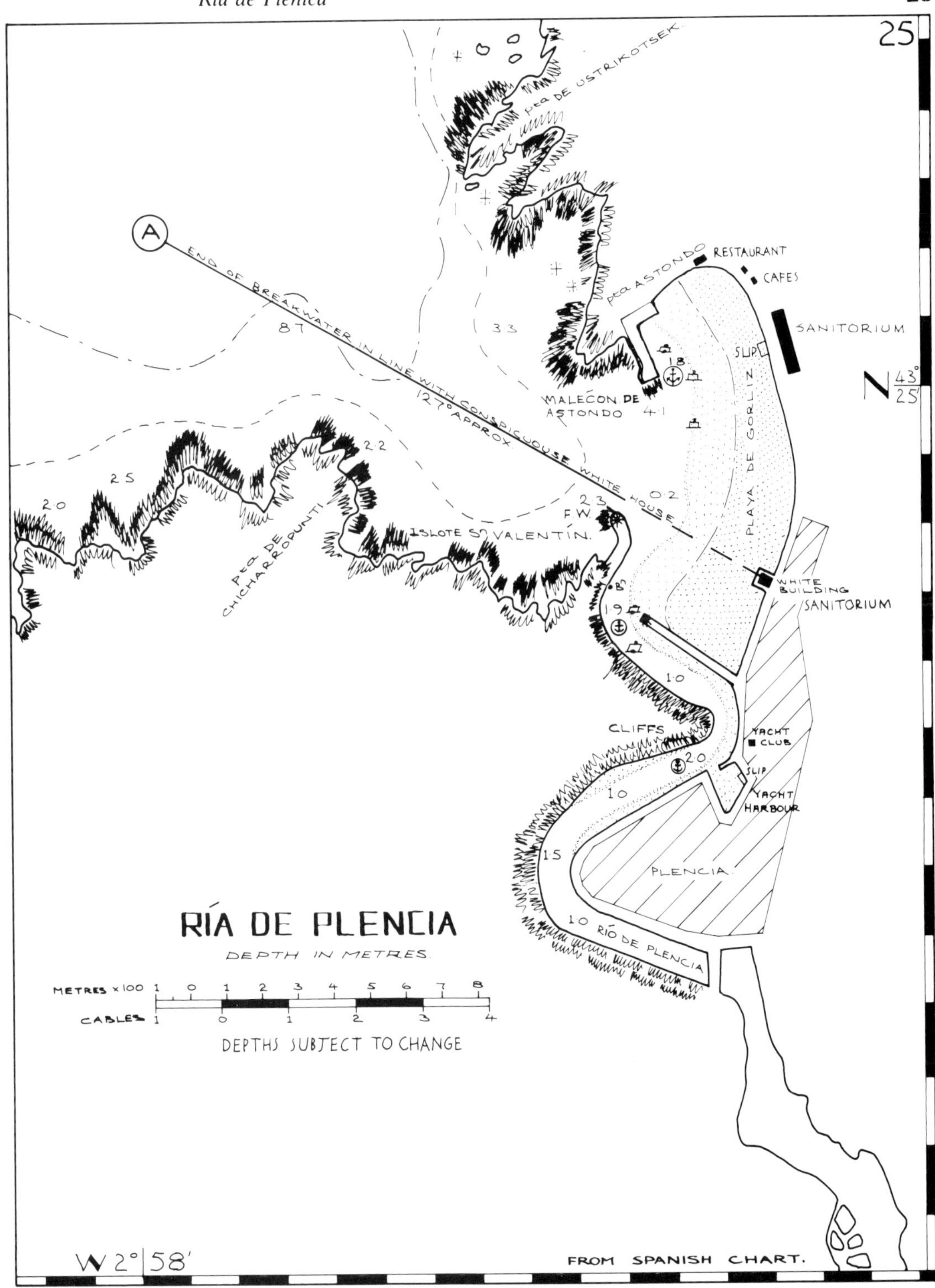
25
RÍA DE PLENCIA
DEPTH IN METRES
DEPTHS SUBJECT TO CHANGE
METRES x 100
CABLES
END OF BREAKWATER IN LINE WITH CONSPICUOUS WHITE HOUSE 127° APPROX
Pta DE USTRIKOTSEK
Pta ASTONDO
RESTAURANT
CAFES
SANITORIUM
SLIP
MALECON DE ASTONDO
PLAYA DE GORLIZ
ISLOTE Sn VALENTÍN
Pta DE CHICHARROPUNTI
F.W.
WHITE BUILDING
SANITORIUM
CLIFFS
YACHT CLUB
SLIP
YACHT HARBOUR
PLENCIA
RÍO DE PLENCIA
N 43° 25'
W 2° 58'
FROM SPANISH CHART.

Ría de Plencia—leading marks—high water.

Ría de Plencia—high water.

Night Not recommended unless familiar with this port as there are no navigational lights and dangers are unmarked.

Anchorages

Behind **Malecón de Astondo** in 2 m (1 fathom) sand, halfway along the breakwater and about 9 m (10 yards) away from it. Note there are rocks around head of breakwater.

In **Río de Plencia** about 23 m (25 yards) upriver from concrete beacon and about 17 m (20 yards) from W bank oppos:te the yacht harbour. Subject to silting.

Moorings

Mooring buoys are established behind **Malecón de Astondo.**

Ría de Plencia – from **Punta Astondo** looking E–SE–S–SW–W.

Ría de Plencia—anchorage behind Malecón de Astondo.

Berths

Drying berth is possible for craft with under 1·2 m (4 ft) draft in small inner harbour.

Yachts which can dry out are advised to do so above the first bend to starboard as the ground there is less covered with small stones and boulders.

Formalities

Nil.

Facilities

Water From cafés.

Petrol Pump on way out of town.

Shops Simple shops adequate for normal food supplies.

Yacht Club Normal facilities. Very helpful (87.60.36).

Visits The famous castle at **Butron** is worth a visit.

Fiestas 2–8 September, festivities of St Antolin.

26 Abra de Bilbao

Population 350,000 Rating 3-1-1 Position 43°20·3′N 3°1·2′W

General

This large commercial port can be entered in all weather conditions and complete shelter obtained. The entrance is easy and anchoring or mooring is possible in up to 6 m (3 fathoms) over a large area. It is also possible to lie alongside temporarily in the **Santurce** boat harbour.

The two yacht clubs provide excellent facilities and welcome visiting yachtsmen. Provisions, water, etc. can be obtained locally and almost any requirements can be met in **Bilbao** city, some 12 km up the river. Sailing up the river between rows of factories, yards and works is not recommended owing to the stench, oil and dirt. **Bilbao** has a close commercial affiliation with Britain and the assistance given the starving city during the Civil War is still remembered.

Warnings

A large breakwater is under construction, which extends 2 miles at 280° from **Punta Galea**. Other harbour works and dredging are constantly in progress. Care must be taken not to impede ships in the narrow entrance between the breakwaters.

If the wind shifts to SE, S or SW yachts are advised to leave, as a blanket of soot and smuts descends on the harbour from the many factories.

Data

Charts

Admiralty Nos. 74, 2925, 1170
Spanish Nos. 197B, 942, 941, 9410
French Nos. 4991, 3836, 6774

Magnetic variation 5°40′W (1984) decreasing by about 5′ each year.

Tidal information Spanish tide tables are available for this port.

	HW		LW		MHWS	MHWN	MLWS	MLWN
Pointe de Grave	0600 1800	1100 2300	0000 1200	0500 1700	5·4 m 17·6 ft	4·2 m 13·8 ft	0·9 m 3·0 ft	2·1 m 6·8 ft
Abra de Bilbao	−0·40	+0·20	−0·30	−0·25	1·3 m −4·1 ft	1·2 m −3·9 ft	0·5 m −1·8 ft	0·7 m −2·3 ft

Strong winds from the SW, W or NW raise the level of the water by 0·5 m (1·5 ft). Gales from NE, E or S lower it by the same amount. The ebb stream in the river and harbour entrance at springs is 3 knots and neaps 1·5 knots. Flood streams are not so strong.

Lights

Punta Galea. Group Flashing (3) White, 8 seconds, 82 m (269 ft), 19 miles. Stone tower with dwelling, red and white cupola. Visible 011°–227°. 196 m (640 ft) NNW Fog Siren (3), 30 seconds.

Dique de Punta Lucerno head. Fl. Green 4 sec. 23 m (75 ft) 8 M Tripod. Racon.

Dique de Punta Galea head. Group Flashing (3) Red, 8 seconds, 21 m (69 ft), 6 miles. Red metal columns.

Contra Mulle de Algorta. Group Flashing (2) Red, 6 seconds, 18 m (59 ft), 10 miles. White stone tower. Visible 312°–192°.

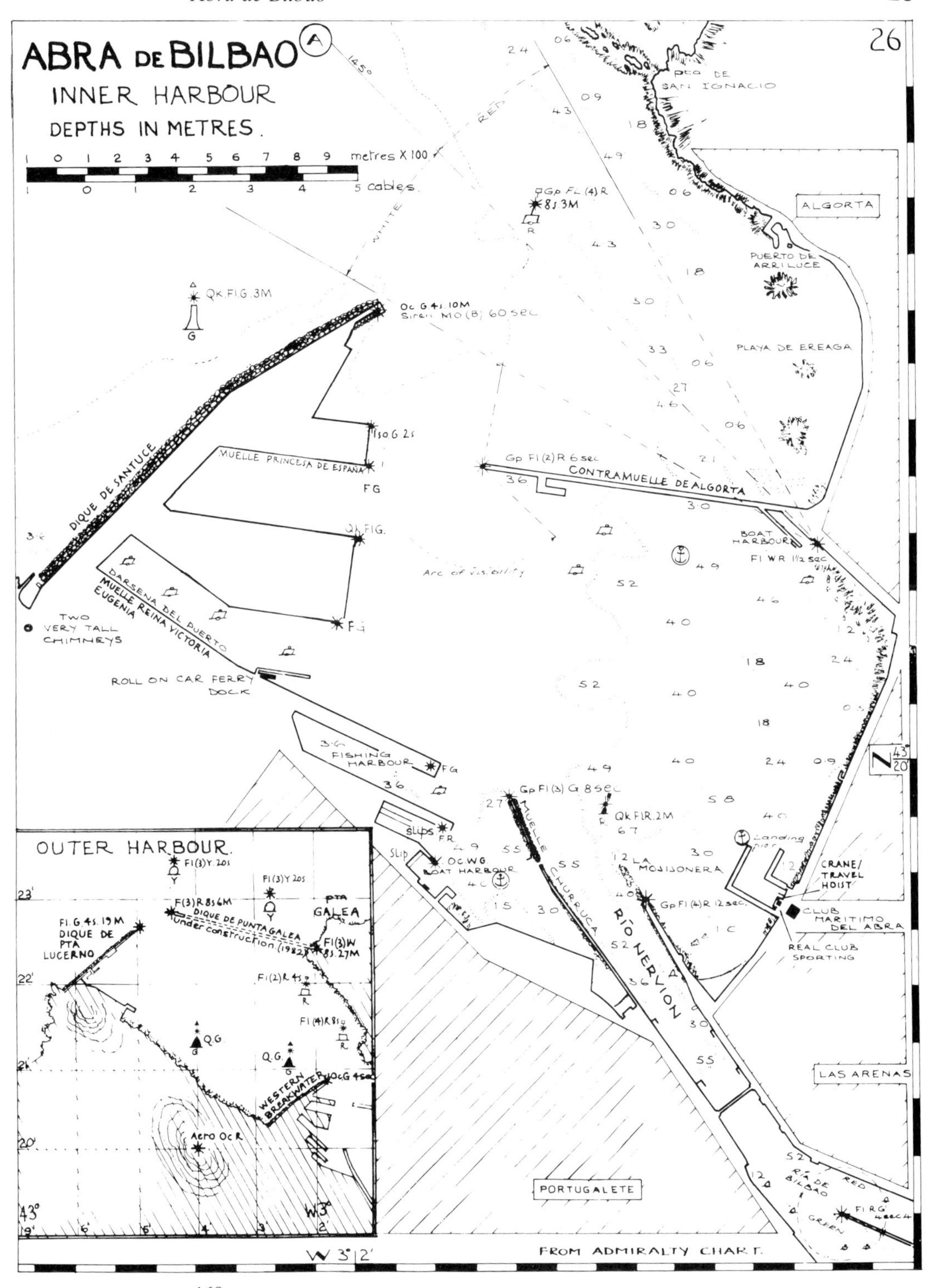
ABRA DE BILBAO
INNER HARBOUR
DEPTHS IN METRES.
metres X 100
cables
26
PTA DE SAN IGNACIO
ALGORTA
PUERTO DE ARRILUCE
PLAYA DE EREAGA
Qk.Fl.G.3M
Oc G 4s 10M Siren MO(B) 60 sec
DIQUE DE SANTUCE
MUELLE PRINCESA DE ESPAÑA
Iso G 2s
FG
Qk Fl G.
Gp Fl (2) R 6 sec
CONTRAMUELLE DE ALGORTA
BOAT HARBOUR
Fl W R 1½ sec
Arc of visibility
DARSENA DEL PUERTO
MUELLE REINA VICTORIA EUGENIA
TWO VERY TALL CHIMNEYS
ROLL ON CAR FERRY DOCK
FISHING HARBOUR
Gp Fl (3) G 8 sec
Qk Fl R. 2M
SLIPS
Oc W G
BOAT HARBOUR
LA MOJIJONERA
Landing pier
CRANE/ TRAVEL HOIST
CLUB MARITIMO DEL ABRA
REAL CLUB SPORTING
Gp Fl (4) R 12 sec.
MUELLE CHURRUCA
RÍO NERVION
LAS ARENAS
PORTUGALETE
RIA DE BILBAO
Fl R G 4 sec
RED
GREEN
WHITE
OUTER HARBOUR
Fl (3) Y 20s
F(3) R 8s 6M
DIQUE DE PUNTA GALEA under construction (1982)
PTA GALEA
Fl (3) W 8s 27M
Fl. G 4s 19M DIQUE DE PTA LUCERNO
Fl (2) R 4s
Fl (4) R 8s
Q.G
WESTERN BREAKWATER
Oc G 4s
Aero Oc R
W 3° 2'
FROM ADMIRALTY CHART.

Punta Lucero and entrance to Bilbao. The new harbour wall is from this point.

Contra Mulle de Algorta. Flashing White, Red sectors, 1·3 seconds, 22·3 m (73 ft), 11 miles. White tower on house with red roof. White 119°–135°, Red 135°–150°.

Dique de Santuce. Occulting Green, 4 seconds, 26 m (85 ft), 10 miles. Concrete tower on building. Fog Siren Morse B (– · · ·), 60 seconds.

Espigón No. 1 head (N corner). Iso Green 2 sec., 13 m (43 ft) 2 M., grey column.

Espigón No. 1 head (S corner). Fixed Green, 1 M., grey tripod on hut.

Espigón No. 2 head (N corner). Q. Green 2 M., grey metal column.

Espigón No. 2 head (S corner). Fixed Green, 10 m (33 ft) 2 M., framework tripod.

Muelle Churruca Group Flashing 3 Green, 8 seconds, 11·9 m (39 ft), 2 miles. Brick tower.

Santurce boat harbour. Occulting White, 4 seconds 7 m (23 ft), 2 miles. Column.

La Mojijonera mole head. Group Flashing (4) Red, 12 seconds, 10·4 m (34 ft), 2 miles. Metal tripod on light grey hut marked '4'.

Monte Serantes. Aero Occulting Red, 3 seconds, 448 m (1470 ft). Occasional.

Fishing harbour. Fixed Red and Fixed Green.

Buoys

Off end of Dique de Santuce. Green conical buoy with tower, Quick Flashing Green 8 seconds. 3 M. Green cone top mark.

Off La Mojijonera. Red can buoy "C" with tower, Group Flashing (4) Red, 8 seconds. 2 M.

Off Algorta. Red can light buoy, Red can top mark, Group Flashing (4) Red, 8 seconds, 5 M. NE off **Dique de Punta Galea** (under construction). 6 Yellow Flashing Yellow and Quick Flashing Yellow light buoys.

Punta Galea and lighthouse. Note light-coloured cliff face. Outer breakwater built from this point.

Signal station 2 cables SSE of lighthouse on **Punta Galea**. For communication by International Code of Flag Signals.

Life saving Life saving apparatus is maintained at **Santurce** and **Portugalete**.

Consul A British Consular Office is at **Bilbao** at Alameda de Urquijo 2–8 (4157600).

Radio Aero radiobeacon, radio weather station (page 17).

Port Radio See page 20.

Approaches

Day *From W* **Punta Lucero**, a high prominent feature with the yellow sandy bay of **Ría Somorrostro** to its W, is easily seen as is the outer breakwater.

From E **Cabo Villano**, a large steep-sided promontory with a very broken and jagged island off it, and the estuary of **Ría de Plencia** are unmistakable as are the whitish cliffs and outer breakwater at **Punta Galea**. The **Abra de Bilbao** is easily recognised by the high stone breakwaters and the smoke and flames of many factories and iron works upriver. Two very tall chimnies with red and white bands at the top and situated at the W end of the breakwater are conspicuous.

Abra de Bilbao—entrance looking south.

Night The lights of **Castello de Santa Ana** (Fl. (4) W. 15 sec. 17 M.), **Punta Galea** (Fl. (3) W. 8 sec. 19 M.), **Cabo Machichaco** (Fl.W. 7 sec. 24 M.), **Monte Serantes** (Aero beacon Oc.R. 3 sec.) enable an approach to the bay to be made at night.

Entrance

Enter between the outer breakwaters and down the middle of the **Abra de Bilbao**, keeping clear of shoals at the sides when there is a heavy sea running. Near the inner entrance keep near to a large red can buoy so that observation can be made inside the harbour to ascertain that no large vessel is leaving. Enter between the inner breakwater heads giving them at least 23 m (25 yards) clearance because of underwater obstructions.

Night Enter between (Fl.G. 4 sec.) and (Fl. (3) R. 8 sec.) then follow the white sector 119°–135° of the light on the root of the E breakwater (Fl.W.R., 1·3 sec. 14 M.) about mid-sector. Pass near a red can buoy (Fl. (4) R. 8 sec.) and if entrance is

Abra de Bilbao—head of western inner breakwater.
Note large concrete blocks which surround most Spanish breakwaters.

clear between W breakwater head (Oc.G. 4 sec. 10 M.) to starboard and E breakwater head (Fl. (2) R. 6 sec. 10 M.) to port. Then leave (Iso.G. 2 sec.), (F.G.), (Q.Fl.G.) and (F.G.) to starboard. The two large oil refineries on the W side of the estuary are very conspicuous at night, having a mass of powerful lights around them.

Anchorages

Anchor either about 100 m (108 yards) NW or N of **Las Arenas** landing pier clear of mooring in 4 m (2 fathoms) mud, or about 200 m (208 yards) W of boat harbour at E breakwater root. These are convenient for landing and are near the yacht clubs.

Anchorage is also possible between the **Muelle Churruca** and the **Santurce** boat harbour.

Berths

Secure to N pontoon of the yacht harbour in SE corner of the **Abra**. There are two small drying harbours in the bay: on the E coast below **Algorta** is **Puerto de Arriluce** and on the W, near **Nogales**, is **Puerto de Ciévrana**.

Moorings

Vacant moorings may be allocated by a club boatman or can be picked up temporarily near both anchorages detailed above.

Formalities

Yachts may be visited by a number of officials of various organisations, all requiring different information.

Facilities

Water From **Las Arenas** yacht harbour (white building on SW corner).

Diesel **Las Arenas** yacht harbour; also there is a bunkering supply point.

Petrol **Las Arenas** yacht harbour.

Shops Adequate shops exist at **Las Arenas** between the landing pier and the transporter bridge and at **Santurce**, also at **Algorta**. At **Bilbao**, a half hour's trip in bus or train, shops of every kind exist. There are chandlery shops on the way to and in **Bilbao** itself.

Yacht yards A yacht building and repair yard exists at the S side of **Darsena de Axpe**, half way to **Bilbao** (278065).

Yacht clubs The **Reál Sporting Club**, a very old-established yachting club, has a full size yacht club on piles near the yacht harbour. The **Club Maritimo del Abra** has a palatial club just SW of the landing stage with the entrance from the road just behind it. Both clubs welcome visiting yachtsmen.

Visits A bus trip to **Bilbao** from **Las Arenas** is worth while. The road runs alongside **Río Nervion** which is lined with factories, works, yards etc. The castle at **Somorrostro** above **Santurce** and the old buildings at **Santa Maria** can be visited in addition to the city of **Bilbao**.

Fiestas Anniversary of the Liberation of the City of **Bilbao** on 19 June. 13 August–11 September, August festivities.

British Consulate General
Alameda de Urquijo 2–8 Bilbao 8 (Tel: 41:57:600, 41-57-711, 41-57-722).

Albra de Bilbao—looking north. *Photo: Alarde*

27 Puerto de Castro Urdiales

Population 12,500 Rating 1-2-2 Position 43°23′N 3°12·9′W

General

A most delightful and picturesque old Spanish town with a Knights Templars' castle and old church, very good restaurants, cafés, shops and sandy beathing beaches. The entrance is easy and the port has a good anchorage, a friendly yacht club and above all, is very clean. Subject to swell with NE–N winds.

Warnings

The bottom of the harbour is mud and sand on rock and in heavy winds anchors may drag.

Data

Charts

Admiralty Nos. 2925, 75
Spanish Nos. 128, 941, 165A
French Nos. 4991, 3542

Magnetic variation 5°46′W (1984) decreasing by about 5′ each year.

Tidal information

	HW		LW		MHWS	MHWN	MLWS	MLWN
Pointe de Grave	0600 1800	1100 2300	0000 1200	0500 1700	5·4 m 17·6 ft	4·2 m 13·8 ft	0·9 m 3·0 ft	2·1 m 6·8 ft
Castro Urdiales	−0·30	−0·40	−0·25	−0·05	−1·4 m −4·5 ft	−1·3 m −4·4 ft	−0·6 m −1·9 ft	−0·7 m −2·1 ft

Lights

Castillo de Santa Ana. Group Flashing 4 White, 15 seconds, 46·3 m (152 ft), 17 miles. White conical tower on old fortress. Fog Siren Morse C (– · – ·), 60 seconds.
Rompeolas Norte head. Flashing Green, 3 seconds, 12·2 m (40 ft), 7 miles. 8-sided tower.
Contradique head. Group Flashing (2) Red, 6 seconds, 8·2 m (27 ft), 6 miles. Red structure.
Muelle Norte, S end. Fixed Green, 6·1 m (20 ft), 4 miles. Concrete column.
Muelle SW, N end. Fixed Red, 6·1 m (20 ft), 4 miles. Concrete column.

Life saving A line throwing apparatus is maintained.

Approaches

Day

From W The large mountain **Montaña Candiña** with the wide sandy estuary **Ensenada de Oriñón** E of the low **Cabo Cebollero** are a group of features easily identified. **Castro Urdiales** itself is not seen until **Punta del Rabanal**, with its conspicuous cemetery, is rounded.

From E The buildings, skyscrapers, castle and church of **Castro Urdiales** can be

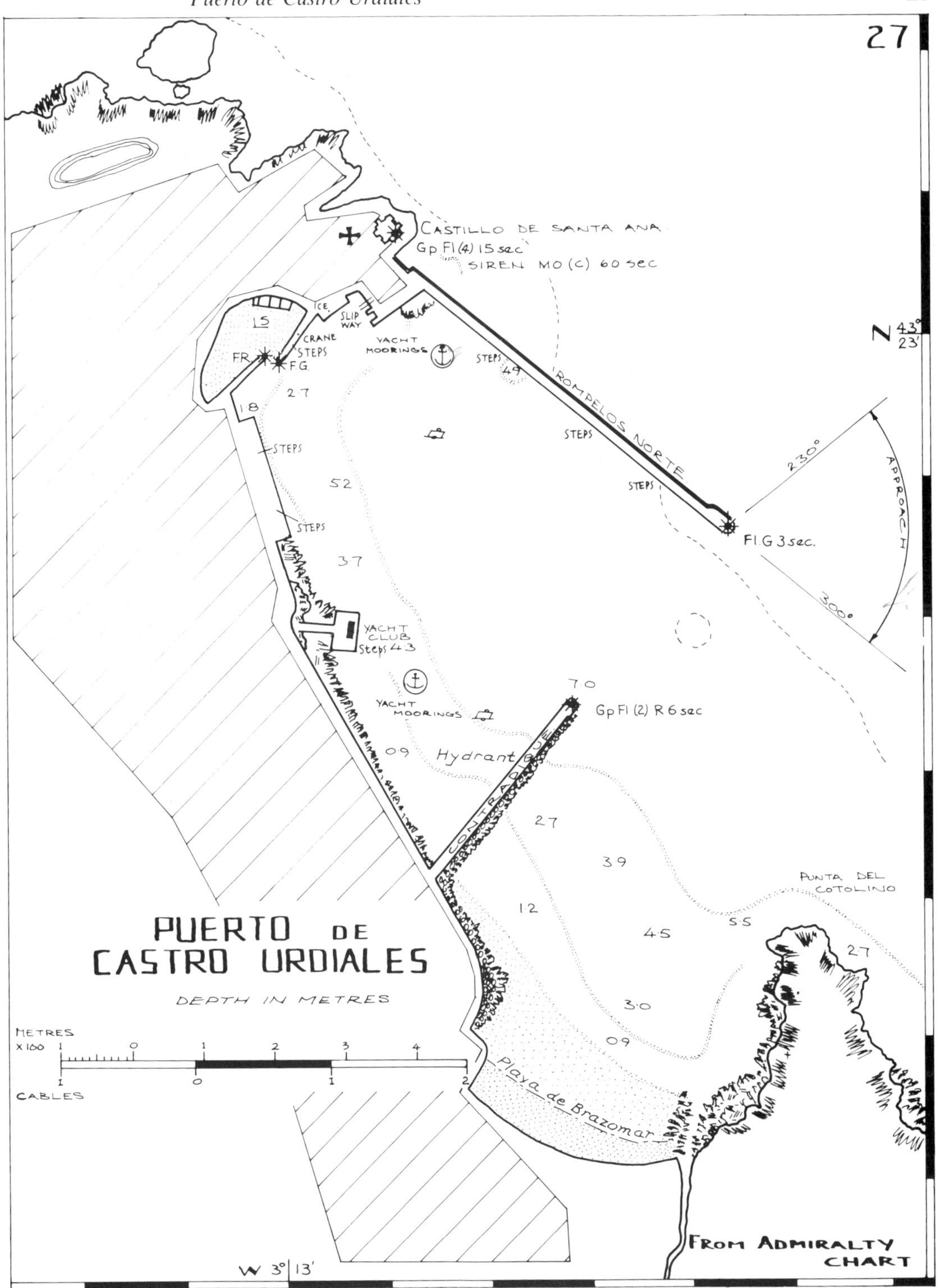
27
CASTILLO DE SANTA ANA
Gp Fl (4) 15 sec
SIREN MO (C) 60 sec
ICE
SLIP WAY
CRANE
STEPS
YACHT MOORINGS
STEPS
FR
F.G.
ROMPELOS NORTE
STEPS
STEPS
STEPS
STEPS
230°
APPROACH
Fl G 3 sec.
300°
YACHT CLUB
Steps
YACHT MOORINGS
Gp Fl (2) R 6 sec
Hydrant
CONTRADIQUE
PUNTA DEL COTOLINO
PUERTO DE CASTRO URDIALES
DEPTH IN METRES
METRES x100
CABLES
Playa de Brazomar
FROM ADMIRALTY CHART
W 3° 13'
N 43° 23'

Puerto de Castro Urdiales—approach from east.

seen afar against a background of dark green steep hills. Approach until the lighthouse on the castle bears due W ½ mile.

Night Using the lighthouses of **Punta del Caballo** (Oc. (4) W. 15 sec. 12 M.), **Castello de Santa Ana** (Fl. (4) W. 15 sec. 17 M.) and **Punta Galea** (Fl. (3) W. 8 sec. 19 M.) navigate to a position where the light of **Castello de Santa Ana** bears due W ½ mile.

Entrance

Day From the position above proceed towards the mole heads on a bearing between 230° and 300° and enter between allowing about 24 m (25 yards) from them for underwater obstruction.

Night From the above position, in *approach, night*, sail on a bearing between 230° and 300° towards the entrance lights and enter between Fl.G. 3 sec. to starboard and Gp.Fl. (2) R. 6 sec. to port, giving clearance of at least 24 m (25 yards) to the mole heads.

Anchorages

Anchor in up to 10 m (5 fathoms) mud/sand/rock, in NW corner of outer harbour. Two anchors are advised as holding is poor. Alternatively, anchor off the yacht club in 4 m (2 fathoms) sand/mud, but buoy anchors.

Moorings

There are several small private moorings in the N of the harbour and by the club some of which can be used in conjunction with an anchor. Do not use the large white buoys near the inner harbour. These are used by tunny fishing boats, which may return at all hours of the night.

Berths

It is possible to lie alongside the moles of the inner harbour just inside the entrance. There is 2 m (1 fathom) for the first 19 m (20 yards) from the entrance on the NW side of the N mole and about 1 m (½ fathom) for the same distance along the SW mole. It would also be possible to dry out further up the harbour, but reconnoitre first at LW as there are many mooring lines and also a grid which is situated along the N wall. In calm weather, yachts may lie alongside the inside of the **Dique Rompeolas Norte.**

Puerto de Castro Urdiales—entrance to inner harbour—low water.

Formalities

A local official will board with the usual kind of proforma to complete but may require visiting yachtsmen to go to his office.

Facilities

Water From the local ice factory near the slip by prior arrangement, or from the water point on the **Contradique** or from the yacht club.

Diesel From pump near SW mole of inner harbour.

Petrol From petrol station behind market.

Shops Excellent shops within easy reach of harbour and a good market.

Slipway There is a very good slip in the N corner of the harbour.

Hotels Several, but mainly for holiday visitors.

Yacht club **Club Nautico de Castro Urdiales** welcomes visiting yachtsmen and is a yachting as opposed to a social club. Showers, drinks and sometimes light refreshments are also available (861234).

Visits A walk to the statue on the hill above the town gives a tremendous panoramic view of the coast.

Beaches The **Playa de Brazomar** is a pleasant sandy bay but tends to get crowded. As the water is so clean one can bathe from the yacht.

Fiestas 26 June, *Romeria* of St Pelayo.
3 August, festivities of Coso Blanco.
15 August, festivities in honour of the Assumption.
23 August, festivities commemorating the Liberation.

28 Puerto de Laredo

Population 8,093 winter, 30,000 summer Rating 3-3-2 Position 43°24·8′N 3°25′W

General

A small fishing port which almost dries out at LW. It is fairly easy to enter and has a very pleasant town with good shops and a small market. A vast sandy beach nearby is being developed into a holiday area typical of the Mediterranean coast, but as it is so large it is not spoiled as yet.

Warnings

Submerged rocky training walls are S of the harbour entrance, unmarked. Dredging is in progress in the harbour but a shelf and rocks extend from the walls.

Data

Charts

Admiralty Nos. 2925, 75
Spanish Nos. 24B, 128, 940, 941
French Nos. 4991, 3542

Magnetic variation 5°46′W (1984) decreasing by 5′ each year.

Tidal information

	HW		LW		MHWS	MHWN	MLWS	MLWN
Pointe de Grave	0600 1800	1100 2300	0000 1200	0500 1700	5·4 m 17·6 ft	4·2 m 13·8 ft	0·9 m 3·0 ft	2·1 m 6·8 ft
Puerto de Laredo	−0·00	−0·10	+0·05	+0·25	−1·3 m −4·1 ft	−1·2 m −4·0 ft	−0·5 m −1·6 ft	−0·6 m −1·8 ft

Lights

Punta Pescador. Group Flashing (3+1) White, 15 seconds, 37·2 m (122 ft), 17 miles. Conical stone tower on square building.
Punta del Caballo. Group Occulting (4) White, 14 seconds, 24·1 m (79 ft), 12 miles. Blue conical stone tower, white dwelling.
Espignón Norte head. Fixed Red, 8·8 m (29 ft), 2 miles. Square concrete tower.

Approaches

Day

From W **Cabo Ajo** and **Quejo** two very large and steep-sided rocky promontories, are quite unmistakable with the sandy **Río Ajo** between them, as is **Montaña Santoña** with its conspicuous lighthouses. This mountain appears like an island when viewed from a distance.

From E **Cabo Cebollero**, a low cape with the noticeably sandy **Ensenada de Oriñón** to its E and a very large mountain feature **Montaña Candiña** to its W are very conspicuous, as is **Montaña Santoña** which appears as an island from this direction. Approach to a position where **Punta del Caballo** is 1 mile at 340°.

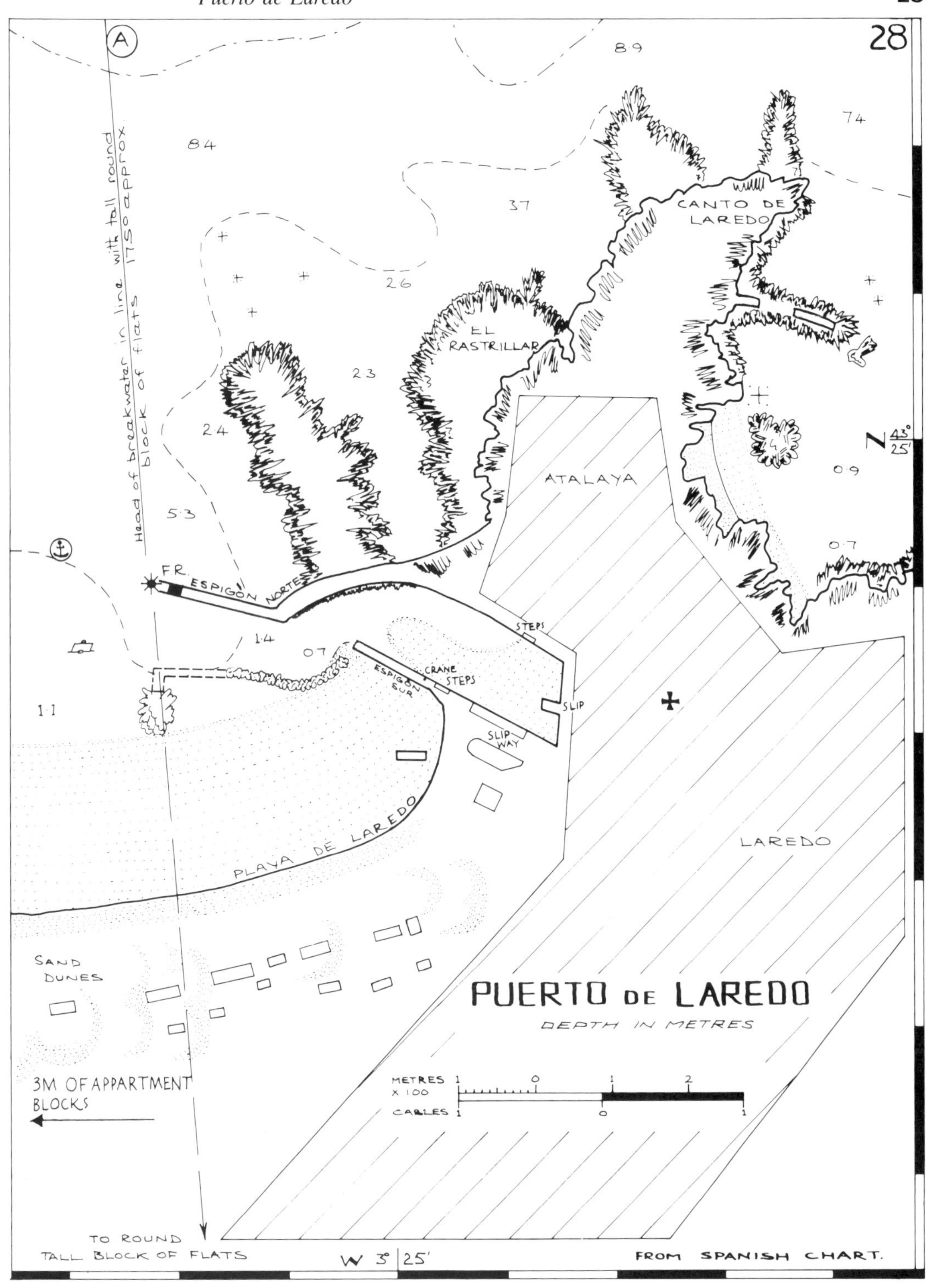
28
Head of breakwater in line with tall round block of flats 175° approx
CANTO DE LAREDO
EL RASTRILLAR
ATALAYA
FR.
ESPIGON NORTE
STEPS
CRANE
STEPS
ESPIGON SUR
SLIP
SLIP WAY
PLAYA DE LAREDO
LAREDO
SAND DUNES
3M OF APPARTMENT BLOCKS
PUERTO DE LAREDO
DEPTH IN METRES
METRES x 100
CABLES
TO ROUND TALL BLOCK OF FLATS
W 3° 25'
N 43° 25'
FROM SPANISH CHART.

Night The lights of **Cabo Ajo** (Oc (3) W. 12 sec. 13 M.), **Punta del Pescador** (Fl. (3+1) W. 15 sec. 17 M.), **Punta del Caballo** (Oc. (4) W. 14 sec. 12 M.) and **Castillo de Santa Ana** (Fl. (4) W. 15 sec. 17 M.) enable a position to be obtained where **Punta del Caballo** is 1 mile at 340°. The harbour light of **Laredo** (F.R. 2 M.) will also assist.

Entrance

Day From the position given above set course 175°, Line Ⓐ, towards the head of the mole on which there is a white building. The town remains obscured until close approach but a large circular block of flats will be easily seen above the end of the mole. Round the end of the mole at about 5 m (5 yards) and follow it along at the same distance into the harbour. Watch out for the rocky training walls to starboard.

Ría de Santoña—entrance—looking south.

Night From the position given above in *approach, night*, sail on a course of 175°, Line Ⓐ, towards the (F.R.) light at the end of the mole. Round this close to at 5 m (5 yards) and follow the mole into the harbour entrance.

Moorings

A mooring buoy is laid ½ cable SW of the harbour entrance in 4 m (2 fathoms) sand.

Puerto de Laredo – anchorage and pontoons at **Punta del Puntal.**

Puerto de Laredo—leading marks.

Anchorages

It is possible when weather permits to anchor in 4 m (2 fathoms) sand, with the end of the mole 145 m (150 yards) at 120°.

Berths

The only berths with any water, about 1·3 m (4·5 ft), are just inside the harbour to port against wood piles with rubber tyres, if not already occupied by fishing boats.

It would be possible to dry out further up the harbour on legs or against the harbour wall.

Puerto de Laredo—looking north west half tide. *Photo: Persa*

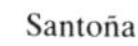

Puerto de Laredo—looking south—high water neaps.

Formalities

Local officials are not very interested, but eventually will require the usual information.

Facilities

Water From bars and cafés near harbour.

Diesel From pump on quay.

Petrol From pump on outskirts of town.

Shops Good shops concentrated in the second road back from the harbour.

Visits Thirteenth century church is worth a visit.

Fiestas 25 August, Battle of Flowers.

Slipway SW side of the harbour.

Puntal del Pasaje

A new yacht harbour has been developed 4 M to NW of **Laredo** behind **Puntal de Pasaje** with floating pontoons and many moorings. Extensions are planned. There is a large club house belonging to the **Club Nautico de Laredo** (CNL) (605942) with all facilities nearby. A slipway, 3 cranes, workshops and covered storage are already provided and more facilities are planned.

Training walls
Berth

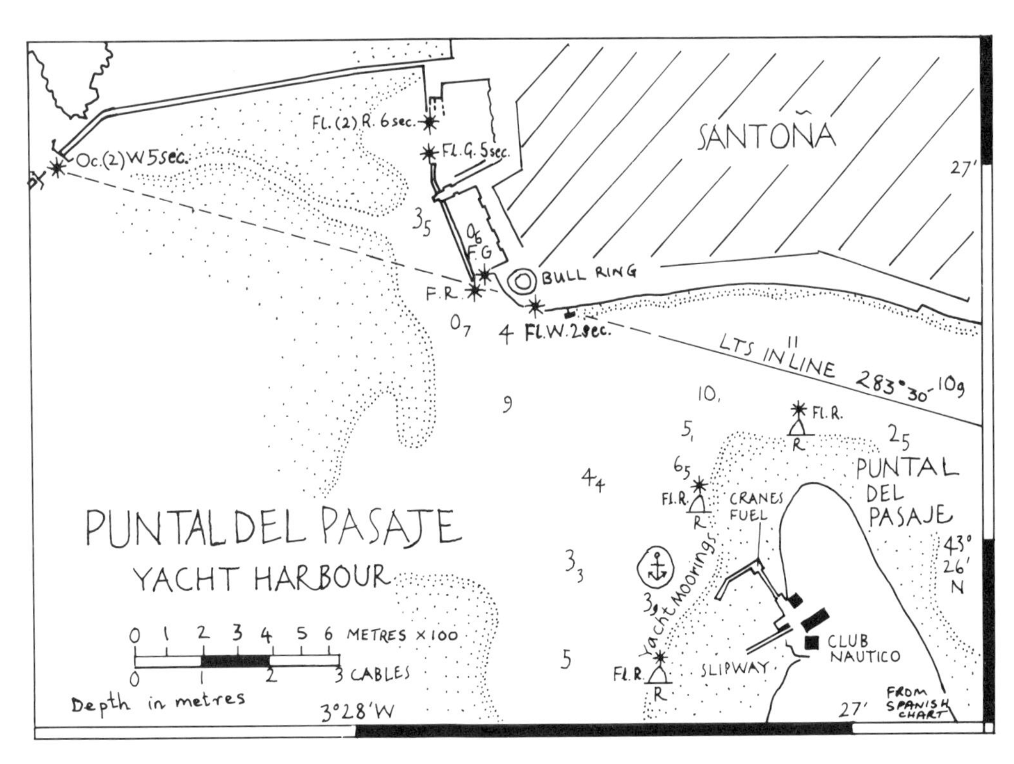
SANTOÑA
Oc.(2)W 5sec.
Fl.(2) R. 6sec.
Fl. G. 5sec.
F.G
F.R.
BULL RING
4 Fl.W.2sec.
LTS IN LINE 283°30'
Fl. R.
R
PUNTAL DEL PASAJE
CRANES
FUEL
Yacht moorings
CLUB NAUTICO
SLIPWAY
PUNTAL DEL PASAJE
YACHT HARBOUR
0 1 2 3 4 5 6 METRES x100
0 1 2 3 CABLES
Depth in metres
3°28'W
27'
43° 26' N
FROM SPANISH CHART

29 Ría y Puerto de Santoña

Population 10,004 Rating 3-3-3 Position 43°26·5′N 3°27·8′W

General

A sardine fishing and canning village and also a military post with two small basins where yachts can moor in up to 4 m (2 fathoms). The approach is not difficult. The town has a colonial air about it. The shops and market are not very good. There is a huge area of beautiful sandy beach opposite and several others nearby. Christopher Columbus's *Santa Maria* was built here.

E and S winds make this harbour uncomfortable at times because of swell from the **Canal de Colindres** at the head of which is a small harbour.

Warnings

The leading marks, which are not easy to see, are on a line passing close to a shoal patch which is being dredged.

Data

Charts

Admiralty Nos. 2925, 75
Spanish Nos. 24B, 128, 940, 941
French Nos. 4991, 3542

Magnetic variation 5°46′W (1984) decreasing by about 5′ each year.

Tidal information

	HW		LW		MHWS	MHWN	MLWS	MLWN
Pointe de Grave	0600 1800	1100 2300	0000 1200	0500 1700	5·4 m 17·6 ft	4·2 m 13·8 ft	0·9 m 3·0 ft	2·1 m 6·8 ft
Puerto de Santoña	−0·00	−0·10	+0·05	+0·25	−1·3 m −4·1 ft	−1·2 m −4·0 ft	−0·5 m −1·6 ft	−0·6 m −1·8 ft

The ebb stream reaches 3 knots at springs and is stronger when **Río Marrón** is in flood.

Lights

Punta Pescador. Group Flashing (3+1) W 15 seconds, 37·2 m (122 ft), 17 miles. Conical stone tower on square dwelling.
Punta del Caballo. Group Occulting (4) White, 14 seconds, 24·1 m (79 ft), 12 miles. Blue conical stone tower, white dwelling.
Leading lights 285·5° Line Ⓐ .
Front: Flashing White, 2 seconds, 5·5 m (18 ft), 9 miles. Triangle on top of grey metal framework tower on quay near bull ring.
Rear: Group Occulting 2 White, 5 seconds, 12·5 m (41 ft), 11 miles. Disc on grey metal framework tower S of road bridge. Visible 281·5°–289·5°.
Old Basin W side. Fixed Red, 6·1 m (20 ft), 4 miles. Column.
Old Basin E side. Fixed Green, 6·1 m (20 ft), 4 miles. Column.
Dársena Nueva N side. Group Flashing 2 Red, 6 seconds, 7 m (23 ft), 4 miles.
Dársena Nueva S side. Flashing Green, 5 seconds, 7 m (23 ft), 3 miles.
Canal de Colindres. Flashing Red, 5 seconds, 1 mile. Triangular metal tower.
Colindres Bridge. Fixed Green.

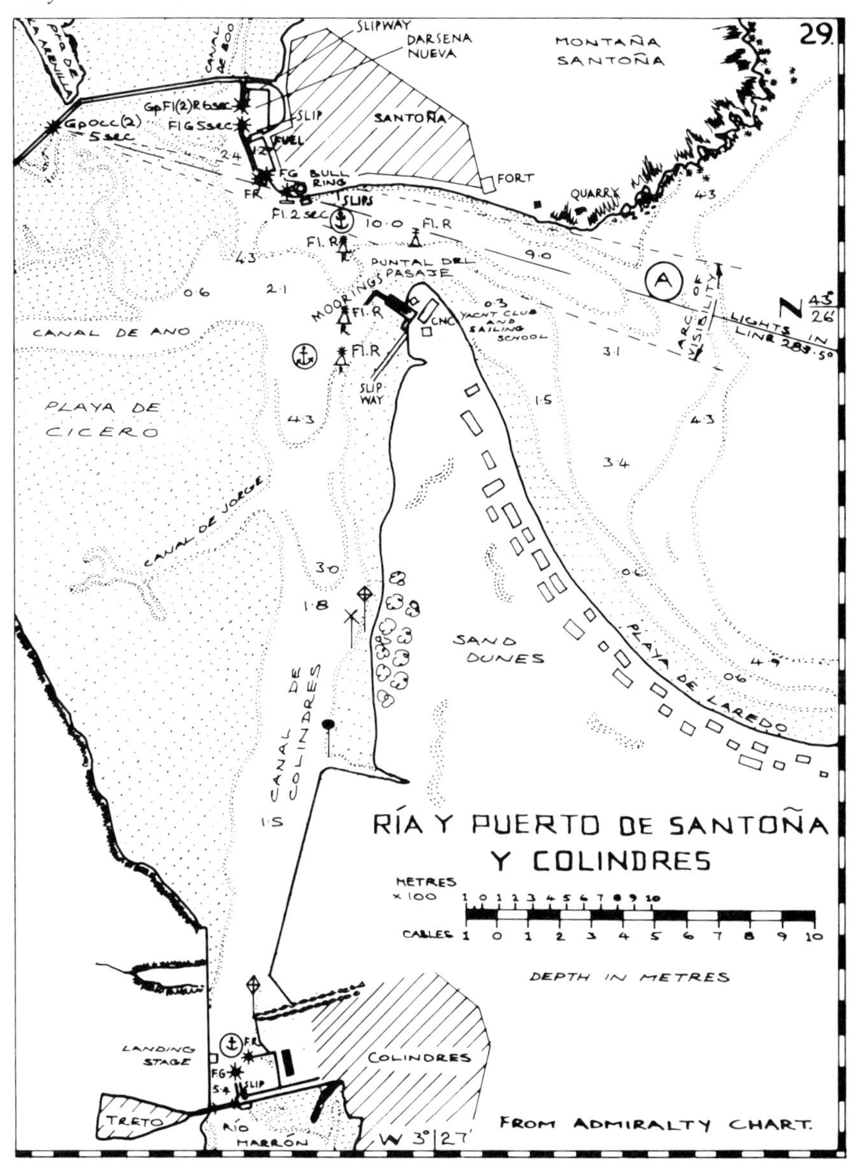

Buoys Four Red conical lightbuoys (Fl.R.) located at **Puntal des Pasaje**.

Port Radio See page 20.

Approaches

Day *From W* **Cabos Ajo** and **Quejo**, two very large and steep-sided rocky promontories, are quite unmistakable with the sandy **Río Ajo** between them, as is **Montaña Santoña** with its two conspicuous lighthouses. This mountain appears like an island when seen from a distance.

Puerto de Santoña—leading lights.

From E **Cabo Cebollero**, a low cape with the sandy **Ensenada de Oriñón** to its E and a very large mountain feature to its W, **Montaña Candiña**, are very conspicuous; also **Montaña Santoña** which appears as an island from this direction. Aproach to a position where **Punta del Caballo** is 1 mile at 340°.

Night The lights of **Cabo Ajo** (Oc. (3) W. 12 sec. 13 M.), **Punta del Pescador** (Fl. (3+1) W. 15 sec. 17 M.), **Punta Caballo** (Oc. (4) W. 14 sec. 12 M.) and **Castillo de Santa Ana** (Fl. (4) W. 15 sec. 17 M.) enable a position to be obtained where **Punta del Caballo** is 1 mile on 340°. The harbour lights at **Laredo** (F.R. 2 M.) will assist.

Entrance

Day From the position above sail SW until the S edge of **Santoña** village, the bull ring, bears 285°. Turn onto this bearing and identify the leading marks on Line Ⓐ, (*Front:* a grey metal lattice tower with triangular topmark 5·5 m (18 ft) high on quay near the bull ring. *Rear:* a similar tower with circular disc topmark 12·2 m (41 ft) high just S of a road bridge. Sometimes difficult to see.)

Puerto de Santoña—entrance to old harbour—half tide.

Follow this line or keep just N of it where the channel is deeper. Pass some 24 m (25 yards) S of a small 'T' jetty. Off the bull ring turn to starboard and enter the Old Basin.

Night From the position given in *approach, night*, above, sail SW until the leading lights are in line on 285·5°, Line Ⓐ (*Front:* Fl.W. 2 sec. 9 M. *Rear:* Oc. (2) W. 5 sec. 14 M.).

Follow this line or keep a little N of it until the 'T' jetty near the bull ring is seen; pass this 24 m (25 yards) to starboard and follow the wall round at the same distance. Enter Old Basin between F.R. and F.G. lights, or pass outside this basin following the wall at 24 m (25 yards) to **Dársena Nueva** entrance, Fl. (2) R. 6 sec. to port and Fl.G. 5 sec to starboard.

Anchorages

It is possible to anchor in up to 12 m (6 fathoms) sand S of **Santoña**: 98 m (100 yards) S of the bull ring is convenient. Anchorage is also possible near the bridge at **Colindres**, and there are many places where shallow draft or craft which can dry out can anchor in the **Canals de Colindres** and **Ano**. Anchor lights/shapes advised.

Moorings

It is advisable to either moor off the N wall of the Old Basin with an anchor astern and a bow line to the wall near the hard in 2 m (1 fathom) mud and sand, or to go to the **Dársena Nueva** and moor in the SW corner in 4 m (2 fathoms) mud/sand.

Berths

It is only possible to lie alongside the walls of **Dársena Nueva** as the walls of the Old Basin slope. It is sometimes possible to find room to lie alongside the inner side of the jetty in the small harbour at **Colindres** in 2 m (1 fathom) near the head of the jetty, although usually this space is occupied by fishing craft, or on the other side of the river at **Treto**.

Formalities

Normal except that papers and passports may have to be produced to the Customs officials at their office E of the bull ring.

Puerto de Santoña – old basin looking SE at high water.

Facilities

Water From ice factory between **Dársena Nueva** and Old Basin.

Diesel From pump on quay in Old Basin and at **Colindres**.

Petrol From pump in village on road N.

Shops Very spread out around the village but most normal requirements can be met.

Hards Good hard available in **Dársena Nueva** and at **Colindres**.

Visits A trip in a dinghy up the **Canal de Colindres** is worth while and if strong enough, a climb to the top of **Montaña Santoña** has a rewarding view. The thirteenth century church is also worth a visit.

Fiestas 8 May *Romeria*, also others during July, August and September.

Puerto de Santoña – Darsena Nueva looking NE at high water.

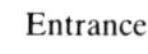

Ría y Puerto de Santoña – looking SW–W

30 Ría y Puerto de Santander

Population 160,000 Rating 1-1-1 Position 43°27·7′N 3°47·8′W

General

A delightful, clean and attractive city, harbour and port that has almost all the facilities that a yachtsman can want. Entrance is possible by day and night under all conditions; sheltered anchorages, berths and moorings are available. A first class yacht club, shops, repair facilities and beaches are avaialble.

Warnings

Under storm conditions the **Isla Mouro** should be left to starboard and the E entrance used. Considerable land reclamations are taking place.

Buoys marking the narrows are moved when this channel changes.

Data

Charts

Admiralty Nos. 2926 or 2925, 76
Spanish Nos. 663A, 660, 940, 128
French Nos. 4991, 3308

Magnetic variation 5°51′W (1984) decreasing by about 5′ each year.

Tidal information Spanish tide tables are available for this port.

	HW		LW		MHWS	MHWN	MLWS	MLWN
Pointe de Grave	0600 1800	1100 2300	0000 1200	0500 1700	5·4 m 17·6 ft	4·2 m 13·8 ft	0·9 m 3·0 ft	2·1 m 6·8 ft
Puerto de Santander	−0·30	−1·00	−0·20	−0·10	−0·9 m −2·7 ft	−0·8 m −2·5 ft	−0·1 m −0·3 ft	−0·2 m −0·7 ft

Gales from SW through W to NW cause a rise of up to 0·5 m (1·5 ft), and those from NE through E to SE decrease the water levels by the same amount. The ebb stream can reach 3 knots at springs.

Lights

Cabo Mayor. Group Flashing (2) White, 10 seconds, 89 m (291 ft), 21 miles. White Tower, first storey 8-sided, remainder round. Fog horn (2) 40 sec. Ro.Bn.
Cabo Ajo. Group Occulting (3) White, 12 seconds, 69 m (227 ft), 13 miles. Grey round tower, aluminium cupola in front of grey dwelling with red roof.
Isla Mouro. Group Flashing (2+1) White, 15 seconds, 36·6 m (120 ft), 8 miles. White conical tower on dwelling.
La Cerda. Group Flashing (4+1) White, 13·5 seconds, 21·9 m (72 ft), 8 miles. White square tower. Obscured on bearings less than 160°. Fixed Red lights on two nearby radio masts.
Peña (Isla) Horadada. Flashing Green, 6 seconds, 5 m (16 ft), 9 miles. Black and white checkered round masonry tower marked 'I'.
Dársena de Molnedo, W mole. Fixed Red. **E mole.** Fixed Green. 6 m (20 ft), 2/3 miles. Metal columns.

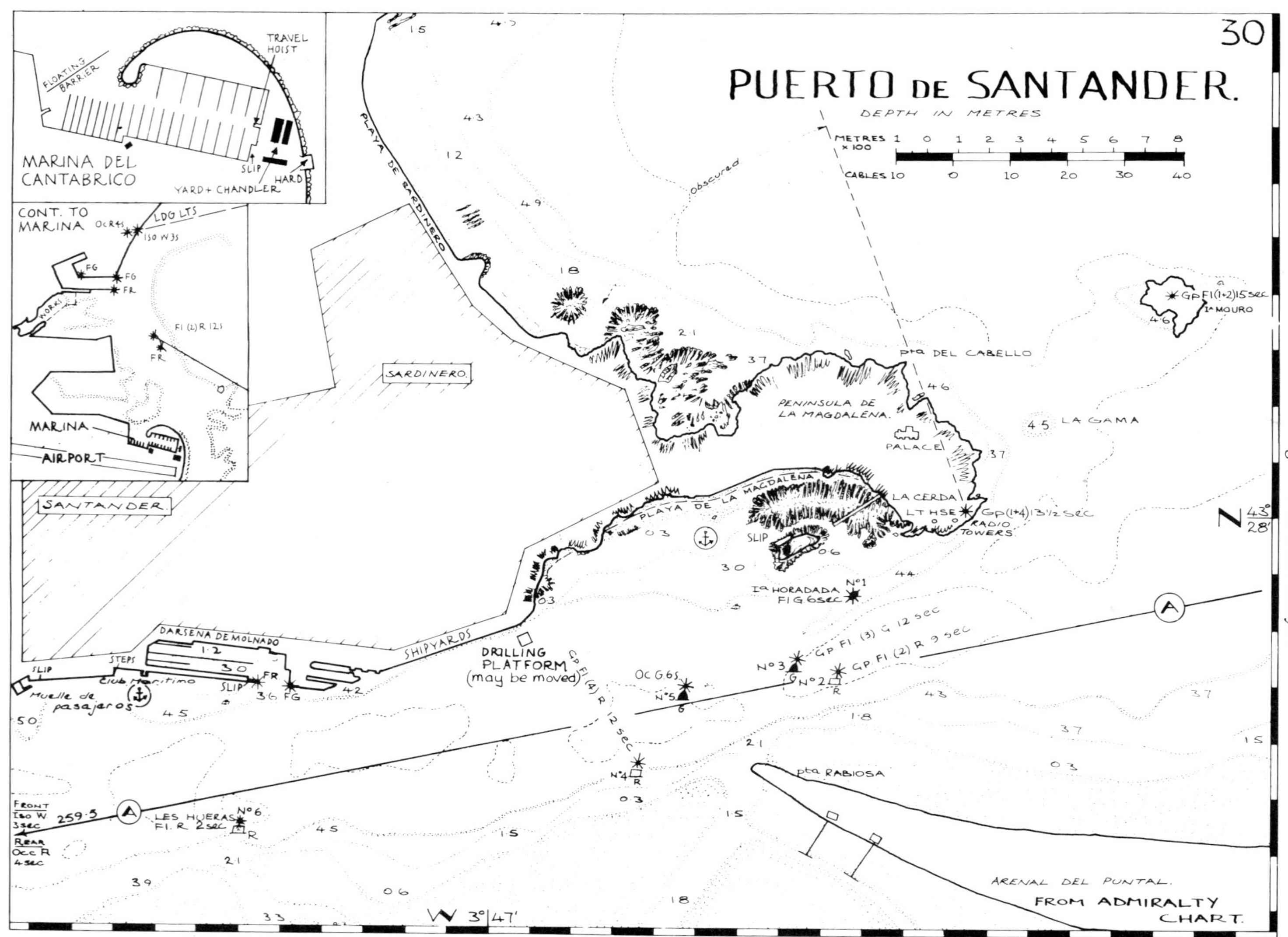
30
PUERTO DE SANTANDER.
DEPTH IN METRES
METRES ×100
CABLES
obscured
Iª MOURO
Gp Fl (1+2) 15 sec
Pta DEL CABELLO
LA GAMA
PENINSULA DE LA MAGDALENA.
PALACE
LA CERDA LT HSE
Gp (1+4) 13½ sec
RADIO TOWERS
PLAYA DE LA MAGDALENA
SLIP
Iª HORADADA Fl G 6 sec
Gp Fl (3) G 12 sec
Gp Fl (2) R 9 sec
Oc G 6s
Gp Fl (4) R 12 sec
DRILLING PLATFORM (may be moved)
SHIPYARDS
PLAYA DE SARDINERO
SARDINERO
SANTANDER
DARSENA DE MOLNADO
STEPS
SLIP
Club Maritimo
Muelle de pasajeros
Pta RABIOSA
ARENAL DEL PUNTAL.
FROM ADMIRALTY CHART.
LES HUERAS Fl. R 2 sec
FRONT Iso W. 3 sec
REAR Occ R 4 sec
259·5
W 3°47'
N 43° 28'
MARINA DEL CANTABRICO
FLOATING BARRIER
TRAVEL HOIST
SLIP
HARD
YARD + CHANDLER
CONT. TO MARINA
LDG LTS
Fl (2) R 12s
MARINA
AIRPORT

Leading lights 259·5° Line Ⓐ.
Front: Isophase White, 3 seconds, 21·6 m (71 ft), 7 miles. Yellow metal tower, black bands on white hut. Visible 183° to 336°.
Rear: Occulting Red, 4 seconds, 33·2 m (109 ft), 7 miles. Red brick building, white stone sides, grey lantern. Visible 256°–262°.
Note: There are more lights further up the river leading to the commercial harbour of **Dársena de Maliaño**.

Buoys Marking the narrows S of **Peninsula de la Magdalena.**
Starboard No. 3, Group Flashing (3) Green, 12 seconds. Green conical buoy.
No. 5, Occulting G. 14 seconds. Green conical buoy.
Port No. 2, Group Flashing (2) Red, 9 seconds. Red can buoy.
No. 4, Group Flashing (4) Red, 12 seconds. Red can buoy.
No. 6 **Las Hueras**. Flashing Red, 2 seconds. Red can buoy.
Note: the starboard hand lights are a very pale green, almost yellow.

Signal station A signal station in a white and grey building near the radio station 4·5 cables WSW of **Cabo Mayor** is manned from half an hour before sunrise to half an hour after sunset. Communication by International Code of Flag Signals.

Life saving A line throwing apparatus is maintained.

Radio A marine beacon operates from **Cabo Mayor** lighthouse on 296·5 kHz, 50 miles, MY (– – / – · – –) period 6 minutes.

Port Radio See page 20.

Approaches

Day *From W* The tower of the large white lighthouse on **Cabo Mayor** and the two nearby radio masts can be seen a good distance off. The hill of **Liencres** is the only high feature W of **Cabo Mayor** and is easily identified. The houses and skyscrapers of **Cueto** N of the city of **Santander** are conspicuous in the offing.

From E The very high, steep sided **Cabo Ajo** and its lighthouse and the houses at **Sardinero** above its sandy bay are easily recognised. The lighthouse on **Cabo Mayor** is also conspicuous from this direction.

Night The lighthouses of **Suances** (Oc. (2) W. 10 sec. 12 M.), **Cabo Mayor** Fl. (2) W. 10 sec. 21 M.), **Isla Mouro** (Fl. (2+1) W. 15 sec. 8 M.) and **Cabo Ajo** (Oc. (3) W. 12 sec. 13 M.) make night approach easy from E and W.

Puerto de Santander—Peninsula de la Magdalena and Palace from the north.

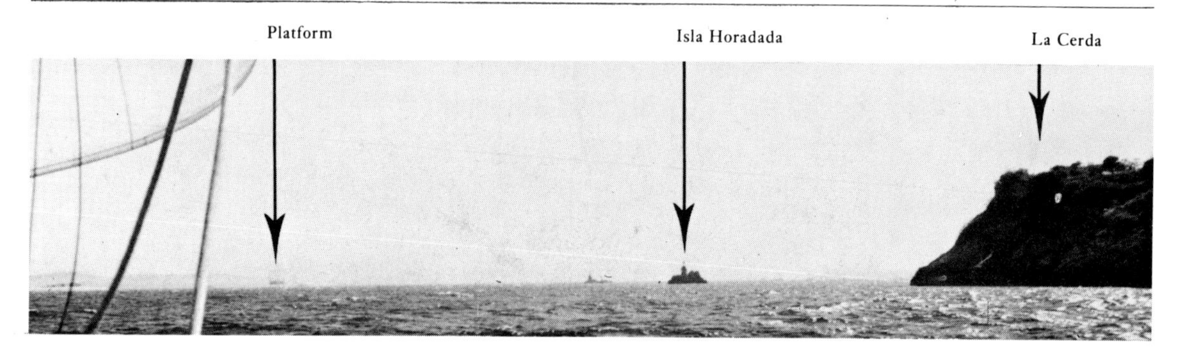

Puerto de Santander—off Peninsula de la Magdalena—looking west.

Anchorages in the approaches

In fair weather it is possible to anchor in the **Fondeadero de Sardinero** as far W as draft will permit; also SW of **Isla de Santa Marina** as close inshore as possible in calm weather.

Entrance

Day There are two entrances either side of the steep-sided rocky **Isla Mouro**. The NW entrance between this island and the **Peninsula de la Magdalena**, on which stands a very conspicuous **Palacio Real** (now a university), should be taken so as to avoid the **La Gama** shoal, especially in heavy weather. The E entrance is between **Isla Mouro** and the sands of **Arenal del Puntal** and care should be taken in bad weather to avoid **Quebrantas** shoals, and to pass about ¼ mile S of **Isla Mouro.**

From both entrances pass 1 to 2 cables S of **La Cerda** lighthouse from whence the small **Isla Horadada** and the buoys marking the narrows can be seen. There are usually dredgers working in the vicinity and there are other unlighted buoys and obstructions either side of the channel, the most conspicuous being a platform with four tall legs to the S, which may be moved and used for traffic control. Pass through the marked narrows near the port hand side and then proceed up the harbour about 2 cables S of the various harbour walls, docks etc.

Night Using the lights of **Cabo Mayor** (Fl. (2) W. 10 sec. 12 M.), **Isla Mouro** (Fl. (2+1) W. 15 sec. 8 M.) and **La Cerda** (Fl. (4+1) W. 13·5 sec. 8 M.) proceed through one of the entrances as detailed above until the light on **Isla Horadada** (Fl.G. 6 sec. 7 M.) and the channel marking buoys *Starboard:* No. 3 Fl. (3) G. 12 sec., No. 5 Oc.G. 6 sec. *Port:* No. 2 Fl. (2)R. 9 sec., No. 4 Fl. (4) R. 12 sec. No. 6 Fl.R. 2 sec. can be seen. In clear weather the leading lights on 259·5° Line Ⓐ (*Front:* Iso.W. 3 sec. 7 M. *Rear:* Oc. R. 4 sec. 7 M.) can be seen.
Proceed between the channel buoys near to the port hand side and then continue up to the harbour about 2 cables from the starboard hand side.
Note: Green lights weak and yellowish.

Moorings

A few private moorings near the yacht club may be used as a temporary measure in the absence of owners' yachts. Apply to the Club Nautico.

Yacht club
La Cerda
Arenal del Puntal

Puerto de Santander—looking east. *Photo: Alsar*

Anchorages

Anchor 50 to 100 m to the SW or SE of the yacht club in 3 m (10 ft) mud.
Note: keep clear of established moorings and also of the race start line which is at 90° to the centre front of the clubhouse. This anchorage is very convenient but a constant stream of fast ferries pass at close range from early till late.

Many other anchorages are available upriver as far as **Astillero.** Use an anchor tripline and show anchor light/shape.

Berths

Apply to the Club Nautico for a berth in the **Dársena de Molnedo** which now has marina-type floating pontoons on its W end. A free berth is unlikely but it may be possible to squeeze in between the yachts already moored to the S wall with a line on to this wall and a stern line to a buoy in 2·7 m to 3·7 m (9–12 ft) mud. The **Marina del Cantabrico**, a modern yacht harbour is located at the E end of the airport; 1335 berths and all facilities are available. Follow the buoyed channel past the head of the large oil terminal, soon afterwards leaving two buoys to starboard, then turning to 241° towards the leading lights near the marina entrance. It is a long way from the shops.

Formalities

Take documents to the customs building at the car ferry terminal, 800 m W of the yacht club, directly on arrival. Other officials may turn up later for similar information.
A yacht club hand may visit with a form to be completed for honorary membership of the club.

Facilities

Water	From hose in front of yacht club and from pontoons.
Diesel, petrol	From pump on NW corner of **Dársena de Molnedo**. Also a bunkering supply point further up the harbour, also at the Marina.

Shops — Almost everything available including some yachting chandlery. There is an excellent market at the rear of the **Banco de Santander**, a conspicuous building on the waterfront. Many food and two chandlery shops near yacht club.

Repairs — As might be expected in a large seaport, all types of repair can be undertaken and slips to suit all sizes of yachts are available at the Marina.

Hards — Good ones are available at **Dársena de Molnedo** at the Marina.

Sail repair — Snr. Pedraja, *Toldos, Travesia, Canaejas 4* is a tent/blind maker but has the equipment to repair sails if shown exactly what is required.

Yacht club — **Real Club Maritimo de Santander** stands on piles near the **Dársena de Molnedo** and visiting yachtsmen are often made honorary members. This is a club which caters for yachts and yachtsmen in addition to the social side. Hot showers, drinks and food are available (273750). Another club to be built at the Marina.

Hotels, cafés, restaurants — Many to suit all tastes. Two De Luxe hotels, one first class A, three first class B, seven second class, and three third class.

Beaches — Several excellent sandy beaches are available—**Playa de Sardinero** is rather like an English south coast resort. **Arenal del Puntal** is a vast area of sand with some cafés. Ferries go to **Pedrena** and **Somo** for this area from **Muelle de Pasajeros**.

Visits — Besides local visits, details of which can be obtained from the information bureau, there are the prehistoric caves **Cuevas de Santián, Altamira** and **El Pendo** not far away. Also the famous preserved medieval town of **Santillana del Mar**.

Information bureau — In the gardens just past the **Muelle de Pasajeros** and another in the square near the **Banco de Santander**.

Fiestas — 27 July–4 August, festivities in connection with St James the Elder; 21 September in connection with La Virgen de La Bien-Aparecida. Also many other attractions during the summer months.

Chapter 4

The coast between Cabo Mayor and Cabo Peñas

The coast between Cabo Mayor and Cabo Peñas

31 General description

Costa Verde

Asturias, Santander and Oviedo

General

This section of the coast is distinguished by the range of mountains, the **Picos de Europa**, some 20 miles inland between **San Vicente de la Barquera** and **Ribadesella**, which are snow covered all the year and visible from considerable distance out at sea in clear weather. They are fronted in the same area by a lower and parallel coastal range of hills having near-vertical cliffs interspersed with many small gaps that have sandy beaches at their heads. The coast to the E and W of this area consists of lower hills intersected by a few river estuaries, and with points and capes which in general are inconspicuous.

There are no outlying dangers and almost all the coast is steep-to.

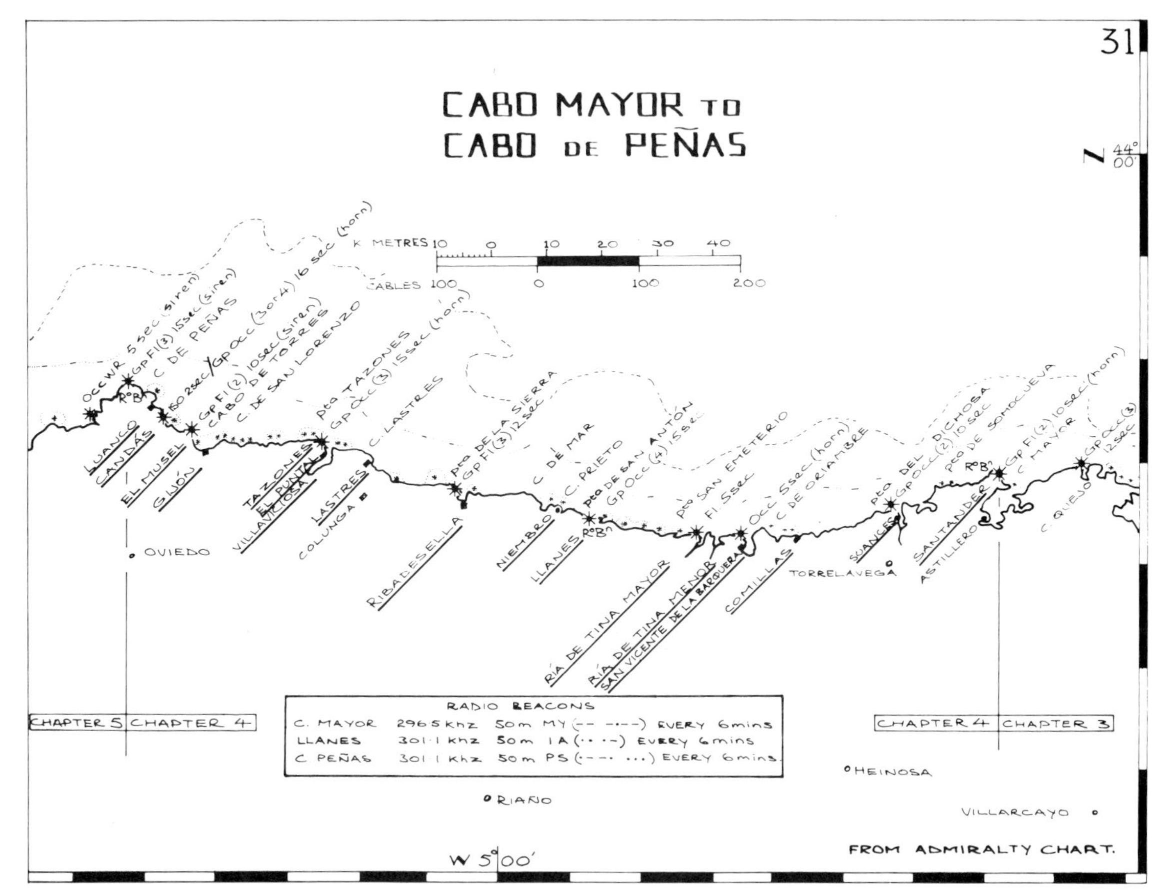

Coast from Ribadesella—looking east towards Cabo de Mar. Note the distinctive nearly vertical cliff face and high range of mountains inland.

Warnings

Winds from a S quarter can sweep down from the higher mountains in gusts much stronger than the normal wind blowing at the time.

Data

Charts

Admiralty	No. 2526
Spanish	Nos. 935, 936, 937, 938, 939, 940, 40
French	Nos. 4991, 5009

Tidal information The current is normally E-going but during and after NE winds it may be reversed. Its strength depends on the strength of the wind and the number of days that it has blown from one direction. It can reach 4 knots in an E direction after strong W winds.

Inshore and off capes the flood stream runs E. It can be strong enough to reverse the general trend of the current.

Cabo Mayor—looking south. Note rock, unique formation and 'face' on the point.

Ensenada de Caldron—looking south.

Major lights

Cabo Mayor (Santander). Group Flashing (2) White, 10 seconds, 88·5 m (291 ft), 21 miles. White tower, first story 8-sided, remainder round. Fog Horn (2), 40 seconds. Radiobeacon.

Punta del Torco (Suances). Group Occulting (2) White, 10 seconds, 33·2 m (109 ft), 12 miles. White conical tower and dwelling. Obscured 091°–113° close inshore.

Punta Silla (San Vicente de la Barquera). Occulting White, 3·5 seconds, 42 m (137 ft), 13 miles. Visible 115°–250°. White stone tower and dwelling. Fog Horn Morse V (· · · –), 30 seconds.

Punta San Emeterio (Tina Mayor). Flashing White, 5 seconds, 65·8 m (216 ft), 20 miles. Bluish-white conical tower on N face of house.

Punta de San Antón (Llanes). Group occulting (4) White, 15 seconds, 16·5 m (54 ft), 15 miles. White 8-sided tower on dwelling. Radiobeacon.

Punta de Somos (Ribadesella). Group Flashing (2+1) White, 12 seconds, 113 m (371 ft), 21 miles. 10-sided tower in centre of house.

Punta de Tazones. Group Occulting (3) White, 15 seconds, 125 m (410 ft), 15 miles. Grey tower, yellow corners and dwelling, aluminium cupola. Fog Horn V (· · · –), 30 seconds.

Cabo de Torres (Gijón). Group Flashing (2) White, 10 seconds, 80 m (263 ft), 18 miles. White 8-sided tower on square dwelling. Fog Siren Morse G (– – ·), 30 seconds.

Punta Tazones—looking south east.

Punta San Emeterio—looking south east. A prehistoric cave dwelling lies just behind the cliff face.

Punta del Cuerno (Candás). Group Occulting (1+2) or (1+3) White, 16 seconds, *or* Isophase White 2 seconds, 37·8 m (124 ft), 12 miles. Reddish tower, white cupola, grey dwelling. Fog Horn C (– · – ·), 60 seconds.
Cabo Peñas. Group Flashing (3) White, 15 seconds, 115·5 m (379 ft), 21 miles. Grey 8-sided tower and dwelling. Fog Siren Morse P (· – – ·), 60 seconds. Radiobeacon.

Life saving Life saving appliances are established at **Llanes** and a lifeboat and line throwing apparatus at **Ribadesella**.

Radio *Radiobeacons* The radiobeacons in this area are as follows; for other beacons outside this area see page 16.

Ría la Franca or Tina del Oeste or Ría de Santiuste.

Punta de la Silla—looking south east.

Station	Frequency kHz	Range miles	Call sign	Period minutes	Group Remarks
Cabo Mayor lightouse	296·5	50	MY (– – / – · – –)	6	**Cap Ferret** FT (· · – · / –) **Cabo Machichaco** MA (– – / · –)
Llanes lighthouse	301·1	50	IA (· · / · –)	6	Grouped with **Estaca de Bares** BA (– · · · / · –)
Cabo Peñas lighthouse	301·1	50	PS (· – – · / · · ·)	6	
Gijón (Austurias) air beacon 43°33′30″N 06°01′37″W	325	60	AVS (· – / · · · – / · · ·)		Continuous

Coast, port and pilot radio stations, weather and navigational messages, see pages 19–20.

Signal stations Ship to shore signals by International Code of Flag Signals may be passed to **Gijón (Muelles Locales)** local messages only.

Trasierra and **Nuestra Senora de Los Remedios** near Comillas.

Ports, harbours, anchorages and landing places

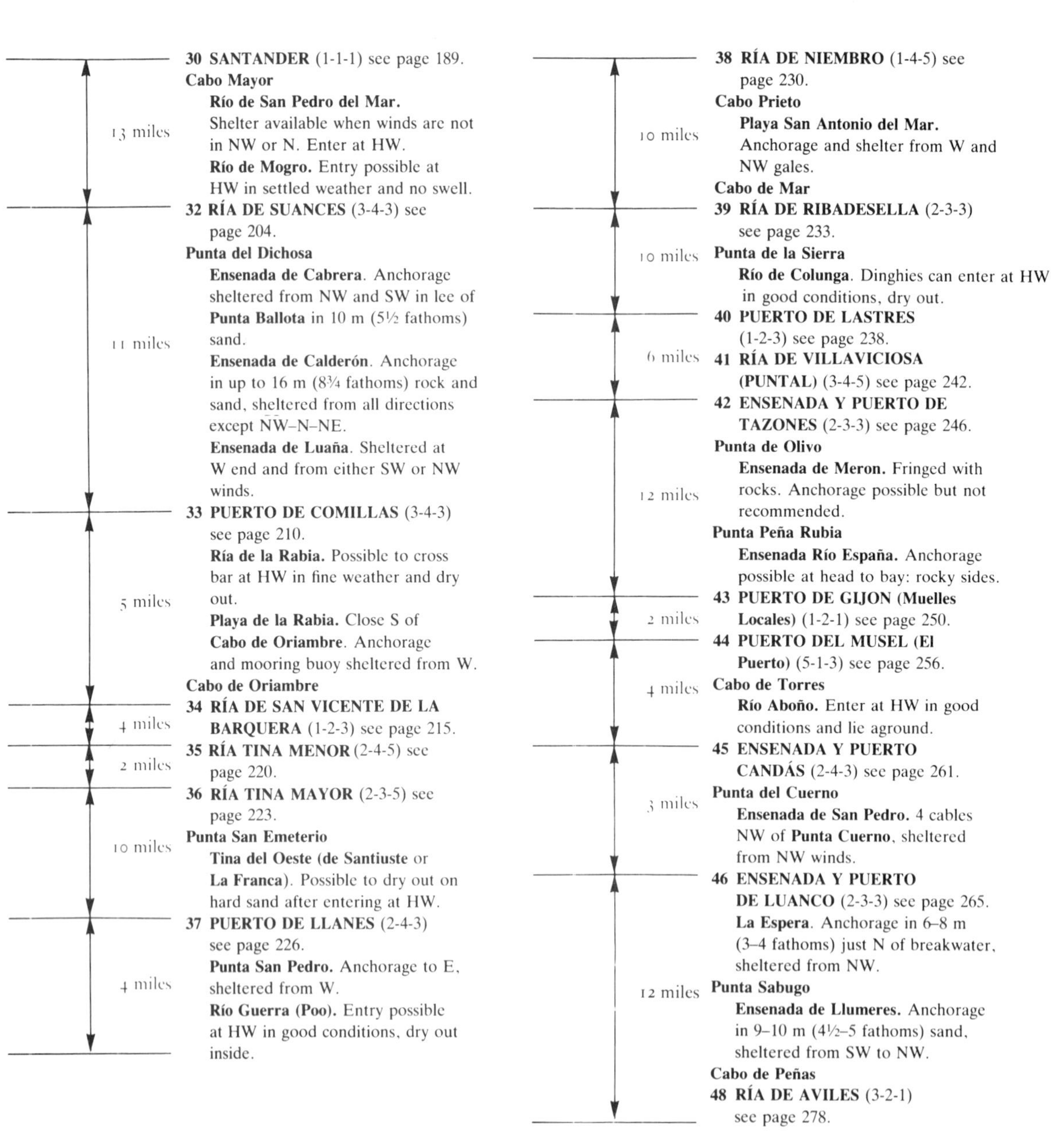

30 SANTANDER (1-1-1) see page 189.
Cabo Mayor

13 miles

Río de San Pedro del Mar. Shelter available when winds are not in NW or N. Enter at HW.
Río de Mogro. Entry possible at HW in settled weather and no swell.

32 RÍA DE SUANCES (3-4-3) see page 204.
Punta del Dichosa

11 miles

Ensenada de Cabrera. Anchorage sheltered from NW and SW in lee of **Punta Ballota** in 10 m (5½ fathoms) sand.
Ensenada de Calderón. Anchorage in up to 16 m (8¾ fathoms) rock and sand, sheltered from all directions except NW–N–NE.
Ensenada de Luaña. Sheltered at W end and from either SW or NW winds.

33 PUERTO DE COMILLAS (3-4-3) see page 210.

5 miles

Ría de la Rabia. Possible to cross bar at HW in fine weather and dry out.
Playa de la Rabia. Close S of **Cabo de Oriambre**. Anchorage and mooring buoy sheltered from W.
Cabo de Oriambre

4 miles

34 RÍA DE SAN VICENTE DE LA BARQUERA (1-2-3) see page 215.

2 miles

35 RÍA TINA MENOR (2-4-5) see page 220.

10 miles

36 RÍA TINA MAYOR (2-3-5) see page 223.
Punta San Emeterio
Tina del Oeste (de Santiuste or **La Franca)**. Possible to dry out on hard sand after entering at HW.

37 PUERTO DE LLANES (2-4-3) see page 226.

4 miles

Punta San Pedro. Anchorage to E, sheltered from W.
Río Guerra (Poo). Entry possible at HW in good conditions, dry out inside.

38 RÍA DE NIEMBRO (1-4-5) see page 230.
Cabo Prieto

10 miles

Playa San Antonio del Mar. Anchorage and shelter from W and NW gales.
Cabo de Mar

39 RÍA DE RIBADESELLA (2-3-3) see page 233.

10 miles

Punta de la Sierra
Río de Colunga. Dinghies can enter at HW in good conditions, dry out.

40 PUERTO DE LASTRES (1-2-3) see page 238.

6 miles

41 RÍA DE VILLAVICIOSA (PUNTAL) (3-4-5) see page 242.

42 ENSENADA Y PUERTO DE TAZONES (2-3-3) see page 246.

12 miles

Punta de Olivo
Ensenada de Meron. Fringed with rocks. Anchorage possible but not recommended.
Punta Peña Rubia
Ensenada Río España. Anchorage possible at head to bay: rocky sides.

43 PUERTO DE GIJON (Muelles Locales) (1-2-1) see page 250.

2 miles

44 PUERTO DEL MUSEL (El Puerto) (5-1-3) see page 256.

4 miles

Cabo de Torres
Río Aboño. Enter at HW in good conditions and lie aground.

45 ENSENADA Y PUERTO CANDÁS (2-4-3) see page 261.

3 miles

Punta del Cuerno
Ensenada de San Pedro. 4 cables NW of **Punta Cuerno**, sheltered from NW winds.

46 ENSENADA Y PUERTO DE LUANCO (2-3-3) see page 265.

12 miles

La Espera. Anchorage in 6–8 m (3–4 fathoms) just N of breakwater, sheltered from NW.
Punta Sabugo
Ensenada de Llumeres. Anchorage in 9–10 m (4½–5 fathoms) sand, sheltered from SW to NW.
Cabo de Peñas

48 RÍA DE AVILES (3-2-1) see page 278.

Cabo de Mar looking south.

Punta del Cuerno looking north west.

32 Ría de Suances (or Ría de San Martin de la Arena)

Population 4,866 Rating 3-4-3 Position 43°25·7′N 4°2′W

General

A canalised river with a bar at its mouth which breaks during heavy swell from the N. Vessels drawing up to 5·5 m (3 fathoms) can enter at HW and anchor. The minimum depth at LW springs is 1·4 m (4·5 ft). Entry is not difficult but the channel is narrow with breaking water on each side. There are several attractive beaches. It is possible, though not recommended due to the smell of factory effluent in the water, to go some 3·5 miles up the river past some attractive countryside. Shopping facilities are about ¾ mile away up a steep hill.

Warnings

The bar should not be crossed on the ebb stream when there are freshets in the river as the heavy flow of water causes the bar to break if there is any swell from the N.

Data

Charts
Admiralty Nos. 2926, 75
Spanish Nos. 659, 939
French Nos. 2042–4991

Magnetic variation 5°45′W (1984) decreasing by about 5′ each year.

Tidal information

	HW		LW		MHWS	MHWN	MLWS	MLWN
Pointe de Grave	0600 1800	1100 2300	0000 1200	0500 1700	5·4 m 17·6 ft	4·2 m 13·8 ft	0·9 m 3·0 ft	2·1 m 6·8 ft
Ría de Suances	+0·10	0	+0·15	+0·35	−1·4 m −4·5 ft	−1·3 m −4·4 ft	−0·6 m −1·9 ft	−0·7 m −2·1 ft

Fresh winds from SW, W and NW cause a tidal rise of up to 0·6 m (2 ft) and winds from NE, E and SE cause a similar fall. The current at the entrance can reach 3 knots on the ebb and is increased when freshets occur.

Lights **Suances, Punta del Torco.** Group Occulting (2) White, 10 seconds, 33·2 m (109 ft) 12 miles. White conical tower and dwelling. Obscured close inshore 091°–113°.
Leading lights 146° Line Ⓐ.
Front Quick Flashing White, 8·2 m (27 ft) 6 miles. White conical tower on E training mole.
Rear Isophase White, 4 seconds, 12·2 m (40 ft), 6 miles. White conical tower on square base at foot of **Punta Marzán.**
E training wall. Fixed Red.

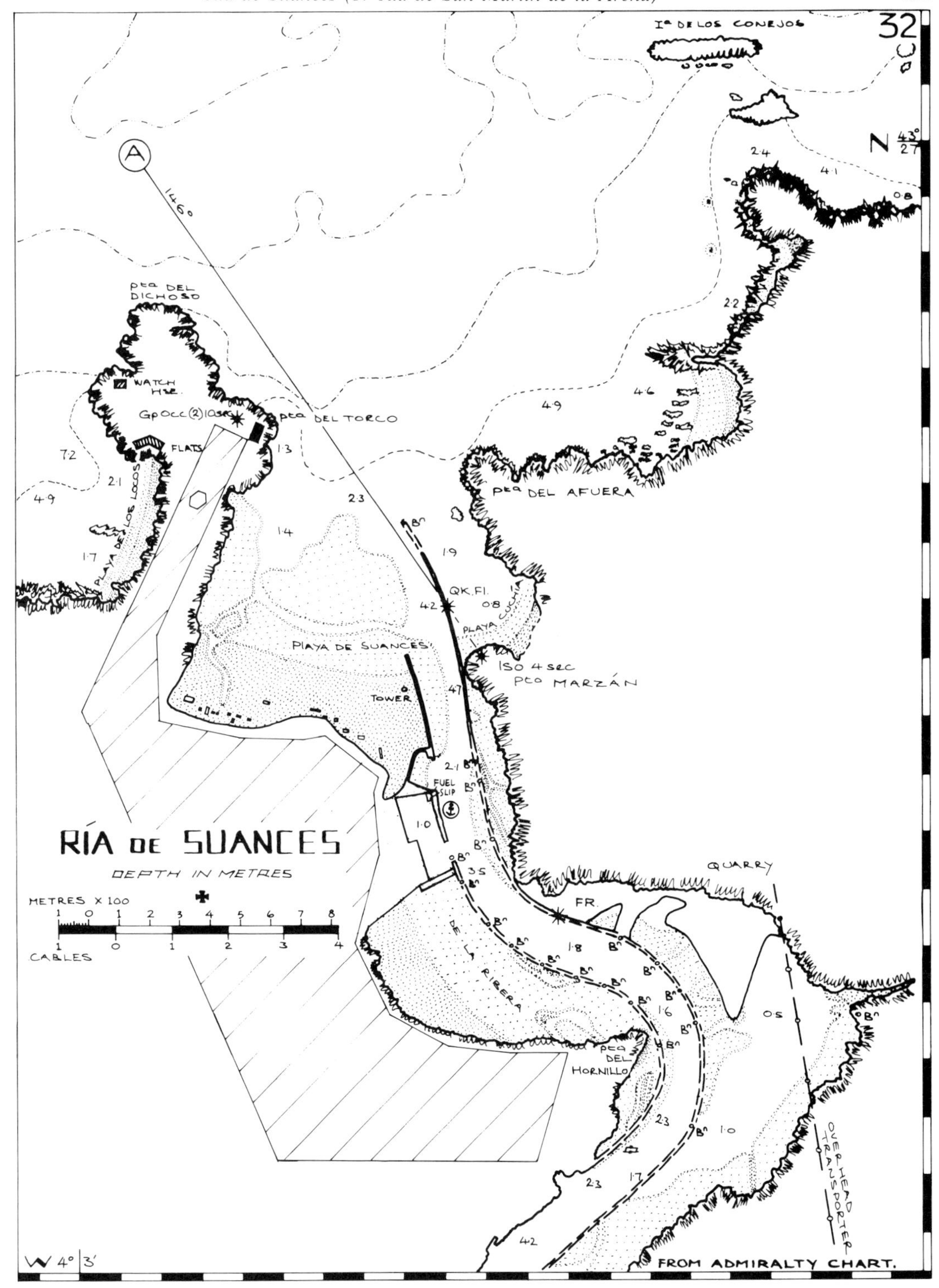
32
Iª DE LOS CONEJOS
N
43°
27'
W 4° 3'
146°
Ptª DEL DICHOSO
WATCH HSE.
Gp Occ (2) 10 sec
Ptª DEL TORCO
FLATS
PLAYA DE LOS LOCOS
Ptª DEL AFUERA
PLAYA DE SUANCES
QK. Fl.
PLAYA CUCHIA
Iso 4 sec
Ptª MARZÁN
TOWER
FUEL SLIP
QUARRY
FR.
DE LA RIBERA
Ptª DEL HORNILLO
OVERHEAD TRANSPORTER
RÍA DE SUANCES
DEPTH IN METRES
METRES X 100
CABLES
FROM ADMIRALTY CHART.

Ría de Suances—looking south east—low water. Note bar breaking in medium swell but deep-water channel is clear of breaking waves.

Pilots Pilots usually meet yachts and will advise or assist as necessary.

Pilot signals If pilots cannot leave harbour they will signal from inside breakers with a white flag as follows:

Signal	Meaning
Waved rapidly from side to side	Stand off, entry not practical.
Held stationary, vertically overhead	Entrance may be attempted, follow present course towards entrance.
Held overhead and lowered out of sight	Insufficient water, heave to outside bar and wait.
Held overhead and inclined towards one side	Alter course towards this direction until flag is moved to vertical position.

Approaches

Day *From W* **Punta del Dichoso** with **Suances** lighthouse and a few buildings and flats on top, flanked on the W by a large sandy bay, is easily identified.

From E The group of islands and in particular **Isla de los Conejos**, which is high and steep-sided, can be recognised at once. The **Playa de Suances**, a large sandy beach backed by flats and houses W of the entrance, also **Punta Marzán** a steep-sided hill with the smaller **Playa Cuchia** to its E, are visible some way off. Steer to a position ½ mile due N of **Punta del Dichoso**.

Night The lights of **Punta de la Silla** (Oc. W. 3·5 sec. 13 M.) are at extreme range and are obscured inshore by **Cabo de Oriambre**, but **Cabo Mayor** light (Fl. (2) W. 10 sec. 21 M.) can be seen close inshore. **Suances** light (Oc. (2) W. 10 sec. 12 M.) is obscured between 091°–113° when close inshore. Navigate to a position ½ mile due N of **Punta del Dichoso**, when the leading lights should be seen.

Ría de Suances—entrances looking south west.

Entrance

Entrance is best made in the last two hours of the flood if there is any sea running. Under calm conditions entry can be made at any time during the top half of the tide.

Day From the position given above the leading marks should be seen. (*Front:* A conical white tower on E training mole. *Rear:* A thin conical tower on top of an octagonal building at the foot of **Punta Marzán**. *Also* the tall red metal pole with a ball on top marking the end (submerged at HW) of the E training mole.) Keeping the leading marks in line on 146°, Line Ⓐ, leave the red metal pole about 14 m (15 yards) to port and follow the line of the training mole at this distance until the gap in the W mole with a sandy bay is abeam, then cross over and follow the W mole at the same distance.

Night From the position in *approaches*, *night*, given above, bring the leading lights into line, Line Ⓐ, and approach the entrance. Care must be exercised in the close approach to keep carefully to this line until the E training mole is reached, when it should be followed at a distance of 14 m (15 yards) until the lights of the café are abeam, when the river should be crossed to 14 m (15 yards) from the bank. Night entry for the first time unless under very calm conditions is not recommended.

Anchorages

Anchor to the side of the channel above the jetty anywhere draft permits. The stretch of water upstream from the jetty and about 22 m (25 yards) from the W bank is handy for going ashore. Keep the centre of the channel clear for commercial shipping.

Anchorage is also possible above **Punta del Hornillo** in rural surroundings, but unless there is a good wind blowing it is not recommended owing to the stench from the river. Further upriver the training walls are marked by metal poles: red and white with square topmarks to port, black and white with triangular topmarks to starboard. There are also several sets of leading marks.

Berths

A small marina above the fuel berth (1·0 m).

Formalities

Officials will come out in a fishing boat from **Suances**. The information required is normal.

Ría de Suances—leading marks.

Ría de Suances—looking south up river—low water.

Facilities

Water From cafés near landing jetty.

Diesel From jetty. Note: only the upriver side of the jetty has enough water. The downriver side is silted up.

Petrol From **Suances** village.

Shops At **Suances** village, where all normal requirements can be met.

Beaches **Playa de Suances**, a good beach, tends to get crowded, but **Playa de Cuchia** is not so crowded, nor is **Playa de los Locos** where there is good surf bathing.

Visits A visit by taxi to **Santillana del Mar** and the **Cuevas de las Aguas**, **Museo** and **de la Clotilde**—prehistoric cave dwellings—is worth while.

Fiestas 16 July, maritime procession of Our Lady of Mount Carmel.

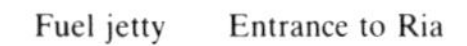

Ría de Saunces – harbour entrance looking N.

33 Puerto de Comillas

Population 3,500 Rating 3-4-3 Position 43°23·5′N 4°17·4′W

General

A little port which dries out. It is situated in a pleasant part of the country, with a good sandy beach and adequate shops nearby. The approach is not difficult though narrow. Two sets of very clear leading marks show the way in through a rock infested bay similar to the Brittany coast. Not for use in bad weather, heavy swell or poor visibility. The harbour is usually full of fishing craft. Charming village.

Warnings

Night approach and entrance for the first time is not recommended. If seas are breaking on **La Molar** rock, ½ mile NW of **Cabo de Oriambre**, they are also breaking at the entrance to **Puerto de Comillas**. Do not attempt to enter in conditions of heavy swell or wind.

Keep close to the line of the leading marks as the channel is narrow.

Data

Charts Admiralty No. 2926
Spanish Nos. 939, 938
French Nos. 2042, 4991

Magnetic variation 5°45′W (1984) decreasing by about 5′ each year.

Tidal information

	HW		LW		MHWS	MHWN	MLWS	MLWN
Pointe de Grave	0600 1800	1100 2300	0000 1200	0500 1700	5·4 m 17·6 ft	4·2 m 13·8 ft	0·9 m 3·0 ft	2·1 m 6·8 ft
Puerto de Comillas	0	−0·15	+0·05	+0·15	−1·3 m −4·2 ft	−1·2 m −4·1 ft	−0·5 m −1·7 ft	−0·6 m −1·9 ft

Lights **Outer leading lights** 194° Line Ⓐ.
Front Isophase White, 2 seconds, 34·1 m (112 ft), 5 miles. White conical pillar 4·3 m (14 ft) high.
Rear Occulting White, 4 seconds, 37·8 m (124 ft), 5 miles. White conical pillar 4·3 m (14 ft) high.
Inner leading lights 245° Line Ⓑ.
Front Isophase White, 2 seconds, 14 m (46 ft), 3 miles. Tower 4·3 m (14 ft)
Rear Fixed Red, 18·3 m (60 ft), 3 miles. Tower 4·3 m (14 ft)
Note: both are obscured on a bearing less than 231°.
Breakwater outer end. Fixed Green, 5·5 m (18 ft), 6 miles. Concrete column 3·6 m (12 ft) high.
Contradique head. Fixed Red. 11 miles. Concrete column.

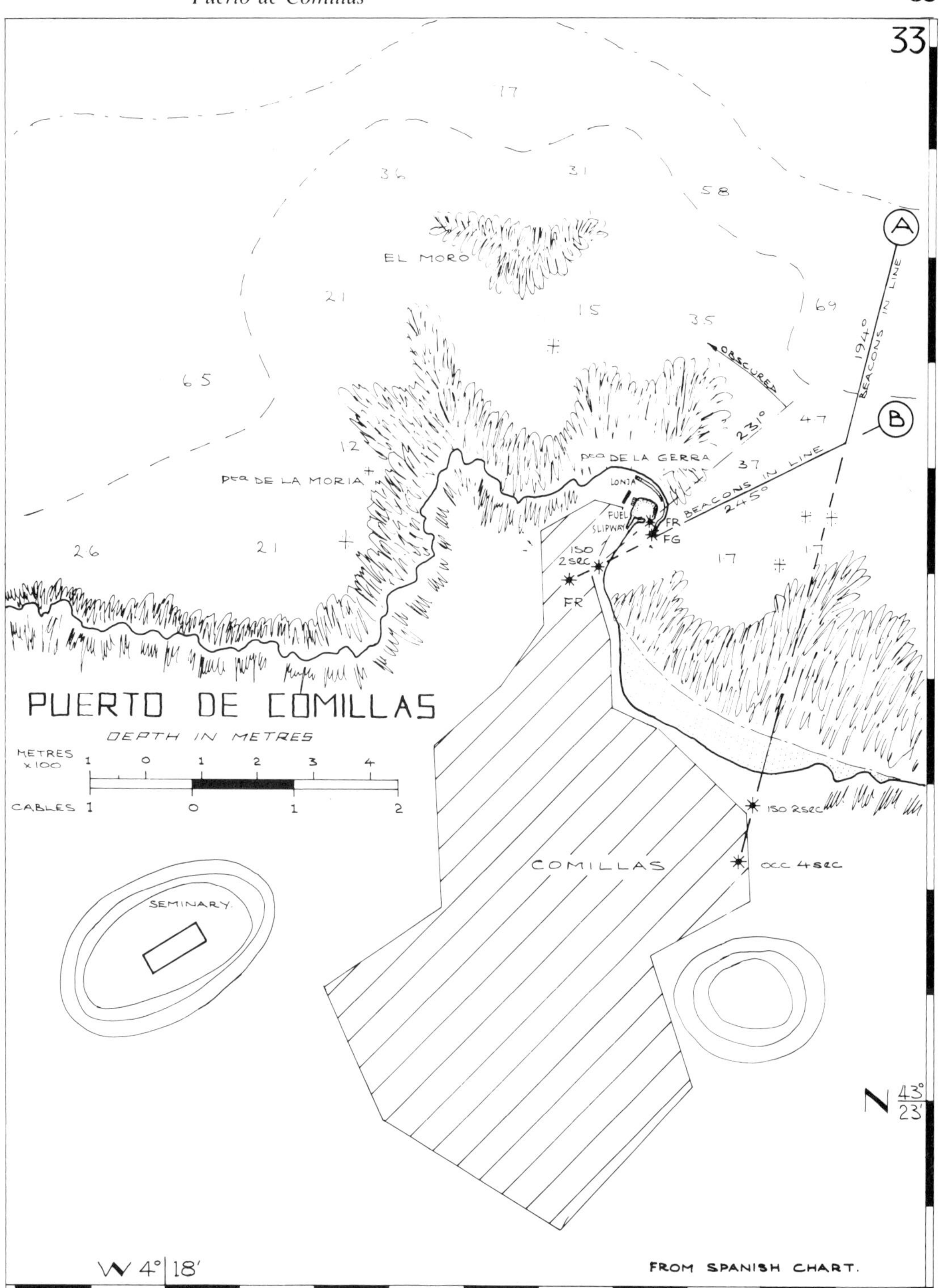
33
EL MORO
Pta DE LA MORIA
Pta DE LA GERRA
LONJA
FUEL
SLIPWAY
FR
FG
ISO 2sec
OBSCURED
231°
194° BEACONS IN LINE
BEACONS IN LINE 245°
ISO 2sec
occ 4sec
PUERTO DE COMILLAS
DEPTH IN METRES
METRES x100
CABLES
COMILLAS
SEMINARY
N 43° 23'
W 4° 18'
FROM SPANISH CHART.

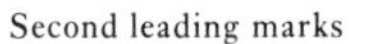

Puerto de Comillas—looking east. *Photo: Alarde*

Approaches

Day *From W* **Cabo de Oriambre**, a low but prominent feature dropping back sharply into the **Ría de la Rabia**, and a very large red brick seminary are both easily identified.

From E A hill feature **Trasierra**, with a very conspicuous isolated church, **Nuestra Señora de los Remedios**, to its W, are easily identified. There are also very large caves in the cliff face in this area. The buildings around the bay SE of the port are only visible when approaching from the E. From the W **Punta de la Moria** hides them until the last moment. When the centre of this bay is due S about 1 mile, turn in this direction and approach the first set of leading marks on 194°, line Ⓐ .

Night The lights of **Punta de la Silla** (Oc. W. 3·5 sec. 13 M.) and the first set of leading lights, Line Ⓐ (*Front:* Iso. W. 2 sec. 5 M. *Rear:* Oc. W. 4 sec. 5 M.) make approach possible, aided to a certain extent by the light on **Punta del Torco** (Oc. (2) W. 10 sec. 12 M.) which is visible in the offing.

Entrance

Day Manoeuvre until the first pair of leading marks, two 4·3 m (14 ft) white conical towers with a black line down them, are in line on 194°, Line Ⓐ . These marks are situated halfway up the hill near a Victorian style house. Follow the line of these marks until the second and similar pair of marks situated just S of the port are in line on 245°, Line Ⓑ . Turn onto this course. When level with the head of the outer breakwater turn to starboard and enter the port.

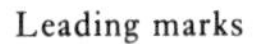

Puerto de Comillas—first pair of leading marks.

Night

Bring the first pair of lights into line on 194°, Line Ⓐ (*Front:* Iso. W. 2 sec. *Rear:* Oc. W. 4 sec.) and approach the bay. When the second pair (*Front:* Iso. W. 2 sec. *Rear:* F.R.) are in line, turn on to 245°, Line Ⓑ , and follow these until the light at the entrance of the harbour is almost abeam, when turn to starboard and enter the port leaving the (F.G.) light to starboard. Note that the second pair of leading lights are obscured on a bearing of less than 231°.

Berths

Berth alongside and dry out if no fishing boats are in the way; otherwise dry out in the middle of the harbour clear of the entrance. W quay best for drying out. Look out for long running mooring lines from the quay.

Formalities

Normal.

Puerto de Comillas—second pair of leading marks.

Puerto de Comillas.

Facilities

Water From **Lonja de Pescadores** on quayside.

Fuel From pump on quay.

Shops About ½ mile away.

Beaches A large sandy beach next to the harbour.

Visits **Cueva las Aguas** at **Novales**, a prehistoric cave, and Pontifical University Palace of the Marquis de Comillas are worth visiting.

Fiestas 30 March, holy week; 29 June, festivities in honour of St Peter; 15 July, festivities in honour of Santo Cristo del Amparo; 25 July, fiesta.

Slip *SW side of the harbour.*

Puerto de Comillas – entrance to harbour looking N.

34 Ría de San Vicente de la Barquera

Population 3,850 Rating 1-2-3 Position 43°23·2′N 4°23·8′W

General

A delightful town and **ría** in beautiful surroundings with good facilities, adequate moorings and berths alongside in up to 3·6 m (2 fathoms). The entrance is not difficult at or near HW by day but should not be attempted by night for the first time, nor under conditions of storm or heavy swell from N or NE.

Warnings

If the sea is breaking on the shoals of **Pedro Gill** and **La Regatona** 6 cables WNW of **Punta Liñera**, it is usually breaking on the bar at **San Vicente de la Barquera**.

The bar breaks in any swell from the N or NE below half tide, especially on the ebb. The ebb stream is very strong at the bridge during springs.

The channel is not quite as shown on either the Admiralty or Spanish charts (1980) and tends to alter due to new harbour works and silt up.

Data

Charts

Admiralty Nos. 2926, 77
Spanish Nos. 4021, 938
French Nos. 6381, 4991

Magnetic variation 6°11′W (1984), decreasing by about 5′ each year.

Tidal information

	HW		LW		MHWS	MHWN	MLWS	MLWN
Pointe de Grave	0600 1800	1100 2300	0000 1200	0500 1700	5·4 m 17·6 ft	4·2 m 13·8 ft	0·9 m 3·6 ft	2·1 m 6·8 ft
San Vicente de la Barquera	−0·10	−0·20	−0·10	+0·10	−1·3 m −4·1 ft	−1·2 m −4·0 ft	−0·5 m −1·6 ft	−0·6 m −1·8 ft

Strong winds from SW through W to N raise the level of tide by 0·5 m (1·5 ft). NE, E and SE strong winds cause a drop by a similar amount.

The ebb stream runs at up to 3 knots at springs.

Lights

Punta de la Silla. Occulting White, 3·5 seconds, 42 m (105 ft), 13 miles. White stone tower and dwelling. Visible 115°–250°. Fog Horn Morse V (· · · –), 30 seconds.
Malecón del Oeste head. Flashing White Green sectors 2 seconds. 7 M. Green 175°–235°; White 235°–045°.
Escollera del Este head. Group Flashing (2) Red 8 seconds, 6 M.
Punta de la Espina. Fixed Green 8 m 4 M. White top red tower.
Note: two flashing street lights at the W end of **Puente de la Maza** are *not* leading lights, but these are being established on the **Arenal de Enmedio**.

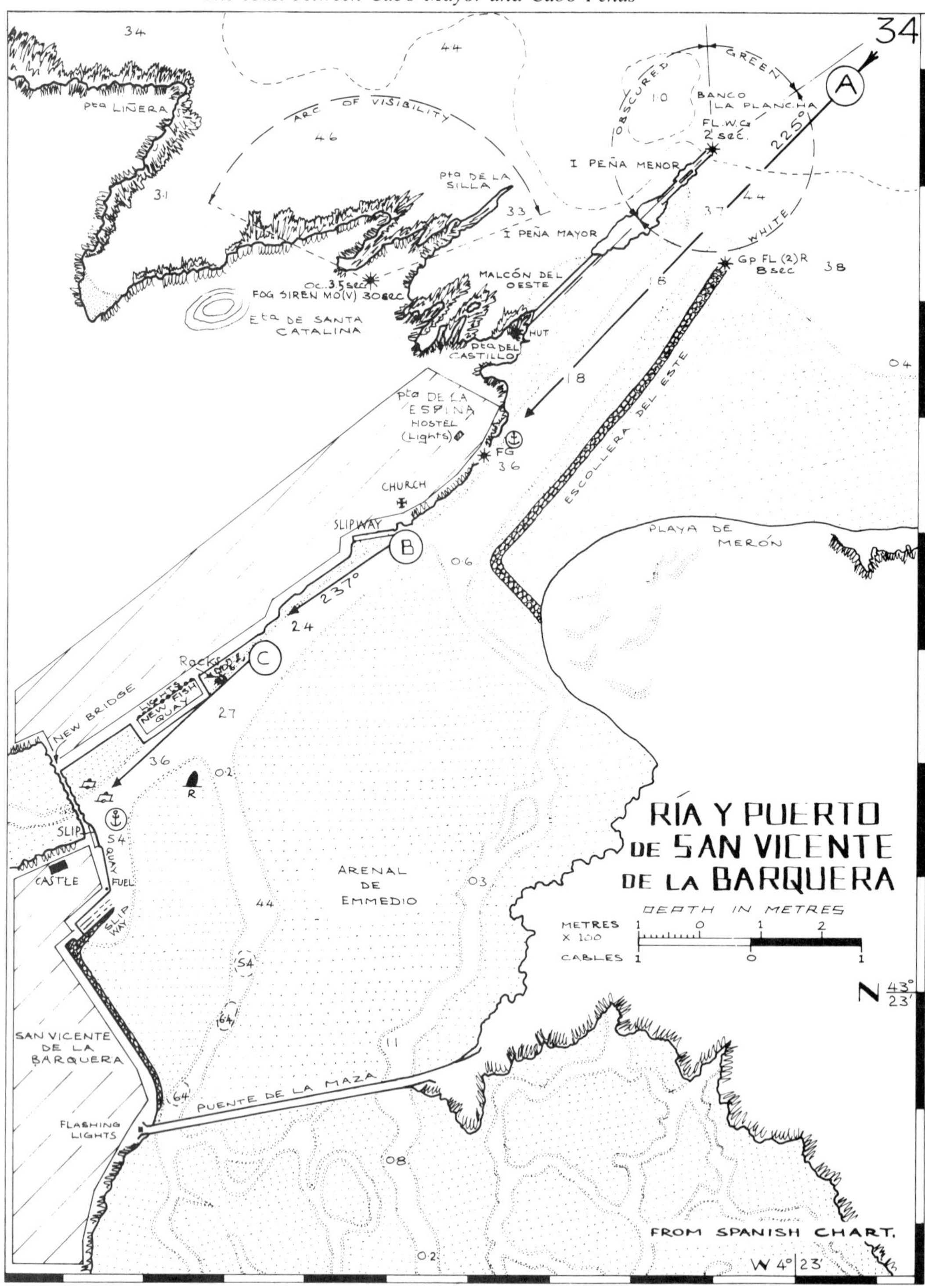
34
A
B
C
Pta LIÑERA
ARC OF VISIBILITY
Pta DE LA SILLA
I PEÑA MENOR
I PEÑA MAYOR
BANCO LA PLANCHA
FL.W.G 2 sec.
OBSCURED
GREEN
WHITE
225°
Oc. 3.5 sec
FOG SIREN MO(V) 30 sec
Eta DE SANTA CATALINA
MALCÓN DEL OESTE
Gp FL (2) R 8 sec
HUT
Pta DEL CASTILLO
Pta DE LA ESPINA
HOSTEL (Lights)
FG
CHURCH
SLIPWAY
ESCOLLERA DEL ESTE
PLAYA DE MERÓN
237°
Rocks
NEW BRIDGE
NEW FISH QUAY
SLIP
CASTLE
QUAY
FUEL
SLIP WAY
ARENAL DE EMMEDIO
SAN VICENTE DE LA BARQUERA
PUENTE DE LA MAZA
FLASHING LIGHTS
RÍA Y PUERTO DE SAN VICENTE DE LA BARQUERA
DEPTH IN METRES
METRES X 100
CABLES
N 43° 23'
W 4° 23'
FROM SPANISH CHART.

San Vicente de la Barquera—entrance looking south.

Approaches

Day *From W* **Punta San Emeterio** with its lighthouse perched on the edge of near-vertical cliffs; the television tower on the hill between the narrow entrances to **Tina Mayor** and **Menor** are unmistakable, as is the lighthouse on **Punta de la Silla**. The E end of the range of high snow-covered mountains, the **Picos de Europa**, stands behind this area. Obtain a position where the harbour entrance bears SW (225°) ½ mile.

From E The only conspicuous and easily identified objects are the very large red brick seminary near **Puerto de Comillas** and the sandy **Playa de Merón** near the harbour entrance. Manoeuvre to a position where the harbour entrance bears SW (225°) ½ mile.

Night The lights on **Punta San Emeterio** (Fl.W. 5 sec. 20 M.) and **Punta de la Silla** (Oc. W. 3·5 sec. 13 M.) enable a position to be obtained where the harbour entrance bears SW (225°) ½ mile.

San Vicente de la Barquera—Punta de la Espina.

Entrance

Day From the position given above proceed towards the harbour on 225°, Line Ⓐ, and enter approximately halfway between breakwaters to starboard and the training wall to port. Direct course towards the tree covered small cliffs of **Punta de la Espina**. Follow this cliff round at 23 m (25 yards) until the ten light standards on the new fish quay are in line on 237°, Line Ⓑ. Then follow this line until the front edge of the new fish quay is in line with the second span of the bridge from the SE end, Line Ⓒ, and then proceed in this direction.

Night Not recommended without previous visits as there are no suitable inner lights.

Moorings

Two mooring buoys between the second and third arches from the SE end of the bridge can be used if not wanted by local fishing boats. It is advisable to check if any of these boats are due in. Moor between one of these buoys and the rings on the pillars of the bridge in 4 m (2 fathoms) bow upstream or secure alongside a fishing boat.

Anchorages

If the buoys are occupied drop anchor from the stern 70 m (75 yards) NE of the bridge and take bow warps to the rings on the bridge pillars. By using two bow warps (onto neighbouring bridge pillars) it is possible to position the yacht between the arches in 3·6 m (2 fathoms). The first and second arch from the SE are the most suitable. Do not get within 11 m (12 yards) of the pillars owing to underwater obstructions. Heavy traffic crosses the bridge by day and night.

An alternative is to anchor opposite the landing slips at the SE end of the bridge and take lines to the two 'cannon' mooring bollards.

In both cases good strong warps, doubled if possible, should be used owing to very strong currents especially on the spring ebb under the bridge.

Berths

Berths alongside the quay SE of the bridge may be possible in 2 m (1 fathom) if not occupied by fishing craft, or alongside the new fish quay in 3·6 m (2 fathoms).

San Vicente de la Barquera—new fish quay.

San Vicente de la Barquera—anchorage—secure with bow *up* stream.

Formalities

Normal.

Facilities

Water From either of the quays.

Diesel From quay by S end of bridge.

Petrol From SW end of town.

Shops Good shops available in main street off bridge.

Cafés, restaurants, hotels A number to choose from.

Slip A good slip for hauling out SE of town.

Beaches **Playa de Merón** is a beautiful sandy beach and not crowded.

Visits The thirteenth century church is well worth visiting and a taxi trip around the two **Tinas** to the **Cueva del Pindal**, a prehistoric cave with paintings, should be undertaken if time permits.

Fiestas 20 April, fiesta of La Folia in honour of La Virgen de la Barquera; 10 August, song festival; 8 September, festivities of La Santisima Virgen de la Barquera.

35 Ría de Tina Menor

Population Nil Rating 2-4-5 Position 43°23·4′N 4°28·4′W

General

A very attractive, deserted, drying estuary with no facilities nearby, suitable for yachts drawing 2 m (1 fathom) or less if they are prepared to dry out. Entrance is only possible in settled weather and in daylight.

Warnings

Do not confuse this estuary with one of the **Falsas Tinas**, a series of similar estuaries 1·5 to 5·5 miles W of **Llanes**.

The channel is reported to change, but as the water is normally clear this can be seen. However if the **Río Nansa** is in flood the water may be dirty.

Data

Charts, tidal information, lights: see **Ría de Tina Mayor**, page 223.

Approaches

Day

From W **Punta San Emeterio** with its lighthouse perched on the edge of the cliff, and the narrow entrance to **Ría de Tina Mayor** are easily recognised.

From E The entrance to **Ría de San Vicente de la Barquera** with the nearby large sandy beach of **Playa de Merón** can be easily recognised. The E end of the range of high snow-covered mountains, the **Picos de Europa**, form a background to this area.

The entrance to this **ría** is flanked on the E side by **Montaña Jorca**, which has cultivated terraces on its side, and to the W by a hill with a tall television tower. Navigate to a position due N of **Punta de la Vigia** and about ½ mile away.

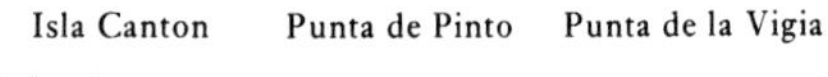

Ría de Tina Menor—entrance looking south south west—low water.

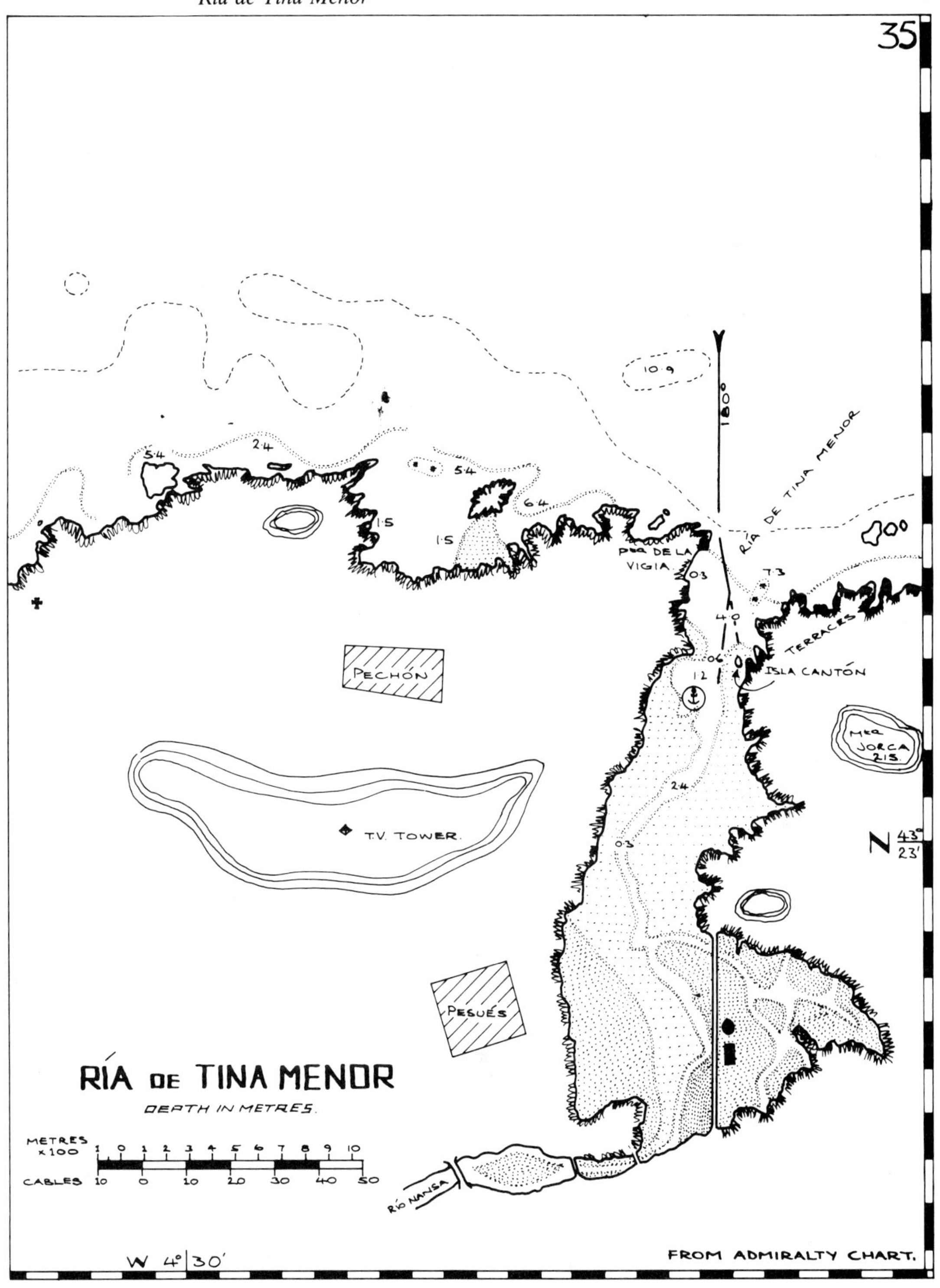
35
RÍA DE TINA MENOR
DEPTH IN METRES
METRES x100
CABLES
PECHÓN
T.V. TOWER
PESUÉS
Pta DE LA VIGIA
ISLA CANTÓN
TERRACES
RÍA DE TINA MENOR
180°
Mte JORCA 215
RÍO NANSA
N 43° 23'
W 4° 30'
FROM ADMIRALTY CHART.

Entrance

At or just before HW approach the entrance close to **Punta de la Vigia** and then steer for **Isla Canton.** When in mid-**ría** alter course to follow the channel, which approximates to the centre of the **ría.**

Berths

Dry out as convenient for wind direction about ½ mile inside the **ría.**

Formalities

Nil.

Facilities

The small villages of **Pesués** or **Pechón** can provide basic supplies, but they are some distance from the **ría.**

Ría de Tina Menor—looking north east towards entrance.

Ría de Tina Menor – looking NE–E–SE at low water.

36 Ría de Tina Mayor

Population Nil   Rating 2-3-5   Position 43°23·4′N   4°28·4′W

General

Another beautiful estuary which almost dries out at LW, with clear water and sandy bottom protected from all directions except N. There are no shops or facilities within easy reach. The entrance is narrow but not difficult. A nice deserted place to visit by day in settled weather in a yacht drawing under 2·7 m (1·5 fathoms) which is prepared to take the ground at LW.

Warnings

Do not confuse this estuary with one of the **Falsas Tinas**—a series of similar estuaries 1·5 to 5·5 miles W of **Llanes.**

Data

Charts
Admiralty No. 77
Spanish No. 938
French No. 4991

Magnetic variation 6°09′W (1984) decreasing by about 5′ each year.

Tidal information

	HW		LW		MHWS	MHWN	MLWS	MLWN
Pointe de Grave	0600 1800	1100 2300	0000 1200	0500 1700	5·4 m 17·6 ft	4·2 m 13·8 ft	0·9 m 3·0 ft	2·1 m 6·8 ft
Tina Mayor	−0·10	−0·20	−0·05	+0·10	1·3 m −4·1 ft	1·2 m −4·0 ft	0·5 m −1·6 ft	0·6 m −1·8 ft

Ría de Tina Mayor—entrance looking south east.

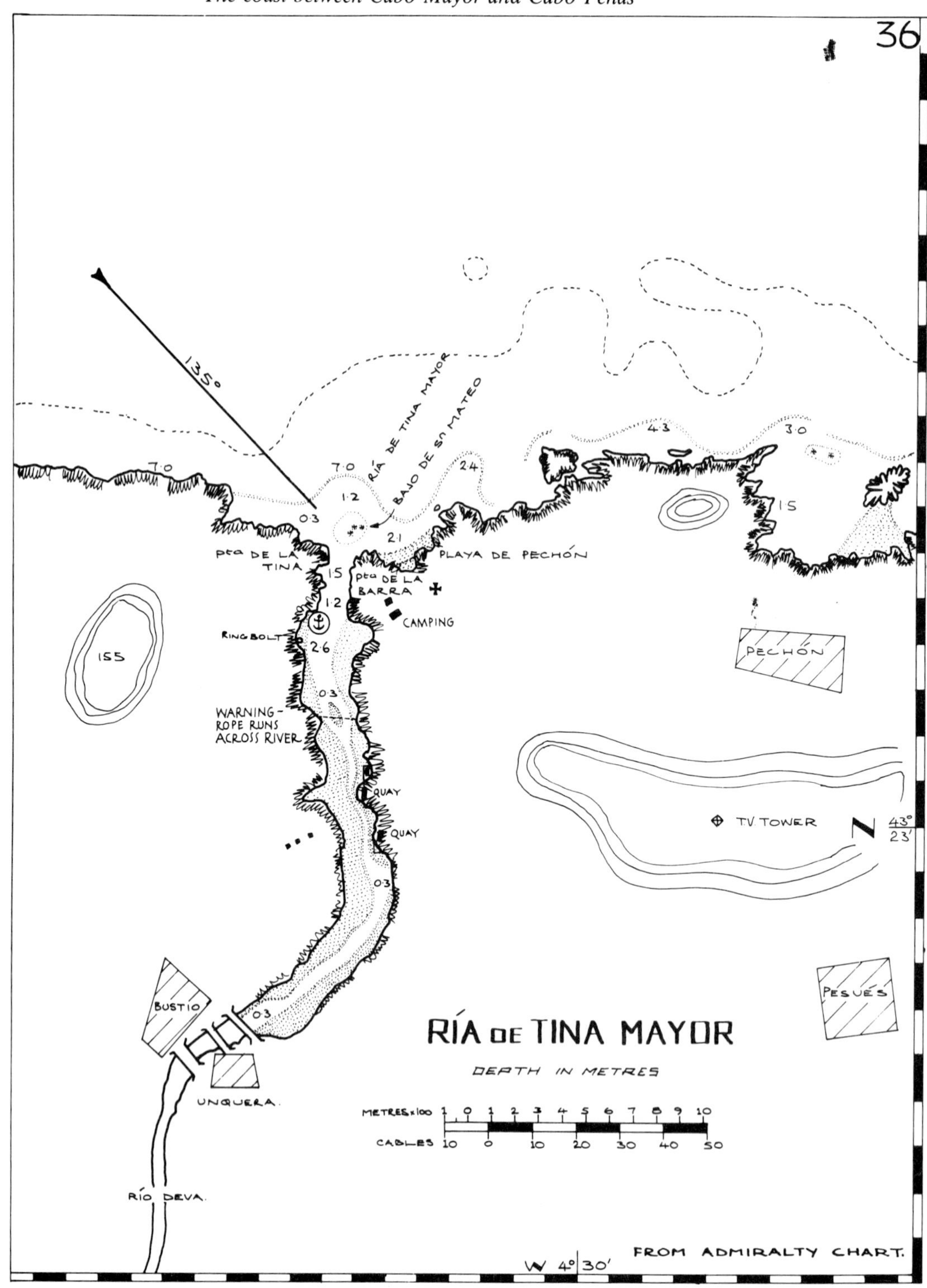
36
135°
RÍA DE TINA MAYOR
BAJO DE Sn MATEO
PLAYA DE PECHÓN
Pta DE LA TINA
Pta DE LA BARRA
CAMPING
RINGBOLT
155
WARNING - ROPE RUNS ACROSS RIVER
QUAY
QUAY
PECHÓN
T.V. TOWER
43° 23'
BUSTIO
UNQUERA
PESUÉS
RÍO DEVA
RÍA DE TINA MAYOR
DEPTH IN METRES
METRES x 100
CABLES
W 4° 30'
FROM ADMIRALTY CHART.

Ría de Tina Mayor—looking south from just inside entrance.

The ebb stream runs up to 3 knots but can, when the **Río Nansa** or **Río Deva** is in spate, reach 8 knots.

Lights **Punta San Emeterio.** Flashing White, 5 seconds, 65·8 m (216 ft), 28 miles. Bluish white conical tower on N face of house.

Approaches

Day *From W* The steep-faced **Punta San Emeterio** and its lighthouse perched on the edge of the cliff are unmistakable.

From E The entrance to the **Ría de San Vicente de la Barquera** with the nearby large sandy **Playa de Merón** can be easily recognised, as can the gap in the hills where lies the **Ría de Tina Menor.** A tall television tower on top of the hill between these two **Tinas** is very conspicuous. The E end of the large snow-covered range of mountains, the **Picos de Europa**, backs the whole of this area and is conspicuous in the approach in clear weather.

Proceed to a position where the entrance to the **ría** lies SW ½ mile.

Night Approach and entrance at night without previous experience of this **ría** is not recommended as there are no navigational lights.

Entrance

Day From the position above, approach on 135° the entrance which lies between two steep-sided hills with the sandy **Playa de Pechón** just to the E. Enter the **ría** about 46 m (50 yards) from **Punta de la Tina**, leaving the drying rocks of **Bajo de San Mateo** to port. Follow the centre of the **ría** for the first 350 m (400 yards) then keep nearer the W shore.

Entrance at or just before HW is advised.

Berths

Dry out anywhere to suit wind direction about ½ mile up the **ría**. Yachts drawing 1·8 m (1 fathom) or less can with care proceed up as far as the railway bridge at **Bustio/Unquera**, but the bottom becomes more and more muddy.

Formalities

Normal if proceeding as far as **Bustio**, otherwise nil.

Facilities

None unless proceeding as far as **Bustio/Unquera**, where there are some shops, cafés and garages and basic supplies can be obtained.

37 Puerto de Llanes

Population 21,000 Rating 2-4-3 Position 43°25·2′N 4°45·3′W

General

An attractive little port and town with good facilities for entrance only in calm weather for yachts drawing up to 2 m (6 ft) which are prepared to lie aground. The harbour dries out at LW as far as the entrance. Enter only at HW.

Warnings

This port is silting up but there is talk of having it dredged in the near future.

Care should be taken to avoid **La Osa** drying rocks. In calm weather seas do not break over them.

Data

Charts

Admiralty No. 2926
Spanish Nos. 937, 938
French No. 5009

Magnetic variation 6°09′W (1984) decreasing by about 5′ each year.

Tidal information

	HW		LW		MHWS	MHWN	MLWS	MLWN
Pointe de Grave	0600 1800	1100 2300	0000 1200	0500 1700	5·4 m 17·6 ft	4·2 m 13·8 ft	0·9 m 3·0 ft	2·1 m 6·8 ft
Puerto de Llanes	−0·20	−0·30	−0·15	+0·10	−1·3 m −4·2 ft	−1·2 m −4·1 ft	−0·5 m −1·7 ft	−0·6 m −1·8 ft

The tidal stream runs up to 1 knot in the entrance.

Lights

Punta de San Antón. Oc. (4), W, 15 seconds, 16·5 m (54 ft), 15 miles. White 8-sided tower on dwelling. Radiobeacon.

Radio

A marine radiobeacon operates from **Punta de San Antón** on 301·1 kHz, 50 miles, IA (· · / · –), period 6 minutes, grouped with **Cabo Peñas**, PS (· – – · / · · ·) and **Estaca de Bares**, BA (– · · · / · –).

Approaches

Day

From W The two sandy beaches W of **Cabo Prieto** and the lighthouse with the two radio towers on **Punta de San Antón** at **Llanes** are the best marks.

From E **Punta San Emeterio** and lighthouse on the edge of a high vertical cliff is very conspicuous. In the offing in clear weather, the range of high snow-covered mountains, the **Picos de Europa**, some distance inland are unmistakable. Manoeuvre until the lighthouse bears WSW ½ mile and the two red and white latticed radio towers are almost in line.

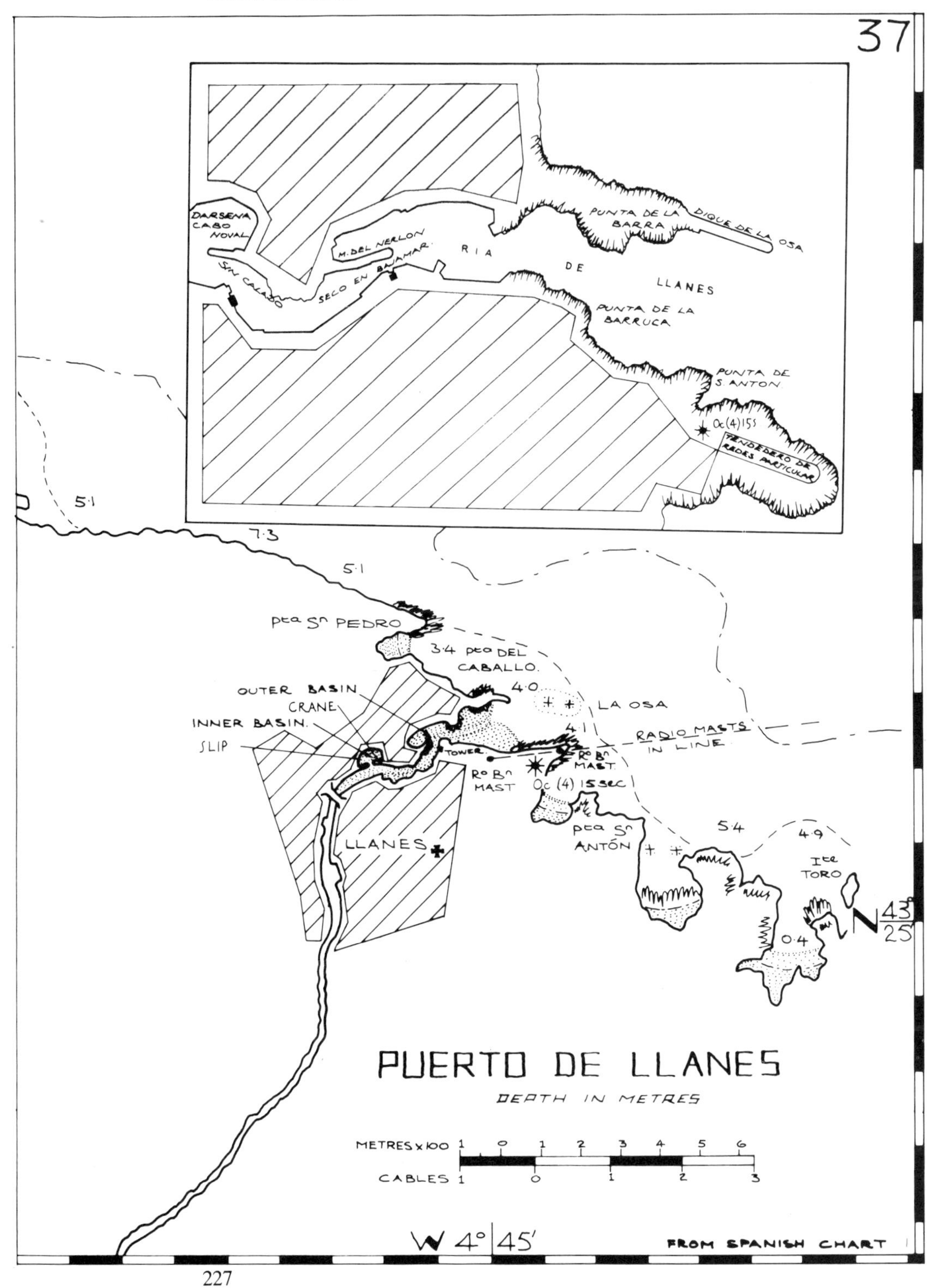
37
DARSENA CABO NOVAL
M. DEL NERLON
SIN CALADO
SECO EN BAJAMAR
RIA DE LLANES
PUNTA DE LA BARRA
DIQUE DE LA OSA
PUNTA DE LA BARRUCA
PUNTA DE S. ANTON
Oc(4)15s
TENDEDERO DE REDES PARTICULAR
5·1
7·3
5·1
pta Sn PEDRO
3·4 pta DEL CABALLO.
OUTER BASIN
CRANE
INNER BASIN.
SLIP
TOWER
4·0
LA OSA
4·1
RADIO MASTS IN LINE
Ro Bn MAST
Ro Bn MAST
Oc (4) 15 sec
pta Sn ANTÓN
5·4
4·9
Ite TORO
0·4
LLANES
N 43° 25'
PUERTO DE LLANES
DEPTH IN METRES
METRES x 100 1 0 1 2 3 4 5 6
CABLES 1 0 1 2 3
W 4° 45'
FROM SPANISH CHART

Puerto de Llanes—looking north east—low water. *Photo: Alarde*

Night The lights on **Punta San Emeterio** (Fl.W. 5 sec. 20 M.) and **Punta de San Antón** (Oc. (4), W. 15 sec. 15 M.) enable navigators to obtain a position where **Punta de San Antón** bears WSW ½ mile.

Entrance

Day Enter the harbour midway between the head of the breakwater to starboard and the cliffs to port and direct course towards the head of the quay which divides the harbour. Then enter either the outer basin or the narrow entrance to the inner harbour which has a tall square tower on the port hand. Follow the curve of the port hand quay at 4 m (5 yards) distance until level with the **Lonja de Pescadores** when keep to mid-channel. Entry at night not recommended.

Berths

Dry out in sand in the outer basin or on muddy sand above the **Lonja de Pescadores**. It would also be possible to dry out alongside the E quay wall between the tower and the **Lonja de Pescadores.**

Formalities

Normal

Facilities

Water From **Lonja de Pescadores.**

Puerto de Llanes—entrance looking west—low water.

Puerto de Llanes – entrance during NW gale – do not enter!

Diesel From pump on quay.

Petrol From pump on the outskirts of town.

Shops A good assortment near harbour.

Visits **Caverna de Avia** and **Cueva del Pindal**, prehistoric dwellings, and the **Picos de Europa** are all worth visiting; also the fifteenth century castle and fifteenth century church.

Fiestas 21 July, feast of St Mary Magdalene. 12–31 August, festivities of St Roch. 7–8 September, festivities of Nuestra Señora de la Guia.

Puerto de Llanes—looking up inner harbour—low water.

38 Ría de Niembro

Population 500 Rating 1-4-5 Position 43°26·2′N 4°50·2′W

General

A beautiful little place entered through a gap in the cliffs at HW, but only for yachts drawing less than 2 m (1 fathom) which can lie aground at LW. Swell and storms from the N would make entrance quite impossible. Night entrance is not recommended. There are no facilities nearby.

Warnings

In calm weather with no swell the sea does not break over **La Vaca** rock at high tide. Care should be taken to avoid this area which is 2 cables ENE of **Cabo Prieto.**

Data

Charts
Admiralty No. 2926
Spanish No. 937
French No. 5009

Magnetic variation 6°10′W (1984) decreasing by about 5′ each year.

Tidal information

	HW		LW		MHWS	MHWN	MLWS	MLWN
Pointe de Grave	0600 1800	1100 2300	0000 1200	0500 1700	5·4 m 17·6 ft	4·2 m 13·8 ft	0·9 m 3·0 ft	2·1 m 6·8 ft
Ría de Niembro	−0·20	−0·30	−0·20	+0·10	−1·3 m −4·2 ft	−1·2 m −4·1 ft	−0·5 m −1·7 ft	−0·6 m −1·8 ft

Tidal stream of up to 1·5 knots at springs: follow the channel.

Lights Nil.

Approach

Day *From W* **Puerto de Ribadesella** and **Punta del Caballo** are easily identified, also **Cabo de Mar**, a low vertical-sided promontory. **Cabo Prieto** is less easily identified but the two sandy beaches W of it are prominent, as is the coast road.

From E **Puerto de Llanes** and its lighthouse with two red and white radio towers can be identified. The islands either side of the entrance to the **Ría de Niembro** enable a close approach to be made to the entrance avoiding **La Vaca** which is covered at HW. This rock is roughly in line with two small islands nearer the coast. Approach the entrance on 210° from at least ½ mile out at sea.

Entrance

The narrow entrance to this **ría**, 146·3 m (160 yards) wide, does not fully open up until it bears due S. Enter in mid-channel and be prepared for a sharp turn to

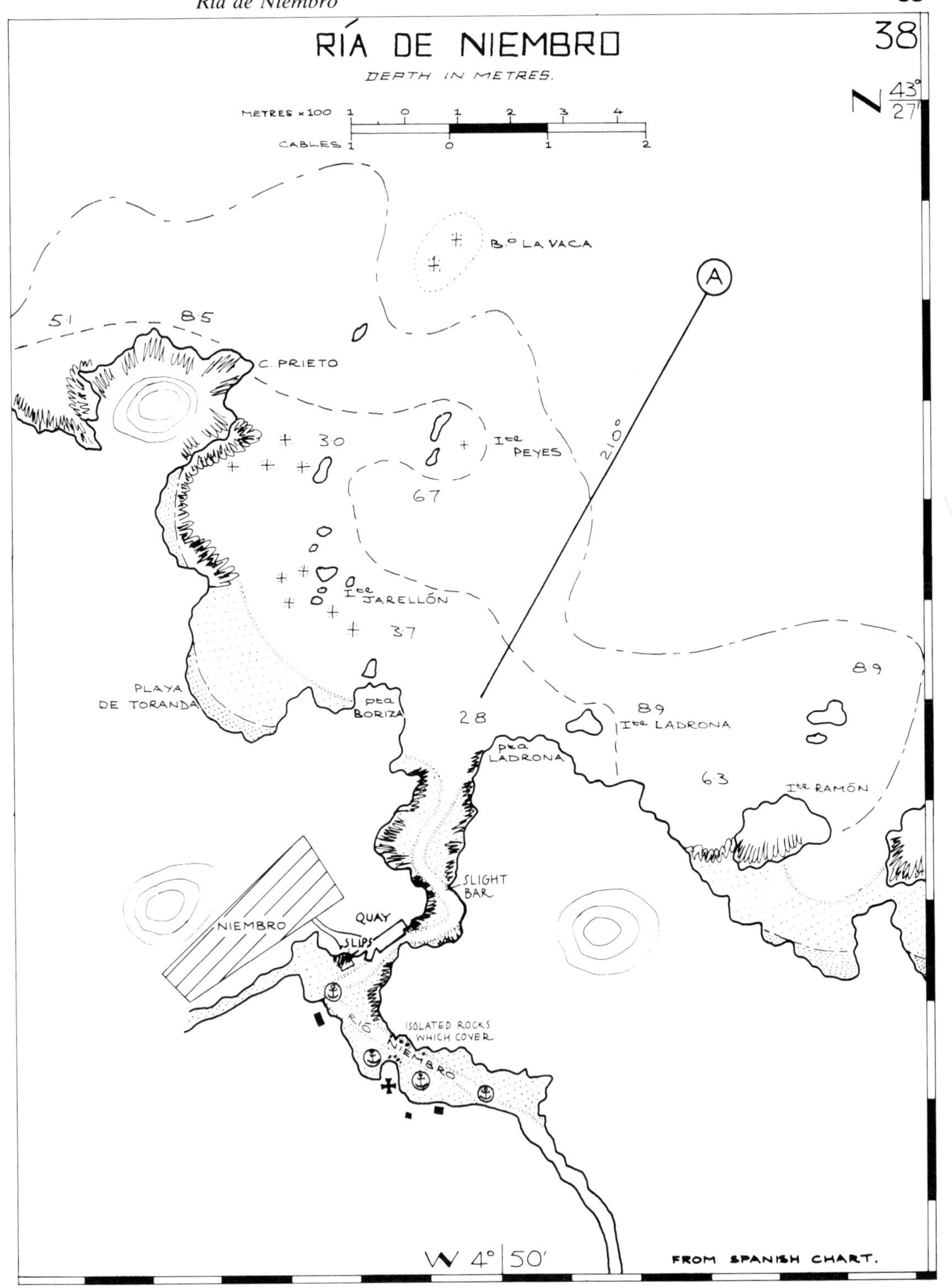
RÍA DE NIEMBRO
DEPTH IN METRES.
38
N 43° 27'
METRES × 100 1 0 1 2 3 4
CABLES 1 0 1 2
B.º LA VACA
A
5·1
8·5
C. PRIETO
210°
3·0
Ite PEYES
6·7
Ite JARELLÓN
3·7
PLAYA DE TORANDA
pta BORIZA
2·8
8·9
Ite LADRONA
8·9
pta LADRONA
6·3
Ite RAMÓN
SLIGHT BAR
QUAY
NIEMBRO
SLIPS
RÍO NIEMBRO
ISOLATED ROCKS WHICH COVER
W 4° 50'
FROM SPANISH CHART.

Ría de Niembro—looking south south west—low water.

port. After this turn keep close to the port hand side until level with the N end of the quay, then cross towards the quay and slip where course should be changed towards the rocky ledge opposite the church. The crystal clear water enables this channel to be followed easily. Isolated rocks near the Church.

Berths

It would be possible to dry out alongside the quay near the slip if it is not occupied by fishing craft. It is normal to dry out between the quay and the church on firm sand or beyond the church in sandy mud.

Facilities

The one pub near the church will provide water, but there is nowhere else where supplies can be obtained locally except for the village of **Niembro** some distance away. Here simple requirements can be met at a general store.

Ría de Niembro – just inside entrance looking W–SW at low water.

39 Puerto de Ribadesella

Population 7,700 Rating 2-3-3 Position 43°27·8′N 5°3·6′W

General

A most attractive port in beautiful surroundings with easy entrance in all but strong winds or swell from N. The bar has a minimum depth of 2 m (6 ft). Good berths can be found alongside in up to 3 m (1·5 fathoms), also fair shops, cafés, restaurants and hotels, with a wonderful beach and some interesting visits.

Warnings

In other than perfect conditions it is important to enter between 2 hours before HW and HW. **Bajo Serropiò** should be avoided in heavy weather.

Data

Charts

Admiralty Nos. 2926, 77
Spanish Nos. 937, 4031
French Nos. 6381, 5009

Magnetic variation 6°16′W (1984) decreasing by about 5′ each year.

Tidal information

	HW		LW		MHWS	MHWN	MLWS	MLWN
Pointe de Grave	0600 1800	1100 2300	0000 1200	0500 1700	5·4 m 17·6 ft	4·2 m 13·8 ft	0·9 m 3·0 ft	2·1 m 6·8 ft
Ribadesella	−0·30	−0·35	−·25	+0·10	−1·3 m −4·1 ft	−1·2 m −4·1 ft	−0·5 m −1·7 ft	−0·6 m −1·8 ft

Puerto de Ribadesella—entrance looking south west.

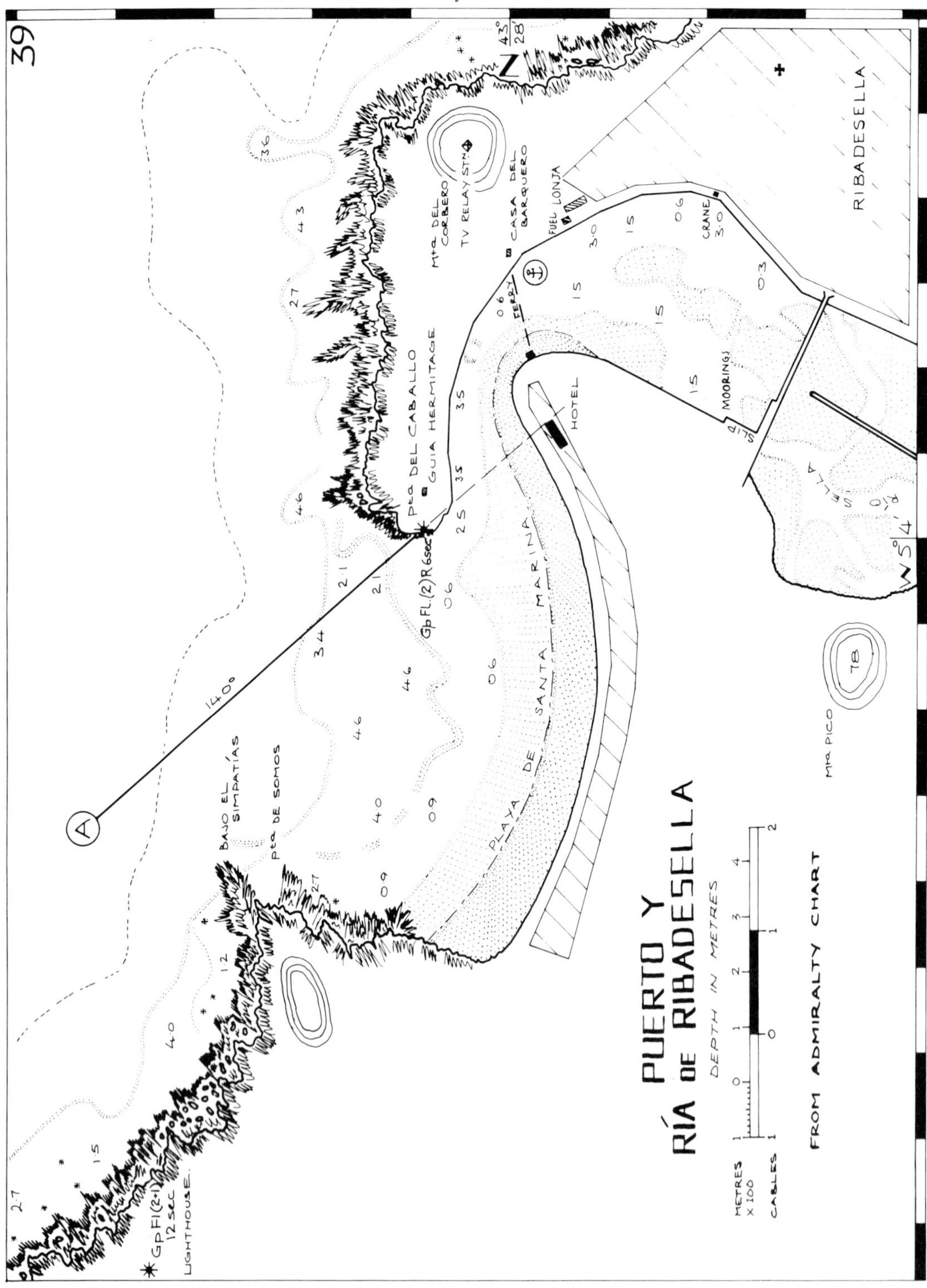
39
PUERTO Y
RÍA DE RIBADESELLA
DEPTH IN METRES
FROM ADMIRALTY CHART
METRES X 100
CABLES
RIBADESELLA
PLAYA DE SANTA MARINA
Pta DEL CABALLO
GUIA HERMITAGE
Mte DEL CORBERO
TV RELAY STN
CASA DEL BARQUERO
FUEL
LONJA
FERRY
CRANE
MOORINGS
HOTEL
RÍO SELLA
Mte PICO
BAJO EL SIMPATÍAS
Pta DE SOMOS
Gp Fl (2+1) 12 sec
LIGHTHOUSE
Gp Fl (2) R 6 sec
140°
43° 28'
5° 4' W

N and NE gales raise the level of the water at the bar as do freshets in the **Río Sella**. NW gales cause sand to build up and may reduce the depth of water at the bar. The outgoing stream runs at 2 knots at springs, but when **Río Sella** is in spate this may reach 5 to 6 knots.

Lights **Punta de Somos.** Group Flashing (2+1) White, 12 seconds, 113 m (371 ft), 30 miles. Square tower in centre of house. F.R. on radio tower 8 M to WNW.
Puntadel Caballo. Group Flashing Red, (2), 6 seconds, 10 m (33 ft), 5 miles. Round red brick tower. Visible 278·4°–212·9° and 117·3°–212·9°.

Pilots Pilots may occasionally direct yachts by leading them in with their own boat or by signals from **Punta del Caballo** as follows:

Signal		**Meaning**
Blue flag	—Vertical	Bar can be crossed *or*— Continue present course.
	—Inclined to Pilot's right	Alter course to port.
	—Inclined to Pilot's left	Alter course to starboard.
	—Waved	Dangerous to enter port or cross bar.
Red pendant *white fly* plus *Blue pendant* *yellow stripes*		Dangerous to enter port or cross bar.

Life saving A lifeboat and line throwing gear are kept at this port.

Approaches

Day *From W* **Punta Misiera** and **Puerto Lastres** are conspicuous as is the tree covered **Punta de Somos** with its lighthouse, a square tower in the centre of a dwelling. The smooth, flat, sloping face of the cliffs of **Punta del Caballo** with the white **Guia Hermitage** on the top are also unmistakable.

From E The coast consists of low vertical cliffs of which **Cabo de Mar**, though low, is the most easily identified. The small white television relay hut on top of **Montagne del Corbero** is very conspicuous as are the cliffs of **Punta del Caballo** referred to above. Make for a position where the lighthouse on **Punta de Somos** is due W and the red brick lighthouse on the quay at **Punta del Caballo** bears 140°.

Night Using the light on **Punta de Somos** (Fl. (2+1) W. 12 sec. 21 M.) and the light on breakwater head (Fl.(2)R. 6 sec. 5 M.) navigate to where the former is due W and the latter bears 140°.

Entrance

In the absence of swell entrance can be attempted during the top half of the tide. If a swell is running the last two hours of the flood are best. In the event of a very heavy swell from NW entrance should not be attempted.

Day Approach the quay on the end of **Punta del Caballo** from the position given above on 140°, Line Ⓐ . The red brick light tower on the quay wall to the NE side of the entrance in transit with the left edge of a large square modern hotel can be used as leading marks. When close to the quay leave it 24 m (25 yards) to port and follow it around into the harbour, keeping parallel with the quay at this distance until a berth is reached. There are some rocks close alongside the quay to the N of the red brick light tower.

Night From the position in *approach*, *night*, above, sail on a bearing of 140°, Line Ⓐ, towards the light on **Punta del Caballo** until 24 m (25 yards) from the quay when follow it around at this distance right into the harbour. The quay and street lights light up the area satisfactorily.

Berths

Berths alongside are available. The most E part of the quay wall is best. Bollards and ladders (partly worn) are available. Avoid the two stretches of pilings under the quay if possible and berth alongside the solid quay wall. Another berth near W end of bridge (dries 1·2 m).

Anchorage

It is possible to anchor in 3 m (1·5 fathoms) 10 m (30 yards) SW of **Casa de Barquero**, a lone building, but the swell will be felt at HW.

Formalities

Normal.

Facilities

Water From **Lonja de Pescadores** on quay, where a short length of hose can be borrowed.

Diesel From pump on quay.

Puerto de Ribadesella—looking north east. *Photo: Alarde*

Puerto de Ribadesella—harbour looking south east from the Hermitage—low water.

Petrol From pump in town near bridge.

Shops Fair shops for most needs near quay.

Hotels Several in town; a good one on E end of **Playa de Santa Marina**.

Yacht Club The Club Maritimo de Ribadesella (160) has a club house at the W side of the harbour with bar, terrace, swimming pool etc.

Repairs Good motor mechanics.

Beaches **Playa de Santa Marina** is first class.

Visits Some newly discovered caves with prehistoric paintings are only ½ hour's walk away. Other caves are the **Gueva de Baxu**, with prehistoric drawings, near **Cangas**, another at **Caverna de Avin** near **Barro**. **Picos de Europa** are well worth a visit in a taxi if the weather is clear and there are no clouds.

Fiestas 9 August, international kayak race down **Río Sella**.

40 Puerto de Lastres

Population 3,000 Rating 1-2-3 Position 43°31′N 5°15·9′W

General

This delightful, attractive and unspoilt old fishing village, clinging to the steep hillside, now has a new harbour with easy entrance and berths alongside in up to 7 m (4 fathoms). Good sandy bathing beaches nearby and fair shopping facilities. However, in a strong E wind and swell it would be an uncomfortable berth. Not as clean as it used to be (1983).

Warnings

Banco de la Plancha should be given a good berth owing to breaking seas.

Data

Charts

Admiralty No. 2926
Spanish Nos. 936, 4032
French No. 5009

Magnetic variation 6°16′W (1984) decreasing by about 5′ each year.

Tidal information

	HW		LW		MHWS	MHWN	MLWS	MLWN
Pointe de Grave	0600 1800	1100 2300	0000 1200	0500 1700	5·4 m 17·6 ft	4·2 m 13·8 ft	0·9 m 3·0 ft	2·1 m 6·8 ft
Puerto de Lastres	−0·35	−0·40	−0·30	+0·05	−1·3 m −4·1 ft	−1·2 m −4·1 ft	−0·5 m −1·7 ft	−0·6 m −1·8 ft

Puerto de Lastres—looking south west.

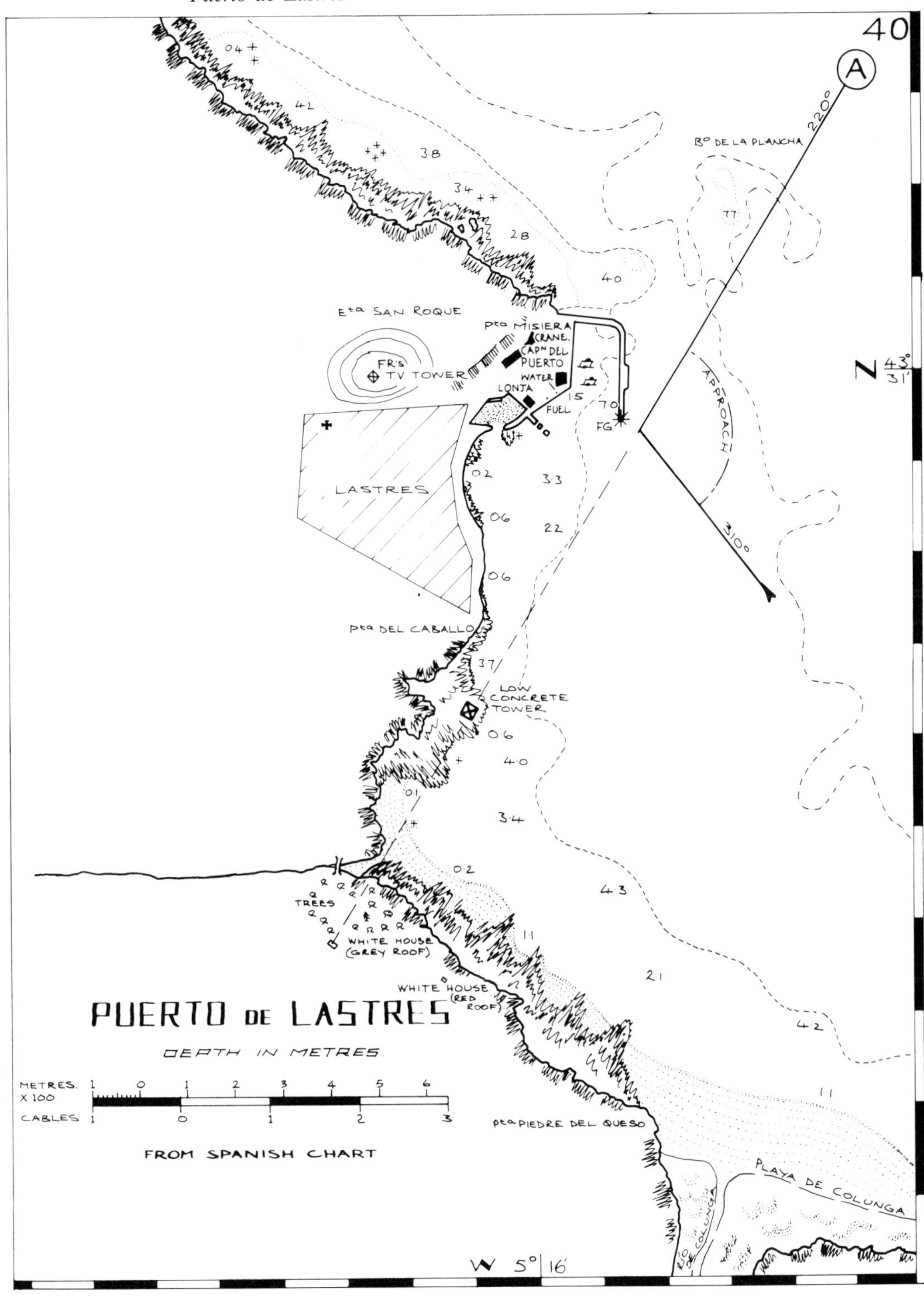
40
A
220°
Bº DE LA PLANCHA
Eta SAN ROQUE
Pta MISIERA
CRANE
CAPN DEL PUERTO
WATER
LONJA
FUEL
FR'S TV TOWER
FG
APPROACH
310°
LASTRES
Pta DEL CABALLO
LOW CONCRETE TOWER
TREES
WHITE HOUSE (GREY ROOF)
WHITE HOUSE (RED ROOF)
PUERTO DE LASTRES
DEPTH IN METRES
METRES X 100
CABLES
FROM SPANISH CHART
Pta PIEDRE DEL QUESO
PLAYA DE COLUNGA
RIO DE COLUNGA
W 5° 16'
N 43° 31'

Lights **Breakwater head.** Fixed Green, 8·8 m (29 ft), 1 mile. Metal post. **TV pylon.** Fixed Red lights.

Approaches

Day *From W* **Punta Tazones**, with an open valley, sandy beach and **Ría de Villaviciosa** to the E are easily recognised. **Cabo Lastres**, though large, does not have an special features except a flat top.

From E The valley and sandy beach of **Ribadesella** by **Punta del Caballo**, and **Punta de la Sierra**, which has trees on its E side and fields on its W, can be identified. The latter should be given a berth of at least 1 mile. A tall television tower on the hill above the port is very conspicuous.

The harbour can be approached on a course between 220° and 310°. When approaching from a W direction care should be taken to clear **Banco de la Plancha**. The leading marks give an approach bearing to the harbour of 220°, Line Ⓐ (*Front:* a low concrete lattice work tower, *Rear:* a lone white house with a grey roof standing in a field with trees below it).

Night Night approach and entrance without previous knowledge or very good visibility are not advised as there are no lights covering the approach. The only light is on the head of the breakwater (F.G. 1 M.).

Entrance

Day Round end of breakwater giving it a berth of at least 23 m (25 yards) and keep a look out for fishing vessels leaving at speed.

Leading mark front
concrete platform

Leading mark rear
grey roofed house above trees

Puerto de Lastres—leading marks.

Puerto de Lastres – harbour looking NE.

Berths

Deep water berths up to 7 m (3·5 fathoms) are possible alongside the harbour wall. There are a few ladders and adequate bollards. The NE corner has the best berth, alongside the E wall. Watch out for masses of mooring cables and lines for dinghies attached to the N wall.

Moorings

Mooring buoys may be available but care should be taken to check with the locals if and when the rightful owners are expected back.

Formalities

Normal, but the local officers have little experience of yachts.

Facilities

Water From a bar near quay.

Diesel From a pump on SW quay.

Shops Adequate but well spread out up the winding street.

Beaches There is a very good sandy beach, **Playa de Colunga**, nearby.

Cafés There are a number of cafés, bars, restaurants which specialise in fish, shellfish and 'cidre' meals.

Visits Fifteenth century *Colegiata* is worth a visit.

41 Puerto del Puntal y Ría de Villaviciosa

Population (Villaviciosa) 20,000 Rating 3-4-5 Position 43°31·6′N 5°23·3′W

General

Something quite different for this part of the coast: a canalised river, a basin with quays and the possibility of mooring in 2 m (1 fathom). There is an open **ría** (estuary) above this port, ending in a narrow river, extending in all over 5 miles. The bar, which has a minimum depth of 1·5 m (5 ft), is only possible in settled weather as it breaks in heavy N winds and swell. Many visitors come to this area by car during weekends, but it is comparatively deserted during the week. Plans for a new yacht harbour 2 M up the river.

Warnings

Entry should only be undertaken during the 2 hours before HW.

The **Bajas de la Mesnada** should be given a wide berth. The channel for the first part is very close to the W training wall and is narrow. The channel and **El Puntal** harbour are subject to silting.

Data

Charts

Admiralty No. 2926
Spanish Nos. 462A, 939
French No. 5009

Magnetic variation 6°23′W (1984) decreasing by about 5′ each year.

Tidal information

	HW		LW		MHWS	MHWN	MLWS	MLWN
Pointe de Grave	0600 1800	1100 2300	0000 1200	0500 1700	5·4 m 17·6 ft	4·2 m 13·8 ft	0·9 m 3·0 ft	2·1 m 6·8 ft
Ría de Villaviciosa	−0·35	−0·40	−0·30	+0·05	−1·3 m −4·1 ft	−1·2 m −4·1 ft	−0·5 m −1·7 ft	−0·6 m −1·8 ft

The stream in the river can run up to 3 knots at springs. Strong W winds raise, and E winds lower, the level of HW by up to 0·5 m (1·5 ft).

Lights

Tazones lighthouse. Group Occulting 3 White, 15 seconds, 125 m (410 ft), 15 miles. Grey tower, yellow corners and building, aluminium cupola. Fog Horn Morse V (· · · –), 30 seconds, 150 m (492 ft) N of lighthouse.

Puerto de Tazones mole head. Fixed Red, 8·5 m (28 ft), 1 mile. Wooden mast.

Approaches

Day

From W The unremarkable coast from **Cabo de San Lorenzo**, consisting of small hills, cliffs and many small rivers, end at **Punta Tazones** which has very high cliffs and a conspicuous lighthouse on its E side.

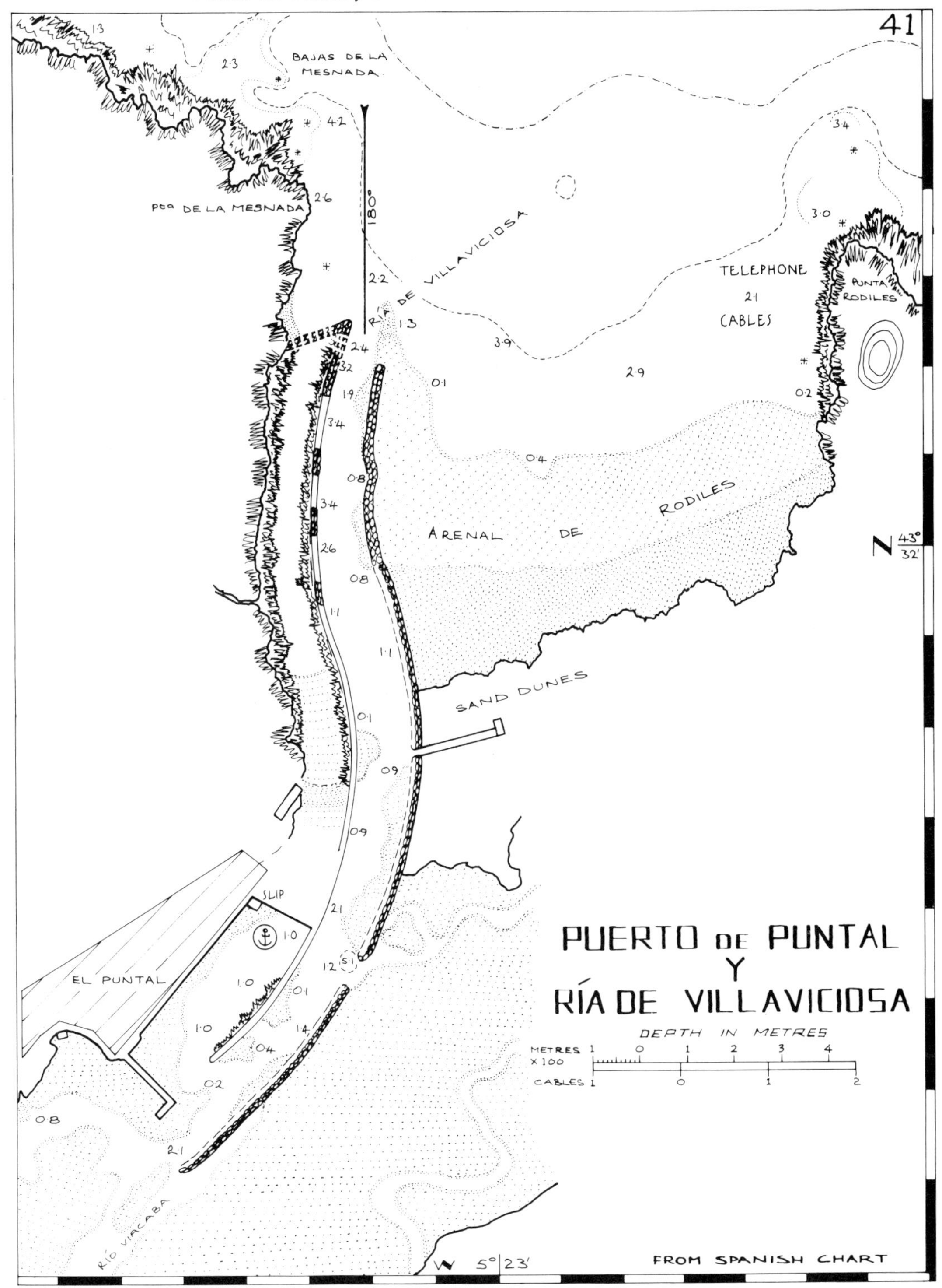
41
BAJAS DE LA MESNADA
Pta DE LA MESNADA
RÍA DE VILLAVICIOSA
TELEPHONE
21
CABLES
PUNTA RODILES
ARENAL DE RODILES
SAND DUNES
SLIP
EL PUNTAL
RÍO VIACABA
PUERTO DE PUNTAL
Y
RÍA DE VILLAVICIOSA
DEPTH IN METRES
METRES x 100
CABLES
FROM SPANISH CHART
N 43° 32'
W 5° 23'

Ría de Villaviciosa—entrance looking south—high water.

From E **Punta Misiera** with its television tower and **Cabo Lastres** with its flat top are easily identified. The entrance to the **ría** is marked to the W by the high **Punta de la Mesnada**, which has a large yellowish scar on its E side, and the sandy beach of **Arenal de Rodiles** to the E. Manoeuvre to a point where the E edge of **Punta de la Mesnada** bears 195° and the lighthouse on **Punta Tazones** is due W.

Night Lights are planned at the entrance, until then **Punta Tazones** (Oc. (3) W. 15 sec. 20 M.) is the only effective light in the area and night entrance is not possible.

Entrance

Day From the position above, proceed due S until the rocky training walls either side of the river can be identified. Approach and enter the river on this bearing close, 14 m (15 yards), to the W training wall, having first made certain that the waves are not breaking in this channel, which is only about 23 m (25 yards) wide. Waves will be breaking either side and will be seen to be breaking further up the channel—they are in fact breaking only on the E side. A similar illusion will also appear when leaving the harbour, and is due to the curve in the training wall.

Keep parallel to the W wall at about 14 m (15 yards) until level with the sand dunes to the E, when alter course and follow the middle of the channel. Keep this position until level with the S end of the wall separating the basin from the river, when turn hard to starboard to enter the basin near the starboard wall. Watch out for the current in this area of the river as it is strong (up to 3 knots).

Night Entrance at night not possible without previous visits to this harbour and adequate natural light.

Moorings

Moor stern to quay on the N side of the basin with anchor out ahead. Keep at least 23 m (25 yards) clear of the quay in 1 to 2 m (½ to 1 fathom) mud and sand.

Formalities

The officials were surprised to have a full size yacht in their harbour as they are more used to motorised runabouts. Only normal details are required.

Facilities

Water From café near the quay.

Shops One shop near café provides simple requirements.

Slip NW corner of **El Puntal** harbour (2 m HW).

Yacht Club Located 2 m above **El Puntal** on W bank. Usual facilities.

Ría de Villaviciosa—looking south from west training wall head—low water.

Beaches There is a first class sandy beach, **Arenal de Rodiles**, but it is crowded at weekends.

Visits A trip in a dinghy with a motor at HW up the **ría** is well worth while. Though it is possible to get to **Villaviciosa** at HW and the old town is well worth a visit, it is not recommended to proceed above the large white factory on the port hand side. The narrow river above this point is very smelly, winding and dirty. It is better to walk from the factory.

Fiestas **Villaviciosa**. 11–15 September, festivities of La Virgen del Portal.

Puerto del Puntal—looking south east.

42 Puerto de Tazones

Population 568 Rating 2-3-3 Position 43°32·7′N 5°23·9′W

General

An unspoilt little fishing village in a steep valley between two hills, much as it must have been a hundred years ago. The harbour has an easy deep-water approach, but the only possible anchorage, in 4 m (2 fathoms) is not protected from the NE and E and would be impossible in heavy weather from this direction. crowded with visitors from **Gijon** at weekends.

Warnings

Except for the shallows, **Bajas de la Mesnada**, there are no off-lying dangers.

Data

Charts

Admiralty No. 2926
Spanish Nos. 939, 4041
French No. 5009

Magnetic variation 6°23′W (1984) decreasing by about 5′ each year.

Tidal information

	HW		LW		MHWS	MHWN	MLWS	MLWN
Pointe de Grave	0600 1800	1100 2300	0000 1200	0500 1700	5·4 m 17·6 ft	4·2 m 13·8 ft	0·9 m 3·0 ft	2·1 m 6·8 ft
Puerto de Tazones	−0·35	−0·40	−0·30	+0·05	−1·3 m −4·1 ft	−1·2 m −4·1 ft	−0·5 m −1·7 ft	−0·6 m −1·8 ft

Lights

Tazones. Group Occulting (3) White, 15 seconds, 125 m (410 ft), 15 miles. Grey tower, yellow corners and dwelling, aluminium cupola. Fog Horn Morse V (· · · –), 30 seconds, 150 m (492 ft) N of lighthouse.
Mole head. Flashing Green, 3 seconds, 8·5 m (28 ft), 1 mile. Wood mast.

Approaches

Day

From W The coast is without any particular distinguishing features and it is not until **Punta de Tazones** is reached that there is any great change. This **Punta** is steep-sided and has a conspicuous lighthouse. The coast here drops back into the **Ría de Villaviciosa**.

From E **Punta Misiera** is similar to **Punta Tazones**, but has a conspicuous television tower. Manoeuvre until the lighthouse on **Punta Tazones** is due W about 1 mile, when the harbour should be seen with the white houses of the village above it.

Night

Approach by night in conditions of good visibility is possible using **Tazones** lighthouse (Oc. (3) W. 15 sec. 20 M.). Navigate to a position where the lighthouse bears due W about 1 mile.

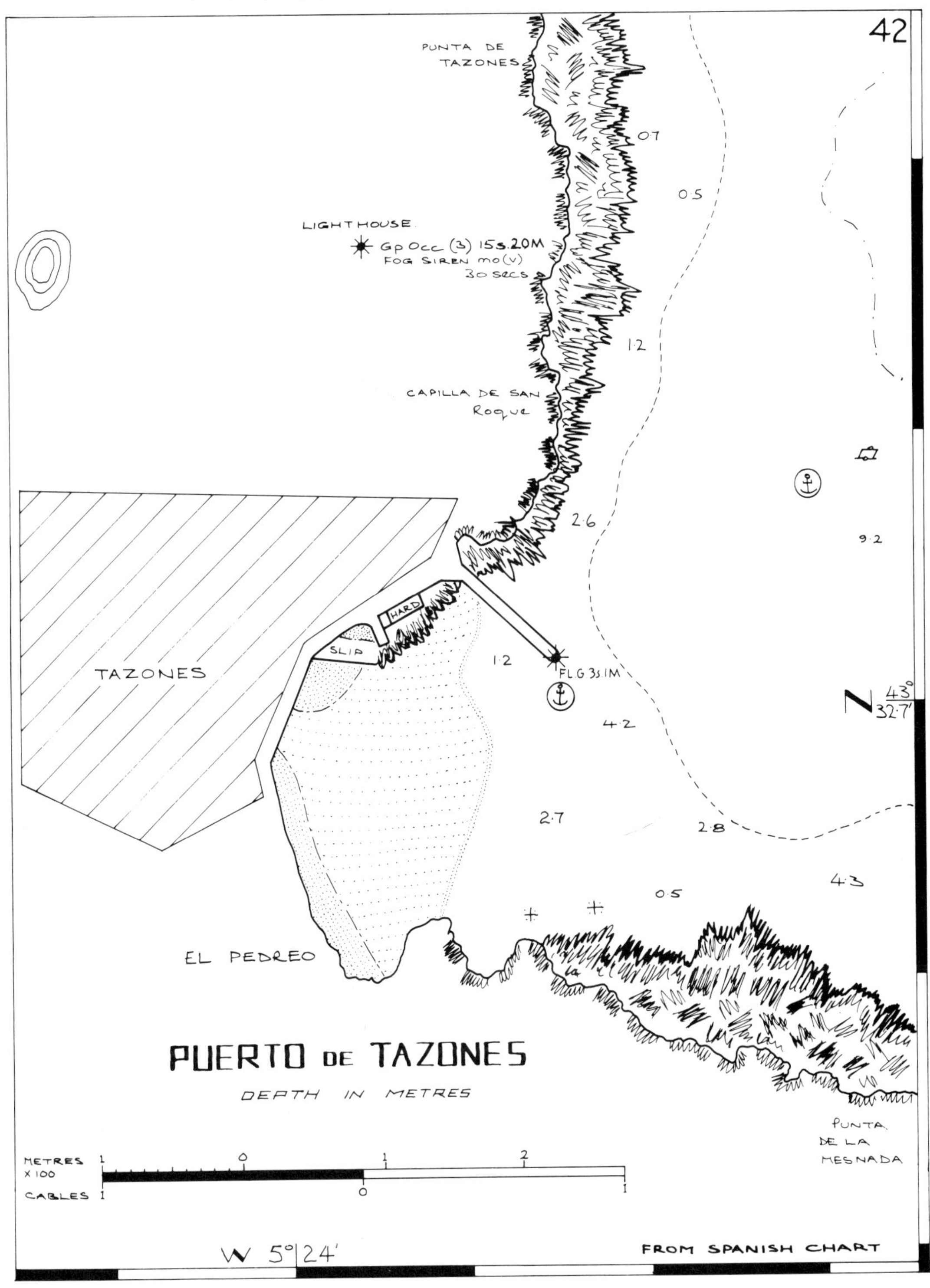
42
PUNTA DE TAZONES
LIGHTHOUSE
Gp Occ (3) 15s.20M
FOG SIREN mo(V) 30 secs
CAPILLA DE SAN Roque
TAZONES
HARD
SLIP
FL.G.3s.1M
EL PEDREO
PUNTA DE LA MESNADA
0.7
0.5
1.2
2.6
9.2
1.2
4.2
2.7
2.8
4.3
0.5
N 43° 32.7'
PUERTO DE TAZONES
DEPTH IN METRES
METRES X 100
CABLES
W 5° 24'
FROM SPANISH CHART

Puerto de Tazones—entrance.

Entrance

Day From the position above approach the head of the breakwater, giving it a berth of about 5 m (17 ft).

Night From the position given in *approach*, *night*, above, direct course towards the mole head light (Fl.G. 3 sec. 1 M.). Keep a look out for a large mooring buoy in this area.

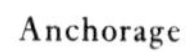

Puerto de Tazones—looking north east.

Anchorages

Anchorage in 2 m (1 fathom) sand 25 m (27 yards) SW of the mole head. At neaps it may be possible to get further inside the harbour and be more protected from the swell. A deep water anchorage 9 m (4·5 fathoms) lies offshore near a mooring buoy.

Formalities

Normal

Facilities

Water From **Lonja de Pescadores** (fish auction room) on quay.

Shops A few basic shops.

Cafés A number of cafés, bars and restaurants which specialise in fish, shellfish and *cidre* meals. These are very crowded at weekends.

Fiestas 16 August, festivities in honour of St Roch.

43 Puerto de Gijón (Muelles Locales)

Population 111,000 Rating 1-2-1 Position 43°32·8′N 5°40·1′W

General

One of the largest cities on the N Spanish coast with two harbour complexes, **Puerto del Musel (El Puerto)** (page 256) and **Puerto de Gijón (Muelles Locales).** The latter can be entered under any conditions except N storms provided visibility is good enough to avoid the banks on which the sea breaks. The bar has a minimum depth of 2·4 m (8 ft). Anchorage or mooring in 2 m (1 fathom) and berths alongside in 3 m (1·5 fathoms) are available. Shopping facilities are first class and there is a palatial yacht club with a section at the harbour. There is a large sandy beach nearby which tends to be very crowded at weekends. The harbour is sometimes oily and dirty and can be crowded.

Warnings

Considerable harbour works are in hand at **Musel** and some are near the approach to **Puerto de Gijón**. Future development will involve the approach to **Puerto de Gijón** itself. Buoys marking harbour works are moved as work progresses. The leading marks are not easy to see in daylight. Rockets and artillery are sometimes fired from **Cabo de San Lorenzo**, so give it a wide berth. When there is a heavy sea running there are eddies at the mouth of the harbour entrance. The harbour is silting, so depths are suspect.

Data

Charts
Admiralty Nos. 2926, 2927, 77
Spanish Nos. 13B, 935
French Nos. 6381, 5009

Magnetic variation 6° 22′W (1984) decreasing by about 5′ each year.

Tidal information Spanish tide tables are available for this port.

	HW		LW		MHWS	MHWN	MLWS	MLWN
Pointe de Grave	0600 1800	1100 2300	0000 1200	0500 1700	5·4 m 17·6 ft	4·2 m 13·8 ft	0·9 m 3·0 ft	2·1 m 6·8 ft
Gijón (Muelles Locales)	−0·40	−0·45	−0·35	0·00	−1·3 m −4·1 ft	−1·2 m −4·1 ft	−0·5 m −1·7 ft	−0·6 m −1·8 ft

The tide levels are lowered up to 0·5 m (1·5 ft) with NE and SE winds. Winds from SW and NW increase them the same amount.

Lights **Cabo de Torres**. Group Flashing (2) White, 10 seconds, 79·9 m (263 ft), 18 miles. White octagonal tower on square dwelling. Fog Siren Morse G (– – ·), 30 seconds.

Pierda del Sacramento (marks **Serrapio de Tierra**). Flashing Green, 1·3 seconds,

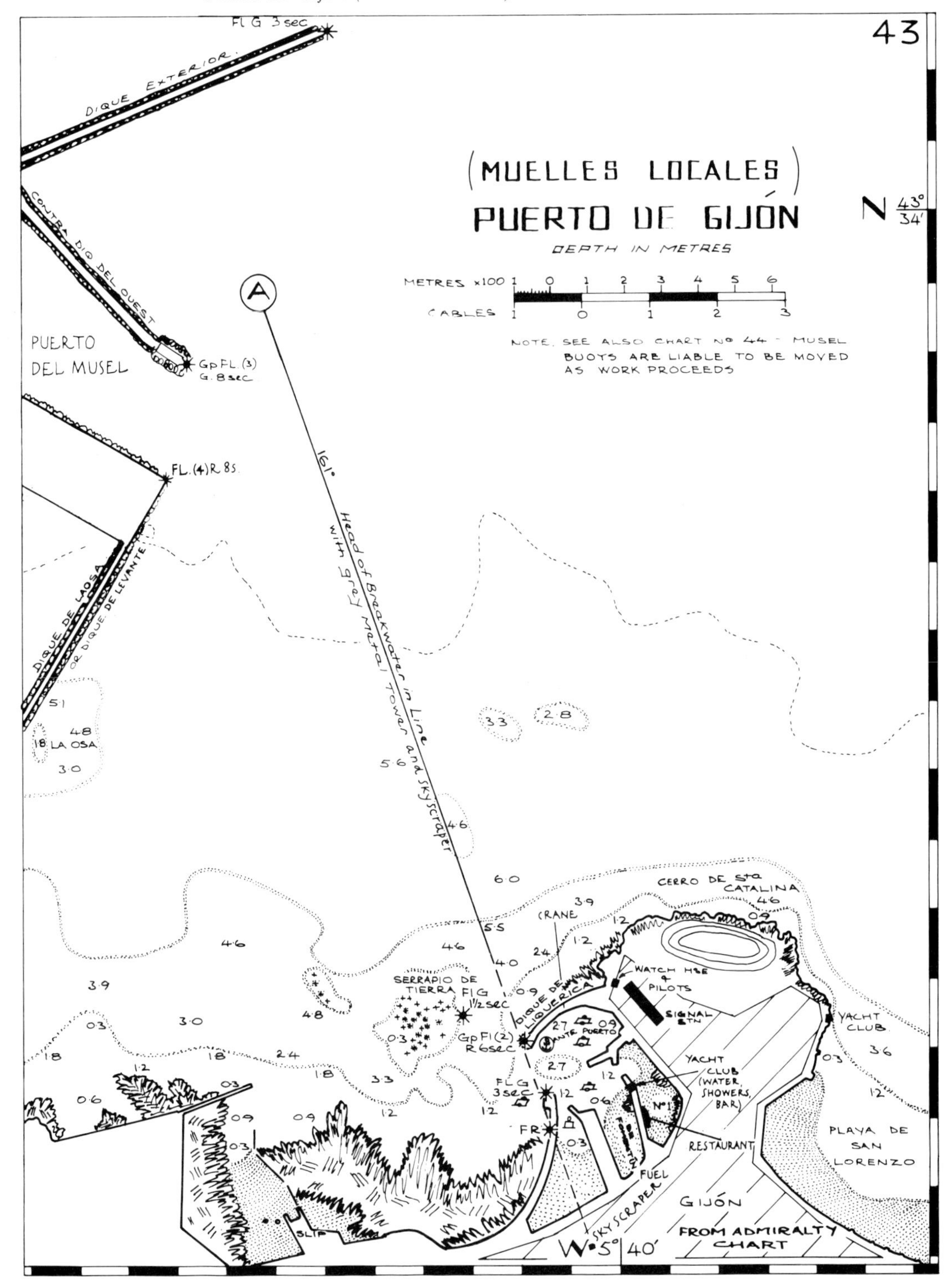
43
(MUELLES LOCALES)
PUERTO DE GIJÓN
DEPTH IN METRES
N 43° 34'
METRES x100
CABLES
NOTE. SEE ALSO CHART Nº 44 - MUSEL
BUOYS ARE LIABLE TO BE MOVED
AS WORK PROCEEDS
Fl G 3sec
DIQUE EXTERIOR
CONTRA DIQ DEL OUEST
PUERTO
DEL MUSEL
Gp FL (3)
G. 8sec
FL.(4)R.8s
DIQUE DE LAOSA
OR DIQUE DE LEVANTE
LA OSA
A
161° Head of Breakwater in Line with grey Metal Tower and Skyscraper
CERRO DE Sta CATALINA
CRANE
WATCH HSE & PILOTS
SIGNAL STN
YACHT CLUB
SERRAPIO DE TIERRA
Fl G 1½sec
Gp Fl (2) R 6sec
DIQUE DE LIQUERICA
ANTE PUERTO
FL G 3sec
FR
YACHT CLUB (WATER, SHOWERS, BAR)
RESTAURANT
FUEL
SLIP
SKY SCRAPER
GIJÓN
PLAYA DE SAN LORENZO
FROM ADMIRALTY CHART
W 5° 40'

6·4 m (21 ft), 4 miles. Octagonal concrete tower, white with black vertical stripes. Unwatched.
Leading lights 161° Line Ⓐ.
Front. **Dique de Liquerica.** Quick Flashing (2) Red, 6 seconds, 6·4 m (21 ft), 6 miles. White column. Red Top.
Rear. **Malecón de Fomento**. Fixed Red, 11 m (36 ft), 6 miles. Grey metal latticework tower. Visible 071°–251°.
Malecón de Fomento head. Flashing Green, 3 seconds, 5·8 m (19 ft), 3 miles. Top of stone wall.
See also **Puerto del Musel (El Puerto)**, page 256, for full details of other lights in the approach.

Radio An air radiobeacon operates near **Gijón** on 325 kHz, 60 miles AVS (· – / · · · – / · · ·), continuous.

Port Radio See page 20.

Signal station There is a signal station by the pilots' lookout house at the root of **Dique de Liquerica** for local signals only. International Code of Flag Signals may be used.

Pilots Pilots in a launch bearing a large letter P may come out and guide yachts in.

Harbour dues A small charge is made

Puerto de Gijón (Muelles Locales)—looking north. Note the new breakwaters at **Musel** are shown by dashed line. *Photo: Alarde*

Approaches

Day *From W* **Cabo Peñas**, a very large white-hued promontory with a large, conical, outlying island, and **Cabo de Torres**, a high, rugged, reddish coloured point with large caves, are very easily identified. **Cabo de Torres** also has three very large spherical white butane storage tanks surrounded by a white wall on top of the ridge, which are very conspicuous. Its lighthouse, a white octagonal tower with an onion-shaped top and rectangular dwelling, is obscured from the N by a pinnacle of rock. The high breakwaters around **Puerto del Musel** are very conspicuous.

From E **Cabo de San Lorenzo** is not particularly conspicuous, but the wide sandy beach backed by blocks of flats E of **Gijón** is easily seen.

The skyscrapers of the city of **Gijón** can be seen some way out at sea, as can the grass covered top of **Cerro de Santa Catalina**. The breakwater N of **Puerto del Musel (El Puerto)** is also very conspicuous.

Navigate to a position near the entrance to **Musel** harbour. Keep **Cabo de Torres** on less than 265° until the head of **Dique Exterior (Ouest)** has been identified.

Night Using the lights of **Cabo de Torres** (Fl. (2) W. 10 sec. 18 M.) and **Puerto del Musel** manoeuvre to a position near **Dique Exterior** head light (Fl.G. 3 sec. 6 M.) at the entrance to **Musel** harbour. Keep **Cabo de Torres** on less than 265° until this light has been identified.

Entrance

Day From the position near the head of **Dique Exterior (Ouest)**, detailed above, sail on a S bearing until a tall, narrow, dark coloured skyscraper bears 161°, Line Ⓐ, keeping the W end of the **Dique de Liquerica** on the W side of the skyscraper until the leading marks (*Front:* small white tower on end of **Dique de Liquerica**, *Rear:* grey latticework tower on **Malecón de Fomento**) can be identified and brought into line. When the top of **Cerro de Santa Catalina** is due E, alter course to 180° to leave the large, conspicuous, concrete octagonal tower with black and white vertical stripes which marks **Serrapio de Tierra** 68 m (75 yards) to starboard, then alter course to enter the harbour. Marks are sometimes hard to spot in certain light.

Night From the position given in *Approach*, *night*, near the Flashing Green 3 seconds, proceed S and bring into line the leading lights (*Front:* on W end of **Dique Liquerica** Fl. (2) R. 6 sec. 6 M. *Rear:* **Malecón de Fomento** F.R. 6 M.) and approach the harbour. When the light marking the **Serrapio de Tierra** (Fl.G. 1·3 sec. 4 M.) bears 210° alter course to 180° and then enter harbour between the *Front* leading light (Fl. (2) R. 6 sec. 6 M.) and the light on the head of **Malecón de Fomento** (Fl.G. 2 sec. 3 M.).

Anchorage

Anchor in mud over rock, 2 m (1 fathom), in entrance to **Antepuerto**. In conditions of heavy swell from the N this anchorage will be uncomfortable and not secure.

Puerto de Gijon – looking E–SE–S from head of **Dique de Liquerica.**

Moorings

Moor stern to one of the large mooring buoys near entrance to the **Antepuerto**, with a kedge ahead towards the harbour entrance.

Berths

Deep-water berths alongside the **Dique de Liquerica** in 3 m (1·5 fathoms) shallowing to 1·5 m (5 ft) as the root is approached may be available. Drying berths are available in the other basins. The E side of **Muelle del Oeste** is satisfactory.

Formalities

Normal information required.

Facilities

Water	From pipe at yacht club on **Muelle del Oeste**, W side at HW.
Diesel	From pump at root of **Muelle del Oeste** at HW. (0·5 at Neaps).
Petrol	May be obtained from pump on the other side of the road at root of **Muelle del Oeste** in cans.
Shops	Almost every type of shop and a good market.
Hotels	There are a number of hotels of all classes.
Bars, cafés and restaurants	Many to suit all tastes are available.
Clubs	**Real Club Astur de Regates** has three centres, a workshop,yard,

clubroom, bar, showers etc. on the **Muelle del Oeste** between **Darsena No. 1** and **Dársena de Fomentín**, a clubroom in the city and a palatial social club house on the E side of the **Cerro de Santa Catalina**. Visiting yachtsmen who are members of recognised yacht clubs are welcome (344202).

Beaches A very large sandy beach, **Playa de San Lorenzo**, is E of the harbour, but tends to be crowded.

Fiestas 24 June, in honour of St John the Baptist; blessing the sea.
29 June, in honour of St Peter; procession of boats.
11–18 August, Feast of the Assumption.

44 Puerto del Musel (El Puerto)

Population 480 Rating 5-1-3 Position 43°33·5′N 5°42′W

General

This is the commercial port of **Gijón** and it covers a huge area. It has facilities for the largest ships of all types. There is a small inner fishing harbour. This port can be entered in any weather conditions and shelter found from storms from all directions. The inner harbour has oily quays and there is a lot of coal dust around. Deep-water berths in up to 5·5 m (3 fathoms) are available. Normal supplies are obtainable from a few shops in the dock area.

Warnings

While harbour works are in progress care should be exercised during approach and entrance as charts, pilot books, etc. may not be up to date.

Data

Charts

Admiralty Nos. 2926, 2927, 77
Spanish Nos. 13B, 935
French Nos. 6381, 5009

Magnetic variation 6°27′W (1984) decreasing by 5′ each year.

Tidal Information

	HW		LW		MHWS	MHWN	MLWS	MLWN
Pointe de Grave	0600 1800	1100 2300	0000 1200	0500 1700	5·4 m 17·6 ft	4·2 m 13·8 ft	0·9 m 3·0 ft	2·1 m 6·8 ft
Musel (El Puerto)	−0·40	−0·45	−0·35	0·00	−1·3 m 4·1 ft	−1·2 m 4·1 ft	−0·5 m −1·7 ft	−0·6 m −1·8 ft

Lights

Cabo de Torres. Group Flashing (2) White, 10 seconds, 79·9 m (263 ft), 18 miles. White 8-sided tower on square dwelling. Fog Siren Morse G (– – ·), 30 seconds.
Dique Exterior (Oeste) Head. Fl.G. 3 sec., 22 m (72 ft) 6 M. White column, black stripes.
Contradique del Oeste Head. Fl. (3) G. 8 sec. 16 m (52 ft). 4 M. Metal tower.
Contradique de La Osa Head. Fl. (4) R. 8 sec. 12 m (39 ft) 4 M. Metal tower.
Dique Norte head. Oc. G. 2·5 seconds. 8 m (28 ft), 5 miles. Black round tower, narrow white stripes.
Espigón II Head. Fixed Red, 4 m (15 ft), 2 miles. White tower.
Espigón I Head. Fixed Red, 6 m (20 ft), 2 miles. White tower.
Puerto Pesquero, Espigón Sur. Fixed Red, 5·5 m (18 ft). 1 mile. Pole.
Nuevos Muelles de la Osa Head. Fixed Red, 8 m (26 ft) 2 miles. White round mast.
Nuevos Muelles de la Osa. N. Corner. Fl. (2) Red, 10 seconds. 9 m (30 ft) 2 miles. Red post.

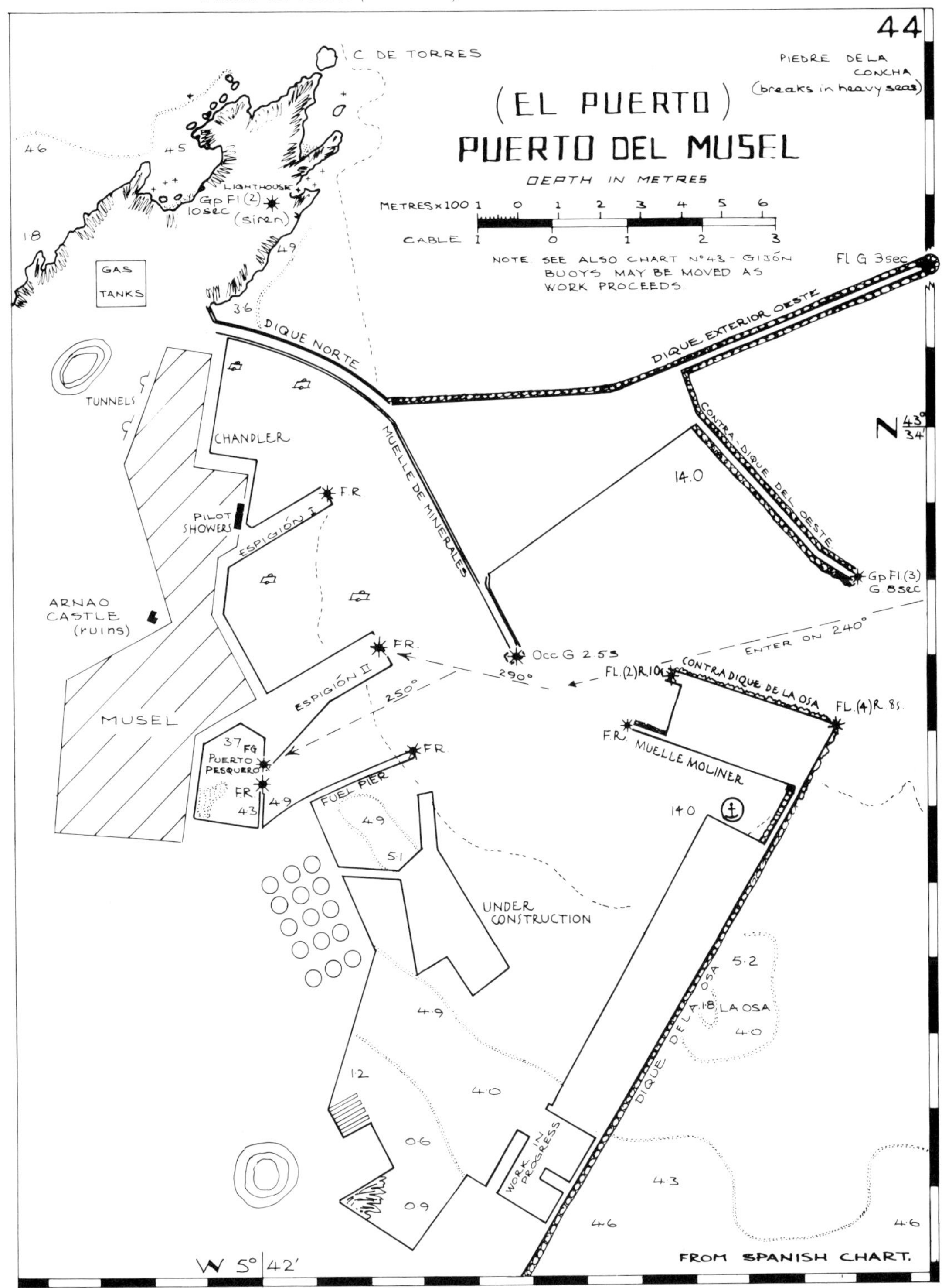
44
C DE TORRES
PIEDRE DE LA CONCHA (breaks in heavy seas)
(EL PUERTO)
PUERTO DEL MUSEL
DEPTH IN METRES
METRES x 100 1 0 1 2 3 4 5 6
CABLE 1 0 1 2 3
NOTE SEE ALSO CHART N°43 - GIJÓN
BUOYS MAY BE MOVED AS WORK PROCEEDS
LIGHTHOUSE Gp Fl (2) 10sec (siren)
GAS TANKS
DIQUE NORTE
DIQUE EXTERIOR OESTE
Fl G 3sec
TUNNELS
CHANDLER
MUELLE DE MINERALES
CONTRA-DIQUE DEL OESTE
Gp Fl.(3) G. 8sec
PILOT SHOWERS
ESPIGIÓN I
FR.
ARNAO CASTLE (ruins)
Occ G 2.5s
290°
ENTER ON 240°
ESPIGIÓN II
250°
FL.(2)R.10s
CONTRA DIQUE DE LA OSA
FL.(4)R. 8s.
MUSEL
FG
PUERTO PESQUERO
FUEL PIER
MUELLE MOLINER
UNDER CONSTRUCTION
DIQUE DE LA OSA
LA OSA
WORK IN PROGRESS
W 5° 42′
N 43° 34′
FROM SPANISH CHART.

Espigón Norte. Fixed Green, 6 m (20 ft). 2 miles. White column, black top.
Fuel pierhead. Fixed Red, Metal tower.

Port Radio See page 20.

Harbour dues A small charge is made.

Puerto del Musel – outer entrance from head of **Dique Exterior Oeste** – looking SW–W–NW.

Approaches

Day *From NW* The rugged **Cabo de Torres** has a conspicuous lighthouse obscured from the N by a pinnacle of rock. On top of the hill are three large white spherical butane tanks which cannot be mistaken.

From E A very large yellow scar in the side of **Cabo de Torres**, where there is a quarry, and the tanks referred to above, are unmistakable as are the high stone breakwaters of the port. Manoeuvre to a position where the new end of **Dique Exterior** head is due W ½ mile.

Night Using the lighthouse of **Cabo de Torres** (Fl. (2) W. 10 sec. 18 M.) with the lights on **Dique Exterior** head (Fl.G. 3 sec., 6 M.), navigate to a position where **Dique Exterior** head is due W ½ mile.

Entrance

Day From the position given above proceed on 240°, leaving the head of **Contradique del Oeste** 150 m to starboard and passing between the heads of **Muelle de Minerales** to starboard and **Contradique de La Osa** to port. Change course to 290° towards the head of **Espigón II** then altering course to 250° towards **Puerto Pesquero**. Enter between jetty heads but watch out for fishing boats leaving at speed. A conspicuous tank farm lies just S of this entrance.

Night From the position given in *approach, night*, above, proceed on 240° leaving (Fl.G. 3 sec.) and (Fl. (3) G. 8 sec.) to starboard and (Fl. (2) R. 10 sec.) to port. Enter between (Oc. G. 2·5 sec.) to starboard and (F.R.) to port. Then on 290° towards

Puerto del Musel – inner entrance from head of **Contradique de Levante** – looking S–SW–W–NW.

(F.R.). When a (F.R.) and a (F.G.) are on 250° turn towards them and enter **Puerto Pesquero** between them.

Anchorages

Although it is possible to anchor almost anywhere inside the outer harbour, this is not favoured by the local authorities and care should be taken to keep clear of the area used by merchant ships: 200 m SW of **Contradique de La Osa** is a possible place to anchor.

Berths

Berths alongside are available in **Puerto Pesquero** in up to 5·4 m (3 fathoms). As the quay wall is dirty see if it is possible to moor alongside a fishing boat which is not going to sea in the immediate future.

Formalities

Local officers are not very interested in all the details usually required at the smaller ports.

Puerto del Musel – looking NE–E–SE.

Facilities

Water From piped supply on quay.

Diesel From piped supply on quay. Bunkering facilities are available in **Puerto Pesquero**.

Showers Near Pilot House.

Shops There are a few basic shops near the quay but there is a good bus service to **Gijón** every 15 minutes, where first class shops exist. Chandlery shop near **Puerte Pesquero**.

Puerto del Musel – Puerto Pesquero looking W from entrance.

45 Ensenada y Puerto de Candás

Population 11,400 Rating 2-4-3 Position 43°35·3′N 5°45·5′W

General

An attractive little fishing harbour and tourist village in a gap between two hills. The approach is fairly easy and anchorage in 2 m (1 fathom) is available. There are also drying berths alongside the quay. This harbour would be impossible in strong NE winds and swell. Normal supplies are available and there are several beaches. There is a small drying river anchorage 2 cables S behind **Punta Peron** which can be used with care in settled weather. Sometimes dirty.

Warnings

The various banks and shoals in the area should be avoided when there is any swell. The harbour should be vacated if strong NE–E winds occur.

Data

Charts

Admiralty No. 2927
Spanish Nos. 748A, 935
French Nos. 2042, 5009

Magnetic variation 6°29′W (1984) decreasing by about 5′ each year.

Tidal information

	HW		LW		MHWS	MHWN	MLWS	MLWN
Pointe de Grave	0600 1800	1100 2300	0000 1200	0500 1700	5·4 m 17·6 ft	4·2 m 13·8 ft	0·9 m 3·0 ft	2·1 m 6·8 ft
Candás	−0·43	−0·48	−0·38	−0·3	−1·3 m −4·3 ft	−1·3 m −4·3 ft	−0·5 m −1·7 ft	−0·5 m −1·8 ft

Lights

Punta del Cuerno. Variable characteristics as warning signal. Group Occulting (1+2) White, 16 seconds, means entry to port practicable; (1+3) White, 16 seconds, means caution necessary; Isophase White, 2 seconds, means entry dangerous. 37·8 m (124 ft), 12 miles. Reddish tower, white cupola, large grey dwelling. Fog Horn Morse C (– · – ·) 60 seconds.
Canal de El Carrero, leading lights 291° Line Ⓐ.
Front Fixed Red, 23·2 m (76 ft), 3 miles. White column in front of lighthouse on **Punta del Cuerno**.
Rear Fixed Red, 62·2 m (204 ft), 3 miles. Lantern on top of stone house, **Casa de la Piedra**.
Nuevo Muelle head. Fixed Green, 9·1 m (30 ft) 4 miles. Grey tower.

Approaches

Day

From NW **La Isla** off **Punta Sombrado** and the high **Punta del Cuerno**, with the church of **Candás** which has two towers showing over the skyline, are easily recognised. Approaching from the NW manoeuvre to a position where the lighthouse on **Punta del Cuerno** bears SW 1 mile.

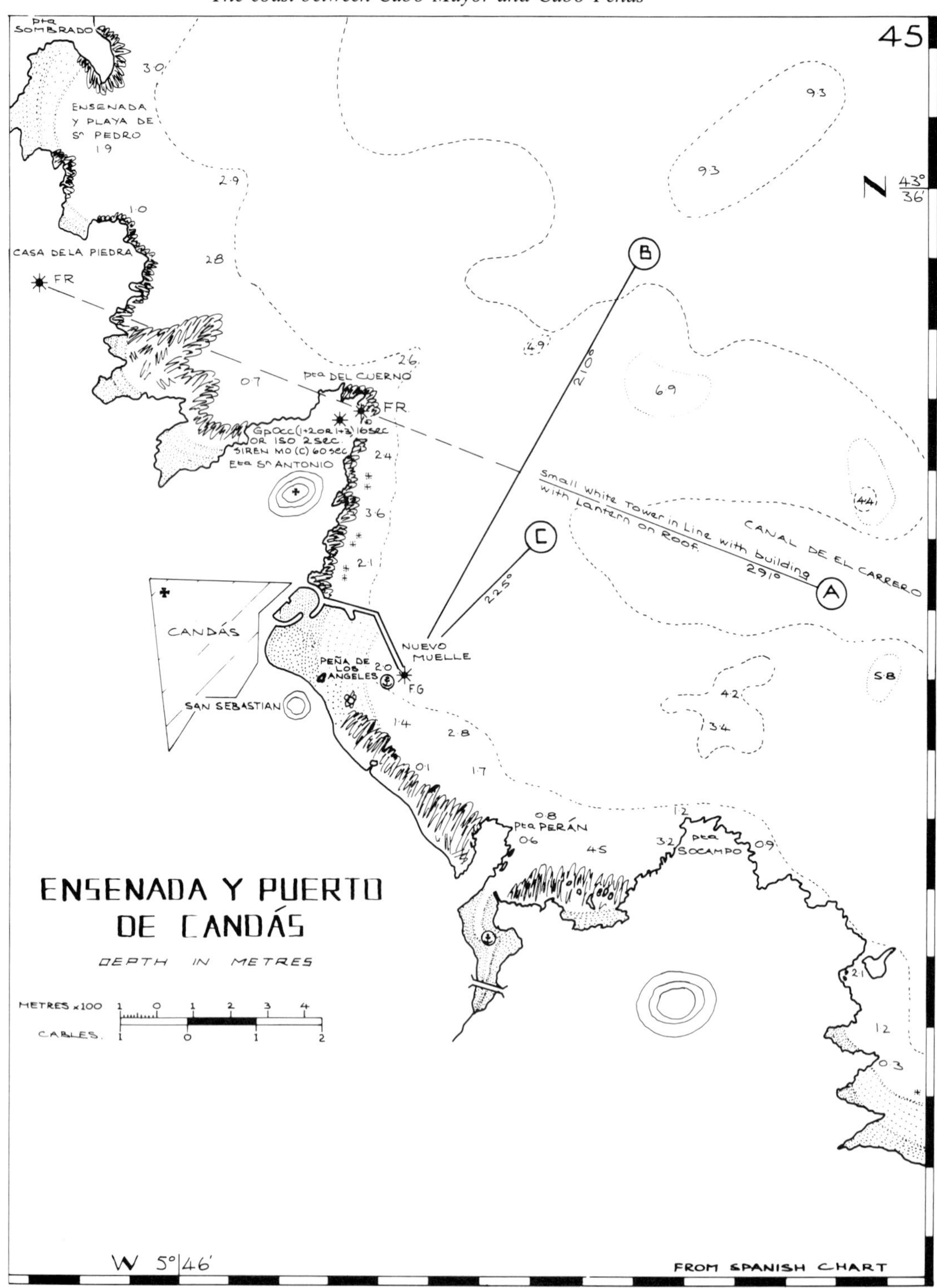
45
Pta SOMBRADO
ENSENADA Y PLAYA DE Sn PEDRO
CASA DE LA PIEDRA
FR
Pta DEL CUERNO
FR
Gp Occ (1+2 or 1+3) 16 sec
or ISO 2 sec
SIREN MO (C) 60 sec
Eta Sn ANTONIO
CANDÁS
PEÑA DE LOS ANGELES
NUEVO MUELLE
FG
SAN SEBASTIAN
Pta PERÁN
Pta SOCAMPO
Small White Tower in Line with building with Lantern on Roof
291°
210°
225°
CANAL DE EL CARRERO
ENSENADA Y PUERTO DE CANDÁS
DEPTH IN METRES
METRES x100
CABLES
W 5°46'
N 43° 36'
FROM SPANISH CHART

From SE **Cabo de Torres**, a high rugged cape with three white spherical butane tanks on it, the reddish-hued cliffs of **San Sebastián** and the red-roofed village of **Candás** are easily seen. From SE approach so that the leading marks are in line on 291°, Line Ⓐ, (*Front:* a white tower on **Punta del Cuerno**, *rear:* a square stone building with a lantern on the roof, the **Casa de la Piedra**).

Night Using the lights of **Cabo de Torres** (Fl. (2) W. 10 sec. 18 M.) and **Punta de Cuerno** (variable characteristics, warning signal: Oc. (1+2) or (1+3) W. 16 sec. 12 M. or Iso. W. 2 sec. 12 M.) manoeuvre to a position where **Punta de Cuerno** light bears 291°, 2 miles.

Entrance

Day *From NE* Approach the harbour on a bearing of 210°, Line Ⓑ, to the head of the breakwater.

From SE Approach the leading marks on a bearing of 291° until the head of the breakwater is SW, when approach it on a bearing of 225°, Line Ⓒ.

Night Entrance at night is not recommended but can be undertaken in settled weather. Follow the leading lights on 291° (*Front* and *Rear:* F.R.) until the light on **Nuevo Muelle** head bears SW, when set course for the light. Note the type of Oc. light on **Punta del Cuerno** and only enter when it is Oc. (1+2). Do not attempt to approach the harbour if it is showing Iso 2 sec., which means that the swell is breaking over shallow patches, or when it is Oc. (1+3), which means that it may be breaking.

Anchorages

Anchor just inside the head of the breakwater so that it bears due E 27 m (30 yards), in 2 m (1 fathom) sand. Drying anchorage in **Río Perán.**

Berths

If not occupied, a berth is possible alongside the first 45 m (50 yards) of the breakwater in 2 m (1 fathom). Drying berths are available further up this breakwater, but not where it makes a bend as there is a hole there.

Formalities

Normal.

Puerto de Candás—looking north west up the harbour.

Puerto de Candas – looking SE–S–SW at low water.

Facilities

Water	From **Cofradia de Pescadores** (fish auction rooms), at the far side of the harbour, and from **Muelle Nuevo.**
Diesel and petrol	At far side of the harbour.
Shops	Adequate for normal supplies.
Beaches	Sandy beaches nearby.
Fiestas	5 April (approx.), Holy Saturday. 14 September, festivities of El Cristo de Candás.
Yacht club	The Sociedad Polideportiva Nautico Carreño has a clubhouse with bar and showers to the NW of the harbour (47).

46 Ensenada y Puerto de Luanco

Population 10,600 Rating 2-3-3 Position 43°37·1′N 5°47′W

General

A pleasant little fishing and tourist port with an anchorage in 2 m (1 fathom) which can only be used in good weather conditions. It would be impossible to use in strong NE winds or swell. The approach is not difficult. There is also a very small drying harbour 2 cables to the S but a local pilot should be used as there are many uncharted rocks off **Ensenada del Dique.**

All normal supplies are available. There is a good sandy beach nearby.

Warnings

Seas break in areas around **La Espiga** and sometimes on **Bajo Juan de Melao**, which should be given a wide berth. In heavy weather seas break all over the bay and it should not be approached in strong winds from N to E.

Data

Charts

Admiralty Nos. 2927, 77
Spanish Nos. 748A, 935
French Nos. 2042, 5009

Magnetic variation 6°29′W (1984) decreasing by about 5′ each year.

Tidal information

	HW		LW		MHWS	MHWN	MLWS	MLWN
Pointe de Grave	0600 1800	1100 2300	0000 1200	0500 1700	5·4 m 17·6 ft	4·2 m 13·8 ft	0·9 m 3·0 ft	2·1 m 6·8 ft
Luanco	−0·45	−0·50	−0·40	0·05	−1·3 m −4·4 ft	−1·3 m −4·4 ft	−0·5 m −1·7 ft	−0·5 m −1·8 ft

Lights

Leading lights 255° Line Ⓐ.
Front Fixed Red, 4·3 m (14 ft), 4 miles. Recessed into wall on mole head.
Rear Fixed Red, 8·2 m (27 ft), 4 miles. Black mast.
Muelle del Gallo head. Flashing Green, 3 seconds, 10·4 m (34 ft), 4 miles. Green concrete column.

Radio

Radiobeacon **Cabo Peñas** 301·1 kHz, 50 miles, PS (· – – · / · · ·), period 6 minutes. Grouped with **Llanes**, IA (· · / · –) and **Estaca de Bares**, BA (– · · · / · –).

Approaches

Day

From NW **Cabo Peñas**, a large whitish-hued promontory, is very conspicuous. The coast between it and **Luanco** is very broken and the several headlands are very similar. **Punta de la Vaca** has to the S some yellowish-hued cliffs. **Luanco** itself is recognised from the NW by the breakwater on **Punta del Gallo** and by the conspicuous church tower. Navigate to a position due E of this church and approach the harbour.

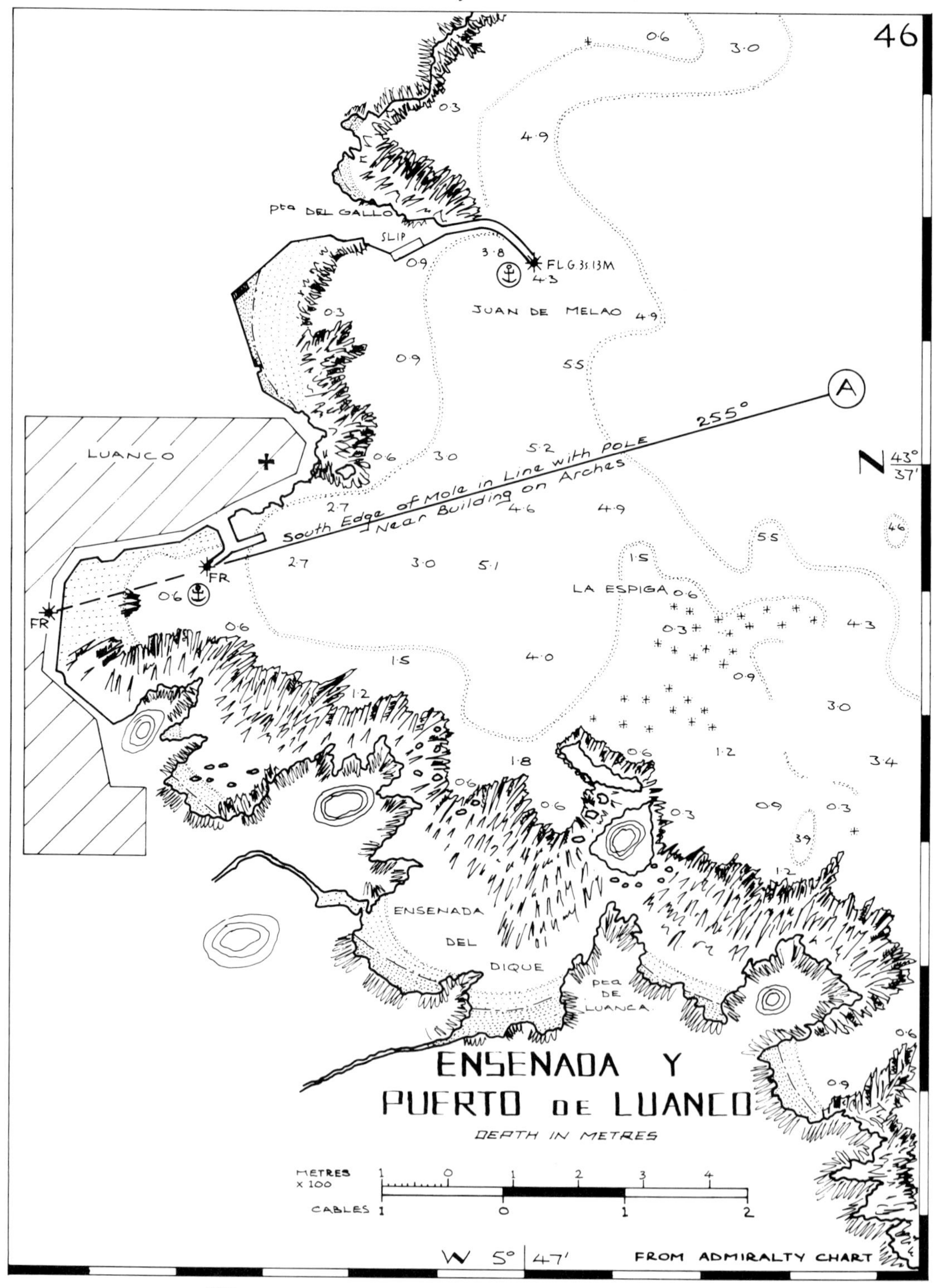
46
Pta DEL GALLO
SLIP
FL G 3s 13M
JUAN DE MELAO
LUANCO
South Edge of Mole in Line with POLE
Near Building on Arches
255°
A
FR
FR
LA ESPIGA
ENSENADA
DEL
DIQUE
Pta
DE
LUANCA
N
43°
37'
ENSENADA Y
PUERTO DE LUANCO
DEPTH IN METRES
METRES
x 100
CABLES
W 5° 47'
FROM ADMIRALTY CHART

Puerto de Luanco—showing leading marks and conspicuous church.

From SE **Cabo de Torres**, with its rugged outline, lighthouse and three spherical white butane tanks, is unmistakable. The coast to **Luanco** is again broken with low cliffs, except either side of **Candás**, where there are high reddish-hued cliffs. Do not mistake this port for **Luanco** when some way out to sea.

Night Using the lights of **Cabo Peñas** (Fl. (3) W. 15 sec. 21 M.), **Punta del Cuerno** (Oc. (1+2) *or* (1+3) W. 16 sec. *or* Iso. 2 sec. W. 12 M.) and **Cabo de Torres** (Fl. (2) W. 10 sec. 18 M.). Navigate to a position where the lights on **Muelle del Gallo** head (Fl.G. 3 sec. 4 M.) bear 285° at ¾ mile.

Puerto de Luanco—outer anchorage—low water—looking east.

Entrance

Day From a position due E of **Luanco** church bring the leading marks into line on 255° and approach the harbour, Line Ⓐ. The *Front* mark is the S edge of the inner harbour mole and the *Rear* a tall pole on the N edge of a large block of flats which has six archways underneath. When due S of the end of the **Muelle del Gallo** turn to starboard and approach the anchorage, or proceed on to the harbour itself.

Night From the position in *approach*, *night*, follow the leading lights on 255° (*Front* and *Rear:* F.R.) Line Ⓐ, until the light on **Muelle del Gallo** (F.W.) bears due N, when turn on to this direction and approach the anchorage. It is not recommended that visitors should enter the inner harbour for the first time at night.

Anchorages

In 2 m (1 fathom) sand, 28 m (30 yards) W of the head of **Muelle del Gallo** or dry out on hard sand to S of inner harbour.

Berths

A temporary berth is possible on the S side of the SW arm of the harbour wall in 2 m (1 fathom). Berths inside the harbour are difficult to find as most spaces are occupied by local fishing craft.

Formalities

These are normal.

Facilities

Water From **Lonja de Pescadores** (fish auction rooms) at the inner harbour.

Diesel and petrol From pumps on inner harbour quay.

Shops Adequate shops in the town.

Beaches There is a pleasant sandy beach N of the town.

Restaurants Several in the town.

Fiestas 5 February, festivities of El Cristo del Socorros.
24–26 June, summer festivities.

Yacht club The Club Nautico Ensidesa has a clubhouse, bar and showers to NW of the inner harbour (880 185).

Chapter 5

The coast between Cabo Peñas and Punta de la Estaca de bares

The coast between Cabo Peñas and Punta de la Estaca de Bares

47 General description

Galicia
Asturias, Lugo and Oviedio

General

The E half of this stretch of coast has high mountains some distance inland. The coast is only slightly indented with ports usually at river mouths. It is steep-to with low rocky cliffs and some outlying islands. The major ports are **Avilés** and **Luarca**. Only **Avilés** can be entered in storm conditions and even this port would be dangerous in a W to NW storm. There are many small ports and anchorages for use in moderate and fair weather.

The other half, W of **Cabo San Sebastián**, has high mountains very near the coast and the coast becomes more and more indented with the deep steep-sided estuaries, the first of the **Rías Atlas**. The major ports and anchorages are in the **Rías de Ribadeo, de Vivero** and **del Barquero**. The latter two can be entered under almost any conditions. There are also a few minor ports and anchorages which can be used only under suitable conditions of fair weather and little swell.

Warnings

Though there are no distant outlying dangers on this coast the main problem is the tremendous swell which occasionally comes in from deep water and breaks with considerable fury over any banks, rocks or obstructions, and makes some harbours and anchorages untenable. It is also impossible to enter or leave those ports which have bars under these conditions.

In N or NE winds the high mountains may be obscured by clouds low enough to limit the range of the higher lighthouses. During night approach to this coast careful watch should be kept on the echo sounder as this may give the first warning of close approach to land. Under storm conditions promontories should be given wide berths as seas break several miles offshore. The wind direction also varies near these large promontories.

Data

Charts

Admiralty Nos. 77, 78, 2927, 1755
Spanish Nos. 931, 932, 933, 934, 935, 40
French No. 5009

Tidal information

Tidal streams Close to the coast and modified by the coastline the flood stream is E and the ebb is W.

Currents in the offing

Cabo Peñas, E-going, stronger E of the **Cabo.**
Ensenada de Avilés, NE-going.
Punta Forcada, NE-going.
Golfo de Foz, W-going, up to 2 knots in summer.

These currents are subject to the effect of recent and prevailing winds. With NE winds strong W currents can be experienced and with NW winds E currents

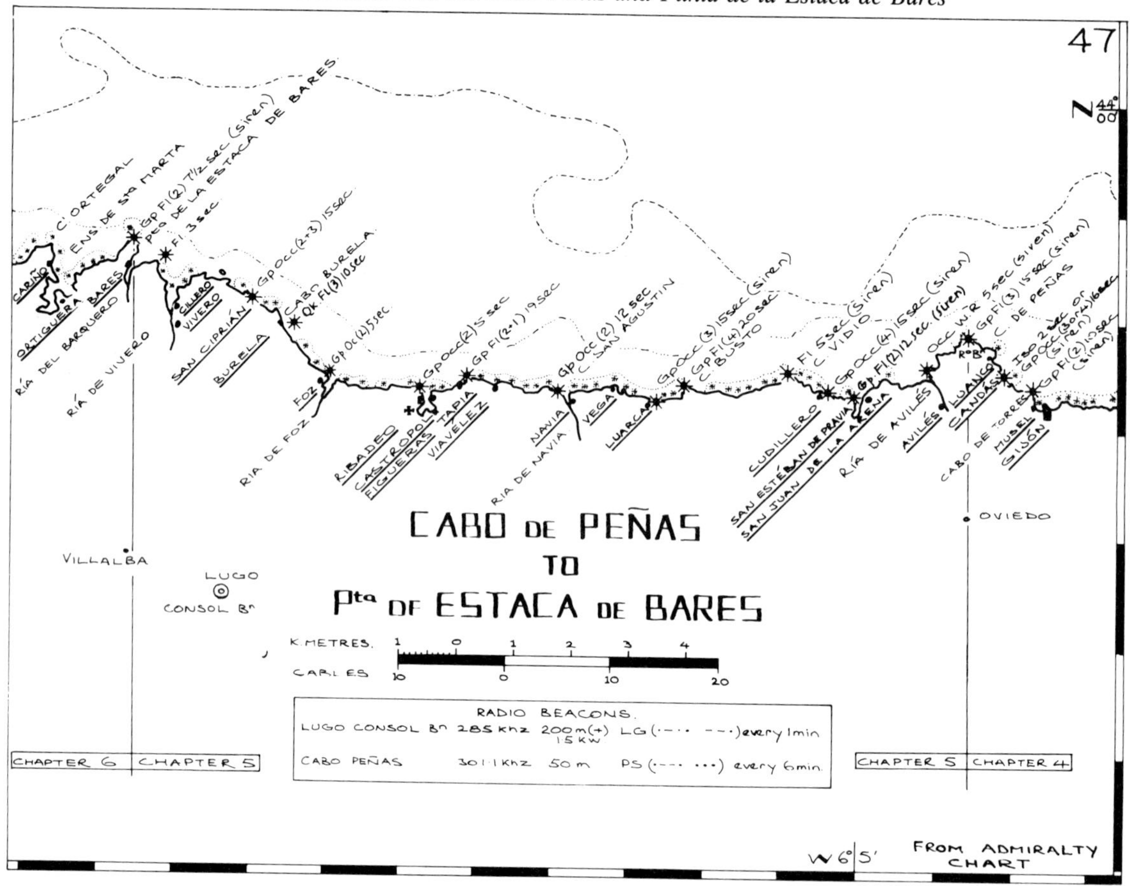

Punta del Castillo (Punta de la Forcada)—Avilés signal station and lighthouse.

Cabo Vidio—lighthouse—note rock formation.

are common. These winds also affect the depth of water. NW winds increase the depth and NE decrease it in the ports and estuaries.

Major lights

Cabo Peñas. Group Flashing (3) White, 15 seconds, 115·5 m (279 ft), 21 miles. Grey 8-sided tower and dwelling. Fog Siren Morse P (· – – ·), 60 seconds. Radiobeacon.

Punta del Castillo (Avilés). Occulting White Red, 5 seconds, 38·1 m (125 ft), White 15/13, Red 17 miles. White square tower. Red 091·5°–113°, White 113°–091·5°. Fog Siren Morse A (· –), 30 seconds. Port Signals.

San Estéban de Pravia W breakwater elbow. Group Flashing (2) White 12 seconds, 13·7 m (45 ft), 14 miles. Red square metal work tower. Fog Siren Morse N (– ·), 30 seconds.

Punta Rebollera (Cudillero). Group Occulting (4) White, 15 seconds, 26·2 m (86 ft), 18 miles. White 8-sided tower on dwelling. Fog Siren Morse D (– · ·), 30 seconds.

Cabo Vidio. Flashing White, 5 seconds, 97·5 m (320 ft), 18 miles. Round masonry tower and dwelling. Aeromarine light. Fog Siren Morse V (· · · –), 60 seconds.

Cabo Busto. Group Flashing (4) White, 20 seconds, 74·3 m (244 ft), 21 miles. White square tower and dwelling. Aeromarine light.

Cabo Busto—lighthouse.

Cabo de San Agustin—Ría de Navia entrance—lighthouse.

Punta Blanca (Luarca). Group Occulting (3) White, 15 seconds, 51·8 m (170 ft), 15 miles. White square tower and dwelling. Fog Siren Morse L (· – · ·), 30 seconds.

Cabo San Agustin (Navia). Group Occulting (2) White, 12 sec. 82 m (269 ft), 18 M. White column black band.

Isla Tapia. Group Flashing (2+1) White, 19 seconds, 21·6 m (71 ft), 18 miles. White granite tower and white dwelling.

Isla Pancha (Ribadeo). Group Occulting (2) White, 5 seconds, 21 m (69 ft), 11 miles. White square tower on dwelling. Obscured 141·5°–145·5°.

Bajo la Rapadoira (Foz). Flashing Green, 3 seconds, 10·4 m (34 ft), 6 miles. White truncated concrete tower.

Piedra Burela. Quick Flashing (3) White 10 seconds, 11·6 m (38 ft), 8 miles. Truncated conical concrete tower.

Punta Atalaya (San Ciprián). Group Occulting (2+3) White, 15 seconds, 35·6 m (117 ft), 9 miles. Grey conical granite tower.

Isla Coelleira (Barquero). Flashing White, 3 seconds, 86·8 m (285 ft), 8 miles. Grey conical granite tower and dwelling.

Punta de la Estaca de Bares. Group Flashing (2) White, 7·5 seconds, 99 m (325 ft), 25 miles. 8-sided tower and dwelling. Fog Signal Morse B (– · · ·), 60 seconds. Aeromarine light, obscured when bearing more than 291°.

Signal stations Signal stations with which yachts may communicate using the International Code of Flag Signals are established as follows:

Punta de la Forcada (Avilés) for local messages only, **Punta Espiritu Santo (Ría de Pravia)**, **Punta de Bares (Ría del Barquero).**

Cabo Blanco and **Atalaya de Porcia.**

Cabo San Sebastian—Isla de Tapia—lighthouse—Tapia.

Life saving Lifeboats and/or line throwing apparatus are maintained at **Avilés**, **San Esteban de Pravia**, **Luarca**, **Ribadeo**.

Radio *Radiobeacons* The radiobeacons in this area are listed below; for those outside the area see page 16.

Station	Frequency kHz	Range miles	Call sign	Period minutes	Group Remarks
Cabo Peñas lighthouse	301·1	50	PS (· – – · / · · ·)	6	**Llanes** IA **Estaca de Bares** BA
Lugo (Consol) beacon 43°14′53″N 07°28′56″W	285	200	LG (· – · · / – – ·)	1	Continuous note

Coast, port and pilot radio stations, weather and navigational messages, see pages 19–20.

Cala Ortiguera.

Ports, harbours, anchorages and landing places

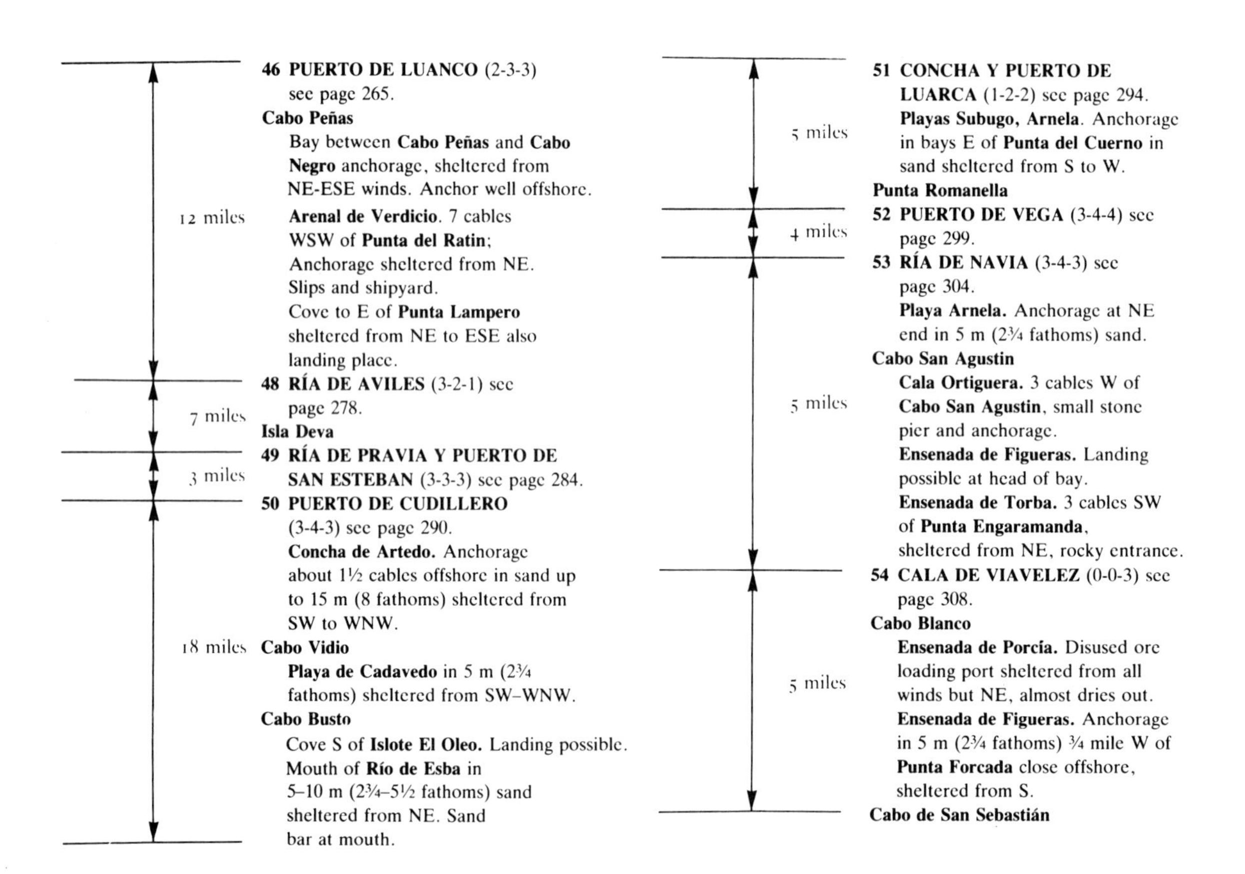

46 PUERTO DE LUANCO (2-3-3) see page 265.

Cabo Peñas

Bay between **Cabo Peñas** and **Cabo Negro** anchorage, sheltered from NE-ESE winds. Anchor well offshore.

Arenal de Verdicio. 7 cables WSW of **Punta del Ratin**; Anchorage sheltered from NE. Slips and shipyard.

Cove to E of **Punta Lampero** sheltered from NE to ESE also landing place.

48 RÍA DE AVILES (3-2-1) see page 278.

Isla Deva

49 RÍA DE PRAVIA Y PUERTO DE SAN ESTEBAN (3-3-3) see page 284.

50 PUERTO DE CUDILLERO (3-4-3) see page 290.

Concha de Artedo. Anchorage about 1½ cables offshore in sand up to 15 m (8 fathoms) sheltered from SW to WNW.

Cabo Vidio

Playa de Cadavedo in 5 m (2¾ fathoms) sheltered from SW–WNW.

Cabo Busto

Cove S of **Islote El Oleo.** Landing possible.

Mouth of **Río de Esba** in 5–10 m (2¾–5½ fathoms) sand sheltered from NE. Sand bar at mouth.

51 CONCHA Y PUERTO DE LUARCA (1-2-2) see page 294.

Playas Subugo, Arnela. Anchorage in bays E of **Punta del Cuerno** in sand sheltered from S to W.

Punta Romanella

52 PUERTO DE VEGA (3-4-4) see page 299.

53 RÍA DE NAVIA (3-4-3) see page 304.

Playa Arnela. Anchorage at NE end in 5 m (2¾ fathoms) sand.

Cabo San Agustin

Cala Ortiguera. 3 cables W of **Cabo San Agustin**, small stone pier and anchorage.

Ensenada de Figueras. Landing possible at head of bay.

Ensenada de Torba. 3 cables SW of **Punta Engaramanda**, sheltered from NE, rocky entrance.

54 CALA DE VIAVELEZ (0-0-3) see page 308.

Cabo Blanco

Ensenada de Porcía. Disused ore loading port sheltered from all winds but NE, almost dries out.

Ensenada de Figueras. Anchorage in 5 m (2¾ fathoms) ¾ mile W of **Punta Forcada** close offshore, sheltered from S.

Cabo de San Sebastián

Isla Pancha—lighthouse—**Ribadeo**—note large white factory.

4 miles

55 PUERTO DE TAPIA (2-4-3) see page 311.

Cove E of **Punta Esguillón.** Anchorage 2 cables W of **Islotes Pantorgas** in 5·9 m (3 fathoms) sand protected from SW to NW.

9 miles

56 RÍA DE RIBADEO (1-2-2) see page 314.

Puerto de Rinlo. E of **Punta Corbeira.** Anchor in small creek in fine weather only. Quay.

Punta Corbeira

Ensenada de la Lousa. W of **Punta Corbeira.** Anchorage sheltered from NE in up to 20·1 m (11 fathoms).

7 miles

57 RÍA DE FOZ (3-4-3) see page 321.

Río de Oro. Silted up sand bar being dredged; can be entered at HW in good conditions.

Cove between **Punta Gralleira** and **Punta Areoura.** Anchor in 4 m (2 fathoms) sand off N beach.

5 miles

58 PUERTO DE BURELA (4-2-3) see page 325.

Cabo Burela

Many landing beaches along this stretch of coast to E and W of **Cabo Burela.**

Río Junco shelter to small craft.

Cabo San Ciprián

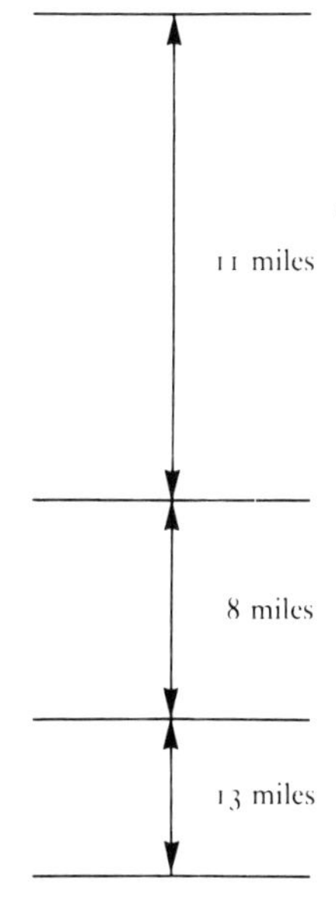

59 PUERTOS DE SAN CIPRIÁN (2-4-4) and (4-1-4) see page 329.

El Portiño. Landing possible.

Playa de Lago. Off mouth of **Río de Largo.** A good anchorage.

Cabo Morás

Río de Porto Celo. Good anchorage in 4 m (2 fathoms) sand near W shore; or lie aground in port.

Punta Saiñas

Landing possible in **Ensenada de Esteiro** S of **Punta Saiñas.**

60 RÍA DE VIVERO (3-2-3) see page 332.

Playa de Teixoso. Landing possible.

Isla Coelleira. Small cove and landing place on W side.

61 RÍA DEL BARQUERO (2-2-4) see page 338.

Punta de la Estaca de Bares

63 ENSENADA DE SANTA MARTA (2-3-3) see page 350.

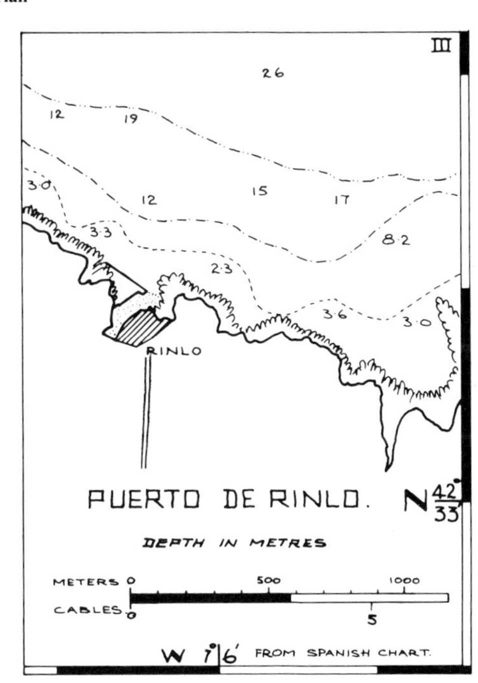

48 Ria de Avilés

Population 75,000 Rating 3-2-1 Position 43°35·1′N 5°55·3′W

General

This commercial harbour has an easy approach and entrance with good berths and anchorages, and a least depth of 4·9 m (16 ft). It can be entered near HW by day or night under any conditions except severe gales from W and NW. Unfortunately, as in most commercial ports, there is a lot of oil on the water and the quays are covered with coal dust. Fouling can be minimised by the use of suitable anchorages. The town is very attractive with good shops and a wonderful market. The nearby village of **Salinas** is a fashionable seaside resort and residential area. It has a palatial yacht club and a large sandy beach.

Warnings

Considerable dredging and harbour works are in hand including a new break water.

Bajo El Petón, off **Cabo Vidrias**, breaks in heavy weather and is in the red sector of the light on **Punta del Castillo**. The inner side of the **Curva de Pachico** is being modified.

Data

Charts Admiralty Nos. 2927, 77
Spanish Nos. 9350, 9351, 9352, 935
French Nos. 6382, 5009

Magnetic variation 7°08′W (1984) decreasing by about 5′ each year.

Tidal information Spanish tide tables are available for this port.

	HW		LW		MHWS	MHWN	MLWS	MLWN
Pointe de Grave	0600 1800	1100 2300	0000 1200	0500 1700	5·4 m 17·6 ft	4·2 m 13·8 ft	0·9 m 3·0 ft	2·1 m 6·8 ft
Ría de Avilés	−0·35	−0·45	−0·25	+0·05	−1·3 m −4·2 ft	−1·2 m −4·1 ft	−0·4 m −1·4 ft	−0·6 m −1·7 ft

The current outside the port is normally NE and can reach 3 knots.

Lights **Punta de la Forcada/Punta del Castillo.** Occulting White Red sectors, 5 seconds, 38 m (125 ft), White 15, Red 13 miles. White square tower. White 113°–091°, Red 091°–113°, covers **Bajo El Petón.** Fog Siren Morse A (· –), 30 seconds. Port signals.

Entrance N side. Group Flashing (2) Red, 10 seconds, 8·8 m (29 ft), 3 miles. Truncated conical concrete tower.

Entrance channel N side (Escollera Norte). 7 small Fixed Red, 11 m (33 ft), 3 miles. Concrete towers.

Entrance S side. Flashing Green, 3 seconds, 12 m (40 ft), 6 miles. White conical tower.

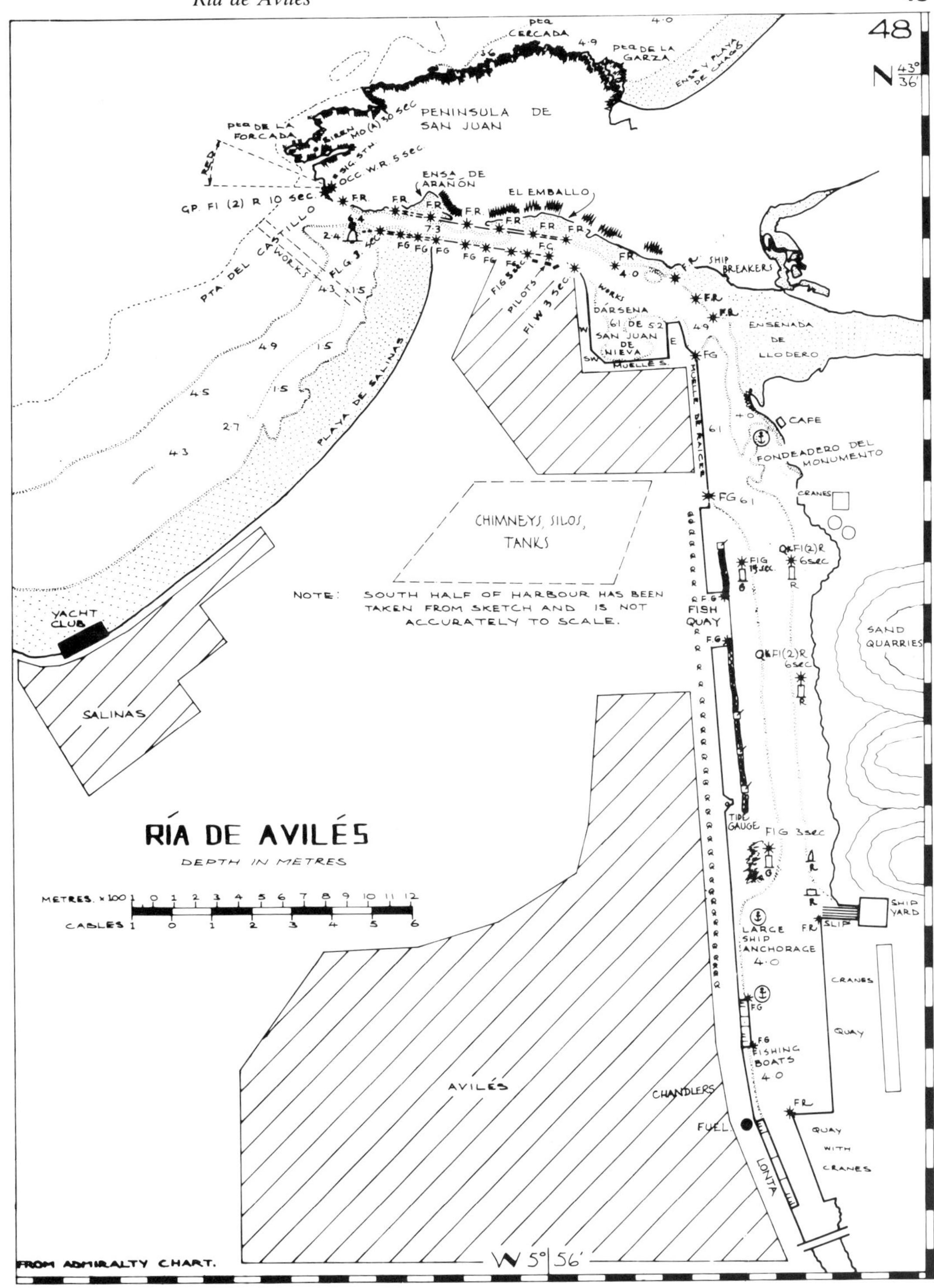
48
PENINSULA DE SAN JUAN
PTA DE LA FORCADA
PTA CERCADA
PTA DE LA GARZA
ENSA Y PLAYA DE CHAGO
ENSA DE ARAÑON
EL EMBALLO
GP. Fl (2) R 10 sec.
OCC W.R. 5 sec.
PTA DEL CASTILLO
WORKS
PLAYA DE SALINAS
SHIP BREAKERS
ENSENADA DE LLODERO
DÁRSENA DE SAN JUAN DE NIEVA
MUELLES
MUELLE DE RAICES
PILOTS
CAFE
FONDEADERO DEL MONUMENTO
CRANES
CHIMNEYS, SILOS, TANKS
NOTE: SOUTH HALF OF HARBOUR HAS BEEN TAKEN FROM SKETCH AND IS NOT ACCURATELY TO SCALE.
YACHT CLUB
SALINAS
FISH QUAY
SAND QUARRIES
TIDE GAUGE
SHIP YARD
SLIP
LARGE SHIP ANCHORAGE
QUAY
FISHING BOATS
CHANDLERS
FUEL
LONTA
QUAY WITH CRANES
AVILÉS
RÍA DE AVILÉS
DEPTH IN METRES
METRES × 100
CABLES
FROM ADMIRALTY CHART.
W 5° 56'

Entrance channel S side (Escollera Sur). 7 small Fixed Green, 10 m (33 ft), 3 miles. Concrete towers.
Flashing Green, 3 seconds, 10 m (33 ft), 3 miles. Concrete towers.
Flashing White, 3 seconds, 10 m (33 ft), 3 miles. Concrete towers.
Curva de Pachico
Port hand. 3 Fixed Red, 10 m (33 ft), 3 miles. Concrete towers.
Starboard hand. 3 Fixed Green, 10 m (33 ft) 3 miles. Concrete towers.
Approach to Avilés
Port. Quick Group Flashing (2) Red, 6 seconds, 6 m (20 ft), 3 miles. Red truncated towers.
Starboard. Group Flashing (3) Green, 15 seconds, 6 m (20 ft) 3 miles. Green truncated towers.
Flashing Green 3 seconds, 2 m (7 ft), 3 miles. Green metal tower on raft.

Port Radio See page 20.

Pilots Pilots may meet yachts and show them suitable anchorages. They have small motor boats with a large P on them.

Traffic signals All vessels including yachts must obey the traffic signals shown from a mast near **Punta del Castillo** lighthouse, from the Pilot House and **Muelle de Raicés**.

Signal station The station at the entrance will also send and receive local signals by International Code of Flag Signals.

Approach

Day *From W* The large conical **Isla Deva** is very conspicuous, as is a large cement works with tall chimneys and the blocks of flat at the W end of **Playa de Salinas**.

Ría de Avilés—entrance—looking east.

Yachts entering harbour.

Signals	Meaning
From mast on Punta de la Forcada *Day* Flag S *Night* One red light.	 A vessel is leaving harbour. Wait until this signal is lowered.
From signal tower near Pilot House *Day or Night* One red light.	 A vessel leaving harbour is in **Curva de Pachico**. Proceed to **Darséna de San Juan de Nieva** until it has passed.

Yachts leaving harbour.

Signals	Meaning
From signal tower on Muelle de Raíces *Day or Night* One green light.	 A vessel entering harbour is in **Curva de Pachico**. Do not enter curved part of the estuary.
From mast on Punta de la Forcada *Day* Red pendant with white circle. Blue pendant with two vertical yellow stripes. *Night* Green over white over red lights.	 This means a vessel is entering harbour. Do not proceed below the Pilot House.

A group of chimneys and silos stand between this **Playa** and the harbour.

From E **Cabo Peñas**, a very large flat-topped white-hued cape with a large outlying island, is easily recognised. **Punta Forcada** with **Punta del Castillo** and lighthouse, at the entrance to the harbour, stand out against the yellow sand of **Playa de Salinas**. Approach the lighthouse until it bears E 2 cables, when the entrance will be visible. There are no outlying dangers in the vicinity other than **Bajo El Petón**.

Night Using the lights of **Ría de Pravia** (Fl. W. 3 sec. 14 M.), **Punta Forcada/del Castillo** (Oc. W.R. 5 sec.15/13 M.) and **Cabo Peñas** (Fl. (3) W. 15 sec. 21 M.) navigate to a position where the lighthouse bears E 2 cables, when the harbour lights should be seen.

Entrance

Day From the position above, observe the signal station on **Punta del Castillo** and check that entry is possible. Enter on 095° midway between cliffs to port and the training wall and breakwater to starboard. Keep to the middle of the marked channel as the seaward end of the starboard hand breakwater extends some 98 m (100 yards) under water and is unmarked.

Night From the position in *approach*, *night*, above, manoeuvre until the lines of (F.R.) and (F.W.) lights are equally disposed port and starboard. Enter harbour on 095° between first (F.W.) and second (F.R.). Keep in mid-channel.

Anchorages

The best and cleanest anchorage is in the **Fondeadero del Monumento**. Anchor 98 m (100 yards) SW of the small **Café del Mar** in 4 m (2 fathoms) sand. There is a small landing stage nearby and buses to **Avilés** pass along a road ½ mile inland every half hour. Alternatively, land at the S end of the **Muelle de Raicés**, where other buses for **Salinas** and **Avilés** pass every fifteen minutes.

It is also possible to anchor bow or stern on with lines ashore to the wall, about ½ mile from **Avilés** in 4 m (2 fathoms) mud or sand. Keep at least 9 m (10 yards) clear of the wall owing to underwater obstructions and use a dinghy to go ashore. Look out for heavy oil fouling on the steps and ladders. Drop anchor well out as the backwash created by merchant ships manoeuvring in this area could cause anchors to drag. The best positions are just below the fishing craft berths or about 98 m (100 yards) above the last black and white channel mark; not between, as this is where merchant ships lie. Yellow water stains hulls.

Berths

It is possible to lie alongside in a deep-water berth in the **Dársena de San Juan de Nieve**. The **Muelle E.** and **Muelle S.**, if unoccupied are the best. Coal dust is the problem in this dock if there is a wind blowing.

Formalities

The usual documents have to be completed. The Customs officers here are very strict and will now allow cameras, etc. to be taken ashore, if they are present when crews disembark.

Facilities

Water From quay in the **Dársena** or fish auction rooms near the station on the quay at **Avilés**.

Diesel From quay at **Avilés** and the **Dársena**.

Petrol From quay at **Avilés**.

Food There is a wonderful market in **Avilés**, one of the best on the coast. Monday morning is 'the' time.

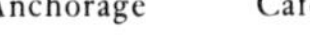

Ría de Avilés—anchorage opposite Muelle de Raicés in Fondeadero del Monumento.

Ría de Avilés—looking south towards the town.

Shops Many attractive shops; several chandlery shops at **San Juan de Nieva**, one in **Avilés.**

Clubs A first class club, **Real Club Nautico** at **Salinas**, will welcome foreign yachtsmen if holding a membership card of an English yacht club, but is really only a social club.

Beaches The **Playa de Salinas** is a very large sandy beach; though crowded at each end it is empty in the middle.

Visits Twelfth century church of **Sabugo** and many fine old buildings are to be found in and around the city.

Fiestas 6 April, fiesta of El Bollu.
18–20 August, festivities of Los Pucheros.
20–31 August, festivities in honour of St Augustine.

Ría de Aviles – looking S–SW–W–NW.

49 Ría de Pravia, Puerto de San Estéban

Population about 1,000   Rating 3-3-3   Position 43°33·2′N   6°5·1′W

General

The **Puerto de San Estéban** is a disused commercial harbour in a sheltered pleasant country river, the **Río Nalon.** Entrance is easy by day or night with a minimum depth of 2·7 m (9 ft). Its main export was coal; consequently there is coal dust everywhere. The towns of **San Estéban** and **San Juan de la Arena** are dirty and unremarkable but the river above the port is clean and attractive. Deep-water berths are available alongside the quays of **San Estéban** and there are also several anchorages in the river. A large sand and coal dust beach is nearby. Water and normal requirements are available in the town. There is some silting due to lack of commercial use.

Warnings

This port cannot be entered under storm conditions from the N and should be entered about 2 hours before HW if there is any swell, as it tends to break on the bar when the tide is ebbing. Care should be taken to keep well clear of the breakwaters and training walls E of the entrance which are unlighted, unmarked and partly submerged. Anchorage in **Puerto chico** is not recommended owing to the swell, underwater obstructions and limited space. Depths unreliable due to silting.

Data

Charts Admiralty Nos. 78, 2927
Spanish Nos. 721B, 934, 935
French Nos. 6381, 5009

Magnetic variation 7°10′W (1984) decreasing by about 5′ each year.

Tidal information

	HW		LW		MHWS	MHWN	MLWS	MLWN
Pointe de Grave	0600 1800	1100 2300	0000 1200	0500 1700	5·4 m 17·6 ft	4·2 m 13·8 ft	0·9 m 3·0 ft	2·1 m 6·8 ft
Puerto de San Estéban	−0·40	−0·45	−0·40	0·00	−1·4 m −4·4 ft	−1·3 m −4·4 ft	−0·5 m −1·7 ft	−0·6 m −1·8 ft

With W winds tides may be 1 m (3 ft) higher than predicted, and with E winds lower. The stream is strong at the bar and may reach 5 knots on the ebb at springs. This stream runs in a NNE direction near the entrance.

Lights **Dique del Oeste elbow.** Fl.(2) W, 12 seconds 13·7 m (45 ft), 14 miles. Red square metal frame tower. Fog Siren Morse N (– ·), 30 seconds. White column, black bands, hut at base.
Dique del Oeste head. Long Flash Green, 6 seconds, 4·3 m (14 ft), 2 miles. Black pyramidal tower.

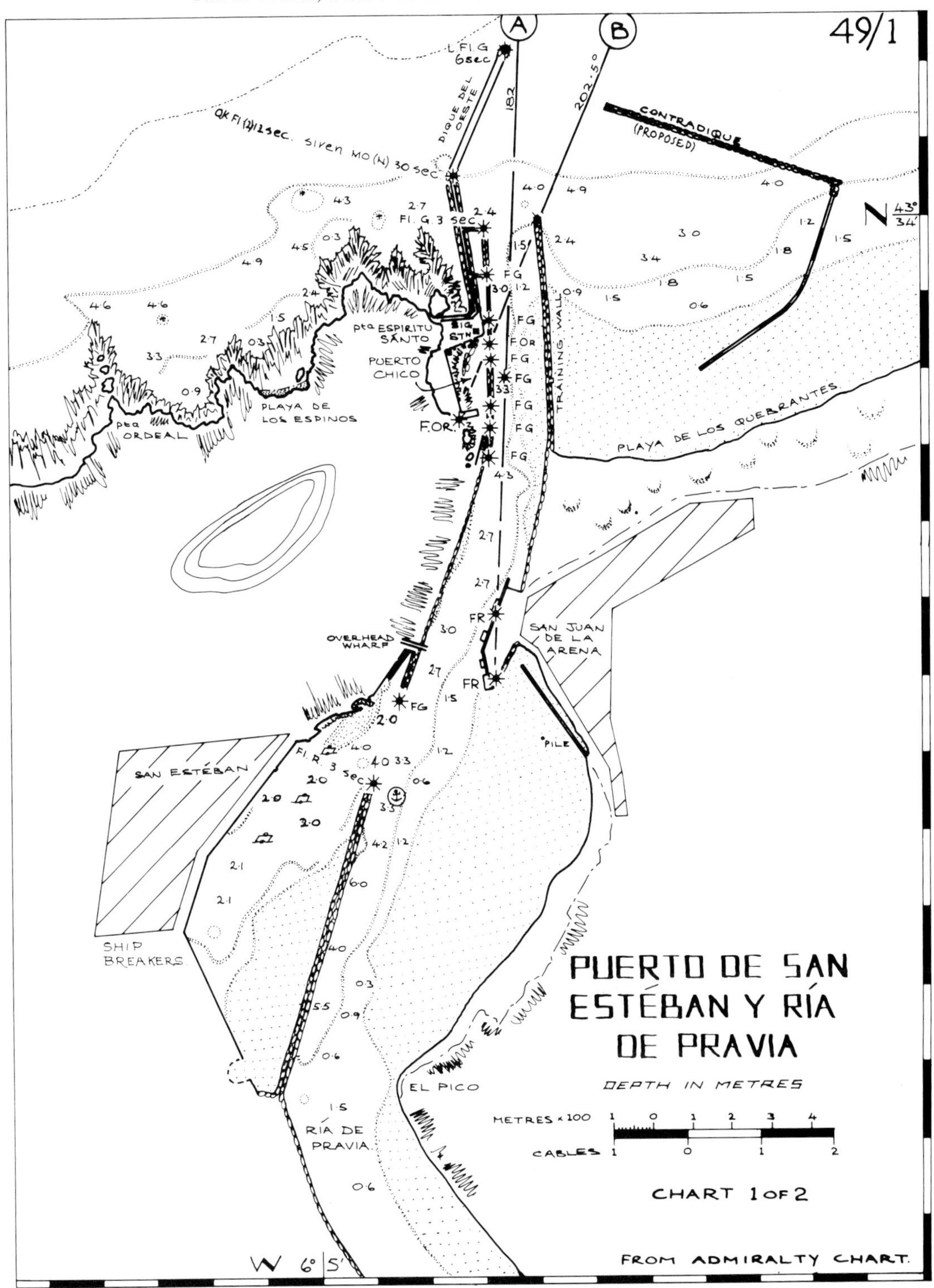
49/1
PUERTO DE SAN ESTÉBAN Y RÍA DE PRAVIA
DEPTH IN METRES
CHART 1 OF 2
FROM ADMIRALTY CHART.
METRES x 100
CABLES
CONTRADIQUE (PROPOSED)
DIQUE DEL OESTE
TRAINING WALL
L Fl. G 6sec
QK Fl (2) 12sec. Siren MO (N) 30 sec
Fl. G. 3 sec
Fl. R. 3 sec
Pta ESPIRITU SANTO
PUERTO CHICO
SIG STN
PLAYA DE LOS ESPINOS
Pta ORDEAL
PLAYA DE LOS QUEBRANTES
OVERHEAD WHARF
SAN JUAN DE LA ARENA
SAN ESTÉBAN
SHIP BREAKERS
PILE
EL PICO
RÍA DE PRAVIA
W 6° 5'
N 43° 34'
182
202.5°

Leading lights 182° Line Ⓐ.
Front Fixed Red, 6·7 m (22 ft), 3 miles. Square concrete pillar, white square, red bands.
Rear Fixed Red, 10·7 m (35 ft), 3 miles. Square concrete pillar, white square, red bands. 160 m from front light.
Left bank training wall spur. Flashing Green, 3 seconds, 2·4 m (8 ft), 3 miles. Grey metal framework tower. Synchronised with W breakwater elbow.
Training wall on left bank. 7 Fixed Greens, 7·0 m (23 ft), 3 miles. Concrete columns.
Leading lights Puerto Chico 202·5° Line Ⓑ. 2 Fixed Oranges, 4 miles. 2 tall poles similar to street lights, 200 m apart.
Basin entrance, starboard. Fixed Green, 5·5 m (18 ft), 4 miles. Grey pyramid.
Mole head, port. Flashing Red, 3 seconds, 5·5 m (18 ft), 6 miles. Grey truncated pyramid.

Signal station At the root of the breakwater on **Punta Espiritu Sánto.**

Pilots Pilots may meet yachts outside harbour and offer help, towing etc.

Life saving Motor lifeboat and line throwing apparatus maintained.

Approaches

Day *From W* **Cabo Vidio**, a large flat-topped cape with three separate points and a small conical off-lying island, is conspicuous as is **Punta Espiritu Sánto**, which is tree-covered to the E and has a hermitage near the top.

From E **Isla Deva**, a large conical island, and the **Playa de Los Quebrantes** are easily seen. Keeping clear of the submerged breakwater E of the harbour, approach the head of the W mole.

Ría de Pravia—entrance looking south.

Ría de Pravia—looking south—from just inside harbour.

Night The lights of **Cabo Vidio** (Fl. W. 5 sec. 18 M.), **Punta Rebollera** (Oc. (4) W. 15 sec. 18 M.), **Punta Forcada (Avilés)** (Oc. W.R. 5 sec. 15/13 M.) enable an approach to be made to the harbour, which has a light on the W breakwater elbow (Fl.(2) W. 12 sec. 14 M.) and also at the head of the breakwater (LFl. G. 6 sec. 2 M.).

Entrance

Day Pass close (23 m (25 yards)) to the E side of the W breakwater and make course towards the first light on the W training wall. The leading marks on 182·5°, Line Ⓐ, consisting of two square towers painted red and white with square tops, located on the sea wall by **San Juan de la Arena**, will be seen. Keep just W of this line and about 23 m (25 yards) from the lights marking the W training wall until the entrance of the harbour basin on the starboard hand can be seen, when a course can be set directly for this. Enter close to port hand wall.

Night Pass close (23 m (25 yards)) E of the W breakwater head light (L.Fl. G. 6 sec. 2 M.) and set course to pass the light on the W training wall head (Fl. G. 3 sec. 3 M.) and the remaining eight lights (two F.G., one F.Or., five F.G.) by a similar distance. The leading lights (F.R.) on 182°, Line Ⓐ, should be left slightly open to the W. Enter the harbour basin between (F.G.) to starboard, to port (Fl. R. 3 sec.), close to the (Fl.R. 3 sec.).

Berths

Deep-water berths are available along the W wall of the harbour basin of **San Estéban** in 2–3 m (1–1·5 fathoms). Keep a lookout for harbour officials who will indicate where to tie up. Berths alongside at **San Juan de la Arena** are not recommended as they are used by fishing boats.

Moorings

If necessary temporary moorings can be taken onto the warping buoys in the basin while awaiting the harbour officials.

Anchorages

Anchoring or mooring in **Puerto Chico** is not recommended due to the swell, obstruction and rocks. Anchorage is possible upriver from the entrance to the basin as follows:

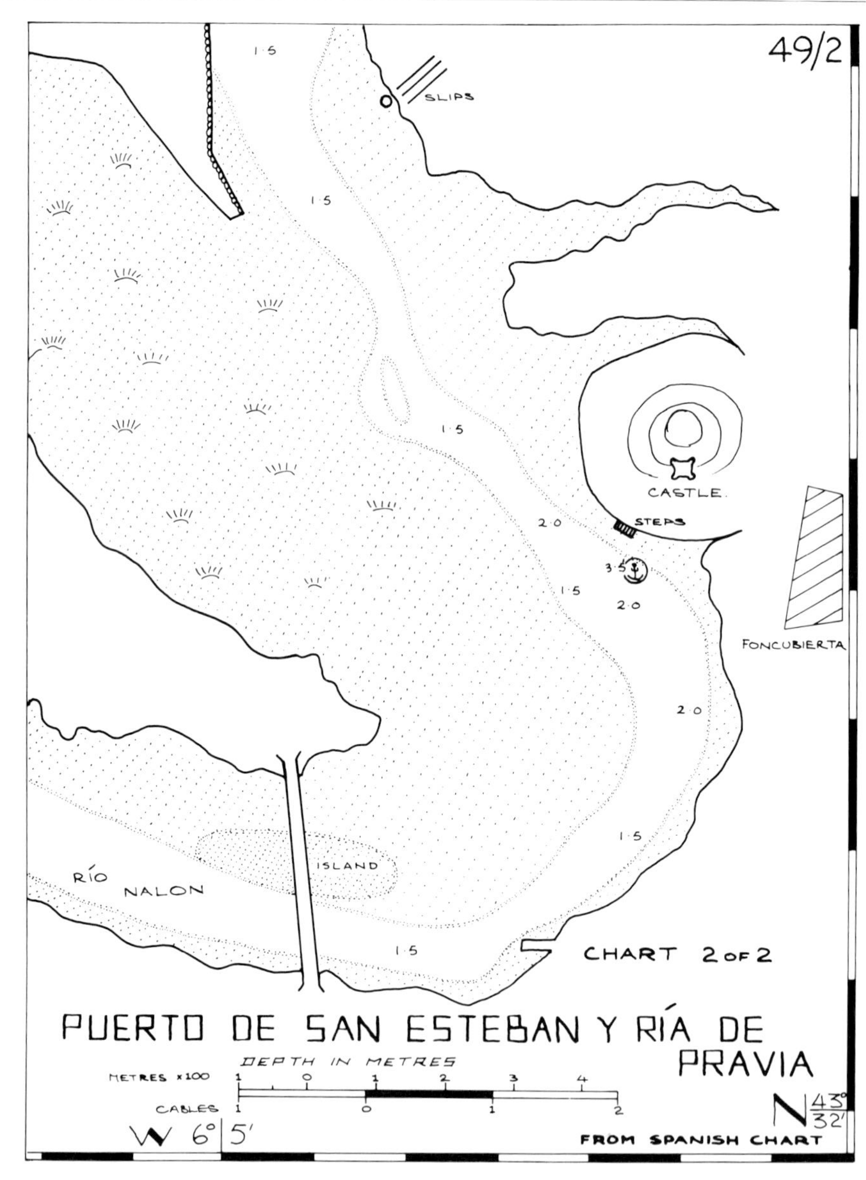

47 m (50 yards) E of the S mole head of the entrance to the basin in 3 m (1·5 fathoms) mud.

23 m (25 yards) SW of the steps leading to the castle located ¾ mile upstream on the port hand in 3 m (1·5 fathoms) rock and sand. Keep to the port side of the river after the first ¼ mile. Use 2 anchors to keep in the area of this deep pool. A reconnaissance with echo sounder or lead before anchoring is advised.

Formalities

Harbour officials, Guardia Civil and Customs may all pay a freindly visit, but only one set of details is required.

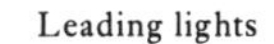

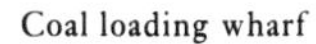

Ría de Pravia—looking south from alongside Puerto Chico.

Facilities

Water Available from pipes on quay. The attendant's office is at the S side of the basin. A small charge is made.

Petrol From pump on the way out of town.

Diesel From pump on quay.

Shops These are poor quality but basic supplies can be obtained.

Beaches A large sandy beach, **Playa de los Quebrantes**, offers exciting bathing in the swell which breaks on it with fury, but unfortunately it is covered with coal dust.

Repairs A limited amount of repair work can be undertaken.

Visits Caves with paintings at **La Peña** near **Pravia**. A dinghy trip up the river is worth while.

Puerto de San Estéban—looking south from alongside coal-loading wharf.

50 Puerto de Cudillero

Population 10,120 Rating 3-4-3 Position 43°33·8′N 6°8·8′W

General

A tiny fishing harbour tucked away in a gap in the cliffs with a picturesque village behind it with many shops. The entrance is narrow and space inside is very limited. It is possible to lie alongside in 2 m (1 fathom) but is unsafe in a N or NW swell. A huge new harbour with all facilities has been built alongside the old harbour.

Warnings

It is advisable to enter on the top half of the tide so as to reduce the effect of the swell. The new harbour is still being finished (1983). Changes may be expected.

Data

Charts

Admiralty No. 2927
Spanish Nos. 934, 935
French No. 5009

Magnetic variation 7°07′W (1984) decreasing by about 5′ each year.

Tidal information

	HW		LW		MHWS	MHWN	MLWS	MLWN
Pointe de Grave	0600 1800	1100 2300	0000 1200	0500 1700	5·4 m 17·6 ft	4·2 m 13·8 ft	0·9 m 3·0 ft	2·1 m 6·8 ft
Puerto de Cudillero	−0·30	−0·35	−0·10	+0·25	−1·3 m −4·4 ft	−1·3 m −4·4 ft	−0·5 m −1·7 ft	−0·6 m −1·8 ft

Lights

Punta Rebollera. Group Occulting (4) White, 15 seconds, 26·2 m (86 ft), 18 miles. White 8-sided tower and dwelling. Fog Siren Morse D (– · ·), 30 seconds.
Dique del Este head. Fixed Red, 7·9 m (26 ft), 2 miles. Metal column.
Old Dique del Oeste. Fixed Green, 2·1 m (7 ft), 2 miles. Concrete pyramid.

Approaches

Day

From W **Cabo Vidio**, a high promontory with a lighthouse and an off-lying small conical island, are easily identified.

Closer to the W, **Islotes las Colinas**, a line of small islands and reefs about ½ mile NW of **Cudillero**, together with the lighthouse situated low down on **Punta Rebollera** to the E, indicate the location of the gap in the cliffs behind which the port lies. The new high **Nuevo Dique del Oeste** is easily seen.

From E The entrance to **Ría de Pravia** with its breakwater is conspicuous as is the **Punta Espiritu Sánto** just to its W. Navigate to a position where **Punta Rebollera** lighthouse bears 200° at about ½ mile. The entrance to the harbour should be seen.

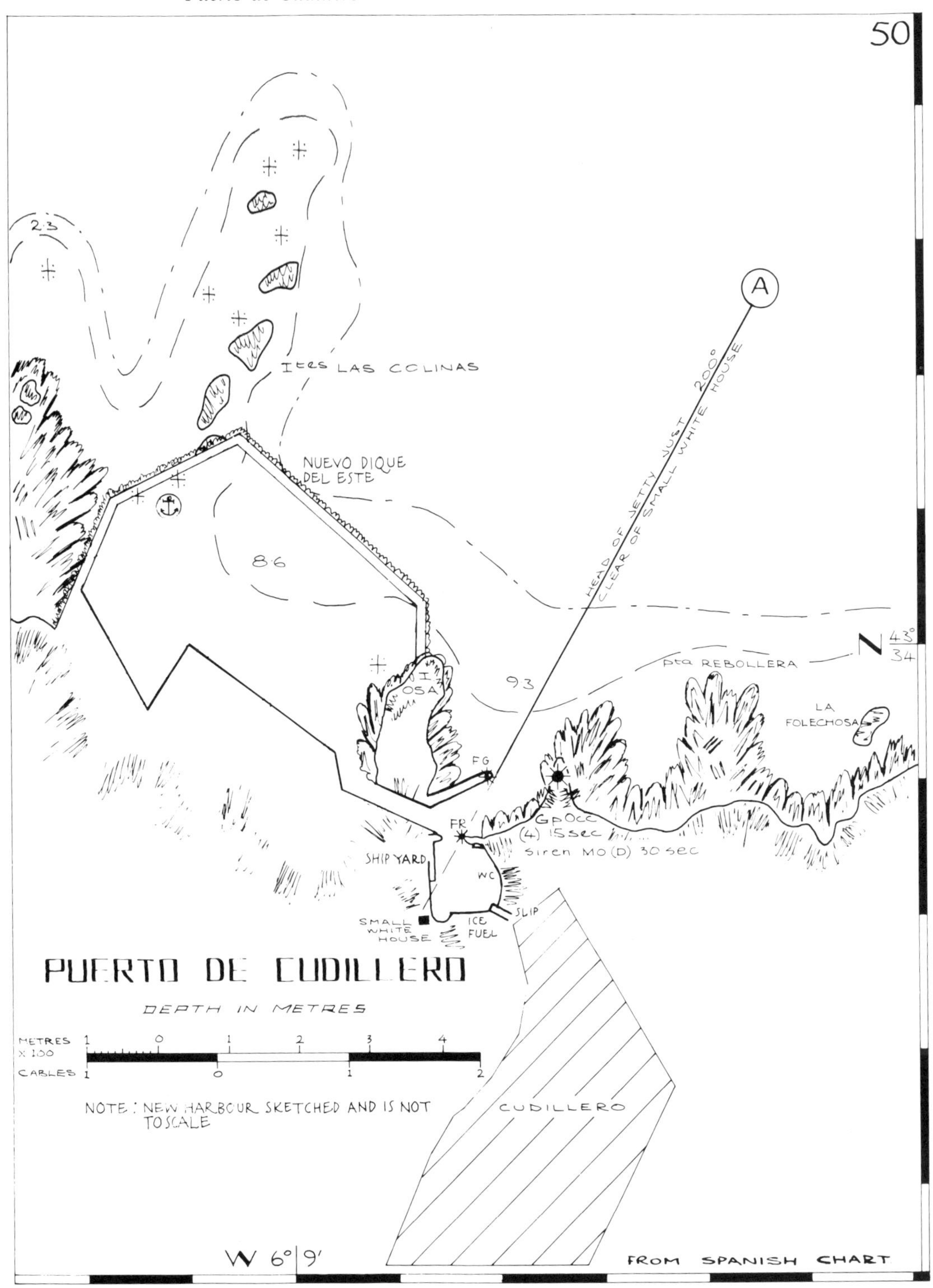
50
A
HEAD OF JETTY JUST 200°
CLEAR OF SMALL WHITE HOUSE
LAS COLINAS
NUEVO DIQUE
DEL ESTE
8·6
2·3
93
N 43° 34
Pta REBOLLERA
LA FOLECHOSA
FG
FR
Gp Occ (4) 15sec
Siren MO (D) 30 sec
SHIP YARD
WC
SLIP
SMALL WHITE HOUSE
ICE FUEL
PUERTO DE CUDILLERO
DEPTH IN METRES
METRES x 100
CABLES
NOTE : NEW HARBOUR SKETCHED AND IS NOT TO SCALE
CUDILLERO
W 6° 9'
FROM SPANISH CHART

Puerto de Cudillero.

Night Using the lights on **Cabo Vidio** (Fl. W. 5 sec. 18 M.). **Ría Pravia** (Fl. W. 3 sec. 15 M.), and **Punta Rebollera** (Oc. (4) W. 15 sec. 18 M.) navigate to a position where the light on **Punta Rebollera** becomes 200° at about ½ mile.

Entrance

Day From the position detailed above, approach the entrance of the harbour on 200° Line Ⓐ, keeping the right hand end of the E breakwater just to the right of a small, white, square building situated at the back of the harbour. Enter the harbour between this breakwater and the remains of the old breakwater and turn hard to port. Entrance to new harbour to starboard behind jetty running NW from **Isla Osa.**

Night Entry at night for the first time is not recommended. It should be noted that the new breakwater obscures the light on the old W breakwater until the approach position detailed above has been reached. Enter with the (F.R.) and (F.G.) lights on the entrance either side of 200°, Line Ⓐ. Extra lights expected.

Berths

A berth alongside the wall in 2 m (1 fathom) rocks at the E side of the harbour. Near the public lavatories is possible, but check the bottom with a lead first as it is uneven. The locals will assist in alloting a berth as this is the part of the harbour where the large fishing boats unload and they know what boats are due to arrive. Anchor in new harbour, use anchor trip line.

Formalities

Normal.

Puerto de Cudillero—leading marks.

Facilities

Water	From a tap near the largest slipway or spring at the bottom of the village main street, and in new harbour.
Diesel and petrol	From pumps on the quay. New harbour, pump to be provided.
Shops	Normal requirements can be met from the many shops.
Beaches	A rather dirty and stony beach nearby to the W.
Fiestas	St Peter's day fishing festival 29th June.

Puerto de Cudillero – new harbour looking N–NE–E.

51 Puerto de Luarca

Population 25,000 Rating 1-2-2 Position 43°32·7′N 6°32′W

General

A very attractive Swiss-style town, in a steep-sided twisting valley, with a small fishing port which can be entered in all weathers except N gales. The approach and entrance are not difficult once the leading marks are seen. Anchorage in the outer harbour or berths alongside the wall of the inner harbour are available in 2 m (1 fathom). Good shops and beaches are nearby.

Warning

The harbour tends to silt up, and is periodically dredged. Do not mistake a red and white television tower on the skyline for one of the leading marks, which are difficult to see against the light.

Data

Charts Admiralty Nos. 78, 2927
Spanish Nos. 731A, 933, 934
French Nos. 6381, 5009

Magnetic variation 7°07′W (1984) decreasing by about 5′ each year.

Tidal information

	HW		LW		MHWS	MHWN	MLWS	MLWN
Pointe de Grave	0600 1800	1100 2300	0000 1200	0500 1700	5·4 m 17·6 ft	4·2 m 13·8 ft	0·9 m 3·0 ft	2·1 m 6·8 ft
Puerto de Luarca	−0·10	−0·15	−0·10	+0·30	−1·4 m −4·4 ft	−1·3 m −4·4 ft	−0·5 m −1·7 ft	−0·6 m −1·8 ft

Lights **Punta Blanca/Focicón**. Group Occulting (3) White, 15 seconds, 51·8 m (170 ft), 15 miles. White square tower and dwellings. Fog Siren Morse L (· – · ·), 30 seconds.
Dique del Canouco head. Group Flashing (2) Red, 6 seconds, 13·4 m (44 ft), 4 miles. Conical concrete tower, red gallery.
Dique del Oeste head. Flashing Green, 3 seconds, 8·3 m (27 ft), 4 miles. Masonry tower.
Dique del Paso. Fixed White, 12·8 m (42 ft), 6 miles. Grey concrete column and staff.
Leading lights 170° Line Ⓐ.
Front Fixed Green, 12·8 m (42 ft), 2 miles. White concrete column red bands.
Rear Fixed Green, 20·7 m (68 ft), 2 miles. Similar white concrete column red bands.

Pilots Pilots may meet yachts and guide them in.

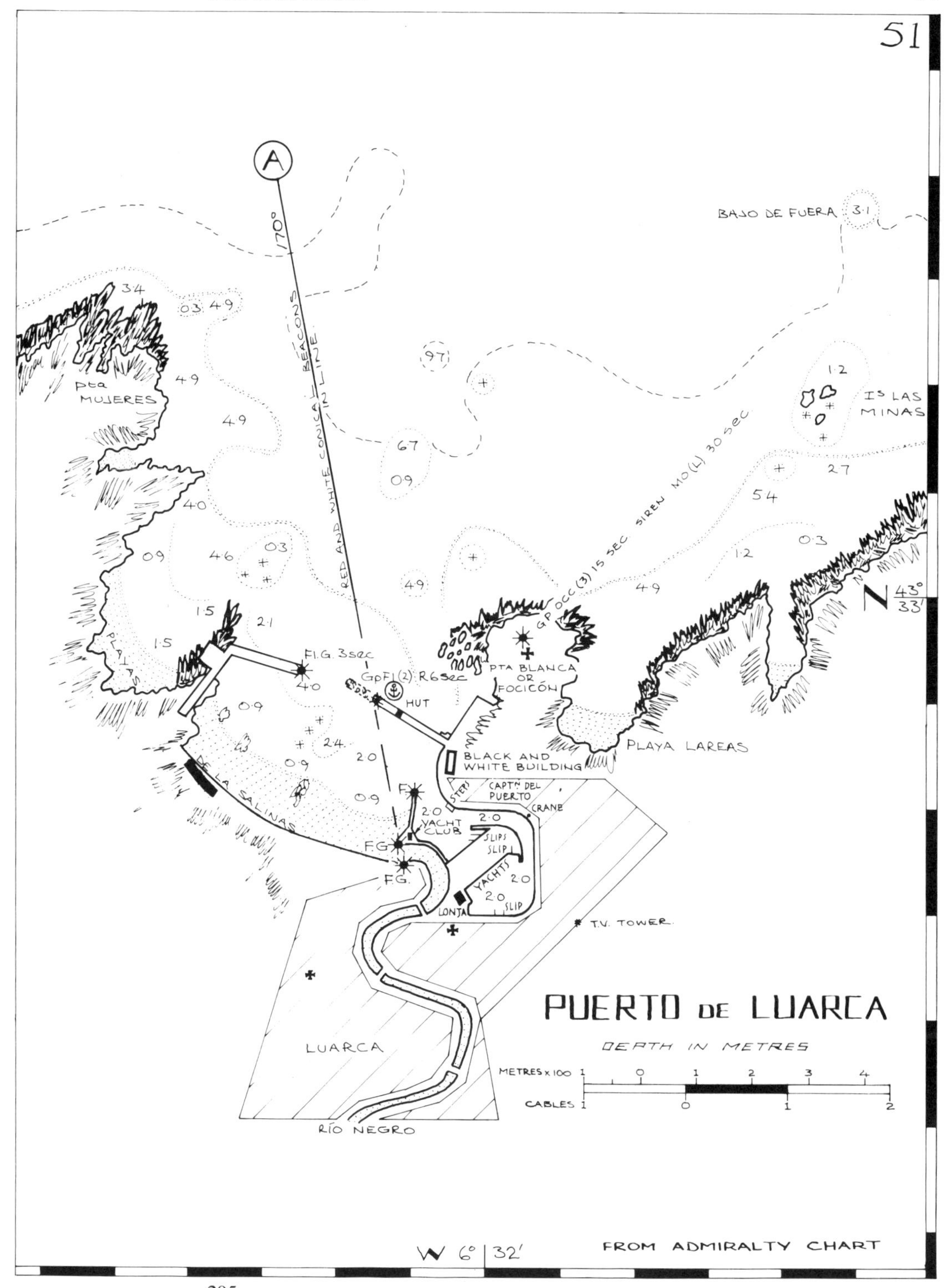
51
BAJO DE FUERA
Pta MUJERES
Is LAS MINAS
RED AND WHITE CONICAL BEACONS IN LINE
170°
G.P. OCC (3) 15 SEC SIREN MO (L) 30 SEC
Fl.G. 3sec
GpFl(2) R.6sec
HUT
PTA BLANCA OR FOCICÓN
PLAYA LAREAS
BLACK AND WHITE BUILDING
STEPS
CAPTN DEL PUERTO
CRANE
YACHT CLUB
SLIPS
SLIP
YACHTS
LONJA
F.G.
T.V. TOWER
PLAYAS
DE LA SALINAS
LUARCA
RÍO NEGRO
PUERTO DE LUARCA
DEPTH IN METRES
METRES x 100
CABLES
N 43° 33'
W 6° 32'
FROM ADMIRALTY CHART

Puerto de Luarca—leading marks.

Life saving Lifeboat and line throwing apparatus maintained.

Approaches

Day *From W* **Punta Romanella**, its outlying islands and the houses around **Puerto de Vega** are easily identified, as is **Cabo Busto**, a flat-topped steep-sided promontory with a conspicuous lighthouse.

From E **Punta Blanca**, located on the E side of the port with **La Blanca** chapel, with a tall tower, and the squat white lighthouse in front of it, are very conspicuous.

The approach from W and N is easy as there are no outlying dangers, but from E care should be taken to pass N of **Bajo de Fuera**, over which seas break. Navigate to a position about 3 cables N of **Punta Mujeres**, from where the entrance to the harbour can be seen.

Night Using **Cabo San Augustín** (Oc. (2) W. 12 sec. 18 M.), **Punta Blanca** (Oc. (3) W. 15 sec. 15 M.) and **Cabo Busto** (Fl. (4) W. 20 sec. 12 M.) navigate to a position 3 cables N of **Punta Mujeres**, from whence the leading lights should be seen.

Entrance

Day From the position detailed above, identify the leading marks. The lower and front is a tall tapering tower painted with red and white bands. The higher and rear mark is a similar tower about half the size of the front mark and near two small stone-coloured houses, to the left of which is a larger white house. This mark is not always easy to see. Enter on a bearing of 170°, Line Ⓐ, until 92 m (100 yards) from the entrance to the outer harbour and then set course to round the port hand breakwater by at least 75 m (82 yards) at LW because of rubble from destroyed head of breakwater. Alter course for the right hand end of a large black and white building, where the entrance to the inner harbour lies.

Night Having reached the position in *approach*, *night*, above, bring the leading lights (F.G. 2 M.) into line, Line Ⓐ, and approach the entrance which is marked by lights to port (Fl. (2) R. 6 sec. 4 M.) and starboard (Fl.G. 3 sec. 4 M.). When about 92 m (100 yards) from these lights alter course to pass between them.

Having passed them turn to port, parallel to the breakwater, and about 23 m (25 yards) away. The starboard hand side of the entrance to the inner harbour is marked by a light (F.W. 6 M.).

Anchorages

Drop anchor on a chain near the centre of the approach to the inner harbour and take a warp to the bollard in the breakwater to keep the yacht clear of this approach, which is constantly used by fishing craft. Up to 4 m (2 fathoms) sand is available but keep 5 m (5 yards) from the breakwater as foundations project underwater. This anchorage should only be used as a temporary measure.

Berths

The whole inner harbour has been dredged to 2 m (1 fathom). Berths alongside, either wet or dry, may be available along the port hand quay halfway to the inner harbour, and in the inner harbour itself on the starboard hand.

Formalities

These are normal except that visitors are asked on arrival to go to the office which is in a grey hut on the quay near the inner harbour or above Restorante Meson del Mara near the entrance.

Facilities

Water Available from a tap at the fish auction shed at the far end of the inner harbour.

Diesel Available from a pump on the quay. There is a ledge exposed at L.W.

Petrol From a pump on the way out of town.

Puerto de Luarca.

Puerto de Luarca – looking NW–N–NE–E–SE. Note: wall is on top of hill from which photo was taken.

Shops These are good and varied. There is an excellent small market.

Clubs A basic **Real Club Nautico** is located near the front leading mark. It has a large green balcony. Drinks are good and cheap here.

Beaches Sandy beaches nearby and really lovely cliff walks.

Visits A climb through the old village to the cliff top is worth while.

Fiestas 28 July, fiesta of the Vaqueiras de Alzada.
3 August, fiesta of the Regalina.
15 August, festivities of the Holy Rosary.
22 August, festivities of St Timothy.

52 Puerto de Vega

Population 1,200 Rating 3-4-4 Position 43°34′N 6°38·8′W

General

This tiny little fishing port has been in use since the days of square-rigged fishing boats, as an old photograph in the local bar proves. The entrance is somewhat hair raising as it is so narrow (12·5 m (41 ft)) and has no less than three 90° turns. Entrance at HW or just before is advised and should not be undertaken in heavy weather or swell from the W or NW. There may be space in the inner harbour to dry out fully protected but if not berths are also available in the outer harbour up to 2 m (1·5 fathoms) which are not so well protected.

Warnings

The approach is not more than 91 m (100 yards) wide and care must be exercised to keep to the leading marks. This is not a port for a large yacht or inexperienced skipper to visit.

Data

Charts

Admiralty No. 2927
Spanish No. 933
French No. 5009

Magnetic variation 7°07′W (1984) decreasing by about 5′ each year.

Tidal information

	HW		LW		MHWS	MHWN	MLWS	MLWN
Pointe de Grave	0600 1800	1100 2300	0000 1200	0500 1700	5·4 m 17·6 ft	4·2 m 13·8 ft	0·9 m 3·0 ft	2·1 m 6·8 ft
Puerto de Vega	−0·15	−0·20	−0·15	+0·25	−1·3 m −4·3 ft	−1·3 m −4·3 ft	−0·5 m −1·7 ft	−0·6 m −1·8 ft

Puerto de Vega

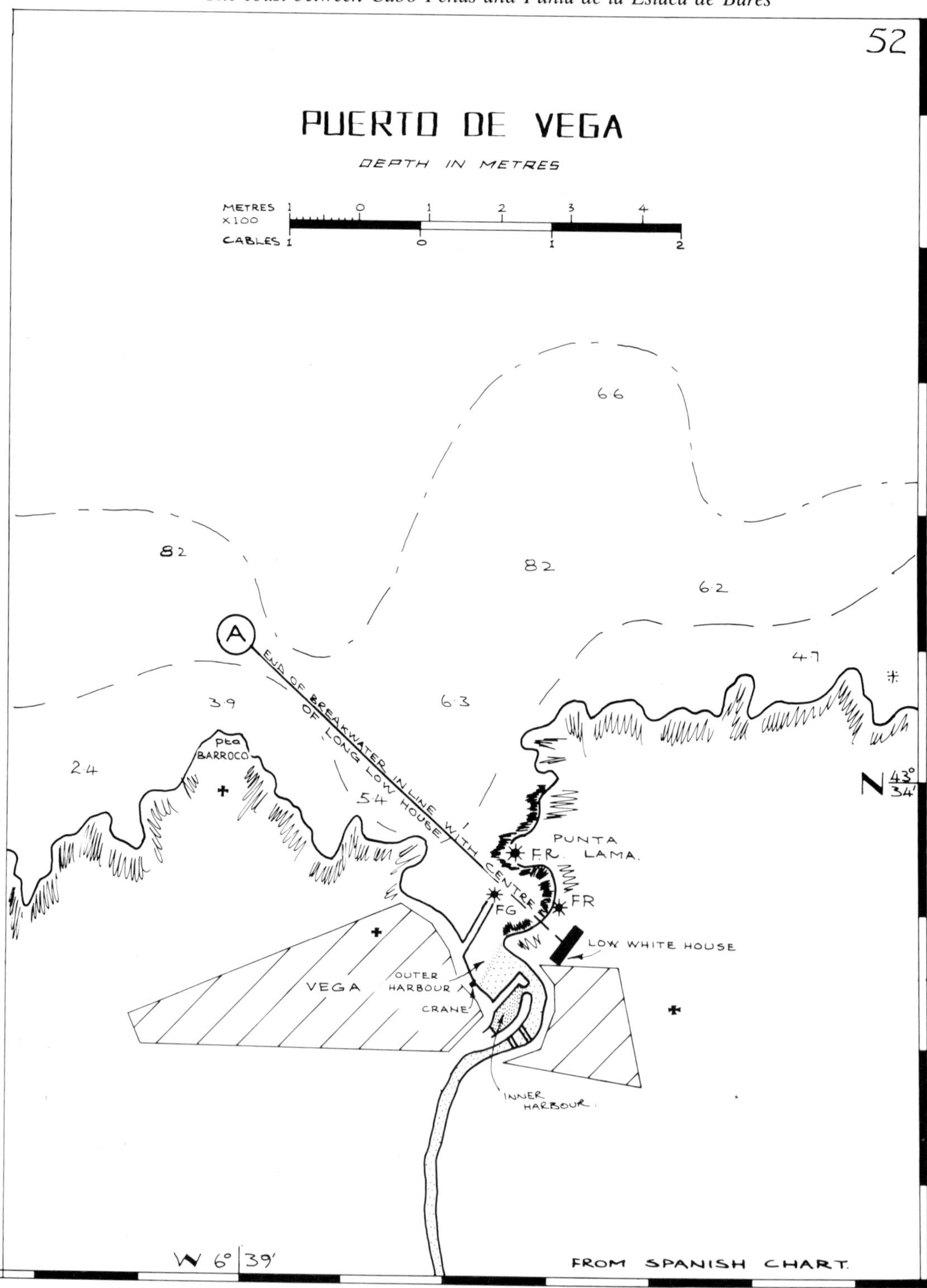
52
PUERTO DE VEGA
DEPTH IN METRES
METRES X100
CABLES
6·6
8·2
8·2
6·2
4·7
3·9
6·3
2·4
5·4
A
END OF BREAKWATER IN LINE WITH CENTRE OF LONG LOW HOUSE
Pta BARROCO
PUNTA LAMA
F.R.
FR
FG
LOW WHITE HOUSE
OUTER HARBOUR
CRANE
VEGA
INNER HARBOUR
N 43° 34'
W 6° 39'
FROM SPANISH CHART

Puerto de Vega—entrance—low water.

Inner harbour Wet berth

Puerto de Vega—entrance to outer harbour—low water.

Lights

Cliff edge. Fixed Red.
Punta Lama. Fixed Red, 12·5 m (41 ft), 6 miles. Grey metal column.
West mole head. Fixed Green, 12·5 m (41 ft), 6 miles. Grey metal column.

Approaches

Day

The **Isla de Vega** to the W and the islands off **Punta Romanella** to the E are easily identified by the surf which breaks around them. **Puerto de Vega** can be identified by a large stone church with two white turrets, some way inland behind the village, and by a chapel on a small headland, **Punta Barroco**, W of the harbour. The white houses of the town on a green background are also easily seen. Navigate to a position about ½ mile NW of **Punta Barroco**, when the harbour entrance should be visible.

Night

Cabo San Agustin (Oc. (2) W. 12 sec. 25 M.) and **Punta Blanca** (Oc. (3) W. 15 sec. 18 M.) enable approach to be made to the entrance as above.

Entrance

Day

At HW approach the entrance with the centre of a long, low, white house with eight windows and a central door in line with the end of the breakwater, Line Ⓐ. In the closer approach, new houses obscure the rear leading mark. Round this breakwater close to and follow it about 3 m (3 yards) away into the outer harbour. It is important to keep close to the breakwater inside the outer harbour as there is very little room.

Night

Entrance at night for the first time is not recommended. There are three lights: (F.G.) on the head of the W breakwater, (F.R.) on the cliffs S of **Punta Lama**, and (F.R.) 91 m (100 yards) N of this on the point itself.

Puerto de Vega—outer harbour—low water.

Puerto de Vega—inner harbour—low water.

Berths

Berth alongside the quay by the crane and check on foot to see if a berth is available in the inner harbour. It is possible to dry out anywhere along the quay of the outer harbour, the deeper water being alongside the outer breakwater.

It is also possible to dry out in the stream above the entrance of the inner harbour and in the lower half of the inner harbour itself.

Formalities

These are normal though yachts are a novelty.

Facilities

Water From spring on the far side of the stream.

Diesel From pump on quay.

Shops There are only limited supplies available in the village.

Visits Attractive cliff walks are well worth the effort.

Fiestas 22 May, festivities of St Rita.

53 Ría de Navia

Population 9,000 Rating 3-4-3 Position 43°32·5′N 6°43·5′W

General

A pleasant country town up an attractive canalised river.Berths alongside in up to 2 m (1 fathom) are available and are sheltered from all weathers. The bar across the mouth of the river which nearly dries has to be crossed near HW and breaks in any heavy swell from W through N to NE. Normal supplies can be found in the town and there are good beaches. Harbour dredged (1982).

Warnings

Observe the bar for not less than 10 minutes before crossing as sometimes on this coast there is a very long swell which will affect the normal waves and may cause some to break. An offshore oil berth 3 M. NE of **Cabo San Agustin** is marked by 3 yellow buoys. The red/yellow beacons transit this terminal.

Data

Charts Admiralty No. 2927
Spanish Nos. 61A, 933
French No. 5009

Magnetic variation 7°07′W (1984) decreasing by about 5′ each year.

Tidal information

	HW		LW		MHWS	MHWN	MLWS	MLWN
Pointe de Grave	0600 1800	1100 2300	0000 1200	0500 1700	5·4 m 17·6 ft	4·2 m 13·8 ft	0·9 m 3·0 ft	2·1 m 6·8 ft
Ría de Navia	−0·15	−0·20	−0·15	+0·25	−1·3 m −4·3 ft	−1·3 m −4·3 ft	−0·5 m −1·7 ft	−0·6 m −1·8 ft

Lights **Cabo San Agustin.** Group occulting (2) White 12 seconds 82 m (269 ft) 18 miles. White column black band on a hut.
Inner harbour entrance N side. Fixed red, 2 miles. Post.
Inner harbour entrance S side. Fixed Green, 2 miles. Post.
Silo. Fixed Red.

Approaches

Day *From W* **Punta Engaramada**, **Cabo San Agustin** and the point between them are conspicuous. There are several large white buildings on **Cabo San Agustin** and on the forward slope a small truncated conical grey tower which is the lighthouse.

From E The sandy bay in the **ría** and a low tree-covered promontory **Punta de la Sierra** on this side can be identified.

Anchorage in the approach There is an anchorage off a small sandy beach, about 2 cables SSE of **Cabo San Agustin** in 4–6 m (2–3 fathoms) sand protected from all winds except N to NE, where boats can await HW and observe the bar.

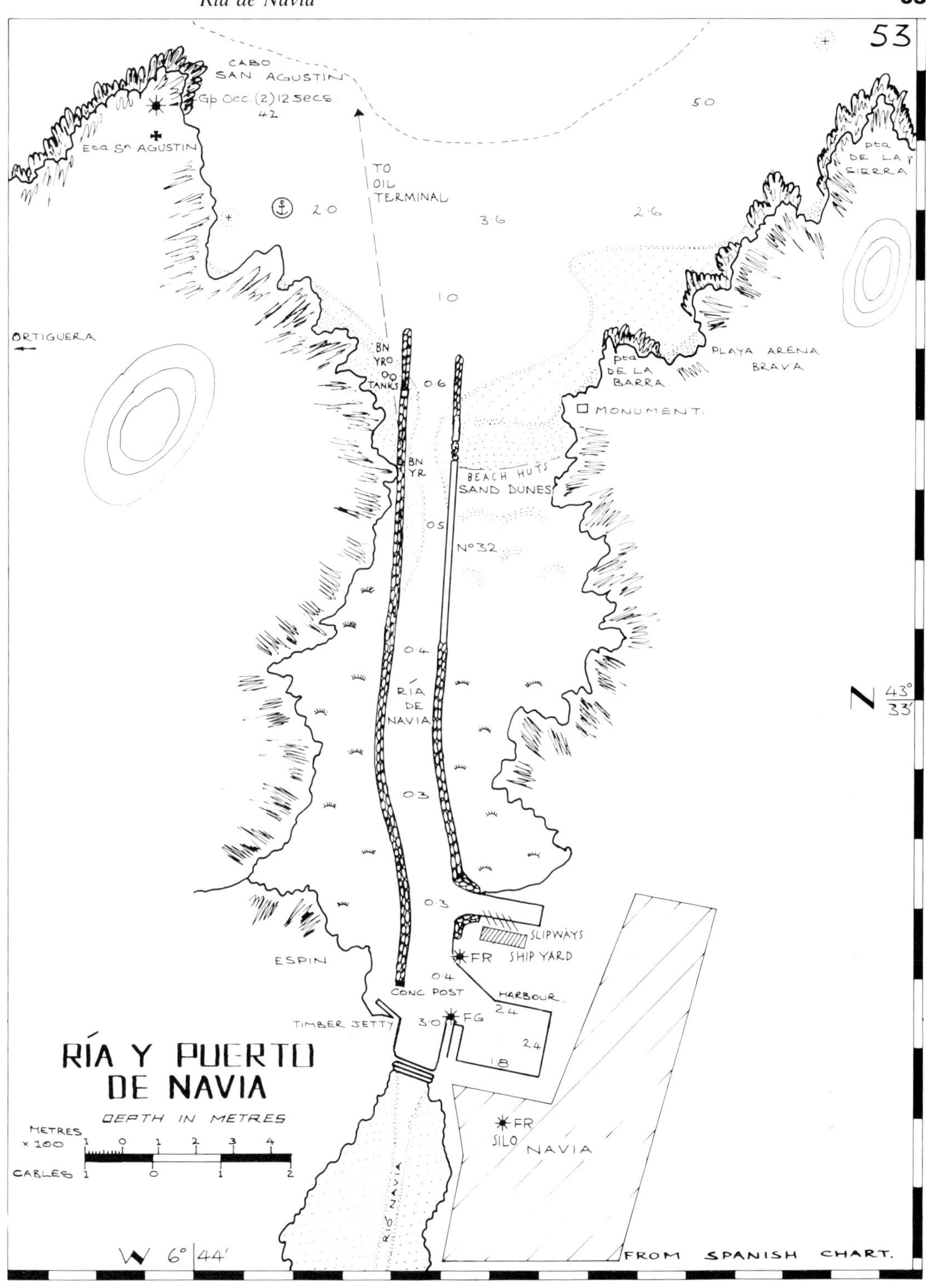
53
CABO
SAN AGUSTIN
Gp Occ. (2) 12 secs.
42
Eta Sn AGUSTIN
TO
OIL
TERMINAL
50
2·0
3·6
2·6
pta
DE LA
SIERRA
1·0
ORTIGUERA
BN
YRO
TANKS
0·6
pta
DE LA
BARRA
PLAYA ARENA
BRAVA
MONUMENT.
BN
YR
BEACH HUTS
SAND DUNES
0·5
Nº32
0·4
RÍA
DE
NAVIA
N 43° 33′
0·3
0·3
SLIPWAYS
FR SHIP YARD
ESPIN
0·4
CONC POST
HARBOUR
TIMBER JETTY
3·0
FG
2·4
2·4
1·8
RÍA Y PUERTO
DE NAVIA
DEPTH IN METRES
METRES
x 100
CABLES
FR
SILO
NAVIA
RÍO NAVIA
W 6° 44′
FROM SPANISH CHART.

Ría de Navia—entrance to Ría—low water—note training walls which are submerged at high water.

Night The light on **Cabo San Agustin** (Oc. (2) 12 sec. 25 M.) leads to this **ría** also **Isla Tapia** (Fl. (2+1) W. 19 sec. 25 M.) may assist.

Entrance

Day Having checked that the bar is not breaking, which can be observed from the anchorage detailed above, set course to a position where the two training walls are about ½ mile due S and the river can be seen between them. Approach to pass between these walls, the E being concrete and the W rocky. Keep nearer the W side of the entrance, then cross over in the first 91 m (100 yards) nearer the E side until No. 32 marked on the concrete wall to port has been passed, when keep to the middle. Note: The yellow/red beacons are not leading marks for the entrance.

Ría de Navia—entrance looking south towards town—low water—note numbers on wall.

About 91 m (100 yards) short of the bridge the entrance to the harbour will be seen to port marked by two poles with lights on them.

Night Night approach and entrance is not recommended without a previous visit and then only in calm weather. The only lights are those of the inner harbour entrance, red and green (port and starboard hand respectively). There is also a red light on the top of a silo on the harbour side of the town just beyond the bridge.

Berths

It is recommended that a berth be taken alongside the N wall of the harbour, if necessary outside a fishing boat, in 2 m (1 fathom) mud.

Puerto de Navia—looking east.

Formalities

The local officials do not know much about yachts. Give them the normal information.

Facilities

Water From a bar on quay.

Petrol From pump at end of an avenue of trees just past bridge.

Diesel From a pump on quay.

Repairs A shipyard can carry out normal repairs.

Shops Normal shops available. Bread shop and bakery 91 m (100 yards) past bridge on right, near a taxi rank and petrol pump.

Beaches There is a fine beach E of the harbour entrance.

Visits It is possible to ascend **Río Navia** by dinghy for many miles through very attractive countryside.

Fiestas 11 August, international swimming races. 17 August, water festivities.

307

54 Puerto de Viavélez

Population 350 Rating 0-0-3 Position 43°33·8′N 6°50·4′W

General

A beautiful little drying port with a narrow twisting entrance should only be entered at HW in settled weather and in the absence of any heavy swell. Drying berths and shallow anchorages exist. Not suitable for large yachts. An experienced navigator is essential.

Warnings

The sea over the shallows of **Cabezo de Viavélez**, 40·2 m (22 fathoms), 2·5 miles NNE off **Cabo Blanco** breaks in heavy weather.

Data

Charts

Admiralty No. 2927
Spanish Nos. 731A, 933
French No. 5009

Magnetic variation 7°06′W (1984) decreasing by about 5′ each year.

Tidal information

	HW		LW		MHWS	MHWN	MLWS	MLWN
Pointe de Grave	0600 1800	1100 2300	0000 1200	0500 1700	5·4 m 17·6 ft	4·2 m 13·8 ft	0·9 m 3·0 ft	2·1 m 6·8 ft
Puerto de Viavélez	−0·20	−0·25	−0·15	+0·20	−1·3 m −4·2 ft	−1·3 m −4·2 ft	−0·5 m −1·7 ft	−0·6 m −1·8 ft

Lights

Cabo San Agustin. Group occulting (2) White, 12 seconds 82 m (269 ft), 18 miles. White column black band.
Isla Tapia. Group Flashing (2+1) White, 19 seconds, 21·6 m (71 ft), 18 miles. White granite tower and dwelling.
Guñin de Afuera head. Group Flashing (2) Red, 5 seconds, 10 m (33 ft), 4 miles. Truncated masonry tower.
Guñin de Adentro head. Flashing Green, 3 seconds, 10 m (33 ft), 4 miles. Truncated masonry tower.

Approaches

Day

From W **Isla Tapia** with its conspicuous lighthouse, the entrance to **Ría de Porcia** with its islands, and **Cabo Blanco**, steep-sided on its E face and whitish-hued on its W face, are the most easily identified places.

From E The **Ría de Navia** with **Cabo San Agustin** alongside to the W and **Punta Engaramada** with its outlying shoals and rocks are conspicuous.

Night

The lights of **Cabo San Agustin** (Oc. (2) W. 12 sec. 18 M.) and **Isla Tapia** (Fl. (2+1) W. 19 sec. 18 M.) enable a night approach to be made.

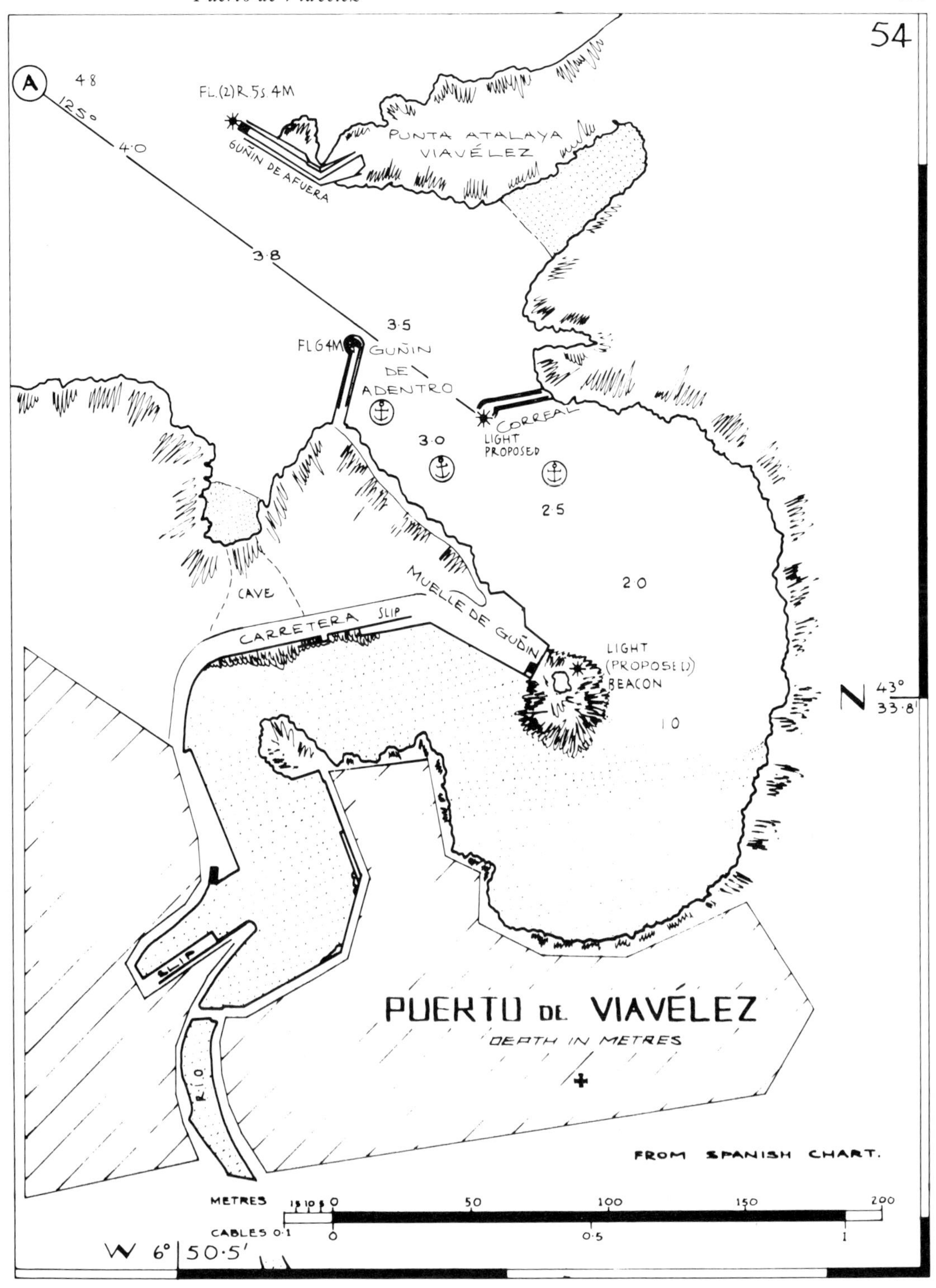
54
A
4·8
125°
4·0
3·8
3·5
FL.(2)R.5s.4M
GUÑIN DE AFUERA
PUNTA ATALAYA
VIAVÉLEZ
FL.G.4M
GUÑIN DE ADENTRO
CORREAL
LIGHT PROPOSED
3·0
2·5
2·0
1·0
CAVE
CARRETERA
SLIP
MUELLE DE GUÑIN
LIGHT (PROPOSED) BEACON
N 43° 33·8'
SLIP
RIO
PUERTO DE VIAVÉLEZ
DEPTH IN METRES
FROM SPANISH CHART.
METRES
0
50
100
150
200
CABLES
0·1
0
0·5
1
W 6° 50·5'

Entrance

Day Approach the breakwaters with the head of **Guñin de Adentro** just open on the head of **Correal** on a course of 125°, Line Ⓐ. Clear the heads of these breakwaters by 10 m (11 yards) and proceed up the harbour taking care to avoid the isolated rocks off **Muelle de Gudin**, which are marked by a stone beacon.

Night Night entrance is not advised without previous daytime visits.

Berths

A drying berth possible alongside the **Muelle de Gudin.**

Anchorage

Anchorage in 1·3 m (4·5 ft) sand is possible 30 m (33 yards) SW of the head of **Correal.**

Formalities

Normal.

Facilities

Water Tap on **Muelle de Gudin.**

Shops Main village of **La Caridad** is a mile and a half inland from the harbour where some shops exist.

Puerto de Viavelez – looking N–NE–E–SE–S. (Continuous panoramic view – right-hand side of top picture joins to left-hand side of lower picture.)

55 Puerto de Tapia

Population 5,088 Rating 2-4-3 Position 43°34·4′N 6°56·8′W

General

A charming little port straight from Devon or Cornwall but without the tourist traps and crowds. Anchorage inside with up to 4 m (2 fathoms) is available. The entrance is narrow but simple. This harbour should not be used when there is a heavy W swell. All normal requirements can be catered for and a good beach is nearby.

Warnings

Entrance by night should only be attempted after a previous visit and then only in good conditions.

Data

Charts Admiralty No. 2927
Spanish No. 933
French No. 5009

Magnetic variation 7°06′W (1984) decreasing by about 5′ each year.

Tidal information

	HW		LW		MHWS	MHWN	MLWS	MLWN
Pointe de Grave	0600 1800	1100 2300	0000 1200	0500 1700	5·4 m 17·6 ft	4·2 m 13·8 ft	0·9 m 3·0 ft	2·1 m 6·8 ft
Puerto de Tapia	−0·25	−0·30	−0·20	+0·15	−1·2 m −4·1 ft	−1·2 m −4·1 ft	−0·5 m −1·7 ft	−0·6 m −1·8 ft

Puerto de Tapia—looking into harbour from entrance—high water.

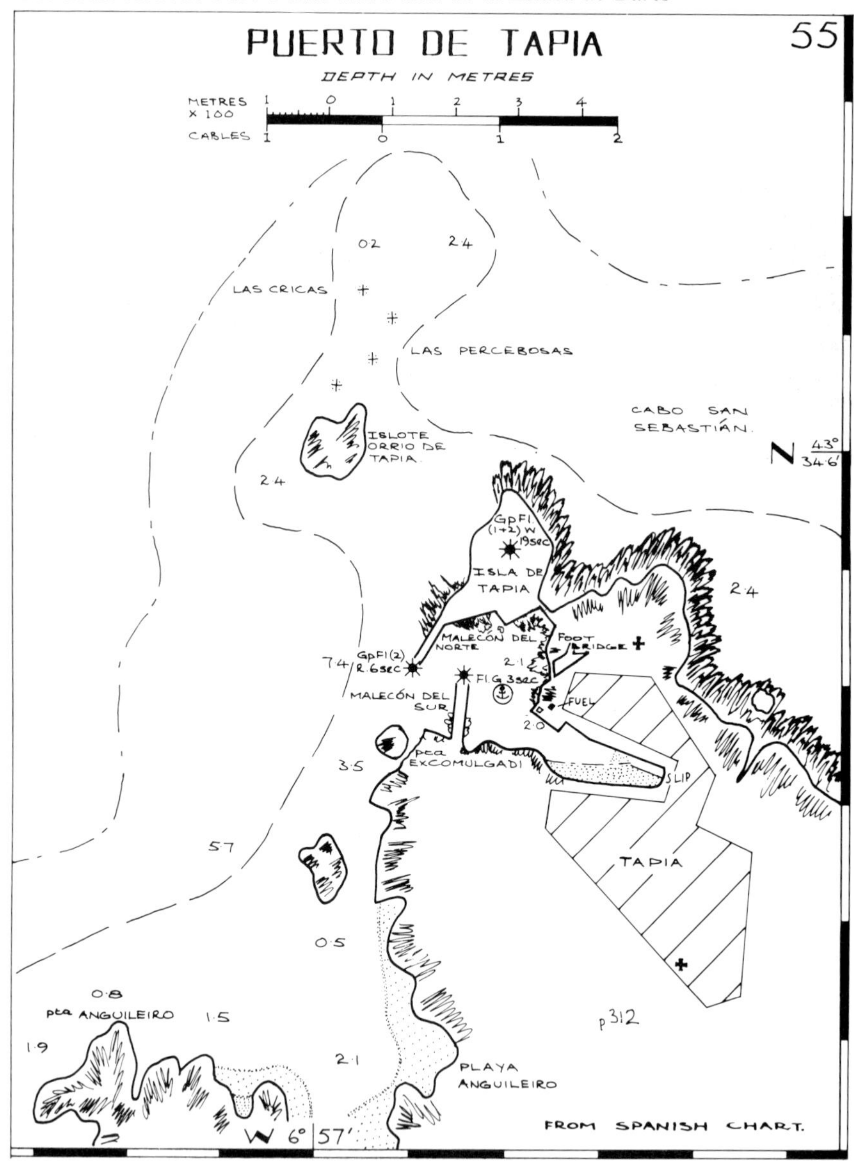

Lights **Isla de Tapia.** Group Flashing (2+1) White, 19 seconds, 21·6 m (71 ft), 18 miles. White granite tower, white dwelling.

Malecón del Norte head. Group Flashing (2) Red, 6 seconds, 9·2 m (30 ft), 5 miles. Truncated conical concrete tower.

Malecón del Sur head. Flashing Green, 3 seconds, 10 m (33 ft), 4 miles. Truncated conical tower.

Approach

Day **Cabo San Sebastián**, the lighthouse on **Isla de Tapia**, the off-lying **Islote Orrio de Tapia** and the town of **Tapia** on the headland, which has a large conspicuous

Puerto de Tapia – looking SE–S–SW.

church with a tower and a statue on top, are all quite unmistakable. Keeping clear of the rocky shallows 2·5 cables N of these islands, navigate to a position due W of the lighthouse and ½ mile away. Approach with breakwater heads in line.

Entrance

Enter between the two truncated conical light towers on either side of the entrance giving them a 10 m berth and then change course about 45° to starboard towards the centre of the S part of the harbour.

Anchorage

Anchor in 2 m (1 fathom) sand near the moorings of the larger fishing boats. Two anchors will be necessary; use tripping lines.

Berths

It is possible in calm weather to lie alongside the fuel quay in 2 m or the **Malecón del Sur** near the light tower but pay attention to an underwater ledge and running moorings.

Formalities

Normal.

Facilities

Water Fountain 180 m (100 yards) up road to E, or from the quay.

Diesel Available from a pump on quay.

Petrol Obtainable from a garage in town.

Shops These are rather spread about the town.

Beaches To be found W of the town.

56 Ría de Ribadeo

Population 9,600 Rating 1-2-2 Position 43°31·8′N 7°2·4′W

General

Probably the most attractive and pleasant to visit of all the beautiful *rías* on this coast. An easy entrance which can be used under all conditions except N storms. There are several anchorages and a pleasant berth alongside a new quay. There are also three entirely different towns to visit and several bathing beaches. Excursions can be made in a dinghy up the river on the flood.

Warnings

In conditions of heavy N swell care should be taken to follow the leading marks accurately. When passing the various rocks and shallows given them 48 m (50 yards) clearance.

Data

Charts

Admiralty Nos. 2627, 78
Spanish Nos. 550A, 932
French Nos. 6383, 5009

Magnetic variation 7°06′W (1984) decreasing by about 5′ each year.

Tidal information

	HW		LW		MHWS	MHWN	MLWS	MLWN
Pointe de Grave	0600 1800	1100 2300	0000 1200	0500 1700	5·4 m 17·6 ft	4·2 m 13·8 ft	0·9 m 3·0 ft	2·1 m 6·8 ft
Ría de Ribadeo	−0·25	−0·30	−0·20	+0·15	−1·3 m −4·1 ft	−1·2 m −4·1 ft	−0·5 m −1·7 ft	−0·6 m −1·8 ft

The height of the water is increased by up to 0·8 m (2·5 ft) with strong W winds and reduced by the same amount in strong E winds.
The stream opposite **Ribadeo** reaches 3 knots on spring tides.

Lights

Isla Pancha. Group Occulting (2) White, 5 seconds, 21 m (69 ft), 11 miles. White square tower and dwelling. Obscured 141·5°–145·5°.
First set of leading lights, Punta Aerojo 140°, Line Ⓐ.
Front Quick Flashing Red, 18·2 m (60 ft), 6 miles. White conical tower. Red diamond.
Rear Occulting Red 4 seconds, 24 m (79 ft), 6 miles. White conical tower. Red diamond.
Second set of leading lights, Muelle del García 203° Line Ⓑ.
Front Very Quick Flashing Red, 8·2 m (27 ft), 4 miles. White conical tower. Red diamond.
Rear Occulting Red 2 seconds, 20 m (68 ft), 4 miles. Lantern on roof of house. Red diamond.
Punta Mirasol quay. NE head. Fixed Green, 9 m (30 ft) 2 miles. Floodlit structure.
Castropol. Light to be established.
Punta Cabanelas. Flashing (3) Green, 11 m (36 ft), 5 miles.

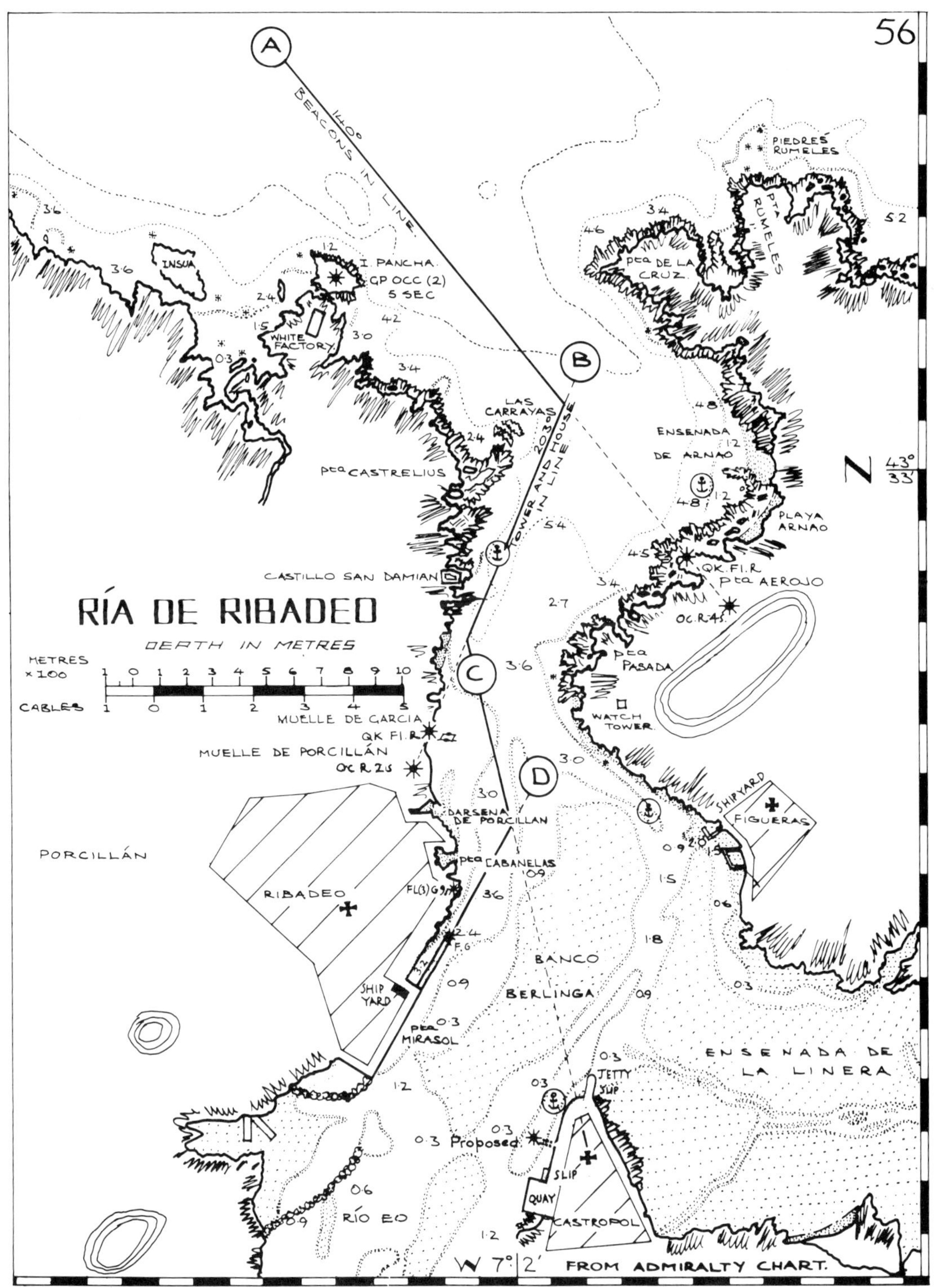
56
RÍA DE RIBADEO
DEPTH IN METRES
METRES ×100
CABLES
BEACONS IN LINE 140°
TOWER AND HOUSE IN LINE 203°
PIEDRES RUMELES
PTA RUMELES
Pta DE LA CRUZ
INSUA
I. PANCHA
GP OCC (2) 5 SEC
WHITE FACTORY
LAS CARRAYAS
Pta CASTRELIUS
ENSENADA DE ARNAO
PLAYA ARNAO
QK FI. R
Pta AEROJO
OC. R. 4s
CASTILLO SAN DAMIAN
Pta PASADA
WATCH TOWER
MUELLE DE GARCIA
QK FI. R
MUELLE DE PORCILLÁN
OC R 2s
DARSENA DE PORCILLAN
SHIPYARD
FIGUERAS
PORCILLÁN
Pta CABANELAS
RIBADEO
FL(3) G 9s
F.G
BANCO BERLINGA
SHIP YARD
Pta MIRASOL
ENSENADA DE LA LINERA
JETTY
SLIP
Proposed
QUAY
CASTROPOL
RÍO EO
W 7° 2′
FROM ADMIRALTY CHART
43° 33′

Ría de Ribadeo—entrance looking south.

Life saving A lifeboat and line throwing apparatus are maintained in the **Ría de Ribadeo.**

Approaches

Day *From W* The low-lying, grass-covered **Punta Promontoira** is easily identified. The **Isla Pancha** at the entrance of this **ría**, has a conspicuous octagonal building with a lighthouse. It is connected to the mainland by a bridge. A very conspicuous large white factory is situated on the mainland nearby.

From E **Cabo San Sebastián**, 4 miles away, also with a conspicuous lighthouse, is easily identified. **Punta Rumeles** and **Punta de la Cruz**, at the entrance of this **ría**, are not particularly conspicuous. Navigate to a position ½ mile N of the lighthouse on **Isla Pancha.**

Night The lights of **Isla Pancha** (Oc (2) W. 5 sec. 11 M.) and **Isla Tapia** (Fl. (2+1) W. 19 sec. 18 M.) enable an easy approach to be made to this **ría**.

Ría de Ribadeo—leading marks Punta Aerojo Line Ⓐ and San Roman watch tower.

Entrance

Day From the position detailed above, identify the two leading marks on **Punta Aerojo**, which consist of two white conical towers with red diamonds, the front on the top of a cliff, the rear near the top of the hill (these are not easy to see in some light conditions). Bring into line on 140°, Line Ⓐ , and enter the **ría.**

When approaching **Las Carrayas** reef, on which the sea breaks, the tallest building in **Ribadeo**, which has a red onion-shaped tower will appear. When it bears 205°, Line Ⓑ , alter course towards it. The next set of leading marks will then be observed. The front and lower mark is on a wooden wharf and consists of a tall white conical tower, with a red diamond. The rear mark is a large six sided building with a small lantern tower on top, painted white with a yellow outline and red diamond. Follow this line until 92 m (100 yards) S of the stone foundations of the dismantled cantilevered wharf when alter course to 165° straight for the tall tower of the church of **Castropol**, Line Ⓒ. After about 274 m

Ría de Ribadeo—2nd set of leading lights—Line Ⓑ.

(300 yards) on this course, the new quay of **Punta Mirasol** will appear from behind **Punta Cabanelas**. Alter course for this quay, Line Ⓓ .

Night Follow the leading lights on **Punta Aerojo** (*Front:* Q.Fl. R. 6 M. *Rear:* Oc. R. 4 sec) on 140°, Line Ⓐ , until the second set of leading lights line up on 205°, Line Ⓑ (*Front:* V.Q.Fl. R. 4 M.) *Rear*: (Oc.R. 2 sec). Then either anchor till dawn 180 m (200 yards) short of the front light or, if visibility is adequate, alter course form this position for the lights of **Castropol Church** which is floodlit on 165°, Line Ⓒ, until the row of yellow lights on the quay of **Punta Mirasol** (F.G.) appear. Then alter course towards this quay, Line Ⓓ , leaving Fl (3) G. 100 m to starboard.

Berths

A good berth alongside the outer side of the new quay at **Punta Mirasol** in 4 m (2 fathoms). This quay has adequate bollards and rings; also ladders, a rarity in Spain. Alternatively use inner side of NE extension of this quay, where it may be necessary to lie outside a fishing boat.

Anchorages

The harbour authorities do not allow yachts to anchor for any length of time off **Ribadeo**, but anchorages are available as follows:

Ría de Ribadeo—2nd set of leading lights—Line Ⓑ.

Ría de Ribadeo—Castropol as seen from Line Ⓑ—Line Ⓒ.

Ensenada de Arnao. Protected from winds from all directions except NW to N in up to 6 m (3 fathoms) off the S half of **Playa Arnao.**
Castillo San Damian. Protected from all winds except N in up to 6 m (3 fathoms) sand, 137 m (150 yards) E of castle.
Figueras. Fully protected in 4 m (2 fathoms) sand, 229 m (250 yards) W of shipyard. Some fishing vessels also lie here.
Castropol. 182 m (200 yards W of **Punta de Castropol** in 4 m (2 fathoms) sand of limited area; use two anchors or dry out alongside quay.

Formalities

Several officials will board and are happy with the completion of one document.

Facilities

Water Available from fishermen's stores yard or café on new quay but should always be boiled. A little spring of water at the foot of the road leading off the quay is reputed to be drinkable. Hose on quay.

Diesel From pump at end of quay. Large diameter hose.

Petrol From pump on road to station.

Ría de Ribadeo—looking south—Line Ⓓ.

Ría de Ribadeo—Figueras—looking east.

Repairs	Excellent mechanics at **Punta Mirasol**. Shipyard at **Figueras.**
Shops	Most stores can be obtained from town, also from café on quay.
Information Bureau	Located on the W corner of main square and will supply maps etc. to visitors.
Hotels	Two official hotels or inns are located just above **Punta Mirasol** and there are several other hotels in the town.
Visits	**Castropol** and **Figueras** are well worth visiting and a trip up the **Río Eo** on the flood tide to **Vegadeo** and beyond is rewarding; also eighteenth century collegiate church in **Ribadeo.**
Fiestas	The first Sunday in August at **Monte de Santa Cruz.** 7 September, festivities of Santa Maria del Campo.
Yacht club	The Club Nautico del Eo has a bar, restaurant, showers etc. on the **Muelle de Porcillan** (110002).

Ría de Ribadeo – harbour at **Punta Mirasol** looking S.

Ría de Ribadeo – harbour at **Figueras** looking NW at low water.

57 Puerto de Foz

Population 2,810 Rating 3-4-3 Position 43°34′N 7°15·2′W

General

A pleasant little town and port with some wonderful sandy beaches. Entrance is only possible in the absence of heavy swell from the N and during the top quarter of the tide across a bar which dries. Berths alongside in up to 3 m (1·5 fathoms) are available. Normal supplies can be provided.

Warnings

As the approach channels can change it would be advisable to wait and follow in the wake of the larger fishing boats, except in very calm weather when the water is clear and the channel can be observed.

The current in the narrow channel NE of the quays can run up to 5 knots at half tide on springs.

Entrance at night without a previous daytime visit is not advisable.

Data

Charts
Admiralty Nos. 1755, 2927
Spanish No. 932
French No. 5009

Magnetic variation 7°18′W (1984) decreasing by about 5′ each year.

Tidal information

	HW		LW		MHWS	MHWN	MLWS	MLWN
Pointe de Grave	0600 1800	1100 2300	0000 1200	0500 1700	5·4 m 17·6 ft	4·2 m 13·8 ft	0·9 m 3·0 ft	2·1 m 6·8 ft
Puerto de Foz	−0·25	−0·30	−0·23	+0·15	−1·3 m −4·2 ft	−1·3 m −4·2 ft	−0·6 m −1·9 ft	−0·7 m −2·0 ft

Puerto de Foz—approach looking south west. *Photo: D. Pownall*

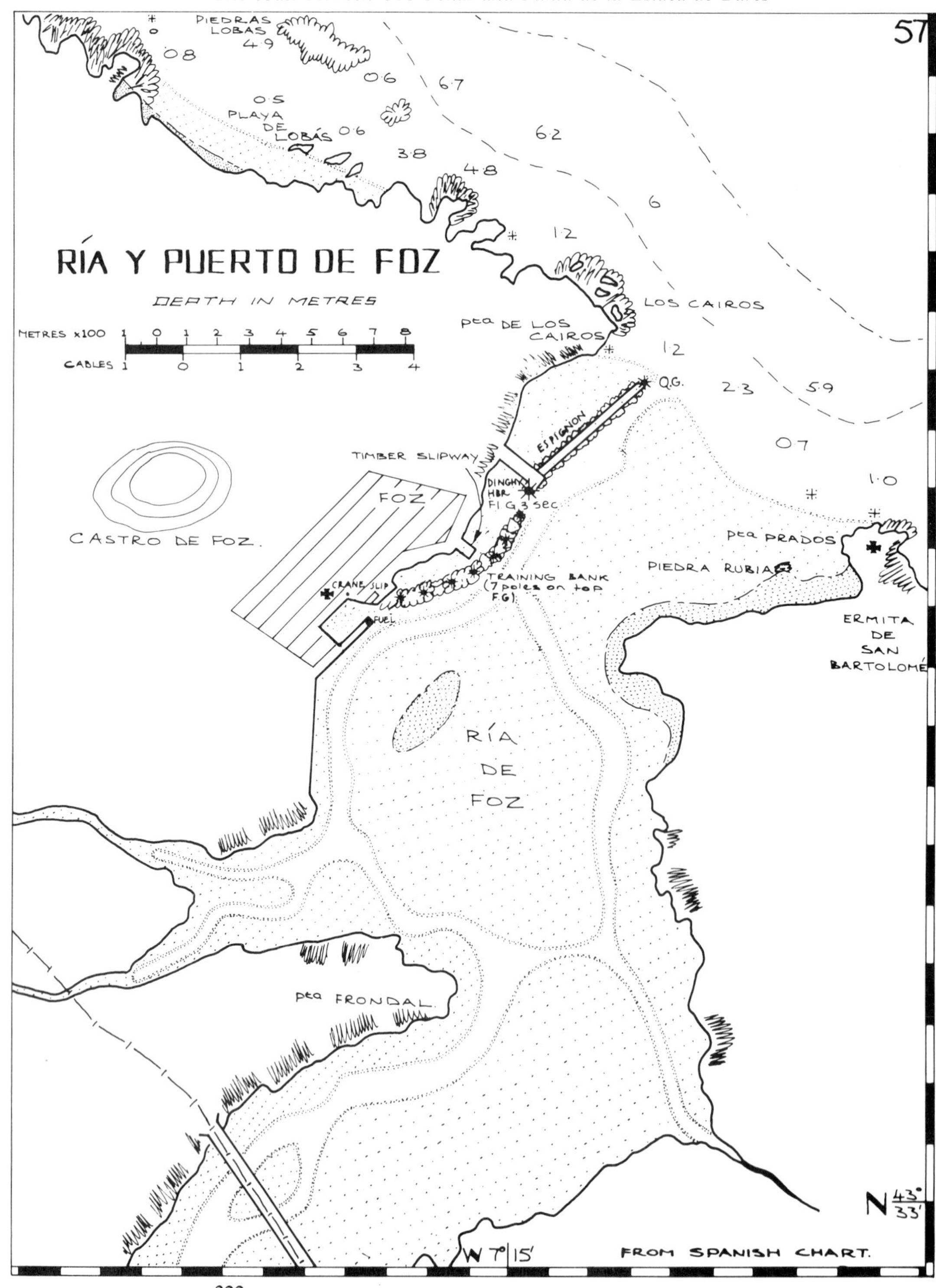
57
PIEDRAS LOBAS
4·9
0·8
0·6
6·7
0·5
PLAYA DE LOBÁS
0·6
6·2
3·8
4·8
6
1·2
RÍA Y PUERTO DE FOZ
DEPTH IN METRES
METRES x100
CABLES
pta DE LOS CAIROS
LOS CAIROS
1·2
Q.G.
2·3
5·9
0·7
1·0
ESPIGÓN
TIMBER SLIPWAY
DINGHY HBR
Fl G 3 sec
FOZ
CASTRO DE FOZ
CRANE
SLIP
FUEL
TRAINING BANK (7 poles on top F.G.)
pta PRADOS
PIEDRA RUBIA
ERMITA DE SAN BARTOLOMÉ
RÍA DE FOZ
pta FRONDAL
N 43° 33'
W 7° 15'
FROM SPANISH CHART.

Puerto de Foz – looking S from **Bajo la Rapadoria** light at high water. Note lights on training wall.

Lights **Isla Pancha (Ribadeo).** Group Occulting (2). White, 5 seconds, 21 m (69 ft) 11 miles. White square tower or building.
Espignon head. Quick Flashing Green. 5 m (16 ft), 6 miles. White concrete tower, green top.
Bajo la Rapadoria. Flashing Green, 3 seconds, 10·4 m (34 ft), 6 miles. White truncated concrete building.
Training Wall. 7 Fixed Green, 1 mile. Posts on breakwater/training wall.
Piedra Burela. Quick Flashing (3) White, 10 seconds, 11·6 m (38 ft), 8 miles. Black truncated conical concrete tower. Yellow band, Topmark two cones base to base.

Approaches

From E **Punta Promontoira**, a low green point with steep cliffs, can be identified when approaching from the E.

From W **Cabo Burela**, a high green point with rocky cliffs, and the houses of **Burela** are conspicuous when approaching from the W. **Punta de los Cairos**, W of the entrance, is a low, fairly conspicuous, cliff-faced point but **Punta Prados** to the E is lower and not so easily seen. A large tree-covered point, **Punta Frondal**, inside the harbour, which has some large white buildings and a white square tower W of the trees, is conspicuous as are the sands at the mouth of the harbour. Navigate to a position about ½ mile NE of **Punta de los Cairos.**

Puerto de Foz—harbour entrance looking south west. *Photo: D. Pownall*

Night A night approach and entrance is not recommended for a first visit due to unreliable lights and a shifting channel.

Entrance

From the position given above, set a course to bring the two white lighthouses into line and approach the outer lighthouse leaving it and the **Espignon** 25 m to starboard. The south end of the **Espignon** has the second lighthouse and the rocky training wall is marked by 7 short poles (F.G.). Follow the rocky training wall at 25m to the harbour entrance.

Berths

Either side of the mole, the outer side having water up to 4 m (2 fathoms), the inner side 3 m (1·5 fathoms).

Formalities

Normal information required.

Facilities

Water From nearby bars or from fishermen.

Diesel From pump on end of mole.

Petrol From pump in town.

Shops To be found up the hill in the town, where most requirements can be met.

Beaches By using a dinghy the completely unspoilt and deserted sands to the E can be visited.

Fiestas 26 May, traditional *Romeria*.
16–17 July, seamen's festivities in honour of Our Lady of Mount Carmel.
8–11 August, festivities of St Lawrence.

Puerto de Foz – harbour looking S.

58 Puerto de Burela

Population 5,699 Rating 4-2-3 Position 43°39·5′N 7°21·2′W

General

A very busy commercial fishing port behind a huge new breakwater which is used by a large number of fishing vessels. It has an easy approach and entrance but only a berth in 2 m (1 fathom) alongside another vessel is normally available. Adequate shops and facilities exist. Not a particularly pleasant harbour to visit.

Warnings

Further extension of the breakwater is expected.

Data

Charts

Admiralty No. 1755
Spanish No. 932
French No. 5009

Magnetic variation 7°18′W (1984) decreasing by about 5′ each year.

Tidal information

	HW		LW		MHWS	MHWN	MLWS	MLWN
Pointe de Grave	0600 1800	1100 2300	0000 1200	0500 1700	5·4 m 17·6 ft	4·2 m 13·8 ft	0·9 m 3·0 ft	2·1 m 6·8 ft
Puerto de Burela	−0·25	−0·30	−0·23	+0·15	−1·3 m −4·2 ft	−1·3 m −4·2 ft	−0·6 m −1·9 ft	−0·7 m −2·0 ft

Lights

Piedra Burela. Quick Flashing (3) White, 10 seconds, 11·6 m (38 ft), 8 miles. Black truncated concrete tower, yellow band. Topmark two cones base to base.
Burela breakwater head. Gp.Fl. (3). Red, Green sectors, 10 seconds, 12 m (39 ft), 4 miles. Round concrete tower. Red 122°–279°, Green elsewhere.
Punta Atalaya (San Ciprián). Group Occulting (2+3) White, 15 seconds, 35·7 m (117 ft), 9 miles. Grey Conical granite tower.

Port Radio

See page 20.

Approaches

Day

From W **Les Farallones** and in particular **El Pié** island are conspicuous. **Cabo Burela** a long, low green headland can be identified by several large white buildings on it and the outlying lighthouse of **Piedra Burela** located further E. The village of **Burela** and the new mole are also easily identified.
From E There are few conspicuous features. Only the **Ría de Foz** with its breakwater and lighthouses and the **Ría de Oro** crossed by two bridges can be easily identified. Navigate to a position about 1 cable E of the outer lighthouse, which is clear of the rocks which lie between it and **Cabo Burela.**

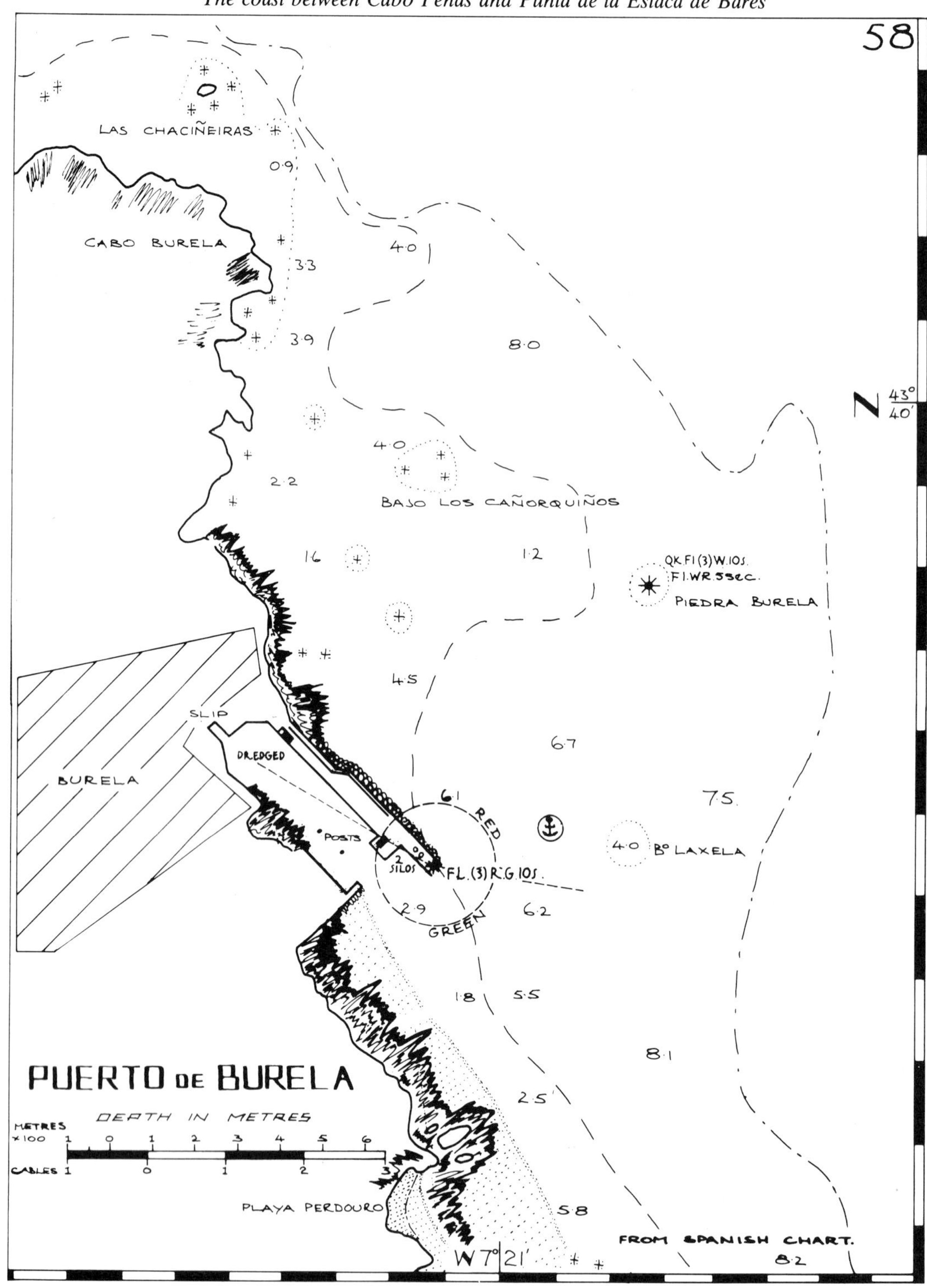
58
LAS CHACIÑEIRAS
0·9
CABO BURELA
3·3
4·0
3·9
8·0
N 43° 40'
4·0
2·2
BAJO LOS CAÑORQUIÑOS
16
1·2
QK Fl (3) W.10s.
Fl.WR.5sec.
PIEDRA BURELA
4·5
SLIP
DREDGED
6·7
BURELA
6·1
RED
7·5
POSTS
4·0
Bº LAXELA
2 SILOS
FL.(3) R.G.10s.
2·9
GREEN
6·2
1·8
5·5
8·1
PUERTO DE BURELA
DEPTH IN METRES
2·5
METRES ×100
CABLES
PLAYA PERDOURO
5·8
FROM SPANISH CHART.
W 7° 21'
8·2

Puerto de Burela—approach looking north west showing Piedra Burela lighthouse and Cabo Burela in the distance. Note: Tower now black with yellow band. Topmark two cones base to base. *Photo: D. Pownall*

Night Using the light on **Punta Atalaya (San Ciprián)** (Oc. (2+3) W. 15 sec. 9 M.) and the outer light of **Piedra Burela** (Q.Fl. (3) W. 10 sec. 8 M.) navigate as above to a position 1 cable E of this outer light.

Entrance

Day Set course to clear the E end of the new mole by 23 m (25 yards) but keep a lookout for large fishing vessels leaving: the masts show above the wall. Round the end of the mole and the harbour opens out ahead.

Night Set course for **Burela breakwater head** light (Fl. (3) RG 10 sec) in the green sector, leaving **Piedra Burela** (Q.Fl. (3) W.10 sec.) to starboard, and then the head of the breakwater 20 m to starboard. Once past the end of the mole the harbour lights illuminate the area.

Berths

As there is no room for anchoring inside the harbour yachts should tie up alongside a fishing boat in about 2 m (1 fathom) or proceed up the harbour where it is possible to dry out against the S side of the mole on hard sand. Greater depths may be found as dredging is taking place.

Puerto de Burela – entrance looking NE.

Anchorage

An exposed anchorage is possible in up to 6·9 m (3·75 fathoms), 2 cables E of the breakwater lights.

Formalities

The local officials will be on board as soon as secured alongside with the usual form. They may require the yacht to go alongside the quay just inside the entrance to complete these formalities before taking up a berth.

Facilities

Water and diesel	From W end of quay.
Petrol	From pump in town.
Shops	A fair selection is to be found up the hill.
Beaches	There are some nearby coves for bathing.
Fiestas	10 June, festivities in honour of St John the Baptist.

59 Puerto de San Ciprián (Old harbour)

Population 727 Rating 2-4-4 Position 43°41·9′N 7°26·6′W

General

A quaint little harbour, anchorage and village, which should not be approached in heavy weather from the N but is protected from E through S to W. The entrance, though narrow, is not difficult but the anchorage in up to 5 m (2·5 fathoms) sand is restricted. Many shops can provide everyday requirements. This port is well worth a visit if weather permits.

Warnings

There are a number of shallow banks around the **Ensenada de San Ciprián** which cause seas to break in heavy weather.

A large number of heavy chain moorings lie on the bottom of the anchorage. Buoy all anchors with trip lines.

The village of **San Ciprián** does not appear from behind its hill until anchorage is reached. Do not mistake the village of **Figueiras** for it in the approach.

Data

Charts

Admiralty	Nos. 1755, 78
Spanish	Nos. 731A, 931, 932
French	Nos. 6383, 5009

Magnetic variation 7°35′W (1984) decreasing by about 5′ each year.

Tidal information

	HW		LW		MHWS	MHWN	MLWS	MLWN
Pointe de Grave	0600 1800	1100 2300	0000 1200	0500 1700	5·4 m 17·6 ft	4·2 m 13·8 ft	0·9 m 3·0 ft	2·1 m 6·8 ft
San Ciprián	−0·25	−0·30	−0·23	+0·15	−1·3 m −4·3 ft	−1·3 m −4·3 ft	−0·6 m −1·9 ft	−0·7 m −2·0 ft

Lights

Piedra Burela. Quick Flashing (3) White, 10 seconds, 11·6 m (38 ft), 8 miles. Black truncated conical concrete tower. Yellowband, Topmark two cones base to base.
Punta Atalaya (San Ciprián). Group Occulting (2+3) White, 15 seconds, 35·7 m (117 ft), 9 miles. Grey conical granite tower.
Leading lights 193° Line Ⓐ . *Front* Q.Fl.R. 9·4 m (31 ft), 5 miles. *Rear* Q.Fl.W. 22·9 m (75 ft), 5 miles. Both white towers with gallery, and red diamonds.
Auzuela Jettyhead. Fl.G. 3 sec. 12 m (39 ft), 3 M. White column.
Mole. F.R. 10 m (33 ft), 3 M. White concrete column.
Isla Coelleira. Flashing White, 3 seconds, 86·9 m (285 ft), 8 miles. Grey conical granite tower and dwelling.

Port Radio See page 20.

Approaches

Day

From E and W The location of this harbour is easily found once the unmistakable **Les Farallones** islands are seen. One of these, **El Pié**, is quite remarkable, being a circular flat-topped rock with almost vertical sides 36 m (118 ft) high. When these are located, navigate to a position halfway between the islands and the lighthouse on **Punta Atalaya** which consists of a small white bungalow with red edges and a low lighthouse tower in its centre front, located on **San Ciprián** hill. Take care to avoid shoal patches in conditions of heavy swell.

Night

Using the lights of **Isla Coelleira** (Fl.W. 3 sec. 8 M.), **Punta Atalaya** (Oc. (2 + 3) W. 15 sec. 9 M.) and **Piedra Burela** (Q.Fl.(3) W. 10 sec. 8 M) navigate to position halfway between **Cabo San Ciprián** and **Les Farallones**. The lights and leading light of the new harbour wall assist.

Entrance

Day

From position halfway between **les Farallones** and **Cabo San Ciprián** bring the W edge of this **Cabo** to the centre of **Figueiras** village and approach the harbour. The breaking waters and the high breakwater of **Anzuela** will be seen. Above and to the left of them the leading marks which consists of latticework towers with a lantern on the top, the bottom two-thirds being covered in and painted with black and white diagonal stripes. The front mark is on the edge of the sand and the rear in a green field and appears in a gap in the houses. Do not mistake a large conspicuous chimney a little to the W for one of these marks. Keeping to 193°, Line Ⓐ, on the leading marks, enter the channel and pass some 9 m (10 yards) W of the rocks on **Cabo San Ciprián** into the anchorage.

Night

From a similar position to the day approach bring the leading lights (*Front:* Qk.Fl. R. 5 M. *Rear:* Q. Fl. W. 5 M.) into line and proceed on this bearing of 193°, Line Ⓐ , into the anchorage leaving (Fl.G. 3 sec) to starboard and (F.R.) to port.

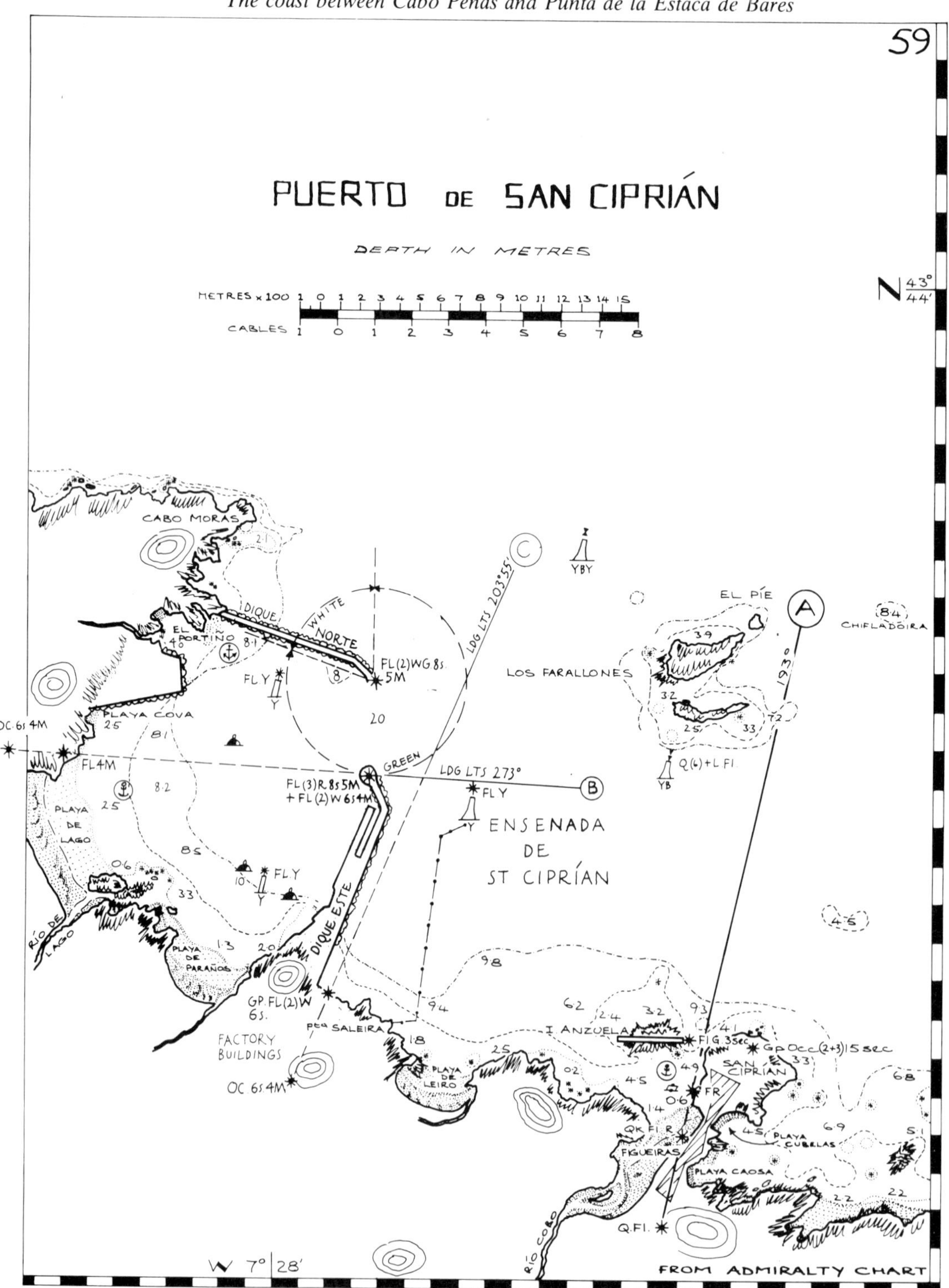
59
PUERTO DE SAN CIPRIÁN
DEPTH IN METRES
METRES x 100
CABLES
CABO MORAS
DIQUE NORTE
WHITE
GREEN
EL PORTINO
PLAYA COVA
PLAYA DE LAGO
RIO DE LAGO
PLAYA DE PARAÑOS
DIQUE ESTE
FACTORY BUILDINGS
Pta SALEIRA
PLAYA DE LEIRO
I. ANZUELA
SAN CIPRIÁN
FIGUEIRAS
PLAYA CAOSA
PLAYA CUBELAS
RIO COBO
LOS FARALLONES
EL PIE
CHIFLADOIRA
ENSENADA DE ST CIPRÍAN
LDG LTS 203°55'
LDG LTS 273°
193°
FL(2)WG 8s 5M
FL(3)R 8s 5M + FL(2)W 6s 4M
OC 6s 4M
FL 4M
GP FL(2)W 6s
Q(6)+L FL
Fl G 3sec
Gp Occ(2+3) 15 sec
FR
QK FL R
Q.Fl.
FROM ADMIRALTY CHART
N 43° 44'
W 7° 28'

Anchorages

Anchor in 5 m (2·5 fathoms) sand about 48 m (50 yards) S of the wall on the **Anzuela** reef and about a similar distance N of a black can mooring buoy. Use a buoyed pair of anchors as room is restricted and there are permanent moorings on the sea bed. Sometimes a mooring is available but check before using. It is not possible to go up **Río Cabo** except at high tide and then only with a draft of 1·3 m (4 ft) or less, and the ability to dry out.

Berths

Temporary berths can be obtained alongside the new jetty provided it is not in use by fishing vessels, but this is not advised if there is any swell.

Formalities

Usual form to complete for port officials.

Facilities

Water On quay or from café on quay.
Petrol From pump in **Figueiras** village.
Diesel From pump on quay.
Shops Shops in **Figueiras** and at **San Ciprián** can supply most requirements.
Beaches There are several sandy beaches nearby.

59A Puerto de San Ciprián (New harbour)

Population 1,000 Rating 4-1-4 Position 43°42·9′N 7°27·5′W

General

A huge commercial harbour serving a large factory. Easy to enter in storm but subject to swell from North. A useful harbour of refuge but little else.

Warnings

Commercial vessels have right of way and must not be hampered.

Data

As for **San Ciprián** (old harbour)

Lights

Dique Norte, head. Fl. (2) WG 8 sec. 18 m (59 ft), 5 M; W 110°–180°, G 180°–110°.
Dique Este, head. Fl. (3) R 8 sec. 18 m (59 ft), 5 M. Grey tower.
Leading Lights 203°55′ *Front:* Fl. (2) W.6 sec. 25 m 4 M. *Rear:* Oc. W. 35 m 4 M 475 m from front. White towers, red bands.
Leading lights 273°14′ *Front:* Fl. (2) W. 6 sec. 40 m 4 M. *Rear:* Oc. W. 6 sec. 44 m 4 M. White towers, red bands.

Buoys

Cardinal W to NW of **Los Farallones**. Cardinal S to SW of **Los Farallones.**

Approaches

Day or Night to W or S of **Los Farallones** using Leading Lights/Marks on 204° or 273°.

Entrance

Straight forward 20 m depth.

Berths

Small quay in **El Portino** W of the entrance.

Anchorage

In NW corner 3 m sand.

Facilities

Virtually nil for yachtsmen.

60 Ría de Vivero

Population Vivero 14,650 Rating 3-2-3 Position 43°40·8′N 7°36′W

General

This is one of the most E of the **Rías Altas**, and is a little more commercial than its neighbours. It has an easy entrance that can be used in moderate weather and shelter can be found from winds from all directions except N in depths up to 8 m (4 fathoms). The town of **Vivero** offers good shopping, restaurants, bars, etc. and a hotel. There are some splendid sandy beaches nearby.

Warnings

In the approach during heavy weather, the three shoal patches of **El Co** and **Co de Estiero** (in two separate patches) should be avoided as the seas break over them.

Harbour construction work is under way at **Cillero** and **Vivero.**

Winds from SW to NW raise the tide level in the **ría** 0·9–1·5 m (3–5 ft) and winds from S lower it up to 0·8 m (2·5 ft).

Data

Charts

Admiralty Nos. 1755, 78
Spanish Nos. 931, 4082
French Nos. 6383, 5009

Magnetic variation 7°42′W (1984) decreasing by about 5′ each year.

Tidal information

	HW		LW		MHWS	MHWN	MLWS	MLWN
Pointe de Grave	0600 1800	1100 2300	0000 1200	0500 1700	5·4 m 17·6 ft	4·2 m 13·8 ft	0·9 m 3·0 ft	2·1 m 6·8 ft
Ría de Vivero	−0·25	−0·30	−0·25	+0·15	−1·4 m −4·4 ft	−1·3 m −4·4 ft	−0·6 m −2·0 ft	−0·7 m −2·1 ft

Entrance **Ría de Vivero** looking south south east. *Photo: D. Pownall*

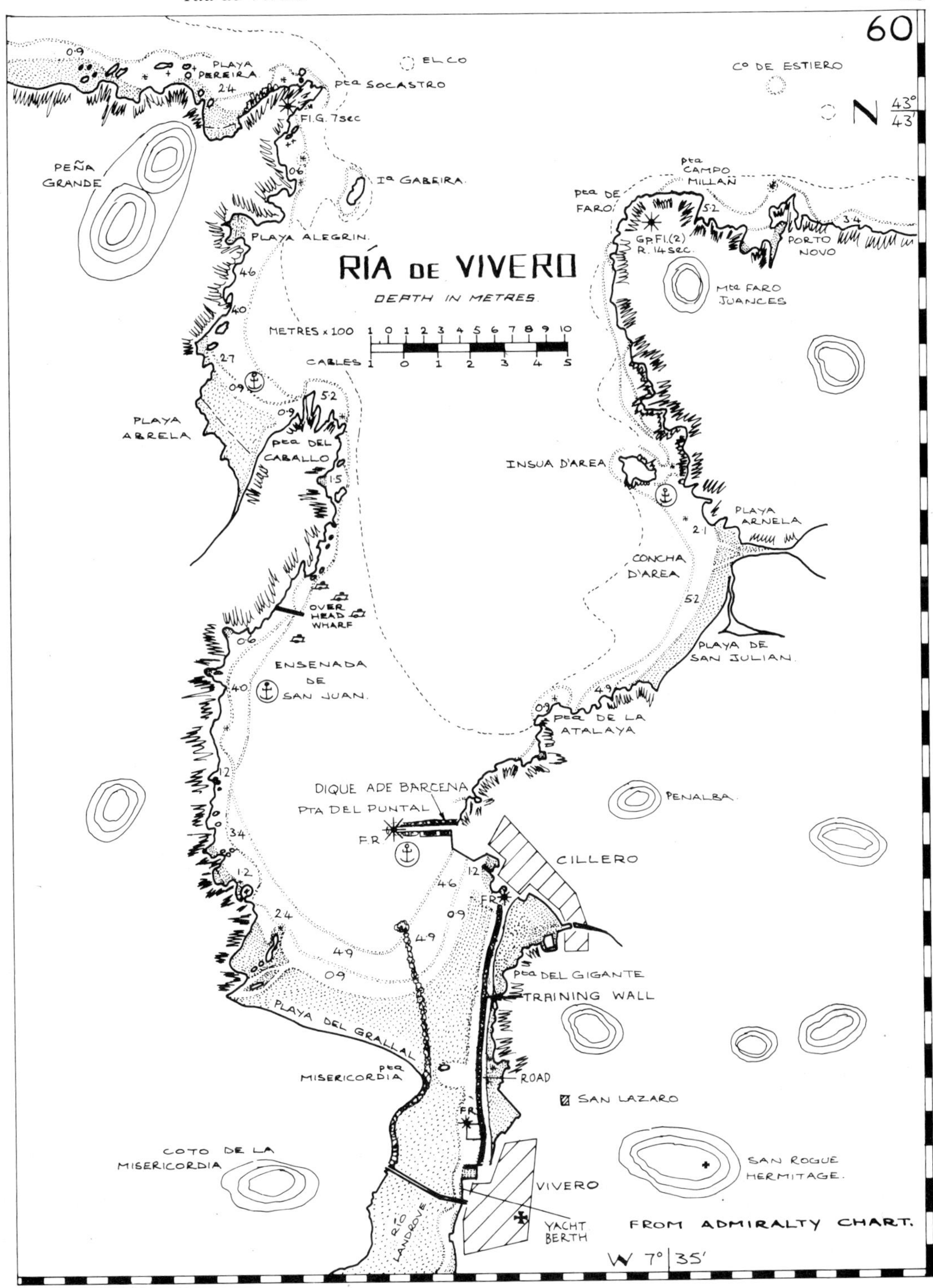
60
RÍA DE VIVERO
DEPTH IN METRES
METRES x 100
CABLES
PLAYA PEREIRA
ELCO
Pta SOCASTRO
Fl.G. 7sec
Iª GABEIRA
PEÑA GRANDE
PLAYA ALEGRIN
Cº DE ESTIERO
N 43° 43'
Pta CAMPO MILLAN
Pta DE FARO
Gp.Fl.(2) R. 14sec.
PORTO NOVO
Mte FARO JUANCES
PLAYA ABRELA
Pta DEL CABALLO
INSUA D'AREA
PLAYA ARNELA
CONCHA D'AREA
OVER HEAD WHARF
PLAYA DE SAN JULIAN
ENSENADA DE SAN JUAN
Pta DE LA ATALAYA
DIQUE ADE BARCENA
PTA DEL PUNTAL
F.R.
PENALBA
CILLERO
Pta DEL GIGANTE
TRAINING WALL
PLAYA DEL GRALLAL
Pta MISERICORDIA
ROAD
SAN LAZARO
COTO DE LA MISERICORDIA
SAN ROQUE HERMITAGE
VIVERO
RIO LANDROVE
YACHT BERTH
FROM ADMIRALTY CHART.
W 7° 35'

Ría de Vivero—Puerto de Cillero looking north west—low water. *Photo: Artes Graficas*

The tidal stream in the river runs up to 3 knots at springs but only reaches 1·5 knots in the middle of the **ría**.

Lights **Punta Atalaya (San Ciprián).** Group Occulting (2+3) White, 15 seconds, 35·7 m (117 ft), 9 miles. Grey conical tower.
Punta Faro. Group Flashing (2) Red, 14 sec., 18 m (59 ft), 6 miles. White tower.
Punta Socastro. Flashing Green 7 sec., 14 m (46 ft), 4 miles. White tower.
Cillero breakwater head. Fixed Red, 2 miles. White mast.
Río Landrove (Cillero). Fixed Red, 2 miles. White concrete pyramid.
Vivero breakwater. Fixed Red, 2 miles. White concrete pyramid.
Isla Coelleira. Flashing White, 3 seonds, 86·9 m (285 ft) 8 miles. Grey conical granite tower and dwelling.
Punta de la Estaca de Bares. Group Flashing (2) White, 7·5 seconds, 99·1 m (325 ft), 25 miles. 8-sided tower and dwelling. Aeromarine light.

Port Radio See page 20.

Approaches

Day The approach to the **ría** is easy. **Punta Socastro**, a low cliff-faced promontory, and the **Isla Gabeira**, backed by **Montaña Pena Grande** on the W side and **Montaña Faro Juances**, a pyramidal mountain on the E side of the **ría**, are easily recognised. The wide, yellow, sandy beaches of **Playa del Grallal** also show up well in the distance, backed by the houses of **Vivero**.

Night The approach to the mouth of the **ría** is also easy using the lights on **Punta de la Estaca de Bares** (Fl. (2) W. 7·5 sec. 25 M.), **Isla Coelleira** (Fl. W. 3 sec. 8 M.) and **Punta Atalaya (San Ciprián)** (Oc. (2+3) W. 15 sec. 9 M.).

Entrance

Day There is no difficulty in entering this **ría**, as there are no outlying dangers and the

Vivero looking south from Cillero. *Photo: D. Pownall*

sea bottom at the sides is smooth sloping mud or sand. The **Puerto de Cillero** at the SE end of the **ría** can be located by a long stone jetty on the **Punta del Puntal** with the houses of **Vivero** appearing beyond it. Round the end of the jetty by ½ cable and the anchorage is ahead.

Night Use **Punta Faro** (Fl. (2) R. 14 sec.) and **Punta Socastro** (Fl.G. 7 sec.) to navigate towards **Cillero** breakwater head (F.R.), which leave 50 m to port and round into the anchorage.

Entrance to Río Landrove and Vivero It is possible to find a drying berth alongside at **Vivero** for boats drawing up to 2·3 m (1·5 fathoms), having first negotiated the river, which virtually dries out at LW. Newcomers are advised to anchor off **Cillero** and walk the 2 miles into **Vivero** at or near LW to observe the trend of the channel and to ascertain if a section of the quay will be free to dry out against, before ascending the **ría** at HW. A training wall has been built along both sides of this river.

Cillero looking east. *Photo: D. Pownall*

The following directions may help.

From a position in deep water approach the small rock just S of **Cillero** with white concrete pyramid, a short pole and red light thereon (rather inconspicuous) on a bearing of 100°. Leave it 18 m (20 yards) to port and direct course for the edge of the cliff to the right of which appears a long vertical scar, a rubbish tip. Keep to this line until 23 m (25 yards) from the foot of the cliffs, when turn S and follow the trend of the rocky training wall with posts on it. Keep this wall 23 m (25 yards) to port and also the quay beyond it.

This ascent is not recommended at night without previous experience.

Anchorages

From winds from E through S to NW

Playa Abrela in up to 10 m (5 fathoms) sand or deeper if required.
Ensenada de San Juan in up to 8 m (4 fathoms) sand, mud and stones.

From winds from NE through S to NW

Concha d'Area in up to 6 m (3 fathoms) sand between **Insua d'Area** and the rock **Congreiras** avoiding fishing hulks.

From all winds

Cillero in up to 4 m (2 fathoms) sand 91 m (100 yards) due W of the old jetty and S of the new quay, allowing sufficient room for fishing boats to warp off from this quay.

Vivero looking south. *Photo: D. Pownall*

Berths

It is possible to berth alongside at **Cillero**, but as the quays are in constant use by large fishing boats it would normally be a temporary measure.

At **Vivero** berth alongside the quay with the bow 9 m (10 yards) below the bridge. Alongside this quay the bottom is of small stones and there are several ring bolts. Neglect the uninitiated advice from the locals and do not moor in the centre of the river opposite the third arch from the W unless drawing under 0·5 m (2 ft). There is a hole there but it is very small and the river runs at a maximum 5 knots. If using it take several strong bow warps onto the bridge itself and anchor the stern down river. Area is noisy due to traffic.

If the wind is from E or NE the yacht will get dirty. The usual mass of spectators will be present at most hours of the day and night.

Formalities

Customs and police will visit the yacht at **Cillero** soon after arrival for the normal data and will also check again at **Vivero**.

Facilities

Water From quay at **Vivero** and at quay at **Cillero**.

Diesel Available at a garage about 366 m (400 yards) S of the berth at **Vivero**; another source about 1 mile N of town. Also from pump on new quay at **Cillero**.

Petrol Available at garages as above.

Shops About six are dotted around **Cillero** and there are many in **Vivero** which can supply most requirements. There is a good market in the square.

Baths A local hotel near the bridge will supply baths.

Beaches **Playa del Grallal**, though huge, does have a few people on it! **Playas Abrela** and **San Julian** are virtually deserted. There are other smaller sandy coves around the coast equally deserted.

Visits Ninth century church and old city gates are worth a visit. A trip by dinghy up the **Río Landrove** through pleasant scenery is worth while.

Fiestas **(Vivero)**
24 June, Feast of St John.
14–20 August, festivities in honour of St Roch and the Assumption.
23–27 August, *Romeria del Naseiro*.

Ría de Vivero—looking SW at high water.

61 Ría del Barquero

Population 300 Rating 2-2-4 Position 43°44·5′N 7°41′W

General

Another beautiful *ría* with an easy approach and entrance. A number of anchorages are available which give excellent shelter in winds from all directions except NE. In addition anchorage is available up the **Río Sor**, which is fully protected from the swell from any direction. Limited shopping facilities exist. There are a number of first class sandy bathing beaches.

The **Puerto del Barquero** up the **Río Sor** can easily be entered near HW and in the absence of any heavy swell from NE.

Warnings

In heavy weather **Punta de la Estaca de Bares** should be given a berth of at least 3 miles and not less than 1 mile in calm weather.

In S to SW gales local intensification of winds up to Force 11 to 12 has been reported off the coast in this area. Ebb stream can be very strong in the river.

Fishermen shoot their nets across the entrance of this *ría* and any small colourful boat should be approached with caution.

Data

Charts

Admiralty Nos. 78, 1755
Spanish Nos. 18A, 931
French Nos. 6383, 5009

Magnetic variation 7°55′W (1984) decreasing by about 5′ each year.

Tidal information

	HW		LW		MHWS	MHWN	MLWS	MLWN
Pointe de Grave	0600 1800	1100 2300	0000 1200	0500 1700	5·4 m 17·6 ft	4·2 m 13·8 ft	0·9 m 3·0 ft	2·1 m 6·8 ft
Ría del Barquero	−0·25	−0·30	−0·25	+0·15	−1·3 m −4·4 ft	−1·3 m −4·4 ft	−0·6 m −2·0 ft	−0·7 m −2·1 ft

Lights

Isla Coelleira. Flashing White, 3 seconds, 86·9 m (285 ft), 8 miles. Grey conical granite tower and dwelling.

Punta del Castro. Group Flashing (2) Red, 6 seconds, 14 m (46 ft), 6 miles. White conical tower. Visible 0°–180°.

Punta de Barra. Flashing Green, 3 seconds, 15 m (49 ft), 6 miles. White conical tower.

Punta de la Estaca de Bares. Group Flashing (2) White, 7·5 seconds, 99·1 m (325 ft), 25 miles. 8-sided tower and dwelling. Fog Siren Morse B (– · · ·), 60 seconds. Aeromarine light. Obscured when more than 291°.

Radio tower. Fixed Red lights, 500 m (1640 ft) E of the lights on **Punta de la Estaca de Bares**.

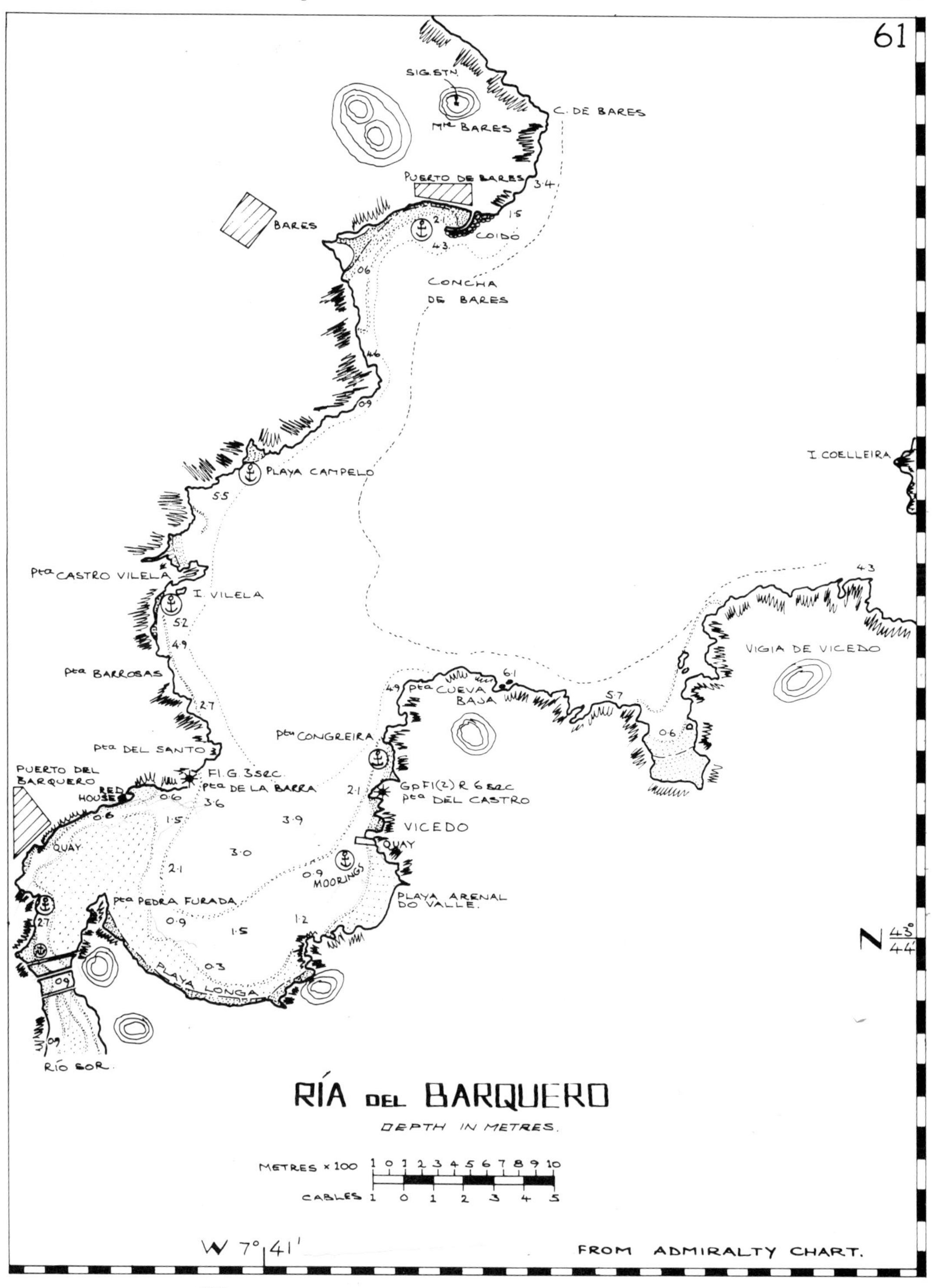
61
SIG. STN.
Mte BARES
C. DE BARES
PUERTO DE BARES
BARES
COIDO
CONCHA DE BARES
PLAYA CAMPELO
I. COELLEIRA
Pta CASTRO VILELA
I. VILELA
Pta BARROSAS
Pta DEL SANTO
PUERTO DEL BARQUERO
RED HOUSE
Fl. G. 3sec.
Pta DE LA BARRA
Pta CONGREIRA
Pta CUEVA BAJA
VIGIA DE VICEDO
Gp Fl (2) R 6 sec
Pta DEL CASTRO
VICEDO
QUAY
MOORINGS
PLAYA ARENAL DO VALLE.
Pta PEDRA FURADA
PLAYA LONGA
RÍO SOR
RÍA DEL BARQUERO
DEPTH IN METRES.
METRES × 100
CABLES
W 7° 41'
N 43° 44'
FROM ADMIRALTY CHART.

Entrance to **Ría del Barquero** looking south east. *Photo: P. White*

Signal and semaphore station A storm signal and semaphore station is located on the top of **Montaña Bares** and is very conspicuous. Vessels can communicate with this station by the International Code of Flag Signals.

Approaches

Day The approach to this **ría** is marked to the NW by **Punta de la Estaca de Bares**, a low rocky headland with a lighthouse on an octagonal tower above a long low building with a red roof, backed by the high **Montaña Bares** with a conspicuous signal station on the top. The NE is **Isla Coelleira**, a high cliff-sided island with a lighthouse in a grey conical tower, with a small building on its highest point to the NE side of the island.

Night The lights on **Isla Coelleira** (Fl. W. 3 sec. 8 M.) and **Punta de la Estaca de Bares** (Fl. (2) W. 7·5 sec. 25 M.), confirmed in the offing in good visibility by **Punta Candelaria** (Fl. (3+1) W. 24 sec. 16 M.) and **Punta Atalaya San Ciprián** (Oc. (2+3) W. 15 sec. 9 M.), enable an easy approach to be made.

Ría del Barquero—Puerto del Barquero looking north—high water. *Photo: Garrabella*

Entrance

As the sides of this **ría** are steep-to the entrance to the **ría** itself presents no problem.

Day *Entrance to Río Sor* Approach the **Punta de la Barra** with its lighthouse just clear of **Punta del Santo** near HW. Steer to leave it 24 m (25 yards) to starboard. Then steer straight for a large red house with white glass-enclosed balcony, which again has to be left 24 m (25 yards) to starboard. Next steer for the end of the jetty at the **Puerto del Barquero**, passing the jetty or berthed fishing boats close to. When clear of the jetty steer for the white railway station on top of a steep embankment. When the promontory halfway to the bridges is in line with the E end of the bridges, steer towards the point of this promonotry to anchor. This entrance would not be practical at night even with previous experience of the river.

Night The lights of **Punta de la Barra** (Fl. G. 3 sec. 6 M.) and **Punta del Castro** (Fl. (2) R. 6 sec. 6 M.) enable navigators to fix their position in the S half of the **ría** and to approach the anchorage.

Anchorages

Sheltered from SE through S and W to N
Puerto de Bares. In up to 6 m (3 fathoms) sand in as shallow water as draft permits due S of the hamlet and clear of local fishing craft.
Playa Campelo. S of cove in sand up to 6 m (3 fathoms).
Isla Vilela. S of island in sand up to 5 m (2·5 fathoms).

Sheltered from winds from N through E and S to SW
Punta del Castro. In up to 5 m (2·5 fathoms) sand NNE of lighthouse.
Playa Arenal de Valle. In 5 m (2·5 fathoms) sand near fishing vessels.

Puerto de Bares—looking west. *Photo: P. White*

341

Ría del Barquero—looking south south west. *Photo: P. White*

Sheltered from all winds
Río Sor in 3 m (1·5 fathoms) sand and mud 23 m (25 yards) E of very small cove off the middle of a small promontory halfway between **Puerto del Barquero** and the road bridges to the S. Use a pair of anchors, one up and one downstream, on short scope so as not to ground at dead LW when lying to the wind, as this anchorage is very limited in area. Land at small cove and walk up the hill to the village of **El Barquero** or along the river to **Puerto de El Barquero**. Another anchorage lies between the road bridge and this promontory.

Berths

Yachts can be moored alongside quay at **Puerto de El Barquero** when not used by fishing boats.

Formalities

Nil.

Facilities

Water Available from springs in the ports of **Bares** and **El Barquero**.
Diesel Available from pump on quay at **El Barquero**.
Petrol Only available from village of **El Barquero** on top of the hill.
Shops A few shops, cafés and restaurants are available on top of the hill in the village of **El Barquero**. A mobile shop visits **Puerto de Bares** at midday with everyday stores. There is a bar in the hamlet.
Beaches The fine sandy beaches of **Bares**, **Playa Longa** and **Xilloy** are virtually deserted. There are also a number of smaller beaches.

Ría del Barquero – anchorage below bridges.

Chapter 6

The coast between Punta de la Estaca de Bares and Punta Herminio

The coast between Punta de la Estaca de Bares and Punta Herminio

62 General description

Galicia and the Rias Altas, Coruña and Lugo

General

This section of the coastline covers the area of the **Rías Altas**, a fjord-like estuary of some considerable size which runs inland between high ranges of hills. There are a number of large promontories between these **rías** and the coast has high steep cliffs. There are no off-lying dangers any distance from this coast and deep water is very close in to the cliffs.

Warnings

The possibility of heavy swell arising from distant storm areas and the problem of the higher mountains and lights being obscured by clouds in NE winds applies also to this stretch of coast.

Very confused seas can be experienced near the coast in storm conditions owing to the reflection of waves from the near-vertical cliffs and disturbances from the uneven bottom. In these conditions the coast and especially any promontories should be given a berth of at least 5 miles.

Exercise Areas. There are submarine exercise and missile firing areas off **El Ferrol**, and a rocket firing range off **Cabo Ortegal**.

Data

Charts

Admiralty No. 1755
Spanish Nos. 40, 929, 930, 931
French No. 3007.

Streams and currents

The tidal stream is up to 2 knots on this coast, NE-going with the flood and SW-going with the ebb. In the offing the current follows the direction of any recent winds that have been blowing, and can be strong. In general the current is SW and becomes the Portugal, and later the Canary Current, further S.

Ensenada de Santa Marta

Cabo Ortegal—Punta de los Aguillones—looking south.

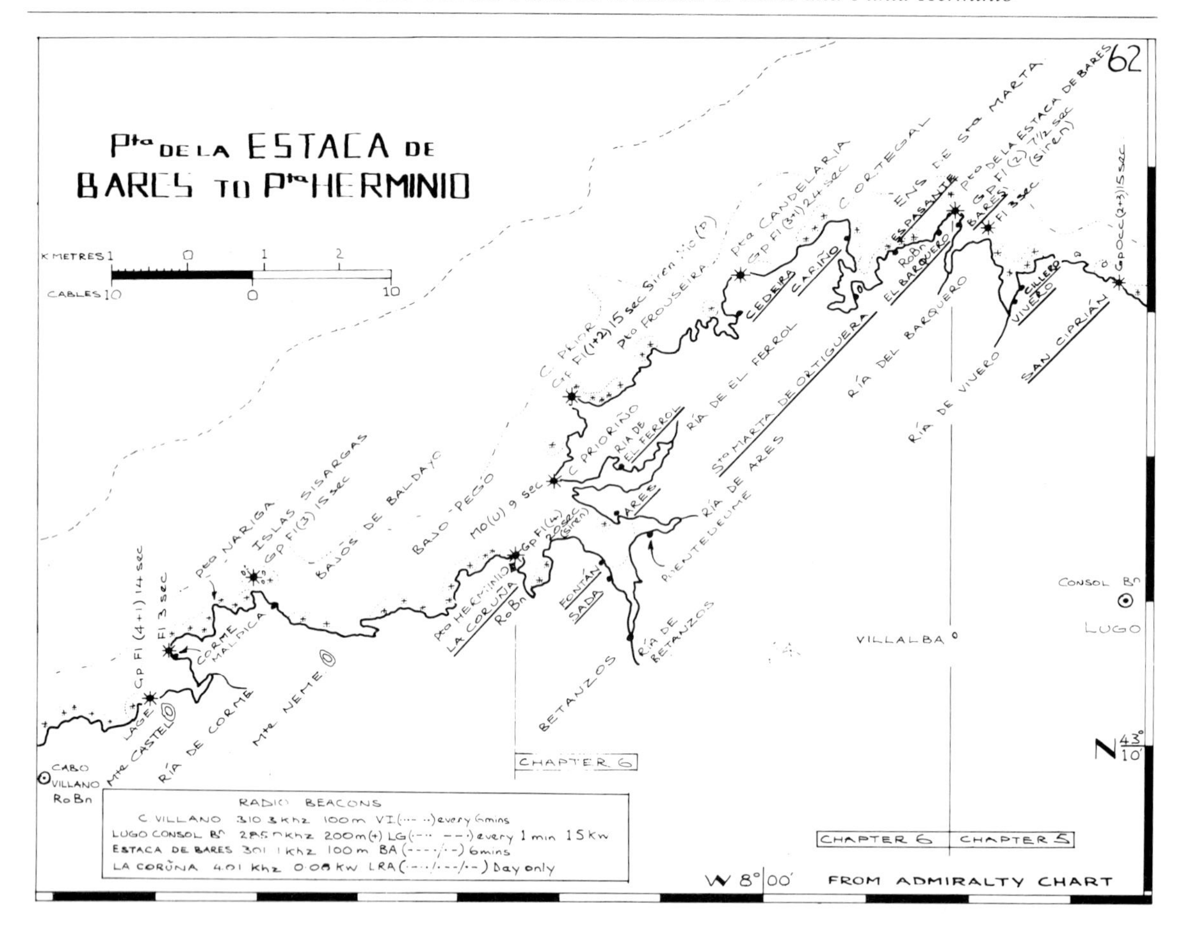

Major lights **Punta de la Estaca de Bares.** Group Flashing (2) White, 7·5 seconds, 99 m (325 ft), 25 miles. 8-sided tower and dwelling. Obscured over 291°. Fog Siren Morse B (– · · ·), 60 seconds. Aeromarine light. Radio beacon.

Punta Candelaria (Cedeira). Group Flashing (3+1) White, 24 seconds, 87·8 m (288 ft), 16 miles. 8-sided tower on brick dwelling.

Cabo Prior. Group Flashing (1+2) White, 15 seconds, 107 m (351 ft), 24 miles. Dark 6-sided brick tower on square dwelling. Fog siren Mo (P).

Cabo Prioriño Chico (El Ferrol). Morse U (· · –) White, 9 seconds, 34·2 m (112 ft), 11 miles. White 8-sided tower on dwelling. Obscured at more than 130°. Radio Beacon.

Punta Herminio (La Coruña), Torre de Hércules. Group Flashing (4) White, 20 seconds, 104 m (341 ft), 23 miles. 8-sided stone tower, lower part square. Siren morse L (· – · ·) 30 seconds. Radio Beacon.

Life saving Line throwing apparatus at **El Ferrol**.

Radio *Radiobeacons* The radiobeacons in this area are listed below; for details of radiobeacons outside this area see page 16.

Cabo Ortegal—looking south west with Punta Candelaria in the distance.

Station	Frequency kHz	Range miles Power	Call sign	Period minutes	Group Remarks
Punta de la Estaca de Bares lighthouse	301·1	100	BA (– · · · / · –)	6	**Lanes** (IA) **Cabo Peñas** (PS)
Lugo (Consol) Beacon 43°14′43″N 07°28′56″W	285	200 1·5 kW	LG (· – · · / – – ·)	1	17·5 sec. continuous note each cycle
La Coruña air beacon 43°22′06″N 08°20′06″W	401	0.08 kW	LRA (· – · · / · – · / · –)	Continuous	Day only

Cabo Prior and lighthouse—looking south east.

Ports, harbours, anchorages and landing places

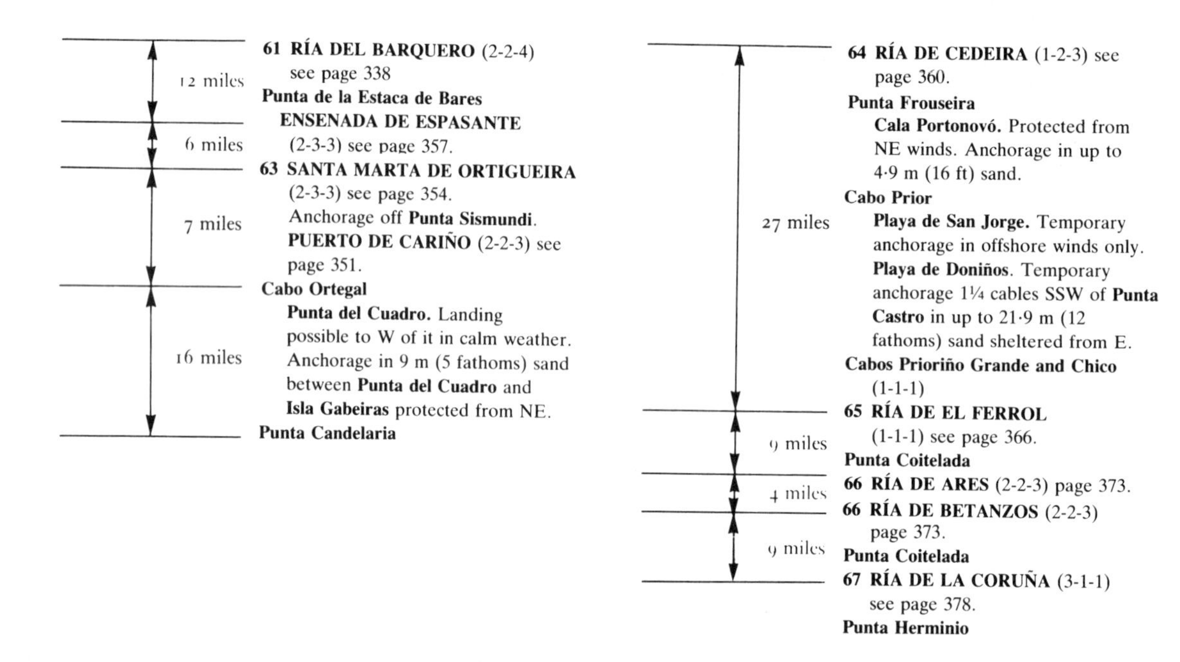

61 RÍA DEL BARQUERO (2-2-4) see page 338
Punta de la Estaca de Bares
ENSENADA DE ESPASANTE (2-3-3) see page 357.
63 SANTA MARTA DE ORTIGUEIRA (2-3-3) see page 354.
Anchorage off **Punta Sismundi**.
PUERTO DE CARIÑO (2-2-3) see page 351.
Cabo Ortegal
Punta del Cuadro. Landing possible to W of it in calm weather. Anchorage in 9 m (5 fathoms) sand between **Punta del Cuadro** and **Isla Gabeiras** protected from NE.
Punta Candelaria

64 RÍA DE CEDEIRA (1-2-3) see page 360.
Punta Frouseira
Cala Portonovó. Protected from NE winds. Anchorage in up to 4·9 m (16 ft) sand.
Cabo Prior
Playa de San Jorge. Temporary anchorage in offshore winds only.
Playa de Doniños. Temporary anchorage 1¼ cables SSW of **Punta Castro** in up to 21·9 m (12 fathoms) sand sheltered from E.
Cabos Prioriño Grande and Chico (1-1-1)
65 RÍA DE EL FERROL (1-1-1) see page 366.
Punta Coitelada
66 RÍA DE ARES (2-2-3) page 373.
66 RÍA DE BETANZOS (2-2-3) page 373.
Punta Coitelada
67 RÍA DE LA CORUÑA (3-1-1) see page 378.
Punta Herminio

Punta Seijo Blanco—Ría de la Coruña looking east—note streaks of white rock.

Cabo Prioriño Chico and lighthouse—looking east.

Puerto de Cariño – looking S–SW.

63 Ensenada de Santa Marta

General

This huge bay on the extreme NW corner of Spain has three attractive places to visit. The harbour of **Cariño**, the completely enclosed **Ría de Santa Marta** with the port of **Santa Marta de Ortigueira** in it, and the anchorage of **Ensenada de Espasante**.

Warnings

The estuary should not be entered in severe storm conditions, according to the *Bay of Biscay Pilot*, but the locals say that this is not correct. However, the **Ensenada** is shallow, 37 m (20 fathoms) shallowing to about 9·1 m (5 fathoms) in the middle of the bay, so heavy seas could be expected in storm conditions.

Data

Charts

Admiralty No. 1755
Spanish Nos 931, 4084
French No. 5009

Magnetic variation 7°47′ W (1984) decreasing by about 5′ each year.

Tidal information

	HW		LW		MHWS	MHWN	MLWS	MLWN
Pointe de Grave	0600 1800	1100 2300	0000 1200	0500 1700	5·4 m 17·6 ft	4·2 m 13·8 ft	0·9 m 3·0 ft	2·1 m 6·8 ft
Ría de S.M. de Ortigueira	+0·20	+0·20	+0·25	+1·05	−1·7 m −5·6 ft	−1·5 m −5·0 ft	−0·5 m −1·7 ft	−0·8 m −2·4 ft

The tidal streams across the mouth of the bay normally run ENE with the flood and WSW with the ebb and are modified by the prevailing wind in the offing. These streams can be up to 3 knots off **Cabo Ortegal** and **Punta de la Estaca de Bares**.

Lights

Punta de la Estaca de Bares. Group Flashing (2) White, 7·5 seconds, 99 m (325 ft), 25 miles. 8-sided tower and dwelling. Aeromarine light. Obscured at more than 291°. Fog Siren Morse B (– · · ·), 60 seconds. Fixed Red lights on radio tower 500 m (1640 ft) E of lights on **Punta.** Radio beacon.
Puerto de Cariño breakwater head. Flashing Green, 2 seconds, 12 m (39 ft), 4 miles. White round tower.
Punta Candelaria. Group Flashing (3+1) White, 24 seconds, 87·8 m (288 ft), 16 miles. 8-sided tower on brick building.

Signal stations A storm warning and signal station is situated at the top of **Montaña Bares**. This station can be communicated with by means of the International Code of Flag Signals.

Approach

Day **Cabo Ortegal**, W of the **Ensenada**, and **Punta de la Bares** to the E are easily located. **Los Aguillones**, a line of sharp-pointed rocks off **Ortegal**, are steep-to, and provided the seas are not too large can be rounded at 2 cables distance. **Punta de la Estaca de Bares** should always be rounded by at least 1 mile, and over 3 miles in heavy sea conditions.

Night The lights of **Punta Candelaria** (Fl. (3+1) W. 24 sec. 16 M.) and **Punta de la estaca de Bares** (Fl. (2) W. 7·5 sec. 35 M.) offer some assistance to the navigator approaching the **Ensenada**, but do not provide a sharp enough cut for accurate location. Under conditions of poor visibility entrance is not advised.

Cariño

Population approximately 3,500 Rating 2-2-3 Position 43°44·2′N 7°52′W

See first **Ensenada de Santa Marta**, page 350.

General

A large, active fishing port in the **Ensenada de Santa Marta** behind **Cabo Ortegal**, which can be entered under all conditions except NE gales. The lights are of low power, but entrance by night should normally be possible. Anchorage up to 6 m (3 fathoms) is available. Everyday requirements are available from the village, where there are many shops, and there are several good sandy beaches.

Warnings

The reef and drying rocks to the SE about 5 cables from the jetty should be located before approaching the entrance from the E. This is not necessary when approaching from the NE. The local fishing vessels swing to a pair of anchors on fairly short scope. New work on quays and breakwater in progress (1983).

Data

See **Ensenada de Santa Marta**, page 350.

Approaches

Day Having entered the **Ensenada de Santa Marta** navigate towards a point on the coast 7 cables SSE of **Punta de los Aguillones** where the high hinterland behind **Cabo Ortegal** falls down to sea level and there is the mouth of a wide valley. The houses around **Cariño** will be observed on close approach and it can be positively identified by a high, conspicuous, church tower.

Night Under conditions of good visibility follow the W side of the **Ensenada** S for 5 cables until the (Fl.G., 2 sec.) light on the S end of the breakwater is observed and also the lights of the higher houses in the village.

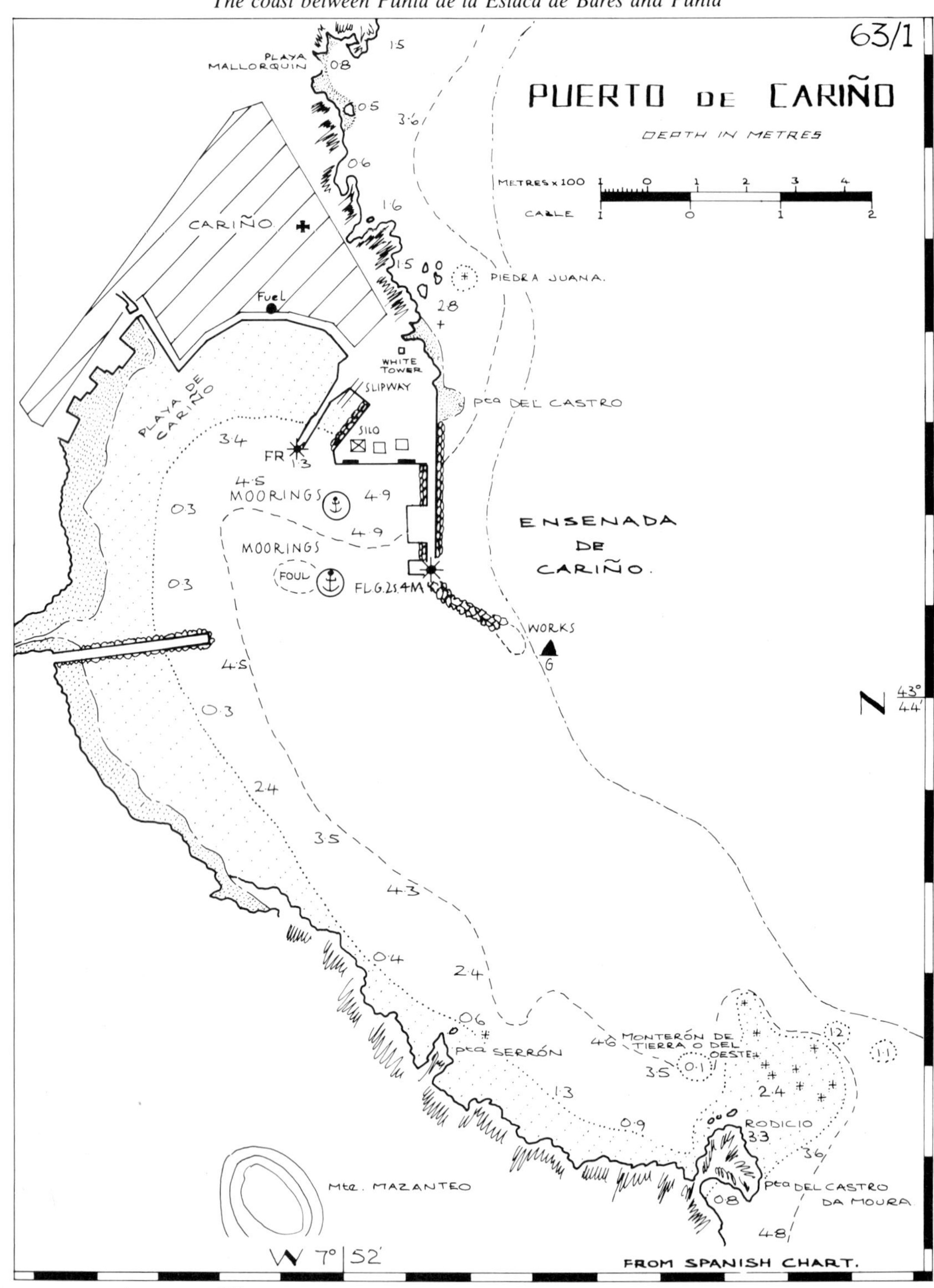
63/1
PUERTO DE CARIÑO
DEPTH IN METRES
METRES x 100
CABLE
PLAYA MALLORQUIN
CARIÑO
Fuel
PIEDRA JUANA
WHITE TOWER
SLIPWAY
SILO
Pta DEL CASTRO
PLAYA DE CARIÑO
FR
MOORINGS
MOORINGS
FOUL
FLG.2s.4M
ENSENADA DE CARIÑO
WORKS
G
MONTERÓN DE TIERRA O DEL OESTE
Pta SERRÓN
RODICIO
Pta DEL CASTRO DA MOURA
Mte. MAZANTEO
W 7° 52'
N 43° 44'
FROM SPANISH CHART.

Entrance

Day and night Round the S end of the jetty at 46 m (50 yards) and proceed to the anchorage to the NW. There is a (F.R.) light on the end of the landing jetty and four street lights on the quay. A green buoy is located off the end of the new breakwater.

Anchorage

In 5–6 m (2·5–3 fathoms) of muddy sand. Anchor between the end of the jetty and the nearest fishing boat or in the case of heavy weather farther up the harbour between the jetty and the fishing boats. Leave room for fishing boats to proceed to the quay and to turn around there. Use a tripping line.

Berths

A temporary berth may be had at the quay if not required by fishing boats.

Formalities

The *Capitan del Puerto* may come out in a fishing boat and request the normal details. He sometimes wants to see passports. His office is in the **Cofredia de Pescadores**, next to the chandlery shop, and is the local centre of social activity.

Facilities

Water	From hose on quay or a tap in the village.
Diesel	From pump on quay.
Petrol	From pump near *Capitan del Puerto*'s house about 92 m (100 yards) beyond his office.
Shops	All normal requirements are available at many shops. These are to be found in the village in the direction of the church.

Puerto de Cariño—high water—looking north west. New building and quays not shown.

Restaurants, bars	Several available.
Chandlery	A shop near the quay has fair supplies of heavy chandlery.
Beaches	The sandy beach S of the harbour is normally deserted and provides good bathing.
Visits	If not proceeding up the **Ría de Santa Marta** by boat, a trip in a bus or taxi to **Santa Marta de Ortigueira** is worth while. It is a beautiful drive, but if going by bus expect a long wait at **Mera**, where you have to change buses.

Ría de Santa Marta and Santa Marta de Ortigueira

Population 16,000 Rating 2-3-3 Position 43°41′N 8° 51′W

General

One of the most beautiful, deserted and unspoilt *rías* on the coast. The entrance to the **ría**, which is at the S end of the **Ensenada** of the same name, is across a bar which frequently changes and a pilot is essential. **Ortigueira** is an attractive little town with good facilities for shopping, restaurants, hotels etc. Anchorages or berths alongside are available in 4 m (2 fathoms). There are miles of deserted sandy beaches near the entrance to the **ría**, which being virtually landlocked is not subject to swell.

Warnings

At half tides springs the current can reach 6 knots in the narrows at the entrance to the **ría**. The bar breaks in any swell from N.

Data

See **Ensenada de Santa Marta** page 350.

Yacht berths

Puerto de Santa Marta de Ortigueira—high water. *Photo: Cusham*

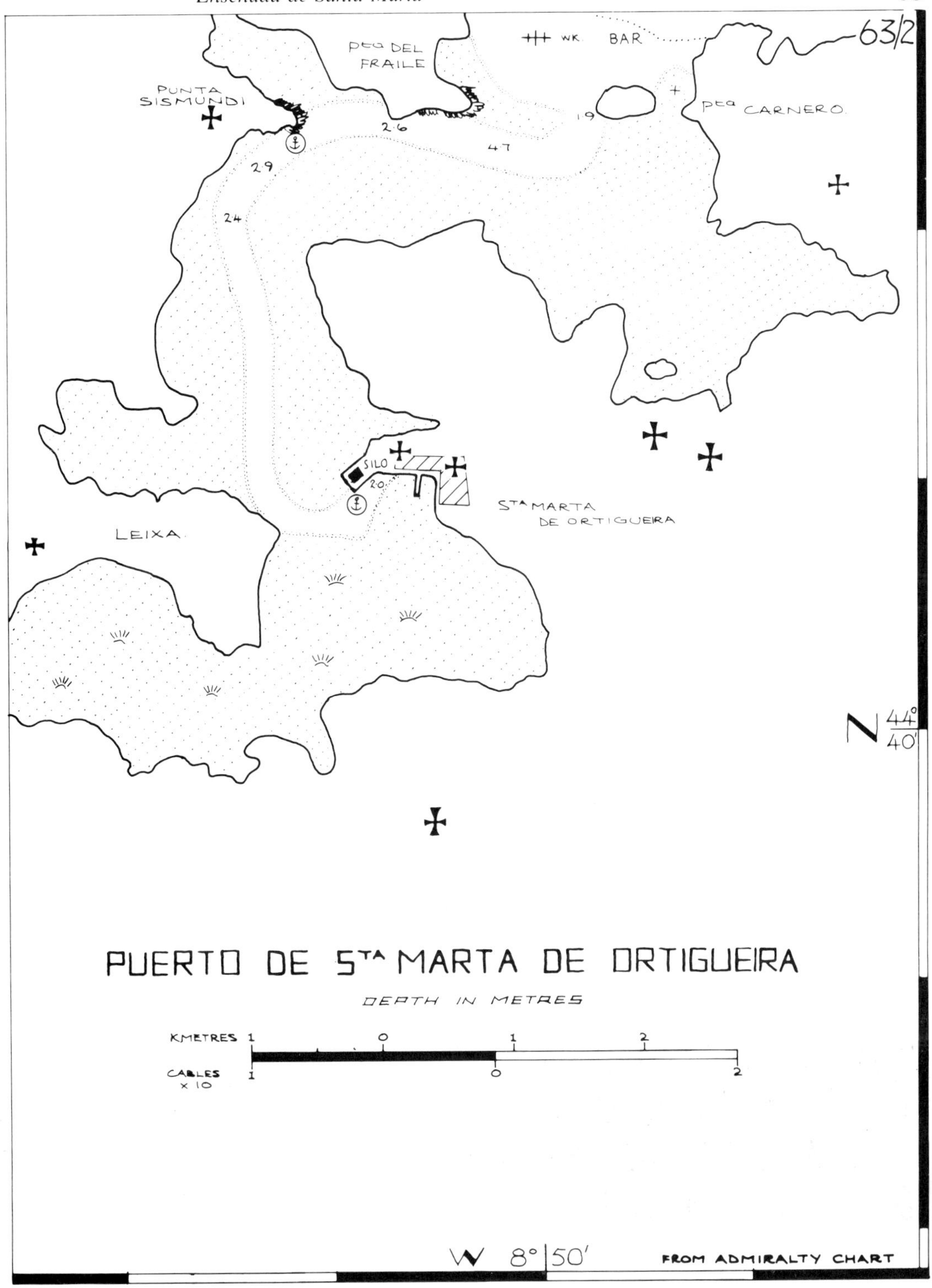
63/2
Pta DEL FRAILE
WK. BAR
PUNTA SISMUNDI
Pta CARNERO
2·6
19
47
29
24
SILO
20
STA MARTA DE ORTIGUEIRA
LEIXA
N 44° 40'
PUERTO DE STA MARTA DE ORTIGUEIRA
DEPTH IN METRES
KMETRES 1 0 1 2
CABLES x 10 1 0 2
W 8° 50'
FROM ADMIRALTY CHART

Approach and entrance

A pilot (**El Pratico**) must be engaged (the cost is not high and well worth while). Apply to the *Capitan del Puerto* at **Cariño** and one will come out from **Ortigueira** by bus. Entrance by night is not possible.

Anchorage

Off **Punta Sismundi**, which lies on the E side of the **ría** 7 cables SW of **Punta del Fraile**, in up to 14 m (2 fathoms) sandy mud with the **Punta** SE 6 cables. The pilot will show the best location.

Off the quay at **Ortigueira** 6 m (3 fathoms) mud.

Berths

Berths alongside the quay at **Ortigueira** are available in 4 m (2 fathoms) mud, between the extreme W corner of the quay and the first set of steps.

A possible berth is in a small basin at **Sismundi**.

Formalities

Nil.

Facilities

Water	Available from a tap at bar on quay.
Diesel and petrol	Available from garage in town.
Shops	½ mile away in town and cover most requirements.
Fiestas	A famous fiesta is held here from 29 July to 2 August in honour of Santa Marta.

Ría de Santa Marta de Ortigueira—looking south—high water.

Ensenada de Espasante

Population 940 Rating 2-3-4 Position 43°43·8′N 7°48·8′W

General

A little village on the E side of the **Ensenada de Santa Marta**, which has an anchorage protected from all winds except strong NW and W winds in depths up to 6 m (3 fathoms) sand. Easy entrance and approach.

Warnings

The group of drying rocks, **Piedras Liseiras**, off **Punta Espasante**, which protects this anchorage from the NW, should be given a berth of at least 2 cables when approaching the anchorage.

Data

See **Ensenada de Santa Marta** page 350.

Approach and entrance

Keep at least 1 mile W of **Punta de Espasante**, which is a steep headland with a watchtower on the summit, until the drying rocks of **Piedras Liseiras** are located when the anchorage may be closed, keeping at least 2 cables from the rocks.

Anchorage

In the centre of the sandy part of the bay up to 6 m (3 fathoms) sand.

Facilities

Normal provisions are available in the village.

Punta Sismundi

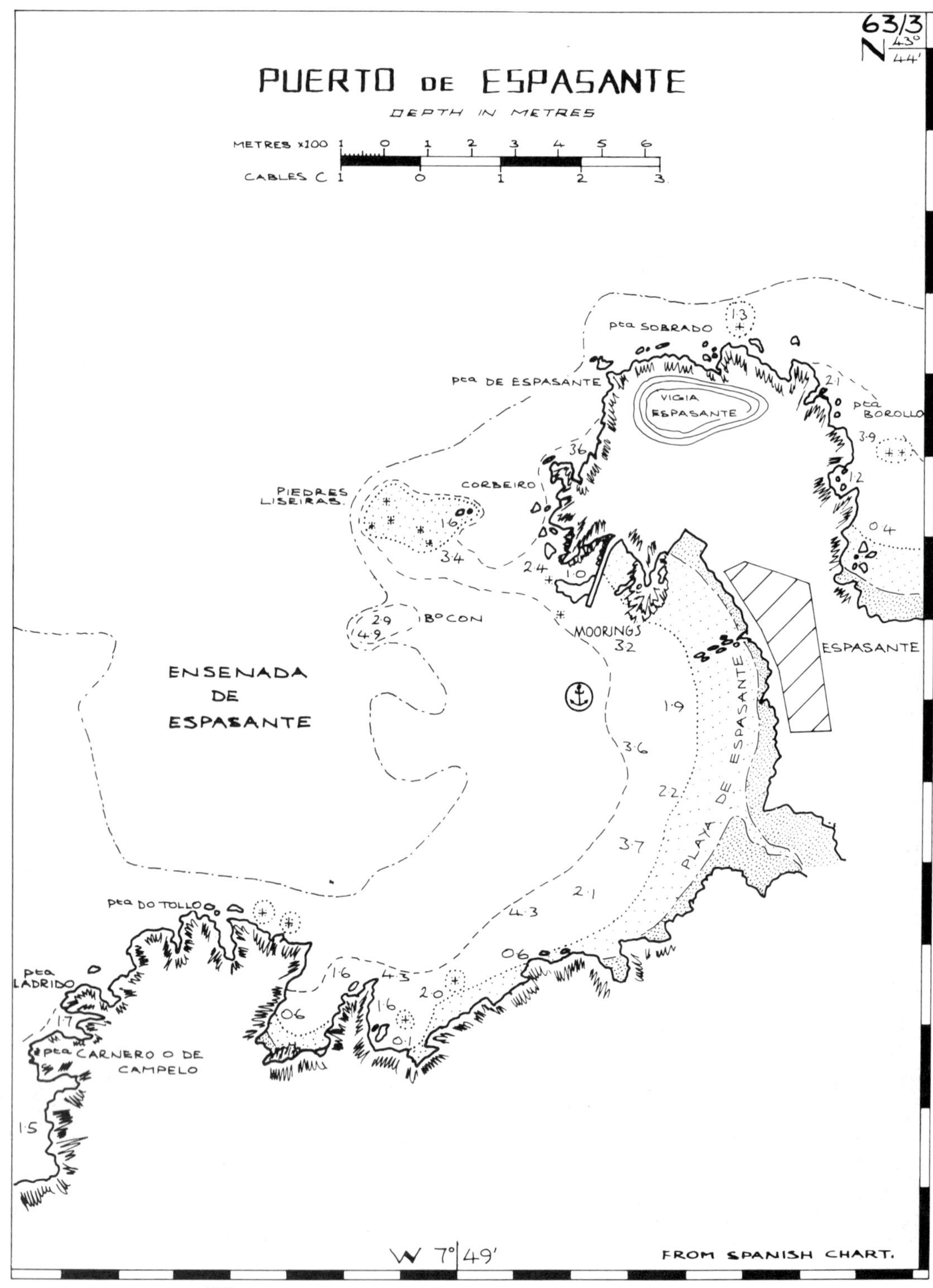

63/3
N 43° 44'
PUERTO DE ESPASANTE
DEPTH IN METRES
METRES x100 1 0 1 2 3 4 5 6
CABLES C 1 0 1 2 3
Pta SOBRADO
Pta DE ESPASANTE
VIGIA ESPASANTE
Pta BOROLLO
PIEDRES LISEIRAS
CORBEIRO
Bº CON
MOORINGS
ESPASANTE
ENSENADA DE ESPASANTE
PLAYA DE ESPASANTE
Pta DO TOLLO
Pta LADRIDO
Pta CARNERO O DE CAMPELO
W 7° 49'
FROM SPANISH CHART.

Ensenada de Santa Marta—Piedras Meas—looking south.

Ensenada de Santa Marta—anchorage at **Espasante**.

64 Ría de Cedeira

Population 3,000 Rating 1-2-3 Position 43°39·4′N 8°4′W

General

An active fishing port in a most attractive **ría**, tucked away behind **Punta Candelaria**. Easy approach and entrance under all conditions by day and night, except perhaps in a SW gale. Good anchorage in up to 6 m (3 fathoms) sand protected from all winds with good deserted sandy bathing beaches and adequate shops, bars, restaurants etc. A new breakwater has been built.

Warnings

The group of covered rocks off **Punta Chirlateira** should be avoided by visitors. A new breakwater extends south from **Punta del Castillo** (Fl. (4) R. 13 sec.).

The small group of rocks in the centre of the **ría**, the **Piedras de Medio Mar**, are either visible above water or can be located by breaking water. These can be avoided by keeping close to **Punta del Castillo**. A tall white beacon tower on **Punta de la Atalaya** is not shown on the Admiralty charts.

Data

Charts

Admiralty Nos. 1755, 78
Spanish No. 930
French Nos. 6383, 3007

Magnetic variation 8°32′W (1984) decreasing by about 5′ each year.

Tidal information

	HW		LW		MHWS	MHWN	MLWS	MLWN
Pointe de Grave	0600 1800	1100 2300	0000 1200	0500 1700	5·4 m 17·6 ft	4·2 m 13·8 ft	0·9 m 3·0 ft	2·1 m 6·8 ft
Ría de Cedeira	−0·15	−0·10	−0·15	+0·55	−1·6 m −5·3 ft	−1·4 m −4·8 ft	−0·5 m −1·6 ft	−0·7 m −2·4 ft

Lights

Punta Candelaria. Group Flashing (3+1) White, 24 seconds, 87·8 m (288 ft), 16 miles. 8-sided tower on brick building.
Punta Promontoiro. Group Occulting (1+3) White, 16 seconds, 24·4 m (80 ft), 11 miles. White 6-sided tower.
Cabo Prior. Group Flashing (2+1) W. 15 sec. 107 m (351 ft) 25 M. Square-sided brick tower.
Breakwater head. Group Flashing (4) Red 13 seconds.

Port Radio See page 20.

Approaches

Day

From N Round **Punta Candelaria**, which is a large promontory running down from a high mountain of the same name. The promontory has a conspicuous white octagonal lighthouse on a brick building halfway down the face of the point. Keeping about 2 cables off the shore, follow it around towards the S, when the entrance of the **ría** will open up.

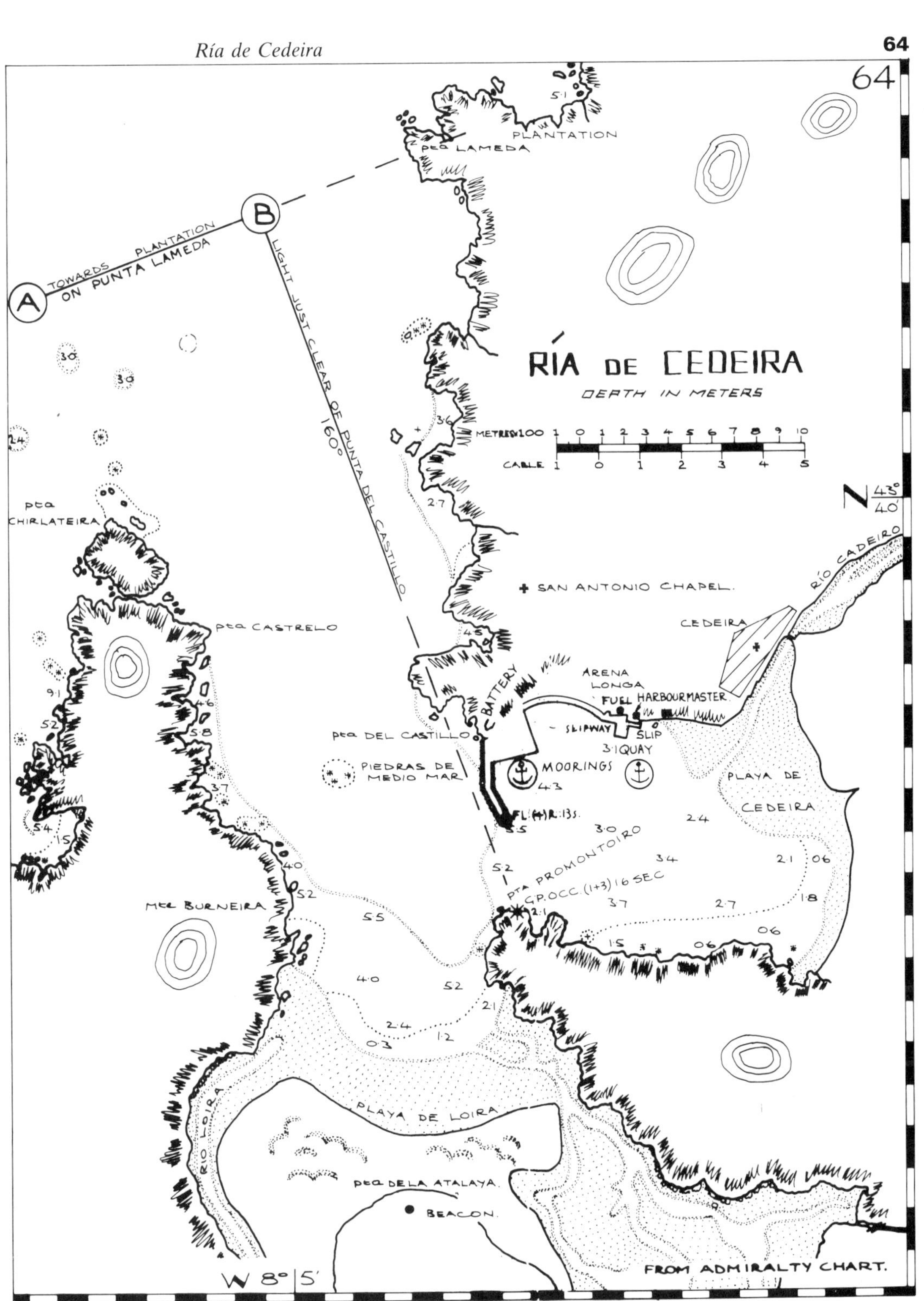
64
RÍA DE CEDEIRA
DEPTH IN METERS
PLANTATION
pta LAMEDA
TOWARDS PLANTATION ON PUNTA LAMEDA
LIGHT JUST CLEAR OF PUNTA DEL CASTILLO 160°
pta CHIRLATEIRA
pta CASTRELO
SAN ANTONIO CHAPEL
CEDEIRA
RÍO CADEIRO
ARENA LONGA
FUEL
HARBOURMASTER
SLIPWAY
SLIP
3·1 QUAY
BATTERY
pta DEL CASTILLO
PIEDRAS DE MEDIO MAR
MOORINGS
FL.(4)R.13s.
PLAYA DE CEDEIRA
pta PROMONTOIRO
GP.OCC.(1+3) 16 SEC
Mte BURNEIRA
PLAYA DE LOIRA
RIO LOIRA
pta DE LA ATALAYA
BEACON
FROM ADMIRALTY CHART.
W 8° 5'
43° 40'
CABLE

Ría de Cedeira—Punta Lameda yellow scar and plantations—Line Ⓐ—070°.

From S Round **Cabo Prior**, a large promontory with a white lighthouse and buildings near the top of the hill, and proceed on a course 055° towards the seaward point of **Punta Candelaria**. When 2 miles from this point **Punta Chirlateira** should be identified. Care should be taken, as this point is not unlike the two just S of it. Close **Punta Candelaria** about 2 miles S of the actual NW point where there is a valley, a few houses and the cliff face is scarred by a landslide. A rocky pimple is on the skyline. Just S of this there are wood plantations on **Punta Lameda**. Direct course towards this **Punta** on 070°, Line Ⓐ. This course clears all dangers off **Punta Chirlateira**. When 4 cables from the cliff face turn S and proceed on 160°, Line Ⓑ, into the **ría**, with the lighthouse on **Punta Promontoiro** just clear of **Punta del Castillo**.

Night Close **Punta Candelaria** (Fl. (3+1) W. 24 sec. 16 M.) and navigate to a position where this light bears 80°, distance 3 miles, when the light of **Punta Promontoiro**

Ría de Cadeira—entrance—looking south—half tide.

Ría de Cedeira – looking N–NE–E from head of new breakwater.

(Oc. (1+3) W. 16 sec. 11 M.) will be seen. Keeping this light just clear of **Punta del Castillo** on 160°, proceed up the **ría**, Line Ⓑ .

Entrance

Day Having closed the E side of the **ría** near **Punta del Castillo** to 2 cables, follow it S. A white beacon tower will be observed on **Punta de la Atalaya** on a bearing which should not exceed 175°, to clear the isolated rocks **Piedras de Medio Mar** which are in the centre of the **ría**. Round **Punta del Castillo**, a small wooded point with some buildings built into the foot, and also a small sandy cove. Then round the head of the breakwater and the anchorage opens up to the E.

Night Having identified the light of **Punta Promontoiro** (Oc. (1+3) W. 16 sec. 11 M.) close in on 160°. This light just clears **Punta del Castillo** on this bearing and the dangers off **Punta Chirlateira** and the rocks in the centre of the **ría**. When past **Punta del Castillo** round the head of the breakwater (Fl. (4) R. 13 sec), the lights around the jetty will appear to the E, and the anchorage may be approached.

Ría de Cedeira—from Punta Promontoiro lighthouse, looking north, high water.

Anchorage

Yachts may anchor anywhere, provided they do not foul the many fishing boats, which lie to a pair of anchors, or obstruct the approach to the quay. It is recommended that visitors anchor about 400 m to SE of **Punta del Castillo** in 3 m (1·5 fathoms) sand or 1 cable S of the jetty, also in 3 m (1·5 fathoms) sand and weed, where the holding is not very good.

Landing may be made on a slip E of the jetty, but haul the dinghy well up as large scends are frequent.

Berths

A temporary berth on the E side of the jetty may be possible, if not required for commercial purposes, but see the *Capitan del Puerto* first. His office is on the quay. There are drying berths at the town quay.

Formalities

A visit from the *Capitan del Puerto* with the usual form of questions is to be expected soon after arrival, but have fenders ready as the local fishing boat in which he visits yachts is without any.

Facilities

Water Obtainable from a tap behind the fish market on the quay, also at a tap on the bridge.

Diesel From a pump at the head of the jetty.

Petrol From a pump about 137 m (150 yards) SE of the bridge.

Repairs Good marine engineers.

Shops All normal requirements for provisions are available in the village, where there are a number of shops, restaurants, cafés and bars.

New breakwater not shown.

Beaches The **Playas de Cedeira** and **de Loira** are large deserted stretches of sand. The latter can be reached by taking a dinghy up **Río Loira**, a worthwhile trip if the seas are not breaking at its mouth. The nearby **Arena Longa** is usually deserted but smaller.

Visits Visits to **La Concepción** castle, the church of **Nuestra Señora Maria del Mar**, the chapel **San Antonio** and **San Andres de Tuxeido** are worthwhile.

Fiestas 14–20 August, festivities in honour of Nuestra Señora Maria del Mar and St Roch.

Ría de Cedeira—looking north west.

65 Ría de El Ferrol

Population 85,000 Rating 1-1-1 Position 43°28·7′N 8°14·7′W

General

Next to **La Coruña**, this is the largest port on the NW corner of Spain. The approach is easy though the entrance is narrow but it can be undertaken in any weather. Good berths and anchorages are available. Shopping facilities are excellent. The town is a bright, well laid out place, and the **ría** attractive and clean.

Warnings

In bad visibility and heavy weather positive identification of **Cabos Prioriño Grande** and **Chico** should be made before attempting an entrance.

Seas break on **Bajo Muela** off **Punta del Segaño** and No. 1 buoy, green (Fl.G. 4 sec) should always be rounded on the N side.

No anchorage is permitted within 2 cables of white pyramid dolphin (Fl. W. 2 sec.) off **Punta Leiras** inside the **ría**.

At night watch out for small boats which do not carry lights while fishing.

Data

Charts

Admiralty Nos. 1755, 79, 80
Spanish Nos. 4122, 4123, 929, 9290
French Nos. 5546, 3007, 6665

Magnetic variation 8°13′W (1984) decreasing by about 5′ each year.

Tidal information

	HW		LW		MHWS	MHWN	MLWS	MLWN
Pointe de Grave	0600 1800	1100 2300	0000 1200	0500 1700	5·4 m 17·6 ft	4·2 m 13·8 ft	0·9 m 3·0 ft	2·1 m 6·8 ft
El Ferrol	−0·55	−0·45	−0·55	−0·15	−1·6 m −5·0 ft	−1·4 m −4·5 ft	−0·5 m −1·5 ft	−0·8 m −2·4 ft

Ría de El Ferrol—Batería de San Cristóbal.

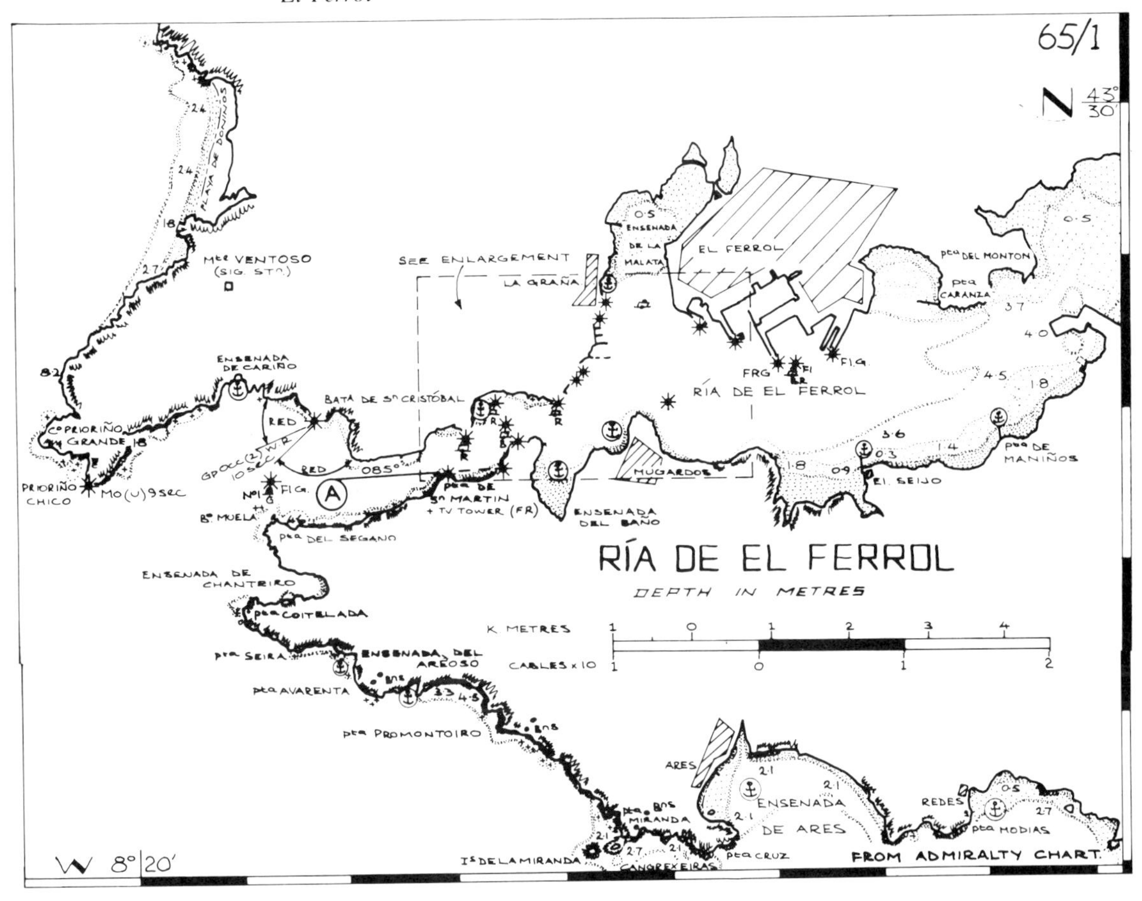

Tidal streams up to 2·5 knots may be experienced in the entrance to this **ría**.

Lights **Cabo Prior.** Group Flashing (1+2) White, 15 seconds, 107 m (351 ft), 24 miles. Dark 6-sided tower with square dwelling. Fog siren Mo(P) 25 seconds.

Cabo Prioriño Chico. Morse U (· · –) White, 9 seconds, 34·1 m (112 ft), 11 miles. White 8-sided tower on dwelling. Obscured over 130°. Radio Beacon.

Batería de San Cristóbal. Group Occulting (2) Red, White sectors, 10 seconds, 19·2 m (63 ft), 4 miles. Low round white tower. White 048°–068°, Red 068°–048°.

Castillo de La Palma. Group Occulting (1+2) White, 7 seconds, 9·1 m (30 ft), 7 miles. Conical granite tower on square dwelling.

Punta de San Martin leading lights 084·5° Line Ⓐ.

Front Fl.R. 1·5 sec 10 m (33 ft), 4 M. White square beacon tower. F.R. on radio tower 0·3M. to SW.

Rear Occulting Red, 4 seconds, 4 miles. White square tower.

Muelle de Concepción Arenal. Group Flashing (4) Red, 8 seconds, 6 m (19 ft), 4 miles. White truncated conical tower.

Dolphin (forbidden area). Flashing White, 2 seconds. White pyramid.

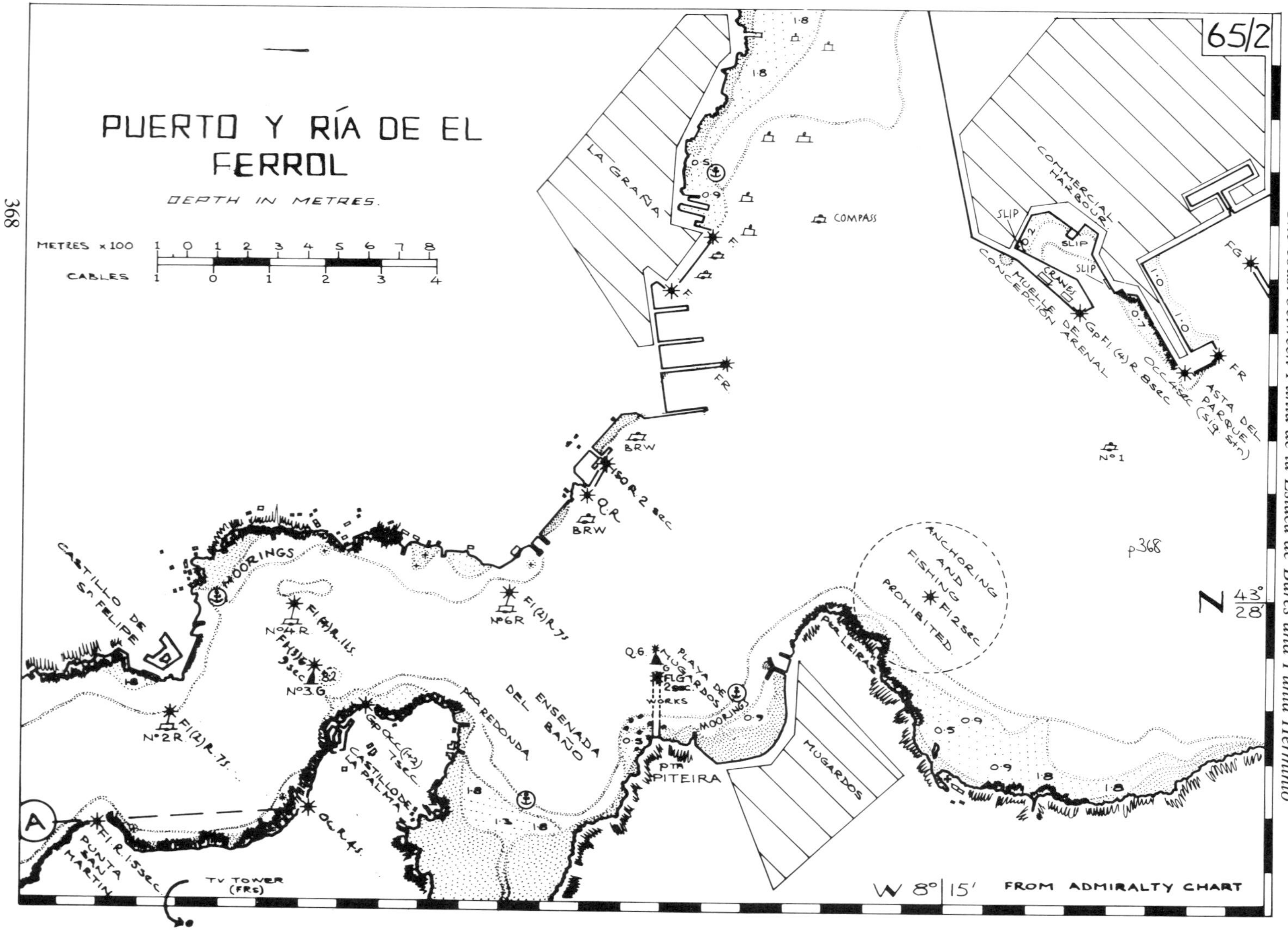
65/2
PUERTO Y RÍA DE EL FERROL
DEPTH IN METRES.
METRES x100
CABLES
COMMERCIAL HARBOUR
SLIP
CRANES
MUELLE DE CONCEPCIÓN ARENAL
ASTA DEL PARQUE
LA GRAÑA
COMPASS
ANCHORING AND FISHING PROHIBITED
MUGARDOS
PLAYA DE MUGARDOS
MOORINGS
WORKS
Pta PITEIRA
Pta LEIRAS
ENSENADA DEL BAÑO
Pta REDONDA
CASTILLO DE LA PALMA
CASTILLO DE Sn FELIPE
PUNTA SAN MARTIN
TV TOWER (FRS)
FROM ADMIRALTY CHART

Radio **La Coruña** air radiobeacon at 43°22′06″N 8°20′W operates continuously by day on 401 kHz, 0·08 kW, call sign LRA (· – · · / · – · / · –).

Port Radio See page 20.

Signal station A signal station is situated on top of **Monte Ventoso** above **Cabo Prioriño Chico**. Messages may be passed by International Code of Flag Signals.

Harbour dues A small charge is made.

Approach

Day

From N Identify and round at 2 cables **Cabos Prioriño Grande** and **Chico**, a pair of rocky headlands similar in outline to **Cabo Prior** but much smaller. A square white building with a squat lighthouse with a metal latticework tower in front stands on **Chico**. The narrow entrance to the **ría** now opens up to the E and the very wide entrance to the **Rías de Betanzos** and **Ares** should be visible S of **Puntas del Segano** and **Coitelada**, two rocky headlands with a cove between.

Proceed on a course of 085° towards No. 1 buoy conical, Green radar reflector (Fl.G. 4·5 sec.) and identify to NE the small and rather inconspicuous low white lighthouse tower at the **Batería de San Cristóbal**.

From S and W Identify and round **Punta Herminio**, backed by the low skyscrapers of the city of **La Coruña**. The wide entrance to **Rías de la Coruña** and **Betanzos/Ares**, is divided by **Punta del Seijo Blanco**, a low rocky headland with white streaks of rock running downwards, which should be easy to identify. Proceed towards the entrance to **El Ferrol**, which appears as a shallow indentation on the coast between the headlands **Cabos Prioriño Grande** and **Chico** and **Puntas del Segano** and **Coitelada**. The signal station on **Monte Ventoso**, on the top of the headland above the **Cabos Prioriño**, is conspicuous. The lighthouses at **Cabo Prioriño Chico** (see above) and **Batería de San Cristóbal** (see above) should be seen and when about halfway between **Cabo Prioriño Chico** and **Puntal del Segano** the **ría** entrance will open up.

Ría de El Ferrol—entrance—note yacht just to left of leading marks.

Ría de El Ferrol—leading marks—line Ⓐ.

Night Using the lights of **Torre de Hércules** (Fl. (4) W. 20 sec. 23 M.) and **Cabo Prioriño Chico** (Morse U (· · –) W. 9 sec. 11 M.), confirmed by the rear light on **Punta Mera** (Oc. (2) W. 10 sec. 8 M.), navigate towards the entrance when the white sector of the light on **Batería de San Cristóbal** (Oc. (2) R.W. 10 sec. 4 M.) and the leading lights on **Punta de San Martin** (*Front: Fl.R. 1·5 sec. 4 ;M. Rear:* Oc. R. 4 sec. 4 M.) will be observed. Leave No. 1 buoy (Fl. G. 4 sec.) to starboard.

Anchorage in approach An anchorage protected from all winds except S–SW is available in 4 m (2 fathoms) sand at **Ensenada de Cariño** on the N side of the **ría** due N of **Punta Segano**. At the head of this bay stand a few houses and a narrow cultivated valley runs up behind it to some trees on the top where a low house stands.

Entrance

Day The leading marks consist of two tall, white, square light towers on the S side of the **ría**. Follow these on 085°, Line Ⓐ, until the buoys marking the narrows and the tall cranes of the dockyard in the distance can be observed, when this line can be left and course set direct for the docks.

Note: large vessels have to make a zig-zag course here to avoid the rock **El Inglés**, 9 m (4·5 fathoms), marked by green buoy No. 3, which should be left to

Ría de El Ferrol—port as seen from the narrows.

starboard. The three red buoys Nos. 2, 4 and 6 should be left to port. Proceed on a course of 060° towards the commercial dock, which has a pair of round white silos to the NW and three cranes, the SE one being of a modern design.

Night Follow the leading lights (*Front:* Fl.R. 1·5 sec. 4 M. *Rear:* Oc. R. 4 sec. 4 M.) on 085°, Line A, until the lighthouse of **Castillo de La Palma** (Oc. (1+2) W. 7 sec. 9 M.) bears 070°, when a course should be set towards it. When past No. 2 buoy to port (Fl. (2) R. 7 sec.) set a course direct for the lights on **Muelle de Concepción Arenal** at the entrance of the commercial dock (Fl. (4) R. 8 sec. 4 M.), leaving buoys No. 4 (Fl. (4) R. 11 sec.) and No. 6 (Fl. (2) R. 7 sec.) to port and leaving buoy No. 3 (Fl. (3) G. 9 sec.) to starboard. It should be noted that there are a lot of navigation, harbour and town lights around and care is needed to select the correct ones.

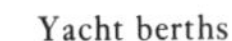

Ría de El Ferrol—commercial harbour from the entrance.

Berths

Yachts can berth alongside the NE wall of the commercial dock in 2 m (1 fathom) near a pair of stone steps. Keep the ramp to the SE clear as this is required for ferry craft. Underwater projections in places on this quay.

The local ferry boats are active from dawn to dusk and can create quite a wash so use good fenders. Winds from SE across the **ría** can cause a swell to enter this dock. Yachts are sometimes directed to the NW corner where there is a ledge which projects 0·5 m underwater.

Anchorage

Anchorages are available as follows but naval authorities have been known to ask yachts to move to the berth detailed above. Clear first with authorities.

La Graña. In 3 m (1·5 fathoms) mud, 1 cable N of small jetty.

Castillo de St Felipe on the E side. Ferry is also available here. Recommended: good facilities ashore, also a drying berth.

Ensenada del Baño. In 4–6 m (2–3 fathoms) mud in the centre of this bay.

Playa de Mugardos. In 4 m (2 fathoms) SW of jetty from which ferry departs for **El Ferrol**. Watch out for fishing boat moorings in this area. 3 slips, crane, quays.

El Seijo. In 2 m (1 fathom) mud, ½ cable E of ferry jetty.
Punta de Maniños. In 2 m (1 fathom) sand, 1 cable NW of ferry jetty head.

Formalities

Normal completion of a single form produced by a very pleasant *Capitan del Puerto* is all that is required. This is essential, no matter where securing.

Facilities

Water	Water is available from a tap on the quay. See *Capitan del Puerto*, whose office is at the head of the dock.
Diesel	Bunkering service in main dock. Pump in commercial basin.
Petrol	Can be collected in cans from a nearby garage.
Shops	Excellent shops are to be found over the top of the hill in new town.
Chandlers	One chandler opposite the commercial dockyard. Two more in the *Plaza N.S. Saturnino*, 91 m (100 yards) to NE.
Repairs	Major repair yards are available and also workshops of all types. Excellent motor mechanic near commercial harbour.
Information	Information and maps of the town and area are obtainable at the *Parador de Turisimo* at the top of the hill next to a naval HQ and from the *Oficina de Informacion* at the far side of the *Plaza de España* at the further end of the town.
Club	The Comision Naval de Regatas near the commercial basin sometimes welcomes visiting yachtsmen (352099).
Beaches	Good beaches are available but public transport is required to get there.
Visits	Curious church at **Chamorra**, about 2 miles NW.
Fiestas	7 January, festivities in honour of St Julian. 18 March, festivities in honour of St Joseph. 31 August, festivities of the *Amboage*.

66 Ría de Betanzos and Ría de Ares

Population: **Sada** 2,100 **Betanzos** 7,200 **Puentedeume** 5,000 Rating 2-2-3
Position 43°24′N 8°14′W

General

Two very attractive and unspoilt *rías*, seldom visited by yachts. There are many beautiful beaches which are quite deserted, and also a number of secure anchorages and several harbours. It is a good 'away from it all' area, with a very easy entrance which can be undertaken in all weathers.

Warnings

In heavy weather seas break on a bank called **Serrón** off **Punta Torrella** and on **Bajo la Miranda**. Dangerous wreck in centre of Ría marked by red pillar light buoy (Fl. 2 sec).

Data

Charts Admiralty Nos. 1755, 79
Spanish Nos. 9290, 929
French Nos. 5009, 6665

Magnetic variation 8°18′W (1984) decreasing by about 5′ each year.

Tidal information

	HW		LW		MHWS	MHWN	MLWS	MLWN
Pointe de Grave	0600 1800	1100 2300	0000 1200	0500 1700	5·4 m 17·6 ft	4·2 m 13·8 ft	0·9 m 3·0 ft	2·1 m 6·8 ft
Rías de Betanzos and **Ares**	−0·55	−0·45	−1·00	−0·20	−1·6 m −5·2 ft	−1·4 m −4·7 ft	−0·5 m −1·6 ft	−0·8 m −2·5 ft

Tide levels may be up to 0·5 m (1·5 ft) above predictions in winds from SW and the same amount below in winds from the NW.

Lights **Cabo Prioriño Chico.** Morse U (· · –) White, 9 seconds, 34 m (112 ft), 11 miles. White 8-sided tower on dwelling. Obscured above 130°.
Puerto de Sada, Malecón Norte head. Group Flashing (3) Green, 8 seconds, 5·8 m (19 ft), 11 miles. Concrete tower.
Escollo Pulgueira. Flashing White, 3 seconds, 4·9 m (16 ft), 4 miles. Red square brick tower.
Malecón Sur. Fixed Red, 5·8 m (19 ft), 2 miles. Tripod. Visible 156°–268·5°.
Torre de Hércules. Group Flashing (4) White, 20 seconds, 103·9 m (341 ft), 23 miles. 8-sided stone tower, lower part square. Fog Siren Mo (L), 30 sec. Radio beacon.

Port Radio See page 20.

Approach

Day *From N* Identify and round **Cabos Prioriño Grande** and **Chico**, which are two rocky headlands somewhat similar to **Cabo Prior** but much smaller. **Cabo Prioriño Chico** has a square white building with a squat lighthouse and a metal latticework

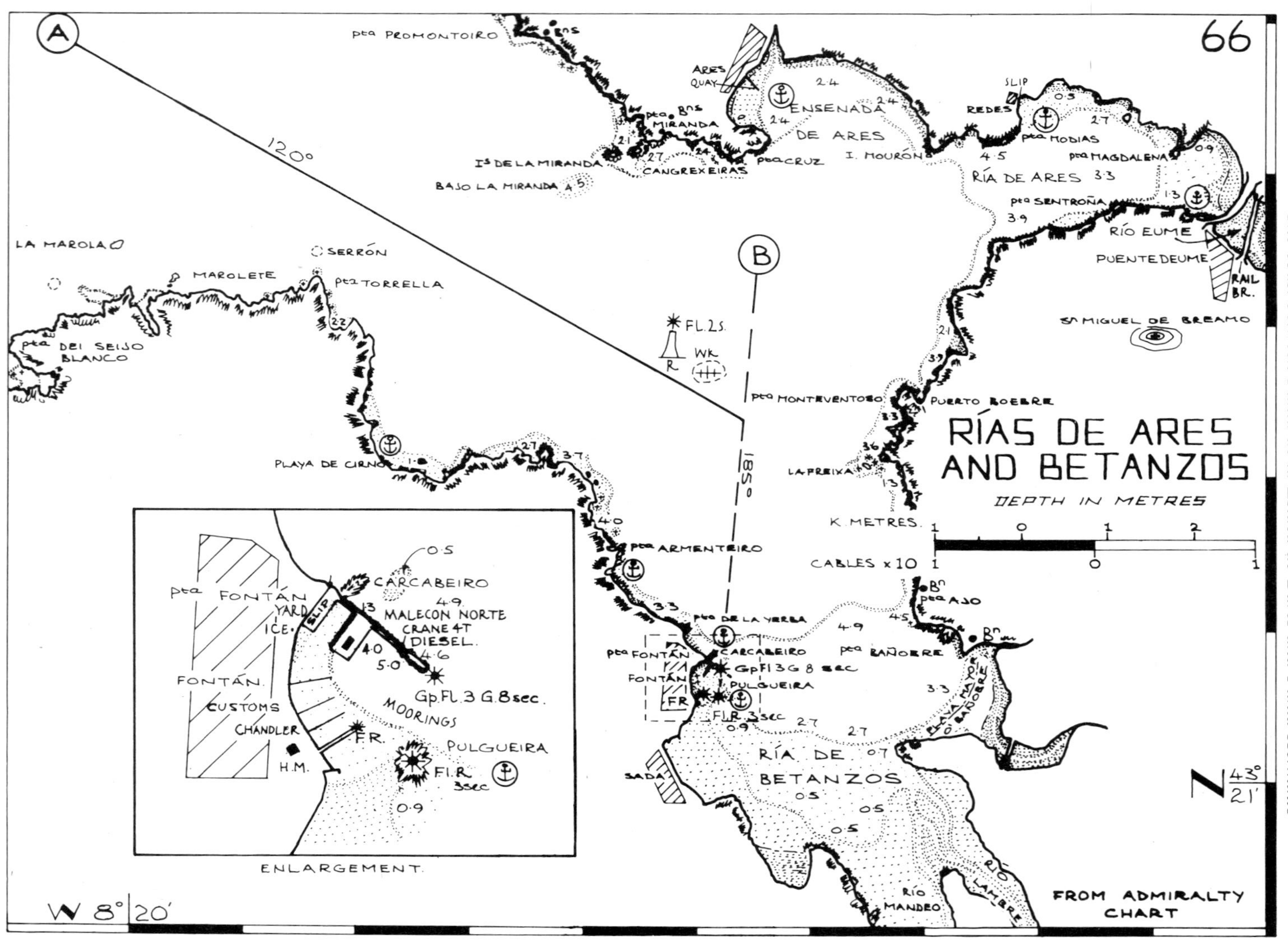
66
RÍAS DE ARES AND BETANZOS
DEPTH IN METRES
K METRES
CABLES x 10
FROM ADMIRALTY CHART
RÍA DE ARES
ENSENADA DE ARES
RÍA DE BETANZOS
RÍO EUME
PUENTEDEUME
Sn MIGUEL DE BREAMO
RAIL BR.
REDES
SLIP
ARES QUAY
I. MOURÓN
Pta MODIAS
Pta MAGDALENA
Pta SENTROÑA
Pta CRUZ
Pta MIRANDA
CANGREXEIRAS
Is DE LA MIRANDA
BAJO LA MIRANDA
Pta PROMONTOIRO
Pta MONTEVENTOSO
PUERTO BOEBRE
LA PREIXA
Pta AJO
Pta BAÑOBRE
Pta DE LA YERBA
Pta ARMENTEIRO
CARCABEIRO
PULGUEIRA
FONTÁN
Pta FONTÁN
SADA
RÍO LAMBRE
RÍO MANDEO
FL.2S.
WK.
185°
120°
SERRÓN
Pta TORRELLA
MAROLETE
LA MAROLA
Pta DEI SEIXO BLANCO
PLAYA DE CIRNO
ENLARGEMENT
MALECON NORTE
CRANE 4T
DIESEL
Gp.FL.3 G 8sec.
MOORINGS
F.I.R. 3sec
F.R.
YARD
ICE
SLIP
CUSTOMS
CHANDLER
H.M.
W 8° 20'
N 43° 21'

tower on its SW side. Cross the entrance to **Ría de El Ferrol**, a narrow deep entrance with high uncultivated hills on each side and a glimpse of the harbour buildings in the distance. Identify **Punta Coitelada**, a low rocky promontory with yellowish rocky face to port and **Punta del Seijo Blanco**, a rocky point with streaks of white rock down it, to starboard. Pass anywhere between them, clearing the coast by 2 cables.

From S and W Identify and round **Punta Herminio** with the lighthouse, **Torre de Hércules**, a very conspicuous octagonal light on a square tower on a large plinth; also identify **Punta del Seijo Blanco** (described above). Do not cross **Banco Yacentes** about 1 mile NE of **Punta Herminio** in heavy weather as seas break on it. Round the small island **La Marola** to the NW of **Punta del Seijo Blanco**. The **Serrón** bank off **Punta Torrella** must also be rounded in heavy weather.

Night Using the powerful lights of **Cabo Prioriño Chico** (Morse Code U (· · –), W. 9 sec. 11 M.), **Torre de Hércules** (Fl. (4) W. 20 sec. 23 M.), also the rear light on **Punta Mera** (Oc. (2) W. 10 sec. 8 M.), navigate to the centre of the entrance to the **rías.**

Entrance

Day Enter these **rías** anywhere within 2 cables of the shore. The following places are conspicuous and will help navigators in these **rías**. The three pairs of tall, 12·2 m (40 ft) high white tower beacons marking two measured miles, situated on **Puntas Averenta**, **Promontoiro** and **Miranda** on the N coast; also the two red and white transit beacon towers on **Puntas Ajo** and **Banobre** on the E coast. On this coast a large wooded hill with a conspicuous building, **St Miguel de Breamo**, on the top is prominent. Attention must be paid to wreck located in the middle of the Ría, marked by red pillar light buoy (Fl. 2 sec).

Night Sail on a bearing of 120°, Line Ⓐ, leaving (Fl. 2 sec.) 300 m to port until the light on the **Malecón Norte** at **Puerto de Sada (Fontán)** (Fl. (3) G. 8 sec. 10 M.) is observed on 185°, Line Ⓑ, when approach may be made to this harbour on this bearing.

Anchorages

S and SW coast Sheltered from the wind from E through S to NW.

Rías de Betanzos and Ares—entrance looking south east.

Puerto de Sada/Fontán – looking NE–E–SE.

Playa de Cirno in 4 m (2 fathoms) sand in the centre of the bay behind the fishing hulks and near moored fishing boats.

One cable S of **Punta Armenterio** near fishing hulks in 4 m (2 fathoms) sand and stone. Check the bottom for good holding ground before anchoring.

Two cables N of light on **Malecón Norte** on **Punta Fontán** in 6 m (3 fathoms) mud.

Two cables SW of this light, in 2 m (1 fathom) sand.

It is also possible to anchor inside the shelter of **Puerto de Sada** at **Fontán**, in 2 m (1 fathom) sand near fishing boats and alongside the quay when permission has been obtained from the *Capitan del Puerto* whose office is at the head of the **Malecón Sur**. Landing is also possible near the head of this mole.

North coast Sheltered from winds from NW through N to SE in 2 m (1 fathom) sand 1 cable SE of **Redes** and in 2 m (1 fathom) sand and mud 2 cables SE of **Ares**, landing in both cases near small jetties. **Ares** very noisy, **Redes** attractive.

Anchor with caution and only in settled weather in a small rocky cove immediately SE of **Punta Avarenta** and also in **Ensenada de Areoso** in 4 m (2 fathoms) sand.

There are numerous anchorages off beaches on the E coast but these may only be used if the NW swell is absent.

Formalities

Officials require the usual form to be completed at **Puerto de Sada (Fontán)** and may also do so at **Redes** and **Ares**.

Facilities

Water Can be obtained from fish market or fish canning factory near quay at **Sada (Fontán)**, or from **Puentedeume** quay.

Diesel From pump on quay, as above.

Petrol From garage in **Sada**, or **Puentedeume** quay.

Repairs Minor repairs may be undertaken at **Sada (Fontán)** and **Ares**.

Shops Adequate shops, hotels, etc. exist for everyday supplies and requirements at **Sada**, also at **Puentedeume** and **Ares**. Chandlers at **Sada**.

Visits A trip 3·5 miles upriver to **Betanzos**, an old Roman city, in a powered dinghy from **Sada (Fontán)** at HW is worth the effort, and if time permits, returning with the subsequent tide.

It is also possible to reach **Puentedeume** in a similar way from **Redes**, which is another old town with a notable church and castle. The fine old bridge is worth seeing.

Fiestas **Sada (Fontán)**
16 July, Feast of Our Lady of Mont Carmel.
15–18 August, festivities in honour of St Roch.
Betanzos
1 May, children's festivals.
14–25 August, festivities in honour of St Roch.
Puentedeume
6–8 August, festivities in honour of La Virgen de las Virtudes and St Nicholas de Tolentine.

Ría de Betanzos y Ares – Puentedeume looking E at high water.

Ría de Betanzos y Ares – Ensenada de Ares looking SW.

67 Ría de La Coruña

Population 190,000 Rating 3-1-1 Position 43°22′N 8°24′W

General

The major port and city on the NW coast of Spain. It has a very easy entrance which can be used at any state of the tide and even under storm conditions. Berths alongside and anchorages are available in several places.

Oil sometimes pollutes all parts of the harbour and is a considerable problem; it is impossible to avoid getting the hull, warps and fenders heavily contaminated. By the choice of suitable anchorages the fouling can be minimised.

All the facilities a yachtsman may require are at hand, including two palatial yacht clubs, both belonging to the **Real Club Nautico de La Coruña**.

The city is unique in that it is an extraordinary mixture of ancient and modern, rich and poor, beautiful and ugly, to be found in close proximity to each other.

Warnings

In storms the sea breaks across the channel between **Banco Yacentes** and **Punta del Seijo Blanco**. A dangerous wreck lies 1·12 M. 099° from **Torre de Hercules**, marked by a green conical light buoy (Fl. (3) G. 10 sec.)

Data

Charts

Admiralty Nos. 79, 1755
Spanish Nos. 4126, 929
French Nos. 3007, 6665

Magnetic variation 8°18′W (1984) decreasing by about 5′ each year.

Tidal information Daily predictions for **La Coruña** are shown in the Spanish tide tables.

	HW		LW		MHWS	MHWN	MLWS	MLWN
Pointe de Grave	0600 1800	1100 2300	0000 1200	0500 1700	5·4 m 17·6 ft	4·2 m 13·8 ft	0·9 m 3·0 ft	2·1 m 6·8 ft
Ría de La Coruña	−0·55	−0·45	−1·05	−0·20	−1·6 m −5·4 ft	−1·5 m −4·9 ft	−0·5 m −1·7 ft	−0·8 m −2·1 ft

Lights

Torre de Hércules. Group Flashing (4) White, 20 seconds, 103·9 m (341 ft), 23 miles. 8-sided stone tower, lower part square. Light obscured over entrance to **Ensenada del Orzán**. Fog siren morse (L) 30 seconds. Radio beacon.

Punta Mera leading lights 108·3°, Line Ⓐ.

Front Fixed Red, 54·5 m (179 ft), 8 miles. White 8-sided tower. Visible 026·8°–146·8°. Racon (M).

Rear Group Occulting (2) White, 10 seconds, 79·3 m (260 ft), 8 miles. White 8-sided tower. Visible 357·5°–177·5°.

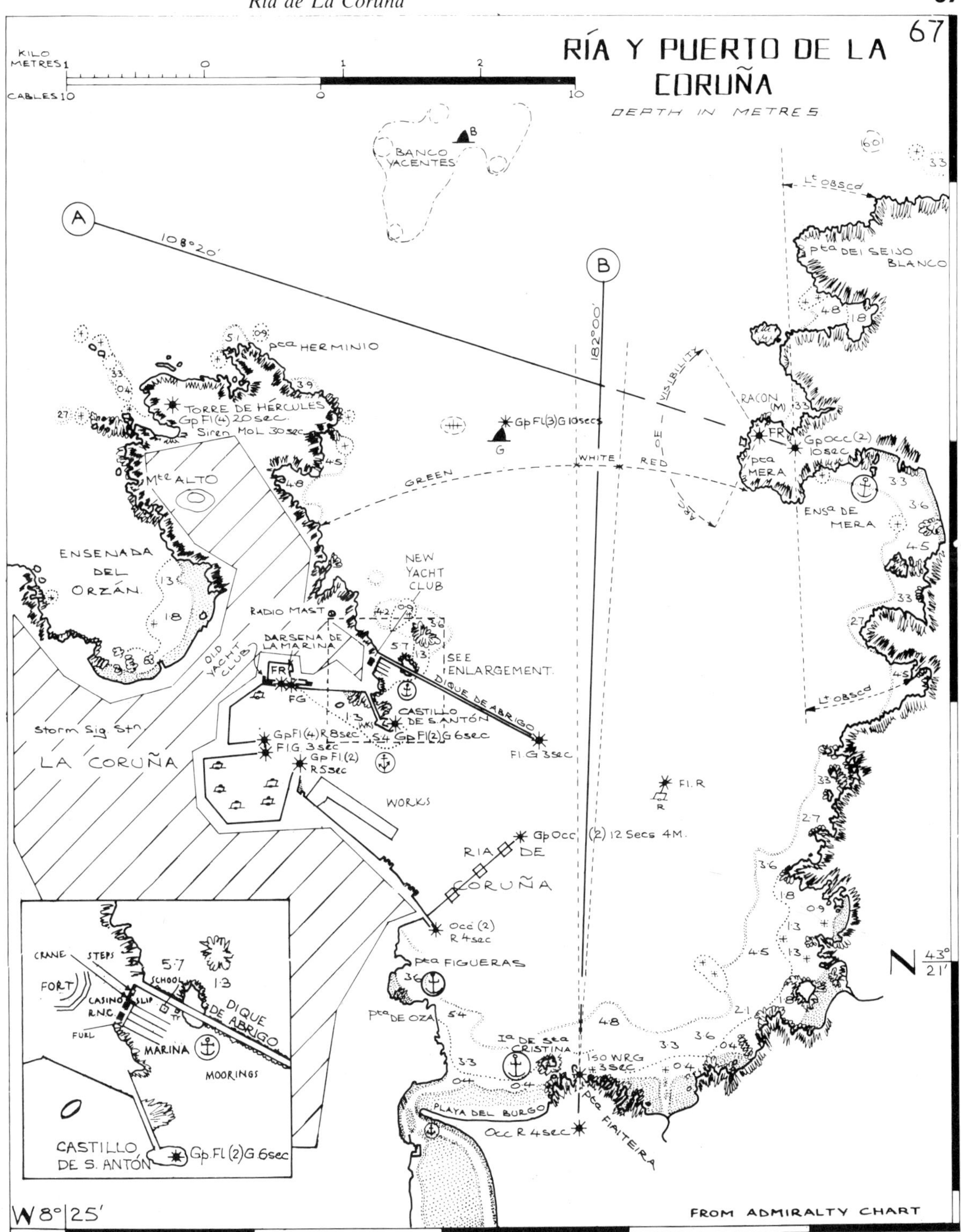

67
RÍA Y PUERTO DE LA CORUÑA
DEPTH IN METRES
KILO METRES 1 0 1 2
CABLES 10 0 10
BANCO YACENTES
Pta HERMINIO
TORRE DE HÉRCULES Gp Fl(4) 20sec. Siren MoL 30sec
Mte ALTO
ENSENADA DEL ORZÁN
Gp Fl(3) G 10secs
GREEN
WHITE
RED
VISIBILITY
RACON (M)
Pta MERA
Gp Occ (2) 10sec
Ensa DE MERA
Pta DEI SEIJO BLANCO
Lt OBSCd
NEW YACHT CLUB
RADIO MAST
DARSENA DE LA MARINA
OLD YACHT CLUB
SEE ENLARGEMENT
DIQUE DE ABRIGO
CASTILLO DE S. ANTÓN
Gp Fl(2) G 6sec
Fl G 3sec
Storm Sig Stn
LA CORUÑA
Gp Fl(4) R 8sec
Fl G 3sec
Gp Fl (2) R 5sec
WORKS
Fl. R
Gp Occ (2) 12 Secs 4M.
RIA DE CORUÑA
Occ (2) R 4sec
Pta FIGUERAS
Pta DE OZA
Ia DE Sta CRISTINA
Iso WRG 3sec
PLAYA DEL BURGO
Occ R 4sec
Pta FIAITEIRA
CRANE
STEPS
FORT
CASINO R.N.C.
SLIP
SCHOOL
FUEL
MARINA
MOORINGS
N 43° 21′
W 8° 25′
FROM ADMIRALTY CHART

Ría de La Corunãa—leading lights—Punta Mera—Line Ⓐ.

Punta Fiaiteira leading lights 182° Line Ⓑ.
Front Isophase White, Red, Green sectors, 2 seconds, 27·7 m (91 ft), White 5, Red 4, Green 3 miles. Round white masonry tower. Green 146·4°—180°, White 180°–184°, Red 184°–217.6°.
Rear Occulting Red, 4 seconds, 52·3 m (173 ft), 4 miles. Round white tower.
Dique de Abrigo head. Flashing Green, 3 seconds, 16·5 m (54 ft) 4 miles. Truncated conical concrete tower.
Castillo de San Antón. Group Flashing (2) Green, 6 seconds, 15·2 m (50 ft), 6 miles. Green 6-sided tower. Visible 276·7°–154°.
Muelle del Este head. Fl. (2) R. 5 sec. 11 m (36 ft) 4 M. Mast.
Dársena de la Marina.
E side of entrance. Fixed Green, 8·5 m (28 ft), 2 miles. Mast.
W side of entrance. Fixed Red, 8·5 m (28 ft), 2 miles. Mast.

Ría de La Coruña—from Punta Mera—looking south east.

Ría de La Coruña—leading lights—Punta Fiaiteira—Line Ⓑ.

Muelle de Trasatlántico head. *N corner.* Fl. (4) R. 8 sec. 8·5 m (28 ft), 4 miles. White tower. *S corner.* Fl. G. 3 sec. 6 m (19 ft) 4 M. White tower.
Oil Pierhead. Oc. (2) R. 4 sec. 6 m (19 ft). 4 M. White tower.
Islas Sisargas. Summit of largest island. Group Flashing (3) White, 15 seconds, 108·2 m (355 ft), 23 miles. 8-sided granite tower on a white building.

Approaches

Day

From N Pass **Cabos Prioriño Grande** and **Prioriño Chico**, two rocky headlands somewhat similar to **Cabo Prior** but much smaller. **Cabo Prioriño Chico** has a square white building with a squat lighthouse on it and a metal latticework tower on its SW side.

Identify to port **Punta del Seijo Blanco**, a rocky promontory with some streaks of white rock down on its face, and also **Punta Mera**, a rounded rocky promontory with two conspicuous white towers (the leading lights for the W entrance). There is also a low square house on this point. To starboard is the **Torre de Hércules**, a very conspicuous octagonal lighthouse with a small off-centre

Ría de La Coruña—Dique de Abrigo head—note fishing hulks since removed.

tower on a tall square tower on a large plinth, all constructed of stone, standing on a rounded green mound which is **Punta Herminio**. These are backed by the low skyscrapers of the city of **La Coruña**. Enter approximately in mid-**ría** on a bearing of 182°. In heavy weather keep more to the E side of the channel as the sea breaks on **Banco Yacentes**.

Note: In storm conditions do not use this channel as the sea breaks right across it.

Continue towards the lighted leading marks on **Punta Fiaiteira**, which consist of two tall white towers with three pale pink bands on each, standing on a green-topped rocky headland with dark trees around it. A group of white houses stands E of these marks with a white curving stairway down to the water.

From W Identify **Punta Herminio** with **Torre de Hércules** on it, and keeping at least 2 cables off this point, proceed on a bearing of 107° towards **Punta Mera** until approximately halfway between **Puntas Herminio** and **Mera** when turn onto 182° towards the lighted leading marks on **Punta Fiaiteira**.

Night *From N* Having left **Cabo Prioriño Chico** (Morse U (· · –), 9 seconds, 11 M.), about 1 mile to port, sail due S until **Torre de Hércules** (Fl. (4) 20 sec. 23 M.) is bearing 240°, when the leading lights on **Punta Fiaiteira** (*Front:* Iso. W.R.G. 2 sec. *Rear:* Oc. R. 4 sec. 4 M.) should be seen on a bearing of 182°, which should be followed in the white sector.

From W Steer so as to pass about ½ mile N of **Torre de Hércules** (Fl. (4) 20 sec. 23 M.) and bring two leading lights on **Punta Mera** into line on 108° (*Front:* F.R. 8 M. *Rear:* Oc. (2) W. 10 sec. 8 M.). Keep on this line until the leading lights on **Punta Fiaiteira** (see above) are abeam on 182°, the white sector, when turn to starboard and follow these marks.

Entrance

Day Proceed on 182° down the middle of the **ría** when a long low mole, the **Dique de Abrigo**, yellowish in colour, will be seen. This has to be rounded to starboard at a distance of 1 cable. A small white-painted light tower is on the E end of this mole and a red can buoy is left to port. Then steer 300° and follow the SW side of this **Dique** towards the pontoons and the New Yacht Club.

Night Follow the white sector of the leading lights on **Punta Fiaiteira** (see above) until the light on the end of **Dique de Abrigo** (Fl. G. 3 sec. 4 M.) bears 300° and a light buoy (Fl.R.) is to port, when turn to starboard to 290° and follow the SW side of this **Dique** towards the pontoons and the New Yacht Club.

Anchorages

Off the new yacht club marina north of Castillo de San Antón. Either pick up a mooring off the marina or anchor in 10 metres. The bottom is thick mud, and the holding good.
Between Punta Figueras and Punta Oza. Anchorage in 6–8 m (3–4 fathoms) sand, between the two points sheltered from NE through W, but rather near the new oil jetties which are under construction.
Near Isla de Santo Cristina. Off **Playa del Burgo** E of the island in 4 m (2 fathoms) sand. Sheltered from NW to W. Regular ferry service to **La Coruña**. This anchorage is behind a number of fishing hulks. Local restaurant and shops available.
South of Castillo de San Antón. A deep-water anchorage in 12 m (6 fathoms) mud is available 1·5 cables SW of this castle and is occasionally used by merchant ships. Rather exposed.
Off **Ensenada de Mera.** In 4 m (2 fathoms) sand near centre of bay sheltered from winds from NE to SE. Regular bus to **La Coruña**. Restaurants and cafés in the village. Taxi available at the barber. Anchor near fishing boats but watch out if the wind changes, as they moor with two anchors out.
Rocks off the head of the jetty.

Berths

Yachts moor alongside the wall on the W side of the entrance to the **Dársena de la Marina** beside the old yacht club. The club boatmen will take lines and allocate berths.

Special warning: at LW springs some parts of the wall which project about 0·5 m (1·5 ft) are exposed and will damage hulls unless large fenders are used. Large fenders will also help prevent damage from the wash of small motor fishing boats which rush past at full speed. The new yacht club marina N of **Castillo de San Antón** is usually full.

Ría de La Coruña—Castillo de San Antón—looking west. New yacht club to right of picture.

Ría de La Coruña—Ensenada de Mera—looking south east.

Drying berths

Yachts may dry out against the wall in the NE corner of the **Dársena de la Marina**, on a hard bottom near some stone steps. Check and if necessary clear small rocks away from area where the keel is going to rest at LW. The wall is very oily.

Formalities

Yacht club staff have immigration forms which will have to be completed. Customs will turn up in due course with another form to complete.

Facilities

All the usual facilities of a large city are available to suit most tastes and pockets, full details of which can be obtained from the officials at the *Bureau de Turisimo* on the NE corner of the **Dársena de la Marina**. They will also provide visitors with maps and leaflets about the city.

Puerto de la Coruña – new yacht harbour looking NE–E–SE from Real Club Nautico.

Water	Available from yacht club hose and from the quays and pontoons. Pumps at the New Yacht Club—difficult to get alongside.
Fuel	Bunkering service available in SW corner of **ría**. Delivery organised by yacht club staff.
Yacht club	The Real Club Nautico has bar, restaurant and showers in two club houses (224500) and (207910).
Shops	A large number within easy reach, covering almost all requirements.
Repairs	A major ship repair yard in E corner of **Dársena de la Marina**. Sailmaker.

La Coruña—looking west. *Photo: Alarde*

Visits The Jardin de San Carlos VI inside the old battlements where Sir John Moore is buried 5 minutes' walk from the New Yacht Club, and the Old Town which lies N of this Jardin.

The **Torre de Hércules**, if energetic and fit. The view from the top of this, the last operational original Roman lighthouse, is well worth seeing. **Santiago de Compostela**, which can be reached by train, bus or taxi, is a beautiful city and is full of interesting places to see. It is one of the great religious centres of Europe.

Beaches The two nearest beaches in the **Ensenada del Orzán** tend to be crowded, but alternatives can be found in the **ría**, of which **Mera** seems to be the best.

Fiestas 1–31 August, summer festivities.

Note. Yachtsmen are recommended to go straight to the yacht club, complete formalities, take on water, fuel and stores and then proceed to an anchorage (**Ensenada de Mera** is probably the best) and to clean off the oil with diesel, petrol or paraffin soaked rags. Visits to the town can be made by bus or taxi.

Index